Advances in Analytics for Learning and Teaching

Series Editors

Dirk Ifenthaler, Learning, Design and Technology, University of Mannheim, Mannheim, Baden-Württemberg, Germany

David Gibson, Teaching and Learning, Curtin University, Bentley, WA, Australia

This book series highlights the latest developments of analytics for learning and teaching as well as providing an arena for the further development of this rapidly developing field.

It provides insight into the emerging paradigms, frameworks, methods, and processes of managing change to better facilitate organizational transformation toward implementation of educational data mining and learning analytics. The series accepts monographs and edited volumes focusing on the above-mentioned scope, and covers a number of subjects. Titles in the series *Advances in Analytics for Learning and Teaching* look at education from K-12 through higher education, as well as vocational, business, and health education. The series also is interested in teaching, learning, and instructional design and organization as well as data analytics and technology adoption.

More information about this series at http://www.springer.com/series/16338

Srinivasa K G • Muralidhar Kurni

A Beginner's Guide to Learning Analytics

Srinivasa K G
National Institute of Technical Teachers
Training and Research
Chandigarh, India

Muralidhar Kurni
Anantha Lakshmi Institute of Technology
and Sciences
Ananthapuram, India

ISSN 2662-2122 ISSN 2662-2130 (electronic)
Advances in Analytics for Learning and Teaching
ISBN 978-3-030-70257-1 ISBN 978-3-030-70258-8 (eBook)
https://doi.org/10.1007/978-3-030-70258-8

© The Editor(s) (if applicable) and The Author(s), under exclusive license to Springer Nature Switzerland AG 2021

This work is subject to copyright. All rights are solely and exclusively licensed by the Publisher, whether the whole or part of the material is concerned, specifically the rights of translation, reprinting, reuse of illustrations, recitation, broadcasting, reproduction on microfilms or in any other physical way, and transmission or information storage and retrieval, electronic adaptation, computer software, or by similar or dissimilar methodology now known or hereafter developed.

The use of general descriptive names, registered names, trademarks, service marks, etc. in this publication does not imply, even in the absence of a specific statement, that such names are exempt from the relevant protective laws and regulations and therefore free for general use.

The publisher, the authors, and the editors are safe to assume that the advice and information in this book are believed to be true and accurate at the date of publication. Neither the publisher nor the authors or the editors give a warranty, expressed or implied, with respect to the material contained herein or for any errors or omissions that may have been made. The publisher remains neutral with regard to jurisdictional claims in published maps and institutional affiliations.

This Springer imprint is published by the registered company Springer Nature Switzerland AG
The registered company address is: Gewerbestrasse 11, 6330 Cham, Switzerland

Preface

Generally speaking, learning analytics refers to the collection and analysis of learner data and their environments to understand and improve learning outcomes. The most cited definition of *learning analytics* comes from the very first Learning Analytics and Knowledge Conference in 2011, where George Siemens and colleagues defined learning analytics as: *"the measurement, collection, analysis and reporting of data for learners and their contexts, for purposes of understanding and optimising learning and the environments in which it occurs."*

A key turning point in the field was imperative to concentrate learning analytics on learning as a core element in its use and application. Since then, more has been done in research and practice in learning and teaching, improved our understanding of the student learning methods and performances, the effect and redesign of design in terms of learning, research, and implementation methodologies.

Learning analytics is where big data in education meets conventional quantitative approaches. Governments, colleges, testing organizations, and MOOC providers capture student data and their learning. However, until recently, when the methods and tools were built, all these data were largely unused. Many of the current data are not available in well-ordered, tidy, and collected formats. It occurs in various forms across networks and places. Analysts need the opportunity to access and process these data now, so we can better understand what students know and how they know it. Translating these data into information and eventually contributing to a better education are learning analytics and educational data mining.

The emphasis on *"understanding and optimizing learning"* where learning analytics departs from the educational data mining and more data-driven practice, a methodology with more important relations with learning theory, the learning design, and a more empirical, evidence-informed practice. A vital, ethical mindset is central to this process of integrating data into teaching and learning practice.

The book, *A Beginner's Guide to Learning Analytics*, is the culmination of decades of experience written by expert thought leaders to help educational institutions develop the culture of sustainable measurement and data-informed decision-making.

Organization of the Book

Chapter 1 provides an overview of learning analytics' evolving field, followed by a short overview of learning analytics' benefits and drawbacks. This chapter also discusses the various ethical and privacy problems involved.

Chapter 2 explores the connection between the two classes, namely LA and EDM. This chapter explores further the improved and official cooperation and collaboration between these two groups to share techniques, research, knowledge mining, and analytical tools to develop EDM and LA areas.

Chapter 3 focuses primarily on how organizations should prepare for learning analytics. How can they organize themselves to advance learning analytics and see the sustainable impacts of learning analytics across traditional services?

Chapter 4 presents and analyzes various data and data usage formats in the learning analytics context to select the best data model for use. This chapter also provides a report on data privacy problems in the learning analytics functions.

Chapter 5 is intended to provide an overview of popular learning analytics tools, including the criteria for selecting the appropriate tool and strategies to effectively develop a learning analytics tool. Eventually, this chapter also presents case studies on learning analytics tools in various educational institutions.

Chapter 6 presents various technologies, viz. big data analytics, data science, AI, ML, and DL, and how can these techniques be used to expand educational system capabilities. This chapter highlights how each technology advances learning analytics' capabilities for reforming higher education practices and helping instructors improve teaching and learning.

Chapter 7 focuses on integrating learning analytics into Massive Open Online Courses (MOOCs), addresses the major challenges of this integration, and examines its potential benefits and limitations.

Chapter 8 highlights the value of pedagogical systems focused on learning analytics and pedagogical intervention design for students to use learning analytics.

Chapter 9 adds remarkable contributions to learning analytics' research by furnishing a substantial and forward-looking view of learning analytics and its related developments and provides a promising path for the twenty-first century in this emerging field.

Chapter 10 explores the usage of learning analytics as recommender systems and in higher education. Additionally, it provides evidence for the use of learning analytics at various educational institutions.

Chapter 11 provides some practice problems to enhance your knowledge and further understand the concepts guided by this book.

The book is well researched and written comprehensively and compellingly, making this book a must-read for all learners, professionals, and teachers. It serves as a practical guide to sound learning analytics practice based on technology and real-world success stories.

Key Features of the Book:

- Clearly provides a basic understanding of the evolving field of learning analytics.
- Provides excellent content on establishing and maintaining learning analytics alignment with various emerging technologies, viz. big data analytics, data science, artificial intelligence, machine learning, and deep learning.
- Gives practical advice for building a solid foundation for your measurement strategy by providing an overview of popular learning analytics tools.
- Analyses various data and data usage formats to ensure that you use the data you gather to improve learning outcomes.
- The content applies not only to readers but also to trainers and practitioners who want to build analytics capability beyond learning, too.

This book is really intended for readers who have no prior knowledge in learning analytics. The book functions as an introductory text to learning analytics for those who want to do more with evaluation/assessment in their organizations. It is useful to all who need to evaluate their learning and teaching strategies. It covers the key concepts linked to learning analytics for researchers and practitioners interested in learning analytics. This book helps those who want to apply analytics to learning and development programs. This book helps educational institutions to identify learners who require support and provide a more personalized learning experience.

Chandigarh, India   Srinivasa K. G.

Ananthapuram, India   Muralidhar Kurni

Acknowledgements

Srinivasa would like to thank Prof. S S Pattnaik, Director, NITTTR Chandigarh, for his kind encouragement for publishing this book. He also would like to thank Prof. Maitryee Dutta, Prof. S S Gill, Prof. C Rama Krishna, and all other faculty members of NITTTR, Chandigarh, for their whole hearted support for publishing this book.

Muralidhar would like to thank the following for all their advice during manuscript preparation: Dr. K. Saritha, P. Sanjeevamma, K. Manushri, Ilayaraja, Thanooj, and K. Somasena Reddy.

Contents

1	**Introduction to Learning Analytics**................................	1
	1.1 Introduction to Learning Analytics	1
	1.2 Learning Analytics: A New and Rapidly Developing Field.........	8
	1.3 Benefits and Challenges of Learning Analytics..................	11
	1.4 Ethical Concerns with Learning Analytics	18
	1.5 Use of Learning Analytics	20
	1.6 Conclusion..	25
	1.7 Review Questions..	26
	References...	26
2	**Educational Data Mining & Learning Analytics**.................	29
	2.1 Introduction...	29
	2.2 Educational Data Mining (EDM).............................	30
	2.3 Educational Data Mining & Learning Analytics	36
	2.4 Educational Data Mining & Learning Analytics Applications	42
	2.5 Conclusion..	56
	2.6 Review Questions..	57
	References...	57
3	**Preparing for Learning Analytics**	61
	3.1 Introduction...	61
	3.2 Role of Psychology in Learning Analytics	62
	3.3 Architecting the Learning Analytics Environment	64
	3.4 Major Barriers to Adopting Learning Analytics	76
	3.5 Case Studies: Adopting/Implementing Learning Analytics at Institutions	82
	3.6 Conclusion..	90
	3.7 Review Questions..	90
	References...	90

4 Data Requirements for Learning Analytics ... 93
- 4.1 Introduction ... 93
- 4.2 Types of Data Used for Learning Analytics ... 94
- 4.3 Data Models Used to Represent Usage Data for Learning Analytics ... 100
- 4.4 Data Privacy Maintenance in Learning Analytics ... 108
- 4.5 Case Studies ... 114
- 4.6 Conclusion ... 118
- 4.7 Review Questions ... 119
- References ... 119

5 Tools for Learning Analytics ... 121
- 5.1 Introduction ... 121
- 5.2 Popular Learning Analytics Tools ... 122
- 5.3 Choosing a Tool ... 126
- 5.4 Strategies to Successfully Deploy a Tool ... 130
- 5.5 Exploring Learning Analytics Tools ... 135
- 5.6 Case Study: Initiation of Learning Analytics Tools Usage at Various Institutions/Organizations ... 135
- 5.7 Developing a Learning Analytics Tool ... 155
- 5.8 Conclusion ... 158
- 5.9 Review Questions ... 159
- References ... 159

6 Other Technology Approaches to Learning Analytics ... 161
- 6.1 Introduction ... 161
- 6.2 Big Data & Learning Analytics ... 179
- 6.3 Data Science & Learning Analytics ... 188
- 6.4 AI & Learning Analytics ... 192
- 6.5 Machine Learning & Learning Analytics ... 196
- 6.6 Deep Learning & Learning Analytics ... 197
- 6.7 Case Studies ... 197
- 6.8 Conclusion ... 199
- 6.9 Review Questions ... 199
- References ... 199

7 Learning Analytics in Massive Open Online Courses ... 203
- 7.1 Introduction to MOOCs ... 203
- 7.2 From MOOCs to Learning Analytics ... 211
- 7.3 Integrating Learning Analytics with MOOCs ... 214
- 7.4 Benefits of Applying Learning Analytics in MOOCs ... 220
- 7.5 Major Concerns of Implementing Learning Analytics in MOOCs ... 222
- 7.6 Limitation of Applying Learning Analytics in MOOCs ... 223
- 7.7 Tools that Support Learning Analytics in MOOCs ... 224

	7.8 Cast Study: Online Learners and their Persistence Within Online Courses Offered on the Coursera Platform	225
	7.9 Conclusion	227
	7.10 Review Questions	227
	References	228
8	**The Pedagogical Perspective of Learning Analytics**	**231**
	8.1 Introduction to Pedagogy	231
	8.2 Learning Analytics Based Pedagogical Framework	240
	8.3 Pedagogical Interventions	243
	8.4 A Preliminary Model of Pedagogical Learning Analytics Intervention Design	252
	8.5 Case Study: Newman University Birmingham's 'Collaborative Development of Pedagogic Interventions Based on Learning Analytics'	253
	8.6 Conclusion	258
	8.7 Review Questions	258
	References	258
9	**Moving Forward**	**261**
	9.1 Self-Learning and Learning Analytics	261
	9.2 Life-Long Learning and Learning Analytics	265
	9.3 Present and Future Trends of Learning Analytics in the World	269
	9.4 Measuring Twenty-First Century Skills Using Learning Analytics	273
	9.5 Moving Forward	274
	9.6 Smart Learning Analytics (Smart LA)	275
	9.7 Case Study. Learning Analytics to Support Self-Regulated Learning in Asynchronous Online Courses: A Case Study at a women's University in South Korea	279
	9.8 Conclusion	281
	9.9 Review Questions	281
	References	282
10	**Case Studies**	**285**
	10.1 Recommender Systems Using Learning Analytics	285
	10.2 Learning Analytics in Higher Education	289
	10.3 Other Evidence on the Use of Learning Analytics	304
	10.4 Conclusion	316
	10.5 Review Questions	316
	References	317
11	**Problems**	**319**

Chapter 1
Introduction to Learning Analytics

1.1 Introduction to Learning Analytics

A key factor that will significantly improve the quality of education is Data (Banihashem & Aliabadi, 2017). Long and Siemens (2014) predicted that in the future, Big Data and Analytics would take a significant factor in higher education as it deals with the things that cannot be seen or touched. Big data deals with large datasets that cannot be analyzed and processed by humans. It has to be computed through a machine to uncover the different trends, associations, patterns specific to human behavior, and interactions (Chen, Mao, & Liu, 2014). For educational institutions, data is critical. Data helps educators to provide better outcomes to their students. Data is analyzed to understand problem instances that provide answers to questions like why a student fails to clear the exam or why an individual chose to quit a course, or why a particular concept was not understood (Reid-Martinez, 2015). Cooper (2012) stated that "analytics is the process of developing actionable insights through problem definition and applying statistical models and analysis against existing and/or simulated future data." Hence, analytics is interpreted as the procedure that uncovers data and processing them to reach implementable insight. From 2008, implementing analytics in education was considered to provide an optimal learning curve for the student. Since 2010, the concept of Learning Analytics has emerged as an independent area (Reid-Martinez, 2015).

"Learning Analytics" incorporates a wide range of techniques used to gather, store, and report data used for administrative, programmatic, and pedagogical purposes. This data ranges from measuring retention, understanding student progress, tracking course tool usage, and providing granular and personalized, student-specific data.

Equally large are the sources for this data, ranging from student information systems, management systems, or task-specific learning tools. This data reporting is descriptive and predictive, using various tools, from business tools to custom algorithms.

Learning Analytics' growth reflects the national surge in evidence-based learning and digital learning content delivery affordability. It remains to be seen if and how the implementation of Learning Analytics would affect pedagogical interest, technical challenges, and cultural barriers.

History Learning Analytics results from understanding two crucial business needs, how the internal organization behaves and the end consumer's behavior. Technological advances enabled businesses to use diverse systems such as PeopleSoft to derive information regarding internal and external behavior through data collection (Shum & Ferguson, 2012). Costello and Mitchell used the phrase Learning Analytics in the year 2000 to analyze international market opportunities for online learning products (Mitchell, 2000). In 2005 the same was used by education technology company Blackboard to describe the compilations provided by its learning management system (LMS) designed for academicians, instructors, and decision-makers (Baepler & Murdoch, 2010).

Knowledge Discovery in Databases (KDD) is an underpinning practice in Data Mining, which centers on gathering and breaking down a considerable amount of data that incorporates several aspects of computing involving logic programming and constructing the decision tree (Romero & Ventura, 2007). According to Baker and Yasef, Educational Data Mining (EDM) can be defined as "an emerging discipline, concerned with developing methods for exploring the unique types of data from educational settings and using those methods to understand better students, and the settings in which they learn" (Baker & Yacef, 2009). Baker and Yasef came up with the EDM concept in 1995.

The Learning Analytics field has been provided a significant boost in implementation across various education fields with affordable LMS systems such as Blackboard, Moodle, and Desire2Learn, which provided an excellent visual representation of large quantities of student information (Shum & Ferguson, 2012).

The Motivation for Learning Analytics The data in educational settings is undoubtedly not new. For decades, institutional-level researchers, managers, and other interested stakeholders have used educational data to analyze and evaluate schools and programs, track graduation and retention levels, and make enrollment and resource predictions.

Data from intelligent agents, learning objects, games, and simulations at the learner level have allowed scientists to inform their pedagogical and cognitive research.

Although educational data is not new, the term "Learning Analytics" has emerged as an essential focal point for higher education in recent years and is often driven by language such as "in the service of improving learning and education" (Macfadyen & Dawson, 2012) or "evaluating the effectiveness of online instruction in delivering user-centric quality undergraduate education" (UCOP, 2010).

Administrators are increasingly using business intelligence software to predict students' recruitment and retention trends. The faculty uses the data from LMS to gain new insights into their classes and students. Vendors enter this market in the hopes of providing institutionally unavailable services. Politicians, corporate executives, and accreditors search for proof of learning from students to ensure quality and validate the public investment.

The current thriving focus on Learning Analytics can be attributed to the availability, scale, and granularity of educational data from multiple new sources being processed via business intelligence tools and predictive statistical methods aimed at various new goals and insights. Contemporary Learning Analytics includes new technologies, applications, reporting methods, descriptive and predictive methods, data mining, and academic and nonacademic accountability pressures.

Vast amounts of information are accumulated and prepared to build up a comprehension of exercises done by people across various businesses, industries, government, and other areas to optimize its process and results.

The expansion of organizations to other sectors depends mainly on analyzing customer's patterns on products. This is achieved using business intelligence and data mining software. In higher education, massive datasets provide information regarding the learners, study environment & patterns of studying. Universities are in a nascent stage, trying to understand how to utilize the available data to enhance their students' educational experience.

Defining Learning Analytics Learning Analytics blends various scholarly disciplines, namely educational data mining and predictive modeling. In 2007 (Campbell, DeBlois, & Oblinger, 2007), analytics could provide opportunities for 'academic analytics' to discover an answer for developing difficulties in the US advanced education, such as the helpless rate of retention. In 2010, Learning Analytics started to associate itself as a discipline (Ferguson, 2012). On the contrary academic analytics was regarded as a tool for institutional businesses focusing on recruitment and less learning. In 2010, The Society for Learning Analytics Research (SoLAR) was incepted. They gave frequently cited interpretation of Learning Analytics (Siemens et al., 2011):

> Learning analytics is the measurement, collection, analysis, and reporting of data about learners and their contexts, for purposes of understanding and optimizing learning and the environments in which it occurs.

There are overlaps between the rapidly evolving three fields like educational data mining, Learning Analytics, and academic analytics. EDM is mainly tailored to technological problems by generating value from Big Data linked to learning. Learning Analytics is about improving the learning elements, whereas academic analytics focuses more on data use marketing and management (Ferguson, 2012; Long & Siemens, 2011). The Learning Analytics field is influenced by many disciplines, including training, psychology, linguistics, philosophy, sociology, learning physics, statistics, IT, computer science, and Artificial Intelligence. The most dominant of the two disciplines (to a large extent) of key field researchers are Information technology and education (Dawson, Gašević, Siemens, & Joksimovic, 2014).

Components of Learning Analytics The three elements (Fig. 1.1) working together for Learning Analytics are Data, Analysis, and Action (CommLab India, n.d.). 'Data' reflects all of the knowledge gathered from the learners and the learning experiences in which they engage. 'Analysis' includes gathering all the data collected and assessing the impact of the training on the organization's productivity and progress. Furthermore, 'Action' is the decisions you take and the changes you make based on the data analysis.

Data Data is a crucial asset in analytics. Data is the raw material that becomes analytical insights. Learning Analytics data is collecting student knowledge, learning environment, learning experiences, and learning outcomes. Typically, this data is collected while the learning process is going on. Data comes from various sources such as Student Information Systems (SIS), providing demographic and academic data, Learning Management Systems (LMS), providing activity reports for students, performance information for students, and other systems providing different information types.

Analysis The analysis uses algorithms on the gathered data and analyzes it for actionable results. Data analysis incorporates machine learning techniques through mathematical and statistical algorithms. In general, the more sophisticated data analysis algorithms you use yield better insights. Alternatively, complex algorithms put forth higher demands on the volume of data to be processed, type of data, timeframe for analysis, etc. The resulting analysis can be categorized into Descriptive Learning Analytics, which understands the past and provides reactive solutions to influence future learning, and Predictive Learning Analytics, which understands the present and provides proactive solutions to improve the existing learning process. Selecting the right data and algorithms provides the best solution to implement the Learning Analytics process.

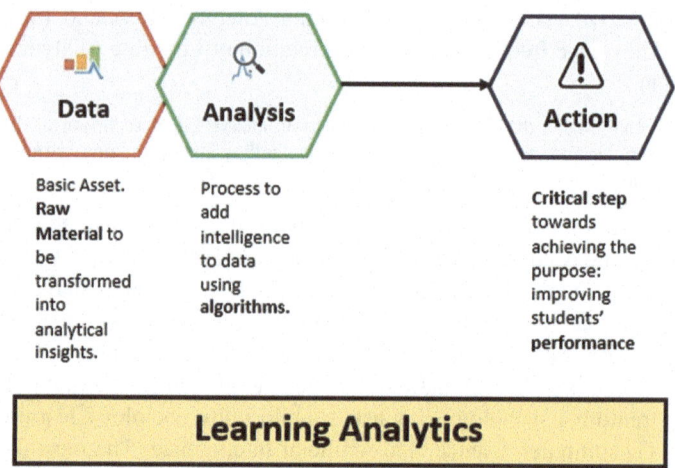

Fig. 1.1 Learning analytics components. (CommLab India, n.d.)

Action Taking action is the ultimate aim of any process of Learning Analytics. Failure to act is a complete failure. It does not matter how good or bad your predictions are if you do not want to or cannot act on them. Your Learning Analytics is incomplete without alterations based on the reportages provided. The results of follow-up actions will determine whether our analytical efforts are successful or failing. Actions are about leadership and culture. As the institution's leadership team must fully embrace the behaviors caused by analytics, school, company, etc., and organizations need to build an internal data-driven culture. The typical behavior pattern for your organization should be intervention following a data analysis process. The right internal processes need to be in place to enable interventions to occur at the end of the day.

What do we do if our empirical analytics reveal at-risk students, missed learning processes, or low-quality training content? Do we want to let that go without any action? We will have to face other ethical considerations if that is the case.

What can I use learning analytics for? Learning Analytics can be used by instructors in various ways (Academic Technology, 2020).

1. *Access Learning Behavior*: Learning Analytics collects user-generated data sourced through learning methods and offers engagement trends in learning. Once we analyze the data, we can see the trends that reveal the students' behavioral learning styles. With this analysis, we can measure the student's engagement behavior rather than focusing on performance, giving the instructor insight into how students understand their course material.
2. *Evaluate Social Learning*: Learning Analytics can be used to analyze the behaviors of a learner on any interactive social network, such as online conversations in Canvas, in order to determine the benefits of social learning. It tests and records interactions between student-to-student and student-to-instructor to understand whether students benefit from social learning in their course.
3. *Improve Learning Materials & Tools*: Learning analytics can track the use of learning materials and means by a student for identifying potential problems or deficiencies and offer an objective assessment of learning materials and tools. It helps teachers to focus on changing strategies deliberately. The teachers can see ways to enhance the learning process or their course structure through aggregated student data.
4. *Individualized Learning*: Learning Analytics allows instructors to be adaptive and customize individualized learning course content for each student. Based on the individual user profile, data is collected and analyzed to produce a more significant personalized learning experience. This approach allows for continuous feedback from individual students to enhance their learning.
5. *Predict Student Performance:* Based on existing data on learning engagement and performance, Learning Analytics employs statistical and automated learning models to predict future learning performance. This will classify potential at-risk students for personalized support. The emphasis is on using data to allow the teacher to intervene quickly and help the student correct the course before it is too late.

6. ***Visualize Learning Activities*:** It tracks all the learning tasks that users conduct in a digital environment to provide visual reporting on the learning process. The reports will assist students and teachers in encouraging learning, improving practices, and enhancing learning performance. The goal is to increase learning habits and understanding of behaviors and self-reflection among students.

Is academic success predictable through analytics? One of the core concepts of Predictive Learning Analytics (Sclater, Peasgood, & Mullan, 2016) is the notion that measuring student participation through VLE, submission of assessments, and additional data can be used as a proxy for learning and, therefore, probable academic success. Many studies confirm that students who are more involved are likely to perform better. For example, a model developed at St. Louis University in Missouri showed that students' exposure to learning material and gradebook contributed to their final grade. However, this was considered an unsurprising finding that offered no useful insights to assist students (Buerck & Mudigonda, 2014). In some studies, the highest rates of participation are not associated with the best outcomes. Even the worst students who work very hard to enhance their performance tend to be the most dedicated.

Nonetheless, a case study in SoLAR's report has clear details and actual results: 730 students in different courses were classified as at risk at the University of South Australia. Of the 549 contacted, the average Grade Point Average (GPA) was 4.29, 66 percent. The average GPA of 52% of at-risk students not contacted is 3.14. This seems to be a crucial finding, suggesting that intervention approaches for the failing students may be highly valuable to institutions: if you are regarded as at risk but are left alone, the outcome is not only much worse but also substantially more likely to fail. However, the lack of such data in the literature and rigorous, empirical, reproducible studies still makes it difficult to justify significant claims regarding the impact of Learning Analytics (Sclater et al., 2016).

Types of Learning Analytics We can find four types (Fig. 1.2) of Learning Analytics (Lewis, n.d.).

Descriptive analytics Descriptive analytics should address questions about what happened. Descriptive analytics collect multi-source data to provide insights into past performance. These data can be used for decision-making related to future training programs. For example, you can take steps to improve the content or use an engaging learning approach if the data suggests higher dropout levels. These findings allow you to improve training programs and even eliminate courses that waste the organization's money and resources. However, descriptive analytics are limited to suggesting something that happened without specifying why.

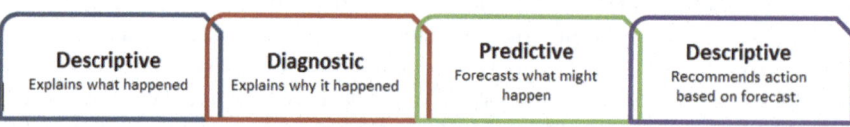

Fig. 1.2 Four types of learning analytics. (Mehta, 2017)

Diagnostic analytics Diagnostic analytics can be used to analyze why something happened and raise questions. You should recognize the dependent elements and locate trends to learn about a particular problem or opportunity. For example, data from the diagnostic analytics may indicate that a customer service eLearning course has been low among senior managers while new hires have found it useful. Further diagnoses found that the course content is too fundamental for senior management, suggesting that the organization requires an advanced level of customer service course. The more thorough research shows that learners' individual needs need to be addressed and that the learning experience needs to be tailored. This will help ensure that the training curriculum is not repetitive while positively affecting all learners' success.

Predictive Analytics Predictive analytics states what is likely to happen. It depends on the effects of current data to forecast the future. However, it is essential to bear in mind that forecasts are just an assessment, and precision is highly dependent on data quality and stability. Therefore, the data should be carefully evaluated. Predictive analytics may help to predict the possible difficulties that learners may encounter in learning. This allows L&D managers to build early intervention and tailor support opportunities. Predictive analytics may also be used to boost training efficiency and increase the commitment ratio. In a post-course survey, for example, we can say that some students do not prefer the eLearning program from a desktop. Since most of you are time-hard and always on the go, you choose to access the training anytime, anywhere on your mobile devices. In this situation, the learner profiles and predictive analytics will allow you to zero-in and deliver microlearning solutions to suit your unique needs.

Prescriptive Analytics Prescriptive analytics aims to find solutions to questions about what should be done. In other words, it would help to understand why it will happen, in addition to seeking answers to what will happen. Also, prescriptive analytics will help you manage training programs strategically. For example, an eLearning course program has to be developed for employees in the manufacturing industry. Two aspects have been revealed by study surveys of courses taken in the past. The courses are theoretically excellent; however, it would be advantageous if students learned how to transfer this learning or apply it to their work. Simulations can gradually be conducted to help students apply the learning in a simulated environment. In effect, this will increase the effectiveness and benefit of the training program.

Again, data powers the world today. Learning Analytics offers decision-makers a deeper understanding of how training courses are aligned with learner objectives and needs. L&D leaders and their stakeholders have a vast opportunity to make data-driven decisions and, above all, use Learning Analytics. When you have not started using Learning Analytics to boost your training programs' efficiency and ROI, it is time for your organization to focus seriously on Learning Analytics.

1.2 Learning Analytics: A New and Rapidly Developing Field

Learning analytics can be regarded as a very complex and onerous field of study. There are different application areas of the method. The processing of large data is the most critical. It is probably an effective approach, particularly in open-source studies and institutions with many participants. To apply this new methodology effectively, such areas should be held, known to, and even trained by researchers. Figure 1.3 below shows nine of these fields. As shown in Fig. 1.3, several skills are required for Learning Analytics, from data analysis to advanced web software languages and methodology. Effective assessment can help clarify and improve the learning process (Astin et al., 1996).

A sufficient number of researchers would, therefore, not be appropriate for Learning Analytics for conventional science. Instead, a larger team of experts can be formed in their fields. In other words, Learning Analytics may be viewed as an interdisciplinary research field focused on education because of its existence.

Elias (2011) notes that Learning Analytics is closely linked to Web analytics, academic analytics, educational data mining, action analytics, and business intelligence. These relationships are summarized in Fig. 1.4. Figure 1.4 indicates that business intelligence applies to the institution's processes to make strategic decisions using data analysis or algorithms, data collection, analysis, and Website usage by visitors, learners, or customers.

Academic analytics is related to the transition to the academia of business intelligence framework concepts and instruments (Goldstein & Katz, 2005). Data mining refers to large-scale data collection, analysis, interpretation, and record of large data. Compared to educational data mining, statistical predictive models in academic analytics seek to enhance decision-making processes.

Audience and Uses "The goal of Learning Analytics is to enable teachers and schools to tailor educational opportunities to each student's level of need and ability" (Johnson, Smith, Willis, Levine, & Haywood, 2011). Learning Analytics will

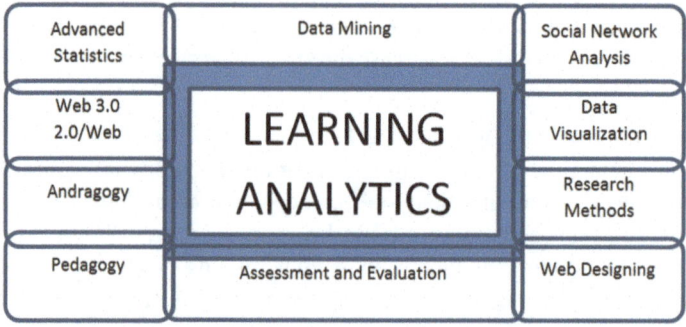

Fig. 1.3 Required fields for learning analytics. (Firat & Yuzer, 2016)

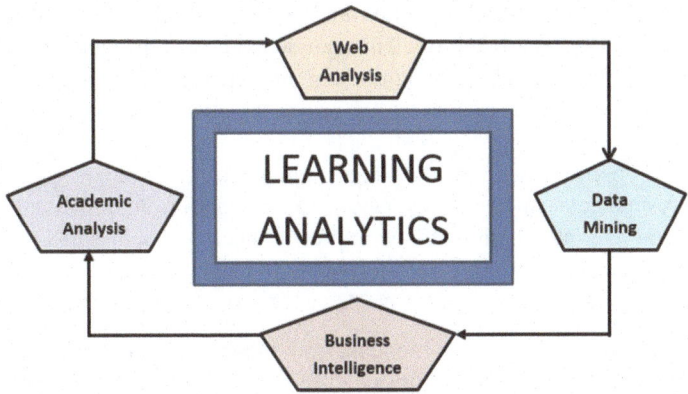

Fig. 1.4 Learning analytics related fields. (Firat & Yuzer, 2016)

give learners, educators, and program coordinators the most significant possible applications. Learning Analytics can benefit the personalization of learning material, enhanced student motivation through immediate feedback, early identification of risky students, and data-driven curriculum and content design (Siemens et al., 2011).

Students Institutes that use Learning Analytics provide their students with resources that allow them to receive feedback on their progress in the course. Dashboards for Learning Analytics will provide necessary information on attendance at seminars and on-line time-to-work events, forum participation rates, online assessments and quiz results, and marks for standardized written assignments and exams. Students can find the system's suggestions particularly to become more effective, focused learners. For example, if a student has a weak understanding of a particular subject area, as identified by a questionnaire, the dashboard will recommend that the student perform specific exercises and readings to enhance their understanding. Alternative learning approaches-based student peers' past experiences or learners with a similar profile can also be provided to students. If a student starts falling behind, the system may suggest strategies to catch up with the rest of the class (Siemens et al., 2011).

Educators Teachers may use Learning Analytic tools to track and get insight into various factors known to influence learners' ongoing participation in the course, use it to adapt their teaching, change their assignments, and suggest teaching as appropriate (Siemens et al., 2011). Training analytical algorithms align online behavior with previous cohort success predictive models. The algorithms used are a mixture of the features of courses taught by a professor, the demographics and learning methods of students, and the technology they employ. The analytics also provide insight into the online student engagement, for example, sentiments by students about a subject, the liveliness of discussion around a topic, or the involvement of various learners (Siemens et al., 2011).

Program Coordinators Program Coordinators may use analytical data to assess the output of a group of students or all their students. They will evaluate information to assess what works in a specific classroom and whether a specific learning plan improves student learning. In general, the program's quantitative learning data may be disaggregated by a subgroup of students, for example, by teacher or year to see how students perform without a course prerequisite or compare their success. Learning system data can help analyze how students learn from individual interventions and how the intervention can be improved. Data can be used to recommend strategies, courses, and administrative systems to enhance teaching, learning, and graduation rates (Bienkowski, Feng, & Means, 2014).

Researchers Researchers use learner data from multiple systems to test with learning concepts and examine the utility of different styles of teaching methods and various elements of course design. Online learning systems researchers may do experiments where several students obtain different teaching or learning methods at random, and program developers may give other users alternate versions of the software: Version A or Version B. An "A/B testing" process will answer student learning questions such as whether students learn better if they are studying at once in a given type of problem ("mass practice") or if work on this type of problem is divided over time ("spaced work")? What about the retention of this skill by students? What sort of practice schedule is superior for supporting retention? For what form of students, and in which contexts (Bienkowski et al., 2014)?

How learning analytics works With online education and increasingly digital content accessed by students, the data sources available to evaluate study are expanding.

Data Sources Most of this is big data that is considered too large to handle traditional database systems (Manyika et al., 2011). The principal source being used for Learning Analytics is the VLE (Virtual Learning Environment), which allows students to view timetables, grades, and course details, access learning materials, communicate with each other through forums, and submit assignments. VLE is commonly used in various modules, courses, and organizations. When used as the primary tool, it is likely to provide a rich source of data, for example, in distance learning programs or MOOCs. Learning Analytics can also provide valuable insights into participating students in courses that do not use VLE. The second primary data source is the SIS (Student Information System), which contains data on students, including prior qualifications, socio-economic status, ethnic group, module selection, and grades. All this is useful material, which can be combined with VLE activity data to predict academic performance.

Other data is also supplemented by VLE and SIS data. There are monitoring systems in some institutions to record students' campus visits or their presence in specific places such as libraries, lecture halls, and refectories. This can be reported from swipe cards, proximity cards, or other entry systems or students' connections to institutional Wi-Fi services. The mix can also be applied to the library info. In some institutions, information such as student library visits, book borrowing records, and access to digital journals is provided to personal tutors on dashboards to facilitate discussions with individuals or groups.

For example, past data analytics for a module may show that frequent access to library resources is associated with success. If the current cohort's statistics reveal that fewer students have visited the library than anticipated so far, a teacher will bring this to the group's attention to improve the students' behavior. They will include documentation from previous students to back up their suggestions.

Technical infrastructure The emerging state of the related technology and the absence of consolidation in the industry are problems for organizations wanting to invest in Learning Analytics. Competition for trade supremacy between VLEs (e.g., Blackboard), SISs (e.g., Tribal), applications of market intelligence, and visualization (e.g., IBM Cognos, Tableau, Qlikview) and emergent personalized Learning Analytics packages (e.g., Civitas Learning) is taking place. The HeLF survey (Newland, Martin, & Ringan, 2015) found that institutions consider various solutions, including their internal developments. This illustrates the results of Jisc of very limited common ground in the learning analytics frameworks of the 13 leading institutions he consulted (Sclater, 2014). One of the higher education community's key demands was for a fundamental Learning Analytics solution, which institutions could experiment with Learning Analytics. Figure 1.5 shows the resulting architecture.

It illustrates how data from sources such as VLE, SIS, library systems, and students' self-declared data flow into the warehouse of Learning Analytics. The Learning Analytics processor, in which prediction analytics are conducted and action controlled by the warning and intervention system, is the architecture's cornerstone. Visualizations of staff analytics are presented in a series of dashboards, and a student app enables students to display their data and compare it to others. The student app provides students information about how they measure their performance and accomplishment to other students, helping them prepare and set their learning expectations and be reinforced motivated by the app when they are met. In the meantime, a student consent service helps protect privacy by requiring students to provide data collection and use authorization.

This platform will be freely accessible to organizations with in the first 2 years as a mix of commercial and open-source platforms providing an open, multi-tenanted cloud solution. This enables organizations to share the same highly scalable architecture while keeping full control over their own data. You can also select individual components if you do not want the entire solution to be deployed.

1.3 Benefits and Challenges of Learning Analytics

When the vast development of comprehensive administrative systems, the collection and interpretation of academic and personal information within educational environments and educational data management is becoming complex. Several

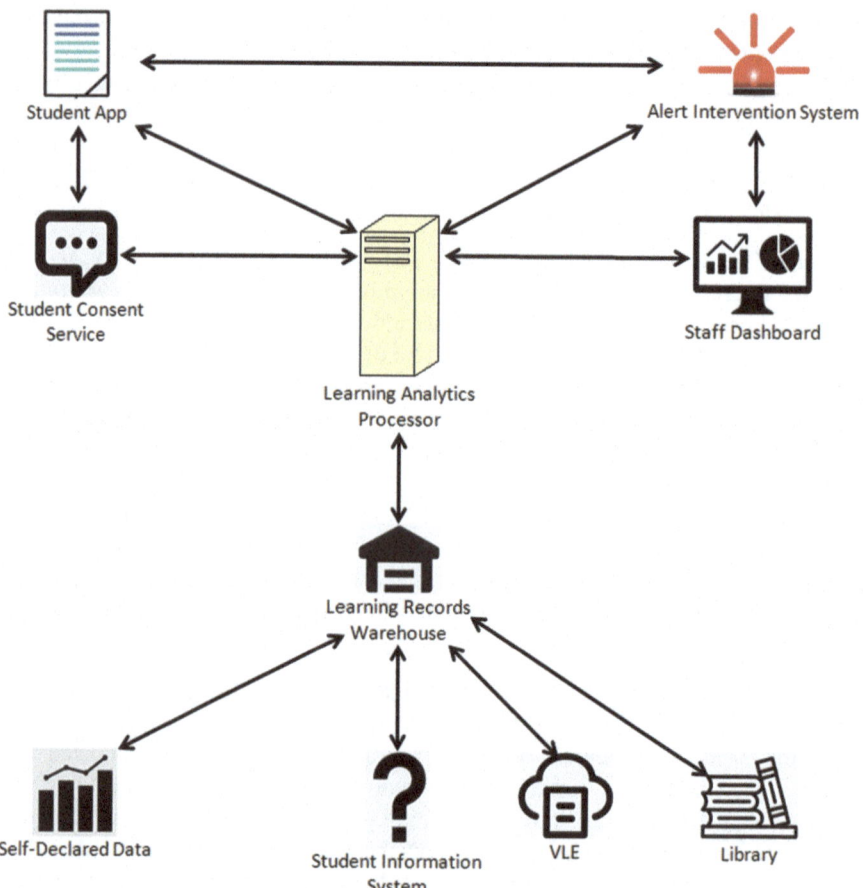

Fig. 1.5 Learning analytics – technical infrastructure. (Sclater et al., 2016)

concepts directly related to collecting of this information include data mining, academic analytics, and Learning Analytics. Such terms are, however, still misunderstood and do not have universally accepted meanings and applicable meanings. The method of extracting valuable information from a wide variety of diverse educational datasets is referred to as educational data mining (EDM). Academic analytics (AA) includes discovering clear trends in education to provide insight into student problems (e.g., retention, success rates). Learning Analytics emphasizes insights and answers to real-time learning processes based on digital learning environments, administrative structures, and social media. Such dynamic information is used to interpret, model, predict and optimize learning, learning environments, and educational decision-making in real-time (Ifenthaler, 2014; Ifenthaler et al., 2014; Ifenthaler & Widanapathirana, 2014).

1.3 Benefits and Challenges of Learning Analytics

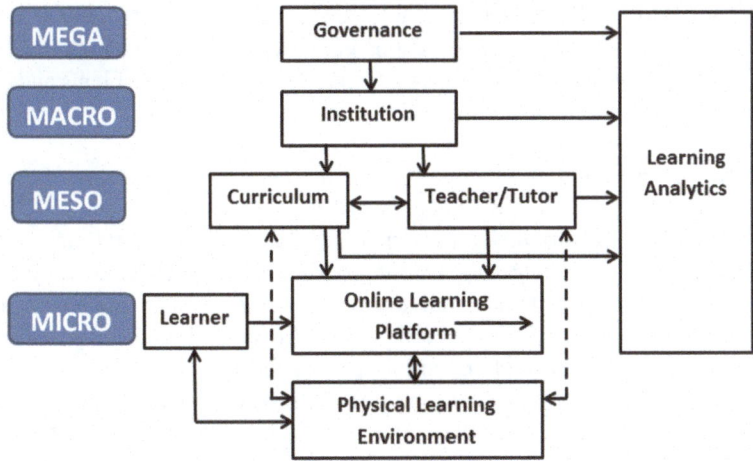

Fig. 1.6 Learning analytics associated with stakeholder levels. (Ifenthaler, 2015)

Benefits of Learning Analytics The benefits of Learning Analytics can be related to four stakeholder levels (Ifenthaler, 2015) (see Fig. 1.6): mega-level (governance), macro-level (institution), and meso-level (curricular, teacher/tutor) as well as micro-level (learner, OLE). Nevertheless, the real-time access, analysis, and modeling of applicable educational information is an essential requirement for Learning Analytics benefits.

The mega-level promotes cross-institutional analytics by integrating data from all layers of the system for Learning Analytics. Such rich datasets allow trends to be recognized and validated within and across institutions, providing useful insights into educational policymaking. The macro-level helps institution-wide analytics better understand learner cohorts to automate related processes and assign vital sources for minimizing dropouts, growing retention, and achieving performance.

The meso-level supports curricula and learning design and offers comprehensive insights into facilitators' learning processes (i.e., teachers, tutors). This knowledge can enhance the overall quality of courses (e.g., sequencing of learning processes, alignment with higher-level results) and improve learning content (e.g., aligning them to expected outcomes and related evaluations).

The analytics of micro-levels supports learners through recommendations and support functions in the OLE. Learners benefit from these flexible and versatile scaffolds and are expected to produce better performance.

Another critical factor for enhancing the advantages of Learning Analytics is the physical environment (e.g., the learner's current emotional state) that is not connected directly to educational knowledge. Therefore, data can be collected by reactive instructions within OLE and linked to available educational information.

Challenges More educational data does not always boost educational results. Learning Analytics, therefore, has its apparent drawbacks, and data obtained from several educational sources may have many meanings. Serious problems and obstacles are also related to the implementation of Learning Analytics (Ifenthaler, 2015):

1. Not all educational data are equal and valid. Therefore, the validity of data and their analysis is critical for producing useful summative, real-time, and predictive insights. This provides a new interdisciplinary field of study in cognitive science, education technology, learning design, psychometry, data processing, web development, artificial intelligence, and statistics. The challenges are to examine complex processes under Learning Analytics frameworks and understand their immediate and long-term impact on learning and teaching.
2. Ethical problems related to the use of educational data for Learning Analytics. This means collecting and storing personal data and analyzing and presenting them to different stakeholders. Therefore, procedures for accessing and using educational data need to be introduced before introducing Learning Analytics frameworks. It also includes the accuracy of applied algorithms and the weighting of predictive modeling educational results. The collection and processing of anonymous personal data is just a small step towards a more robust educational data management system.
3. Restricted access to educational data creates drawbacks for the stakeholders concerned. Invalid predictions, for example, may lead to wrong decisions and unforeseen problems. A misalignment of prior knowledge, pathways, and learning outcomes could increase shifts, at-risk learners' delayed identification may cause discontinuities. A definition of Learning Analytics threshold standards could prevent vast gaps between educational institutions and provide all stakeholders with equal opportunities.
4. Preparing stakeholders for meaningful application of Learning Analytics insights is vital. Stakeholder professional development ensures that issues are recognized and opportunities become concrete acts. Therefore, the expanded implementation of Learning Analytics needs a new generation of experts with specialized interdisciplinary skills. It would also require new logistical and testing facilities to improve Learning Analytics' operations.
5. Distributed networks and unstructured knowledge cannot be specifically related to educational data gathered in an institution's environment. The accumulation of such knowledge and the unregulated association with existing information from education raises the risk of critical prejudice, invalid analysis, predictions, and decisions. The task is to develop mechanisms to filter biased information and to alert stakeholders.
6. Learning Analytics has yet to determine an appropriate data collection and economic response period (seconds, minutes, hours, days, weeks). This includes minimum requirements for valid forecasts and meaningful interventions. The shortage of data is a big obstacle for potential Learning Analytics algorithms.
7. A qualitative study of rich somaticized data (e.g., forum content, open-end evaluation responses) allows a deeper understanding of learners' information and

needs in the context of digital data (e.g., click streams). Developing an automated, natural language processing (NLP) capability is a simple requirement. The critical challenge is to validate algorithms, link quantitative educational data, and build NLPs in real-time.

Summarizing Benefits and Challenges A current research source suggests that the continuous development of higher education institutions is done by learning analytics. This section aims to discuss the opportunities provided by data analytics to higher education and the challenges that bring down its role, adoption, and usage in the different fields of higher education (El Alfy, Gómez, & Dani, 2017).

Table 1.1 summarizes the various challenges facing by Learning Analytics from various stakeholders, and Table 1.2 summarizes the benefits of Learning Analytics for different stakeholders.

Applications of Learning Analytics The different applications of Learning Analytics (Guay, 2016) are discussed in this section. The most common use of data for learning is creating a dashboard that compares one learner's learning way to larger groups, ranging from a single team to a classroom or even a whole organization. This tool is used in environments like Moodle (Enriched Rubric module for learning analytics and SmartKlass™), Brightspace, etc.

The learner's dashboard charts its position using various aspects: progress level, histograms, and the number of visits. One of their key goals is to include students in the management and preparation of their activities. The dashboard of the instructor allows the testing of students with difficulties based on pre-defined criteria. It helps the teacher to move quickly and to provide the necessary assistance. Many methods go as far as to say that the frequency and length of visits in the first 3 weeks of a course are valid indicators of success or failure in a specific course.

Table 1.1 Challenges of learning analytics for stakeholders

S.No.	Area	Challenges
1	Teachers and learners	Learning analytics results are constrained by values of aggregate data, such as marks in summative assessments.
		Lack of adequate skills: hard and soft skills to convey information persuasively.
2	Management	Lack of staff and resources required in theoretical research programs.
		Need for custom research programs that are context-specific and need to develop human and institutional skills.
		The framework for Learning Analytics must be responsive to the peculiarities of the educational institution and its stakeholders.
		Need to promote organizational adoption and cultural transition.
		Unstructured data systematic management.
		Concerns related to data privacy, data ethics, and data security.
		Budgetary problems, societal attitudes that do not value education, and human resistance to change.
3	Research related	Learning analytics are also hard to operationalize.

Table 1.2 Benefits of learning analytics for stakeholders

S.No.	Area	Benefits
1	Teachers and learners	Monitoring the performance and development of students individually as relative to their peers.
		Connect data from different courses to identify patterns of disciplinary behavior for student success.
		Identify the most successful intervention approaches to help students excel at academic risk.
		The opportunity to explain how the teacher's teaching and support activities influence various aspects of student interaction.
		Individual success predictors in a teamwork sense.
		Provide students with real-time feedback on their progress and class participation via SMS notification.
		In educational assessment, Learning Analytics overcomes main measurement obstacles.
		Find out which students are behind and why they are not engaged in online learning.
		Build statistical models of the academic success of students.
		Develop automated tools that foster transparency and intellectual integrity in the e-learning environment by analyzing the student's content trends.
		Tracking and predicting student performance, student learning styles, and curriculum growth.
		The ability to capture data online and offline and to synchronize data online and offline automatically.
		Uncover internal and external factors that influence the performance of students.
		Help for the assessment of academic programs.
		Encouragement of the learner-centered environment.
		It provides detailed measures of the learning process that direct the design and execution of the courses.
		Determination of model for student behavior, performance estimation, increase student self-awareness, boost evaluation input, and suggest resources.
2	Management	Data mining helps HEI decision-makers to create criteria for enrolling students.
		Learning Analytics respond highly to real-time learning processes.
		Capacity to align library resources with institutional priorities and outcomes.
		Revolutionized decision-making powered by data.
		Inform policy on education.
		Registration management, strategic communication, preparation, scheduling, and distribution of resources.
		Academic and technology management of the university.
		Big data and analytics can enhance staff development and training programs, minimize costs, improve productivity and efficiency, and achieve strategic objectives.

(continued)

1.3 Benefits and Challenges of Learning Analytics

Table 1.2 (continued)

S.No.	Area	Benefits
3	Researchers	The mining of educational data facilitates creating new data analytics methods.
		Methods for data analysis include studying social networking data and methods for neural networks that promote model creation and manage large data.
		Clustering algorithms can provide a simple schema of student learning styles and another clustering of educational data.
		Numerous techniques of data mining have solved everyday educational tasks.
		Increase school performance and serious games.
		Identify gaps in knowledge.
4	Course designers	Target course recognition.
		Improve the quality of learning design.
5	Parents	Monitoring the behaviors of students.

Another application is to detect learning difficulties in individual students quickly. Language problems (dysorthography and dyslexia), arithmetic problems, and even problems of motor skills (dyspraxia) can skew learning performance. Rapid diagnosis and remediation may make a huge difference, particularly if all factors resulting from the assessment are taken into account in the intervention.

In some instances, teachers and supervisors may also use a more comprehensive data pool for all students within a single organization. As a result, managers can give employee-specific training, and instructors can confirm a specific student's absentee rate during their course with other colleagues.

Class group analysis can also be done as a fundamental quality control tool. Given that this is no longer an individual coaching effort at this time, best practices should include separating personal data from learning paths in the interests of maintaining anonymity, ensuring confidentiality, and protecting the privacy of all associated parties, including families and learner associates.

Some proponents of Learning Analytics concentrate on automated learning pathways based on personal preferences and material level. Therefore, this task includes access to a detailed and consistent representation of the structure of curricula, a list of associated skills, and a wide set of digital tools with clearly specified parameters. Such information is seldom contained in electronically interoperable formats.

These studies' outcomes should be considered instead of a solid framework for concrete details or reliable prescriptions as a statement or even a suggestion. Predictive trends are based on a simplistic learning model that does not consider individuals' inherent complexity, personal experiences, or the broader learning context.

1.4 Ethical Concerns with Learning Analytics

Learning Analytics provides fantastic incentives for learners but can have legal implications that should not be overlooked (Yupangco, 2018). Many organizations use Learning Analytics to track and understand learners' actions but do not recognize the ethical implications. There is no record of the amount of personal information accessible to the LMS, and online learning experts continue to address all of the data processing and management problems. As a result, companies do not need to follow established ethical standards; therefore, each company needs to think carefully about how the students' personal information is used, who will have access to and what will be shared. The challenges that Learning Analytics poses are fresh and complex. You need to ensure that the information is treated ethically when you use your institution's online learning and collect student data.

1.4.1 What Are the Ethical Concerns with Learning Analytics?

The practical difficulty of Learning Analytics is the matter of the student's privacy. There are plenty of questions (Yupangco, 2018):

- Who has access to the data of students?
- How much do you need to remind LMS users about the processing of their data?
- Do you need permission from learners to use their data?
- Where are the data to be stored? How safe does it have to be?
- Who controls the data of individuals?
- What about data misinterpretation or other data errors?
- Is there an ethical obligation to react to the data we have?

Let us look quickly at each of these issues.

Access to data Who has access to the collected data? Should managers or course designers have the same access as teachers? Should instructors have access to all or only some of the data?

If the students are distributed geographically, it might help to know which city they live in-but that does not mean that teachers will know the street addresses of students. Additional sensitive information may well be off-limits: credit cards (if paid for courses), SSN, passwords, etc.

Transparency How much do you tell students about your collection of information, and how can it be used? Most students know that organizations gather, monitor, and analyze specific quantities of their information. It is a pervasive online experience in contemporary online culture. However, your students probably do not know how much you use their data, particularly in an educational or training environment.

Consent What type of consent should you ask for? Can you use any (or all) of their data without your consent? Do you want students to be anonymous online? There is a consensus that you ethically need some kind of student sign-off, but what the sign-off should contain is not an agreed standard.

Location and Security Where should data be stored? Most organizations do not regulate the storage, location, or protection of the data collected. Data are frequently stored not only outside the institution but outside the country. In the country where data are located, specific laws on security and privacy may not apply, which means that your students' data may be used or sold without their permission.

Ownership of records Who is entitled to determine the use of the data? Can personal information or online learners' behaviors, such as research or marketing, be used for unrelated purposes? May students test how their data are used? How long will the data be preserved until it is deleted?

Misinterpretation Learning Analytics also relies heavily on data interpretation and the relation between dots. This means that teachers often have to rely on experience and assumptions. You can misinterpret the data or view patterns that do not exist. In cases of misinterpretation or inaccurate information, what are the consequences for responsibility and liability?

Obligation Some learning experts believe that once we have the information, we are ethically obliged to act. However, it could be argued that not all actions require action. What is the data that requires action, and what is not the data? Are we responsible for acting on data?

Any organization that gathers student data for Learning Analytics has to deal with these issues. Other businesses' repercussions may be dizzying, but you do not have to work your way around the problems yourself.

1.4.2 How to Protect Learners' Privacy?

What steps must be taken to protect students? Employ these guidelines as a starting point for the code of conduct for Learning Analytics in your organization (Yupangco, 2018).

Set the scope and purpose You need a good idea of what data is being processed, how, and for what purposes. By determining your Learning Analytics' scope and purpose, you establish ethical limitations, which can be explained and defended if students have questions about how their information is used.

Be transparent and get consent Provide students with documentation that clearly explains data collection and analysis processes. Explain how and why the data are to be used and how it is not to be used. Get each student's permission before any information is collected. However, there could be legal situations in which students cannot opt-out; these cases should be obvious.

Protecting confidentiality Restrict student data access. Not all accessors need full access; only staff and administrators grant them the permissions they need. Render learner data anonymous wherever possible. Be sure also that student information is covered for data storage and analysis when contracting with third parties.

Trigger positive interventions You collect data to help students succeed. Set specific guidelines for how and when teachers will intervene to help hard-working students. Specify and who will conduct the sort and purpose of the interventions. Communicate the obligations of learners for self-intervention when feedback data are given.

1.4.3 Are You Ethically Prepared?

Learning Analytics will open up Pandora's box of ethical issues for which you will have to plan. While there is still a broad debate about your ethical responsibilities in the online learning industry, you should create a fundamental code of conduct that protects your business and your learners from information misuse (Yupangco, 2018).

1.5 Use of Learning Analytics

1.5.1 Use of Learning Analytics at the University of Edinburgh

The University invests in the use of Learning Analytics for course design, enhance the student experience and attainment. The area of Learning Analytics and its related online student data analysis methods have significant potential to overcome the challenges faced by educational institutions and educational science. Through advanced data mining techniques combined through existing educational theory, practice, and research, Learning Analytics has provided new, real-time strategies for assessing fundamental problems, such as development and retention of students, the establishment of metrics for acquiring the twenty-first century's skills, and customized and adaptive learning.

The University of Edinburgh has a wide variety of activities in Learning Analytics (The University of Edinburgh, 2020). These activities cross many different educational, organizational, practice, and research boundaries, as seen in Fig. 1.7 below. Led by the Vice Principle of Digital Education, the Center for Research in Digital Education, the School of Informatics, Student Systems, Information Services, and the Institute for Academic Development, Members, Researchers, and professionals from the university's support and study divisions cooperate on a range of project initiatives funded by both internal and external sources. Only some projects use student data from the University of Edinburgh. Many projects are thoroughly explored and have no direct effect on students at the University of Edinburgh,

1.5 Use of Learning Analytics

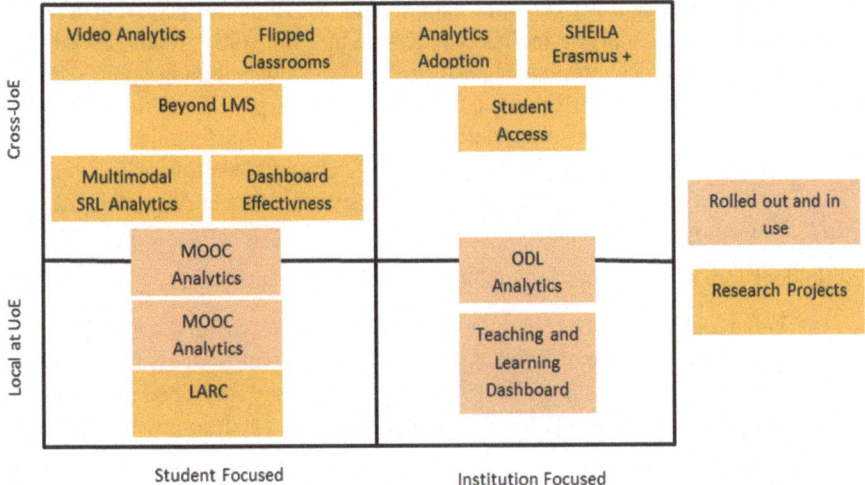

Fig. 1.7 Activities in the field of learning analytics at The University of Edinburgh (2020)

although some discoveries and innovations may be used in the future by the University of Edinburgh. While the university cooperates widely with other universities, no data is shared.

1.5.1.1 Learning Analytics Activities

1. Student-focused activities local at the University of Edinburgh.
    (a) ***The Learning Analytics Report Card (LARC)***: This project asks: "How can University teaching teams develop critical and participatory approaches to educational data analysis?" It aims to develop ways to include students in their selection and study as research collaborators and active participants and encourage a deeper understanding of computational analysis in education. This research was funded by a Principal's Teaching Award grant and included special courses in the Master's in Digital Education for graduates.
    (b) ***VLE Analytics***: Information services have explored other Learning Analytics methods in the Learn and Moodle virtual learning environments operating with a limited number of specific training courses. Projects and tools include those that allow students to display their data and understand their activities and learning patterns. These studies have provided useful insight into student attitudes towards data and privacy and inform many other projects.
    (c) ***MOOC Analytics***: The University of Edinburgh is one of the founders of massive online open courses. Information services analysts, the Digital Education Research Centre, the School of Computers, and the Institute for Academic Development systematically examine the digital trace,

longitudinal, and performance data of students who have been registered in MOOC. The analysis includes understanding the study trends, social networking impact on student performance, and other demographic data on MOOC learners' performance and experience. Experts from the University of Edinburgh have also partnered extensively with the Technical University of Delft, the University of Michigan, Massachusetts Institute of Technology, University of South Australia, the University of Texas at Arlington, and the University of Memphis.

2. Student-focused activities in collaboration with other institutions

   (a) ***Video analytics***: Video analytics work is carried out mainly in collaboration with the University of South Australia, University of Sydney, University of New South Wales, and the University of British Columbia. Analytics is developed to investigate the effects of educational conditions and experience implementing the Online Video Annotations for Learning (OVAL), a video annotation software. Analytics is based on digital traces of OVAL interaction, used in studies with performance and engineering students and faculty members for academic development.

   (b) ***Flipped Classroom analytics***: The work into analytics in flipped classrooms focuses primarily on developing methods for understanding the types of tactics and strategy changes that learners adopt over the academic semester based on the analysis of digital traces recorded by VLEs. Such analytics are used to enhance education and to advance the learning experience. This work is being conducted in collaboration with the University of Sydney, University South Australia, and the University of Belgrade.

   (c) ***Multimodal data of self-regulated learning***: The purpose of this research is to establish measures of students' cognition, metacognition, emotion, and motivation students during learning, supported by the European Association for Research on Learning and Instruction (EARLI) as the Centre for Innovative Research, to encourage the development of more effective and adaptive educational technologies. This research collaborates with Radboud University Nijmegen, University of Oulu, North Carolina State University, Technische Universität München.

   (d) ***Learning dashboard effectiveness:*** This project works to identify common problems faced by teachers and students during online learning and find out the types of Learning Analytics that are useful for teachers to effectively deal with these problems. The project creates a web-based analytics tool named 'Loop' that enables teachers to interpret with Learning Analytics more easily to enhance their teaching and learning practices. This work is carried out in collaboration with the University of Melbourne, the University of South Australia, and Macquarie University.

   (e) ***Learning beyond the LMS***: When educators use new technologies to facilitate learning, assessing the content and essence of student participation in activities using technology related to the Learning Management System (LMS) of the organization poses challenges. This project extends the field of

Learning Analytics by creating an open-source toolkit for a detailed analysis of learners' participation in connected learning environments. This research is conducted in partnership with the University of Sydney, the University of Texas at Arlington, University South Australia, and the University of Technology Sydney.

3. Institution-focused activities local at the University of Edinburgh

   (a) ***Teaching and learning dashboards***: In 2015, Senior Management wanted the Student Systems to

   - develop the use of student data to help improve the student experience, learning & teaching, and operational effectiveness;
   - focus on what is going to make a difference at the school level – support, help to develop insights, and share practice;
   - focus on accessibility, visualization, and data transparency to assist in simplifying and managing complexity;
   - check the use of dashboards to achieve these targets.

   Prototypes were developed using QlikView and BI tools in the second half of 2015 and delivered to various forums with senior officials from schools and colleges. The dashboards received clear and constructive reviews from academics. Funding has been raised to make such dashboards functional for 2016/17, and the dashboards are also used to give the schools more insight. Such dashboards complement the work being done to build Learning Analytics to provide direct support for individual students and better course design.

   (b) ***Learning Analytics Project with Civitas***: A 2-year pilot was conducted with Civitas Learning (the leading U.S. company using data from completely online in-house Masters level programs and courses. A governance group was set up to guide the project. The choice of the online Master programs as the pilot field was essential as it has the advantage of being an easily identifiable and isolated pilot group that is sufficiently large to work within the pilot system. This was a data-rich atmosphere with a clear presence of students in the digital learning system. This project gained expertise in creating Learning Analytics models, strengthened the understanding of teachers and students in this field, improved awareness of the areas where the shortcomings of the data collection occur, and led to developing a policy to support Learning and Teaching Analytics.

4. Institution-focused activities in collaboration with other institutions

   (a) ***SHEILA Erasmus + Project***: To help European universities maturely use and protect their online students' digital data, the SHEILA Project builds a policy development mechanism that encourages formative assessment and personalized learning, using stakeholders' direct participation the development process. It was done from 2016 to 2018.

(b) ***Adoption of Learning Analytics***: Although the interest in Learning Analytics is rapidly expanding, there are limited resources that can inform institutions on how best to start and use Learning Analytics (Ifenthaler & Gibson, 2020). This is a significant challenge as Universities try to engage in Learning Analytics and develop institutional capability. The research focused on how Learning Analytics informs teaching practice, personalized education, and applications to improve retention and identify at-risk students. The work was carried out in collaboration with Macquarie University, The University of Melbourne, University of New England, University of Technology, Sydney, and the Sunshine Coast.

Ethics and Privacy Protection The university is committed to the fair use of data and practices in compliance with national and European legislation that protect consumer privacy. Analytics at the University are primarily used to recognize and increase the students' achievements and learning experiences, increase teaching ability, and inform institutional data development. The University is actively involved in national and international initiatives to promote the ethical and privacy protection of Learning Analytics. All research activities in this field are conducted under the UK Research Integrity Office: Code of Practice for Research. The University's active involvement in creating the Jisc's Code of Practice for Learning Analytics was exceptional. The decisions on Learning Analytics at the University comply with the Jisc Code of Practice standards. Once external organizations are contracted to provide Learning Analytics services, arrangements are concluded that comply with the applicable UK and European regulations on personal data use and processing. The evaluated data were then rendered confidential with state-of-the-art protocols before being exchanged with contracting organizations.

1.5.2 Use of Learning Analytics in Other Recognized Institutions

Several institutions have used Learning Analytics to enhance the success and retention of students. Table 1.3 below shows some of them (Dietz-Uhler & Hurn, 2013). As the information in the table shows, many successful organizations have used or developed Learning Analytics tools that often gave students and teachers a "dashboard." For example, Purdue University has developed SIGNALS to collect data and provide a dashboard for students and teachers to track student advancement. Many schools, such as UMBC, use a Learning Analytics tool built into their LMS to track students' progress. As shown in the third column of Table 1.3, most of these institutions use data to improve their students' performance in a course.

Other educational institutions use analytics successfully to improve teaching, learning, and student performance. Campbell et al. (2007) highlight the institutions that have succeeded in predicting student performance using different data kinds. The University of Alabama, for instance, used first-year student data files to establish a retention model based on different factors, including English course grade and

1.6 Conclusion

Table 1.3 List of institutions that implemented Learning Analytics successfully

S. No.	Institute/University	Purpose
1	University of Central Florida	Data management
2	Rio Salado Community College	Track student progress in courses; intervention
3	Northern Arizona University	Student notifications about academic issues and accomplishments
4	Purdue University	Student feedback on academic issues
5	Ball State University	Boost research on knowledge building
6	University of Michigan	Help and support for students
7	University of Maryland Baltimore County (UMBC)	Track student performance and predict student success
8	Graduate School of Medicine, University of Wollongong	Continuity of care issues

the time taken. For advising and retention, Sinclair Community College established the Student Success Plan (SSP). The collection and analysis of data allowed students to be monitored, and student performance improved.

1.6 Conclusion

The world today is powered by data. Learning Analytics provides decision-makers with greater insight into how training programs' goals and learning requirements are matched with each other. In the last decade, Learning Analytics has become an important research field for technology-enhanced learning. Learning Analytics differentiate themselves by their commitment to providing value for learners in formal, informal, or mixed environments. They are used to understand and improve both the learning and its environments. There are now opportunities for Learning Analytics to exploit the power of feedback loops at the individual teachers and students' level. Measuring and making visible student progress and evaluation gives students the ability to develop skills to track their progress and evaluate how their performance increases their achievements. Teachers gain insights into students' success that help them adapt their lessons or implement initiatives through tutoring, tailor-made tasks, and so on. Learning Analytics allows educators to quickly see the output of modifications and strategies and provide feedback on quality improvement.

It is clear that Learning Analytics are gaining traction and are likely here to stay. There are many benefits of Learning Analytics; in particular, it will enable students to excel. We have large quantities of data available in educational institutions. The capacity to use this data to inform us what to do in the classroom, whether face-to-face or online, lies at heart about Learning Analytics. Institutions such as Purdue University, Rio Salado Community College, and the University of Michigan have paved the way and shown students and faculty the great benefits of Learning Analytics.

Learning Analytics has a significant role to play in higher education in the future. The importance of Learning Analytics can be seen in their role in driving higher education reforms and helping educators improve teaching and learning. Learning Analytics can penetrate the fog of confusion as to how resources are distributed, build competitive advantages, and, above all, increase learning quality and value. Unless your organization has not begun to use Learning Analytics to increase the efficiency and return on its training programs, it is time to think seriously about Learning Analytics. The advantages of Learning Analytics continue to help improve various higher education areas in which problems occur simultaneously.

1.7 Review Questions

Reflect on the concepts of this chapter guided by the following questions.

1. What do we mean by 'learning analytics'?
2. For the student or workplace learner, how can data about their behavior help them improve their performance?
3. Who benefits from Learning Analytics?
4. What will be the fundamental role and impact of learning analytics in Education?
5. Define Learning Analytics.
6. What is Learning Analytics and illustrate its main components?
7. List the various types of Learning Analytics. Explain in brief.
8. How did the Learning Analytics work?
9. How to protect learner's privacy?
10. What are the ethical concerns with Learning Analytics?

References

Academic Technology. (2020). *What are the pedagogical uses of learning analytics?* https://at.doit.wisc.edu/guides/what-are-the-pedagogical-uses-of-learning-analytics/

Astin, A. W., Banta, T. W., Cross, K. P., El-Khawas, E., Ewell, P. T., Hutchings, P., Marchese, T. J., McClenney, K. M., Mentkowski, M., Miller, M. A., Moran, E. T., & Wright, B. D. (1996). *9 Principles of good practice for assessing student learning*. American Association for Higher Education. https://www.dartmouth.edu/oir/assessmenteval/tools/9principles.html

Baepler, P., & Murdoch, C. J. (2010). Academic analytics and data mining in higher education Paul. *International Journal for the Scholarship of Teaching and Learning, 4*(2), 1–9.

Baker, R. S. J. D., & Yacef, K. (2009). The state of educational data mining in 2009: A review and future visions. *Journal of Educational Data Mining, 1*(1), 3–16. https://doi.org/http://doi.ieeecomputersociety.org/10.1109/ASE.2003.1240314

Banihashem, S. K., & Aliabadi, K. (2017). Connectivism: Implications for distance education. *Interdisciplinary Journal of Virtual Learning in Medical Sciences, 8*(3). https://doi.org/10.5812/ijvlms.10030

References

Bienkowski, M., Feng, M., & Means, B. (2014). Enhancing teaching and learning through educational data mining and learning analytics: An issue brief. *Educational Improvement Through Data Mining and Analytics*, 1–60.

Buerck, J. P., & Mudigonda, S. P. (2014). A resource-constrained approach to implementing analytics in an institution of higher education: An experience report. *Journal of Learning Analytics, 1*(1), 129–139. https://doi.org/10.18608/jla.2014.11.7

Campbell, J. P., DeBlois, P. B., & Oblinger, D. G. (2007). Academic analytics: A new tool for a new era. *EDUCAUSE Review, 42*(4), 40–57.

Chen, M., Mao, S., & Liu, Y. (2014). Big data: A survey. *Mobile Networks and Applications, 19*(2), 171–209. https://doi.org/10.1007/s11036-013-0489-0

CommLab India. (n.d.). *Learning analytics 101 the what and the why.*

Cooper, A. (2012). What is "Analytics"? Definition and essential characteristics. *CETIS Analytics Series, 1*(5), 1–10. http://publications.cetis.ac.uk/2012/521

Dawson, S., Gašević, D., Siemens, G., & Joksimovic, S. (2014). Current state and future trends: A citation network analysis of the learning analytics field. *ACM International Conference Proceeding Series*, September 2018, 231–240. https://doi.org/10.1145/2567574.2567585.

Dietz-Uhler, B., & Hurn, J. E. (2013). Using learning analytics to predict (and improve) student success: A faculty perspective. *Journal of Interactive Online Learning, 12*(1), 17–26.

El Alfy, S., Gómez, J. M., & Dani, A. (2017). Exploring the benefits and challenges of learning analytics in higher education institutions: A systematic literature review. *Information Discovery and Delivery, 45*(1), 36–44. http://www.scopus.com/inward/record.url?eid=2-s2.0-67650630322&partnerID=40&md5=24d712ed787dc317fb527b6382ae35fd

Elias, T. (2011). *Learning analytics: Definitions, processes and potential.* Retrieved 10 Feb 2012.

Ferguson, R. (2012). Learning analytics: Drivers, developments and challenges. *International Journal of Technology Enhanced Learning, 4*(5–6), 304–317. https://doi.org/10.1504/IJTEL.2012.051816

Firat, M., & Yuzer, T. V. (2016). Learning analytics: Assessment of mass data in distance education. *International Journal on New Trends in Education and Their Implications, 7*(2)1–8.

Goldstein, P. J., & Katz, R. N. (2005). Academic analytics: The uses of management information and technology in higher education. *Educause Quarterly, 8*(December), 113. https://doi.org/10.1080/17439880802097659

Guay, P.-J. (2016). An introduction to learning analytics. *VTE – Vitrine Technologie Education.* https://doi.org/10.1007/BF00140398

Ifenthaler, D. (2014). Toward automated computer-based visualization and assessment of team-based performance. *Journal of Educational Psychology, 106*(3), 651–665. https://doi.org/10.1037/a0035505

Ifenthaler, D. (2015). *Learning analytics: Benefits and challenges for higher education.* May. https://councilcommunity.org/2015/05/23/learning-analytics-benefits-and-challenges-for-higher-education/

Ifenthaler, D., Adcock, A. B., Erlandson, B. E., Gosper, M., Greiff, S., & Pirnay-Dummer, P. (2014). Challenges for education in a connected world: Digital learning, data rich environments, and computer-based assessment – Introduction to the inaugural special issue of technology, knowledge and learning. *Technology, Knowledge and Learning, 19*(1–2), 121–126. https://doi.org/10.1007/s10758-014-9228-2

Ifenthaler, D., & Gibson, D. C. (Eds.). (2020). *Adoption of data analytics in higher education learning and teaching.* Cham, Switzerland: Springer.

Ifenthaler, D., & Widanapathirana, C. (2014). Development and validation of a learning analytics framework: Two case studies using support vector machines. *Technology, Knowledge and Learning, 19*(1–2), 221–240. https://doi.org/10.1007/s10758-014-9226-4

Johnson, L., Smith, R., Willis, H., Levine, A., & Haywood, K. (2011). *The horizon report.*

Lewis, H. B. (n.d.). *Leveraging learning analytics to maximize training effectiveness practical insights and ideas table of contents.*

Long, P., & Siemens, G. (2011). Penetrating the fog: Analytics in learning and education. *EDUCAUSE Review*. September/October 2011, 31–40.

Long, P. D., & Siemens, G. (2014). Penetrating the fog: Analytics in learning and education. *Italian Journal of Educational Technology, 22*(3), 132–137. https://doi.org/10.17471/2499-4324/195

Macfadyen, L. P., & Dawson, S. (2012). Numbers are not enough. Why e-learning analytics failed to inform an institutional strategic plan. *Educational Technology & Society, 15*(3), 149–163.

Manyika, J., Chui, M., Brown, B., Bughin, J., Dobbs, R., Roxburgh, C., & Hung Byers, A. (2011). *Big data: The next frontier for innovation, competition and productivity* (Issue June). McKinsey Global Institute. https://bigdatawg.nist.gov/pdf/MGI_big_data_full_report.pdf

Mehta, A. (2017). *Four types of business analytics to know*. Analytics Insight. https://www.analyticsinsight.net/four-types-of-business-analytics-to-know/

Mitchell, J. (2000). *International e-VET market research report a report on international market research for. 02.*

Newland, B., Martin, L., & Ringan, N. (2015). *Learning Analytics in UK HE 2015: a HeLF survey report.*

Reid-Martinez, K. (2015). *Big data in education – Harnessing data for better educational outcomes. 3.*

Romero, C., & Ventura, S. (2007). Educational data mining: A survey from 1995 to 2005. *Expert Systems with Applications, 33*(1), 135–146. https://doi.org/10.1016/j.eswa.2006.04.005

Sclater, N. (2014). Learning analytics The current state of play in UK higher and further education. *Jisc*, 1–65. https://repository.jisc.ac.uk/5657/1/Learning_analytics_report.pdf

Sclater, N., Peasgood, A., & Mullan, J. (2016). Learning analytics in higher education. In *JISC*. http://ovidsp.ovid.com/ovidweb.cgi?T=JS&PAGE=reference&D=emed11&NEWS=N&AN=71020726

Shum, S. B., & Ferguson, R. (2012). Social learning analytics. *Educational Technology & Society, 15*(3), 3–26.

Siemens, G., Gasevic, D., Haythornthwaite, C., Dawson, S., Shum, S. B., Ferguson, R., Duval, E., Verbert, K., & Baker, R. S. J. D. (2011). *Open learning analytics: an integrated & modularized platform.* 145–150. https://doi.org/10.1145/3284179.3284206.

The University of Edinburgh. (2020). *Learning analytics.* https://www.ed.ac.uk/information-services/learning-technology/more/learning-analytics

UCOP. (2010). *The UC online instruction pilot project request for letters of intent from UC academic senate faculty.* 1–16.

Yupangco, J. (2018). The essential guide to learning analytics in the age of big data. In *Lambda solutions e-book* e-book (Vol. 4, Issues 5–6). Lambda Solutions: Canada.

Chapter 2
Educational Data Mining & Learning Analytics

2.1 Introduction

There has been increasing interest among researchers and practitioners in Learning Analytics (LA) and Educational Data Mining (EDM) in recent years. Through designing computer-aided learning systems and automated processing of educational data, several attempts were made to improve the learning experience (Schroeder, Thüs, & Technologies 2012). In 2011, the Horizon report claimed for a fruitful future of LA (Johnson, Smith, Willis, Levine, & Haywood, 2011): LA is seen as an essential tool to uncover the knowledge and trends concealed from raw data obtained from the educational environment (Siemens, 2012). For this cause, knowledge of LA is raised, and essential ties with data-driven research fields such as data mining and machine learning (ML) are strengthened.

The combined use of LA, a modern field of research that can have a high potential for impacting current educational models (Siemens, 2012), and EDM, a novice growing field of research in the application of data mining techniques for educational data (Bousbia & Belamri, 2014), leads to new inspections of learner behavior, relationships, and learning pathways. In this connection, LA and EDM can give opportunities and great potential to enhance our understanding of learning processes to improve learning through education systems. We should educate learners, teachers, and their institutions and enable them to understand how such useful tools should offer tremendous advantages in learning and progress in educational outcomes by personalizing and adjusting education based on learners' needs (Greller & Drachsler, 2012). Such prospects have been enhanced by a significant change in data re-sources availability. This is a motivating basis for growing research in the area: PSLC DataShop and enriched educational data from MOOCs are examples (Baker & Yacef, 2009). These repositories are also known as benchmarks for advancing current approaches and algorithms in conjunction with other algorithms (Verbert, Manouselis, Drachsler, & Duval, 2012).

2.2 Educational Data Mining (EDM)

Educational data mining refers to techniques, tools, and research to automatically extract meaning from broad data repositories created by or linked to people's educational activities. Often these data are detailed, fine-grained, and precise. For example, some LMSs monitor details such as the number of times each student viewed the learning object and the number of minutes the learning object was displayed on the computer screen. As another example of intelligent tutoring systems, each time a learner proposes a solution to a problem, they will collect the time of submission, whether or not the solution matches the solution anticipated, time spent since the last submission, the order of solution components entered in the interface, etc. The specific data provides a great deal of process data for review, even in a relatively short session with a computer-based learning environment (e.g., 30 minutes).

In other instances, the results are less fine-grained. For instance, a student's university transcript may include a list of courses taken by the student, the student's degree in each course, and their chosen or changed academic major. EDM uses all data types to identify relevant information about and how different learners learn the domain knowledge structure and the impact of instructional approaches implemented into various learning environments. These analyses offer new information that is hard to distinguish from the raw data. For example, the LMS data analysis will show the connection between students' learning objects and their final grades. Similarly, the analysis of student transcript data can reveal a link between an individual course's degree and its decision to change its academic major. Such knowledge helps students, teachers, school administrators, and educational policy-makers decide how to communicate, deliver, and handle their education resources.

2.2.1 Timeline of Significant Milestones in EDM

Educational data mining can be interpreted in two ways: a research group or a scientific research field. EDM can be used as a sister community for learning analytics as a research environment. In a series of workshops starting in 2005, Educational Data Mining was the first to become an annual conference in 2008 and spawn a journal in 2009 and society, the International Educational Data Mining Society, in 2011. Here you can view a timeline of critical events for the formation of the EDM community (Baker & Inventado, 2014).

- 1995 – Bayesian Knowledge Tracking Paper by Corbett & Anderson – the early primary algorithm still popular today
- 2000 – First workshop related to EDM
- 2001 – Zaiane's theoretical paper on EDM methods
- 2005 – The first workshop using the word "educational data mining."
- 2006 – First EDM book published: "Data mining in E-learning," Romero & Ventura

- 2008 – First Education Data Mining International Conference
- 2009 – First issue of Journal of EDM
- 2010 – EDM first handbook published, Romero, Ventura, Pechenizkiy, and Baker
- 2011 – First conference on Learning Analytics and Knowledge
- 2011 – IEDMS has been established
- 2012 – SoLAR was founded
- 2013 – First Summer Institute for Learning Analytics
- 2022 – Analytics and data mining will be involved in all the educational research.

2.2.2 Goals of EDM

The following four EDM goals were identified by Ryan S. Baker and Kalina Yacef (2009):

1. **Prediction of the future learning behavior of students** through the development of models for students that incorporate detailed information including knowledge, motivation, metacognition, and attitudes;
2. **Discover or develop domain models** characterizing the learning material and optimal instructional sequences;
3. **Studying the impact of various forms of pedagogical support** offered through learning software;
4. **Advancing scientific knowledge about learning and learners** by creating computational models integrating student models, the environment, and the software's pedagogy.

2.2.3 Users and Stakeholders

Four primary users and stakeholders are interested in the mining of educational data (Wikipedia, 2019). Such comprise:

1. **Learners** – Learners want to consider students' needs and approaches to improve learners' understanding and success. For example, learners may also use the information they have gained to recommend activities and tools based on experience with the online learning tool and experiences from the past and the like. Educational data mining can also warn parents about the learning success of their children for younger students. In an online environment, it is also essential to effectively group students. The task is to learn these groups based on complex data and establish models for interpreting these groups.
2. **Educators** – Educators try to understand the nature of learning and the approaches used to develop their teaching methods. EDM applications can be used by educators to assess how the curriculum should be structured and organized, the best approaches for delivering course information, and the resources

to entice students to achieve optimum learning outcomes. In particular, distilling human judgment data offers educators the ability to benefit from EDM, as it allows educators to quickly recognize patterns of behavior, which can promote their learning practices throughout the course or enhance future courses. Educators should identify metrics that reflect student satisfaction and adherence to materials and track success in learning.

3. **Researchers** – Researchers concentrate on designing and testing effective data mining techniques. A yearly international conference started in 2008, followed by the Educational Data Mining Journal in 2009. The broad range of EDM topics includes data mining to increase institutional productivity and student success.
4. **Administrators** – Administrators are responsible for allocating resources in organizations for implementation. As institutions are increasingly accountable for students' achievement, the administration of EDM applications in educational environments is becoming increasingly popular. The faculty and consultants are becoming more involved in recognizing and discussing students at risk. However, often it is a task to provide decision-makers with the knowledge to handle the application quickly and efficiently.

2.2.4 Phases of EDM

With the continued advancement of work in educational data mining, many data mining techniques have been applied to various educational backgrounds. The aim is to turn raw data in each case into concrete knowledge on the learning process to make informed decisions on the design and direction of a learning environment. EDM is thus usually composed of four phases (Romero & Ventura, 2010; (Baker & Yacef, 2009):

1. The first phase of the EDM process (no preprocessing) detects relationships in data. This includes filtering data from an educational environment via a repository to find coherent correlations between variables. Several algorithms have been used to classify these relationships, including classification, regression, clustering, factor analysis, social network analysis, association rules, and sequential pattern mining.
2. To prevent overfitting, discovered relationships must also be validated.
3. Validated relationships are used to predict future events in the learning world.
4. Predictions are used to facilitate strategy and decision-making processes.

During phases 3 and 4, data are also visualized or refined for human interpretation through any other means (Baker, 2010). There has been a significant amount of work into best practices for data visualization.

2.2.5 Main Approaches

In educational data mining, a wide range of current methods are available. These methods fall into the following categories (Baker, 2010).

- Prediction
- Clustering
- Relationship mining
- Discovery with models and
- Distillation of data for human judgment

The first three categories are generally accepted as typical for data mining types (although some have different names). The fourth and fifth groups are especially common in the field of educational data mining.

Prediction In prediction, the aim is to create a model that can infer from a particular combination of certain data aspects (predictive variable) a single aspect of the data. Prediction requires that labels be given for a specific data set in the output variable, where a label reflects some accurate "ground truth" information about the value of the output variable. In some instances, though, it is important to understand how provisional or incomplete these labels can be.

A prediction has two main applications for educational data mining. In some cases, prediction methods may be used to research which characteristics of a model are important for prediction and provide information on the underlying structure. In the second form of application, prediction procedures predict the result value in contexts where the label for that construct cannot be directly obtained.

There are three prediction types:

- Classification
- Regression
- Density estimation

The predicted variable in classification is a binary or categorical variable. Some of the standard classification methods include decision trees, logistic regression, and vector support machines. The expected variable is continuous in the regression. Standard regression methods include linear regression, neural networks, and support vector machine regression in educational data mining. The predicted variable is a probability density function in the density estimation. Several kernel functions can be used, including Gaussian functions. For each prediction form, the input variables can be categorical or constant; depending on the type of input variables used, various prediction methods are more accurate.

Clustering The clustering goal is to find naturally clustered data points, which divide the entire collection of data into a set of clusters. Clustering is particularly useful when the most common categories in the data set are not identified beforehand. If some clusters are optimal within a grouping, every data point is usually more similar than data points in the other clusters. Clusters may be generated in a variety of potential grain sizes, such as the clustering of schools (e.g., to research similarity and difference between schools), the clustering of students (e.g., to examine similarities and differences between students), or the clustering of student activities (e.g., to study behavior patterns).

Clustering algorithms may either start without any previous hypotheses about data clusters (such as the randomized rebooting of the k-mean algorithm) or start from a particular hypothesis that could be generated with a different dataset in prior research (using the Expectation-Maximization algorithm to move on to a cluster hypothesis for the new data set). A clustering algorithm could support the hypothesis that each data point would belong to one cluster (e.g., k-means) or that other points should belong to more than one cluster or no clusters (e.g., Gaussian Mixture Models).

The quality of a set of clusters is generally measured based on how well the set of clusters match the data in contrast with how many matches the number of clusters could only be predicted by chance using statistical methods, for example, the Bayesian Knowledge Criterion.

Relationship Mining Relationship mining discovers relationships between variables in a data set with a wide range of variables. This could be achieved by attempting to decide which variables are most closely correlated with one variable of particular concern or by trying to determine which relationships are strongest between any two variables.

Four forms of relationship mining occur in general:

- association rule mining
- correlation mining
- sequential pattern mining
- causal data mining

In association rule mining, the goal is to decide if-then rules of the form generally have a particular value if any variable values are found. In correlation mining, the objective is to find linear (positive or negative) correlations between variables. The goal of sequential pattern mining is to find temporal associations between events. Causal data mining aims to evaluate whether an event (or observed construct) has been responsible for another event (or observed construct) by evaluating either the covariance of both events or using knowledge about how one event is initiated.

Relationships found by relationship mining must fulfill two criteria: statistical significance and interestingness. Standard statistical tests, such as F-tests, usually determine the statistical significance. Since several checks are performed, it is essential to verify relationships by chance. One approach is to apply post-hoc statistical methods or modifications to the number of tests performed, such as Bonferroni adjustment. This approach will improve confidence that there is no possibility of an individual relationship. An alternative approach is to determine, using Monte Carlo techniques, the overall likelihood of success. This approach tests how likely the overall pattern of outcomes occurred because of chance.

To minimize the set of rules/correlations/causal relations communicated to the data miner, each finding's interestingness is evaluated. Hundreds of thousands of significant relationships can be found in comprehensive data sets. Interestingness measures aim to decide which outcomes are the most distinctive and well supported by the evidence, and others seek to obtain too many similar results. Various measures of interest, including support, confidence, conviction, lift, leverage, coverage, correlation, and cosine.

Discovery with Models In developing a model, a phenomenon model is built by prediction, clustering, or knowledge engineering. This model is then used in another analysis as a component, such as prediction or relationship mining.

In the prediction case, the generated model's predictions are used in predicting a new variable as predictor variables. The relationship between the predictions of the generated model and additional variables are studied in relationship mining. This allows an investigator to examine the relationship between a complex latent construct and a wide range of observed constructs.

Often, model discovery leverages the validated generalization of an integrated prediction model. Generalization in this way depends on adequate validation that the model generalizes correctly across contexts.

Distillation of Data for Human Judgment The distillation of data for human judgment is another area of interest in educational data mining. In some instances, people may conclude data outside the immediate reach of fully automated data mining methods if addressed appropriately. The tools in this area of education data mining are tools for information visualization. The most commonly used visualizations within EDM are often different from those most often used for other information visualization problems.

Data is refined in education data mining for human judgment for two primary purposes: identification and classification. Data are distilled for identification in ways that allow a person to recognize well-known patterns that are difficult to express formally easily. Alternatively, human labeling data may be refined to enable the subsequent development of a prediction model. In this case, sub-sections of a data set are played in visual or text format with human coders named. These labels are then typically used as the basis for predictor growth.

2.2.6 Main Applications

Many educational data mining applications are in practice; this section addresses four applications that have gained considerable attention in the area (Baker, 2010).

One main field of application is *improving student models* that provide detailed information on students' characteristics or conditions such as knowledge, motivation, metacognition, and attitudes. To allow the software to adapt to individual differences, modeling individual differences between students is crucial in educational software research. In recent years, educational data mining methods have allowed student models' complexity to be dramatically expanded. In particular, educational data mining has allowed researchers to obtain more information on students' actions, such as when a student is gaming in the system, when a student has "slipped" (despite knowing an error), and when a student is engaged self-explanation. These richer models were useful in two respects. Firstly, these models improve the ability to forecast student awareness and future success. Second, these models help researchers to investigate what factors causing students to choose a particular learning environment.

A second primary area of application is **discovering or improving models of the knowledge structure of the domain**. Methods for discovering accurate domain models directly from data have been built in educational data mining. These methods typically combine psychometric modeling frameworks with advanced space-searching algorithms and typically present them as predictive problems for model detection purposes (for example, attempting to predict whether individual behavior using different domain models are correct or incorrect is one common way of developing those models).

A third main application field is the **study of pedagogical support** by learning tools. Modern educational software provides students a range of pedagogical support. The discovery of the pedagogical support is most successful for educational data miners was a key area of concern. The decomposition of learning, a form of relationship mining, is a match for exponential learning curves, which link student performance to the quantity of pedagogical help each student receives (with a weight for each form of aid). The weight of each form of pedagogical support shows how successful it is to enhance learning.

A fourth main area for applying educational data mining is a **scientific discovery** into learning and learners. This takes different forms. In each of the three areas listed before, the application of educational data mining can have broader empirical advantages; for instance, the analysis of pedagogical support can have long-term potential to enrich scaffolding theories. However, within these three fields, multiple analyses were geared directly towards scientific discovery. Model discovery is a crucial tool for scientific exploration through educational data mining. Research into whether status factors or features are stronger predictors of how often a student would game the system is a prominent example of this approach within educational data mining research. Learning decomposition methods are another effective form of scientific study on learning and learners.

2.3 Educational Data Mining & Learning Analytics

Educational data has been increased on a large scale through e-learning tools, instrumental educational software, the use of the Internet in education, and the development of state databases of student knowledge. For several years mainstream educational institutions have used information systems that store lots of exciting information. Today, web-based education systems have grown exponentially, allowing us to store many possible data from different sources in various formats and granularities (Romero & Ventura, 2017).

Many students' data is also gathered in different education settings, such as blended training (BL), virtual/enhanced environments, mobile/ubiquitous learning, game learning, etc. These systems generate large quantities of high educational value knowledge, which cannot be analyzed manually. Tools are also essential to automatically analyze this type of data as all of this information offers students a wealth of educational knowledge to explore and manipulate to understand how students learn. The rapid increase of education data and the transformation of these data into new insights that can support learners, teachers, and administrators are currently among the most significant challenges facing education institutions (Baker, 2015).

There were two separate communities in the same field with a shared interest in how educational data can be used in education and learning science (Baker & Inventado, 2014):

- **Educational data mining (EDM)** aims to develop methodologies for exploring specific data types from educational environments (Bakhshinategh, Zaiane, ElAtia, & Ipperciel, 2018). The application of data mining techniques (DM) to this specified form of data set from educational environments could also be described to deal with critical educational issues (Romero & Ventura, 2013).
- The measurement/collection, analysis, and reporting of data concerning learners and their contexts for understanding and optimizing learning and the environments in which it takes place (Lang, 2017) can be described as **Learning Analytics (LA)**.

Both groups share a mutual interest in data-intensive approaches to research in education and share the goal of improving education (Siemens & Baker, 2012; Calvet Liñán & Juan Pérez, 2015). LA focuses on the education issue on the one side, and EDM concentrates on the technical challenge. LA focuses on decision-making based on data and combining the technological and social, and pedagogical aspects of learning through established models. On the other hand, EDM typically explores new data patterns and creates new algorithms and/or models. In the end, the discrepancies among the two groups are focused more on emphasis, study questions, and the potential use of models than the methods used (Baker & Inventado, 2014). Notwithstanding the variations between the LA and EDM communities, both the goals of investigators and the approaches and strategies used in the inquiry have substantial similarities.

EDM and LA are interdisciplinary fields, including knowledge collection, advocacy programs, visual data processing, domain-based data mining, social network analysis, psycho-pedagogical research, cognitive science, psychometrics, etc. They can be drawn as a mixture of three main fields (Fig. 2.1): computer science, education, and statistics. Other sub-areas closely linked to EDM and LA, such as CBE, data mining and machine learning, and educational statistics, are also established at the intersection in these three industries.

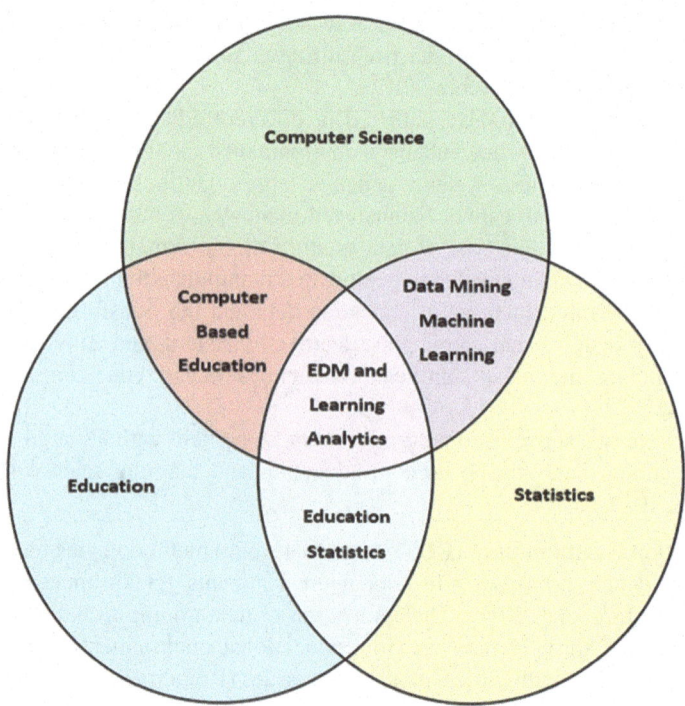

Fig. 2.1 Main areas related to Educational Data Mining/Learning Analytics (Romero & Ventura, 2020)

2.3.1 Benefits of LA and EDM

The advantages of LA and EDM are further clarified in several studies. For example, a UNESCO policy brief defines LA advantages at various micro, meso, and macro levels (Buckingham Shum, 2012). The three key stakeholders are educators, learners, and administrators. Educators are responsible for developing and implementing curriculum programs, and they are most aware of the learning process, the needs, and standard errors of students. The availability of real-time feedback on learners' success allows this community to adapt their teaching activities to students' needs.

Learners seek guidance and input on their learning activities, resources, and paths. The input the students get can be inspiring and encouraging. Finally, administrators handle decision-making and the budget allowance and control the program development and learning process (Vahdat et al., 2015).

Generally speaking, in both fields, the main aim is to enhance learning and get insights into learning processes. LA and EDM are useful for anticipating possible learning patterns to input and adjust implementing methods based on the learner's attitudes. They are also helpful in finding and developing learning domain models

2.3 Educational Data Mining & Learning Analytics

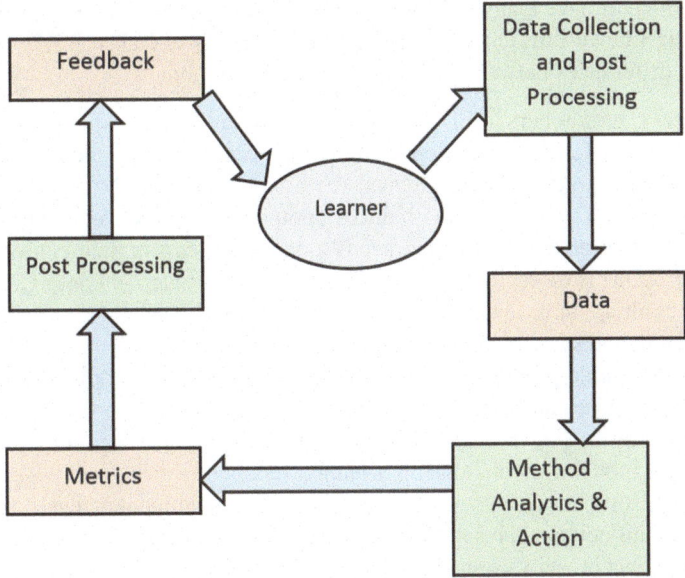

Fig. 2.2 An LA/ EDM process (Vahdat et al., 2015)

and testing learning materials and training tools. They can also advance scientific awareness of students, identify their irregular conduct, and problems and enhance pedagogical support through learning software (Bienkowski, Feng, & Means, 2014; He, 2013). Such study fields are considered complementary, and both present opportunities and challenges (Papamitsiou & Economides, 2014). Figure 2.2 illustrates the LA-EDM process for data collection, processing, and feedback for students to influence and improve the learning outcome.

2.3.2 Similarities and Distinctions

The overlap between the two research fields is important. Nevertheless, there are several variations in the literature. EDM and LA seek to enhance education quality by analyzing vast data quantities to obtain stakeholders' valuable knowledge. Representative organizations in other fields, such as industry, finance, or healthcare, have also adopted statistical, machine-learning, and data-mining technology to boost efficiency through historical data-based decisions. The popularity of these research areas has increased since the beginning of the 2010s, while EDM research began several years earlier. The future gains for students, instructors, administrators, researchers, and society in general, and the importance of current research-based on big data, are expected to continue to be increased in these fields (NMC Horizon Report > 2012 Higher Education Edition, 2012).

LA and EDM have many similarities and common purposes and goals, but there are also significant differences. According to (Siemens & Baker, 2012) following five main differences between EDM and LA are noticeable.

- *Discovery*: researchers in EDM are interested in automated exploration, and it is an instrument for this to exploit human judgment; it is quite the reverse in LA; the aim is to exploit human judgment.
- *Reduction and holistic*: EDM reduces component systems and analyzes them and their relationships, while LA needs to grasp systems in their entirety.
- *Origin*: EDM is rooted in educational software and student modeling; LA roots, on the contrary, have to do with semantic web, "intelligent curriculum," outcome prediction, and systemic interventions.
- *Adaptation and personalization*: EDM accomplishes automatic adaptation, while LA advises and activates instructors and students.
- *Techniques and methods*: EDM employ further classification, clustering, Bavarian modeling, relationship mining, model creation, and visualization; while LA focuses on the study of social networks, sentiment analysis, sentiment analysis, influence analysis, discourse analysis, performance prediction of the learner, concept analysis and sensory models.

Such differences reflect large patterns in each group and, therefore, do not determine the entire scope. A similar concept is articulated in (Baker & Inventado, 2014), where it says that "the overlap and differences between the communities are largely organic, developing from the interests and values of specific researchers rather than reflecting a deeper philosophical split."

Bienkowski et al. (2014) assume that LA is more subject to discipline than EDM. LA is linked to information science and sociology and computer science, statistics, psychology, and learning sciences. Therefore, even though both fields' boundaries are complex and their distinctions are based partly on their backgrounds and patterns, they remain important for these authors. Furthermore, both study groups' co-existence, as upheld in (Siemens & Baker, 2012), contributes to a more diverse and significant contribution to society. Communication and competition between the two should, therefore, be promoted. The significant differences between EDM and LA are discussed in Table 2.1 (Calvet Liñán & Juan Pérez, 2015).

2.3.3 Educational Data Mining/Learning Analytics (EDM/LA) Methods

EMD and LA have a wide variety of standard methods for solving educational or application problems. The most common EDM / LA methods are as follows (Romero & Ventura, 2020).

2.3 Educational Data Mining & Learning Analytics

Table 2.1 Significant differences between EDM and LA

Differences	EDM	LA
Techniques	Clustering, classification, Bayesian modeling, a discovery with models, and relationship mining	Visualization, statistics, sentiment analysis, social network analysis, discourses analysis, influence analysis, concept analysis, and sense-making models
Origins	Student modeling, educational software, and course outcomes prediction	Intelligent curriculum, semantic web, and systematic interventions
Emphasis	Description and comparison of the data mining techniques used	Description of data and results
Type of discovery	Automated	Making use of human judgment
Data used	Mostly administrative data	Pedagogical, administrative, and other types of data
Goals	Inform education practice	Influence education practice

- *Causal mining* – used for causal relationships or for finding causal effects in data. This approach will determine the characteristics of students' behavior that trigger learning, academic failure, drop-out, etc.
- *Clustering* – is used to classify related observation groups. Using this approach, we may group related materials or students based on their study and interaction patterns.
- *Discovery with models* – Used to employ a previously established model of a phenomenon as a component in another analysis. Using this approach, relationships between student behaviors and characteristics or contextual variables are established.
- *Distillation of data for human judgment* – This approach is used for intelligibly representing data using summarization, visualization, and interactive interfaces. This approach can help teachers interpret and evaluate the students' current activities and use of knowledge.
- *Knowledge Tracing* – This approach helps students test abilities, using a cognitive model that maps a problem-solving item with the skills needed and records of correct and incorrect responses to prove their knowledge of a given ability. We can track student awareness over time by using this method.
- *Nonnegative matrix factorization* – this technique is used to describe a matrix of positive numbers with student test outcomes, which can be decomposed into a matrix of items and a matrix of student mastery of skills. We can test student skills using this method.
- *Outlier detection* – This technique is used to denote significantly different people. By using this approach, students with disabilities or abnormal learning processes can be identified.
- *Prediction* – uses this technique to infer from a variety of certain variables, the goal variable. With this approach, we can forecast the success of students and detect behaviors of students.

- *Process mining* – Used to gain process information from event logs. Using this approach, we can find students' actions across the educational system based on traces of their evolution.
- *Recommendation* – Used to predict a user's rating or choice of an item. Using this form, we can give students feedback about their activities or assignments, links to visits, issues, courses to be carried out, etc.
- *Relationship mining* – This approach is used for studying relationships between variables and encoding rules. By using this approach, we can recognize relationships in student behavior patterns and diagnose student problems.
- *Statistics* – This method is used to compute statistics that are descriptive and inferential. This approach helps us to evaluate, interpret, and draw conclusions from educational data.
- *Social network analysis* – This approach is used in networked information to analyze social relationships between individuals. Using this approach, the role and relationship in group activities and experiences with communication tools can be interpreted.
- *Text mining* – This method is used for extracting high-quality information from text. Through using this method, forums, chats, web pages, and documents can be analyzed.
- *Visualization* – This approach is used to display data graphics. Using this approach, we can create data visualizations that allow educators to communicate EDM/LA research results.

2.4 Educational Data Mining & Learning Analytics Applications

Educational data mining and Learning analytics begin to address increasingly complex questions about what students know and whether they are engaged. Researchers have experimented with new model-building techniques and new learning system data that have proven promising to predict students' performance. This section discusses various applications (Alani, Tawfik, Saeed, & Anya, 2018) using EDM and LA technologies to customize and enhance teaching and learning.

- Student knowledge modeling
- Student behavior modeling
- Student experience modeling
- Student profiling
- Domain modeling
- Learning component analysis and instructional principle analysis
- Trend analysis
- Adaptation and Personalization

2.4 Educational Data Mining & Learning Analytics Applications

Each of these areas of application uses specific data sources; this section briefly discusses questions that these categories address and lists the data sources used in such applications (Table 2.2).

Table 2.2 Data sources

Application area	What can be achieved?	What data needed?
Student knowledge modeling	What content does a student know (for instance, necessary skills and concepts, procedural awareness, and higher comprehension skills)	Student answers (correct, incorrect, partly correct), time spent before answering a prompt or question, hits requested, repeating wrong answers, and errors made. The skills a student mastered and all the realistic possibilities. The performance level of students derived from system function or obtained from other sources such as standardized tests
Student behavior modeling	What do student behavior patterns mean for their learning? Are students inspired?	Student answers (proper, wrong, partly correct), time spent before answering a question or prompt, requested tips, replications of incorrect answers, and errors made. Any changes in the context of the classroom/school during the investigation period.
Student experience modeling	Are users satisfied with their experience?	Survey or questionnaire responses. Choices, actions, or performance in subsequent study units or courses.
Student profiling	What groups do users cluster into?	Student answers (correct, incorrect, partly correct), the time it takes to answer a prompt or query, the requested advice, repetition of wrong answers, and mistakes made.
Domain modeling	What is the right standard for separating subjects into modules, and how should they be sequenced?	Student responses (correct, incorrect, and partial) and results on modules with varying grain sizes compared to an external measurement. A taxonomy of the domain model. Associations between issues, expertise, and issues.
Learning component analysis and instructional principle analysis	Which components facilitate learning effectively? What principles of learning work well? How effective are the whole curricula?	Responses of students (correct, wrong, partly correct) and hierarchical output at various levels of detail instead of external steps. A taxonomy of the domain model. Structure of interaction between challenges and skills and issues.

(continued)

Table 2.2 (continued)

Application area	What can be achieved?	What data needed?
Trend analysis	What changes over time, and how?	Depending on what information is of interest, at least three data points will usually be needed longitudinally to discern a pattern. The collected data contains admissions, grades, completion, student source, and high school data over successive years.
Adaptation and personalization	What next steps should the consumer propose? How can the user experience for the next user be changed? How can the user experience be modified in real-time most often?	Varies according to the particular recommendation given. You can need to collect historical data about the user and relevant product or service to be recommended. Academic performance of the students.

2.4.1 Challenges

Although LA and EDM have beneficial advantages, the researchers and practitioners must also find their disadvantages and challenges (Vahdat et al., 2015). As LA and EDM come from different fields of study, data mining, and statistics, it is difficult for them to create relations with cognition, metacognition, and pedagogy, which are important sources for understanding learning processes. Researchers need to concentrate on learning sciences to facilitate successful pedagogy and improve learning design.

The high costs of software and techniques and the challenges of data interoperability and reliability are also factors listed in many studies. Educational data have been standardized, and movement improved, such as the IEEE standard for Learning Technology (IEEE SLT) and the Experience API. However, the present state of interoperability is not adequate to put together all data levels. Concerning reliability, the way users interpret activity data and make sense of the context through unorganized information poses many challenges. Moreover, ethical standards such as privacy and anonymity are becoming more difficult as data resources and significant resources have been increased.

2.4.2 Tools for EDM or LA

This section seeks to explain to the EDM or LA research practitioner the most commonly used, open, and efficient tools available (Slater, Joksimović, Kovanovic, Baker, & Gasevic, 2017). This discussion's direction will essentially follow the route that might be followed when exploring a study problem or evaluating it. The first big challenge is to turn raw and inchoate data streams into usable variables in data mining and other data science fields. Data also come in types and formats that cannot be analyzed; the data need to be converted into a more meaningful format and meaningful variables. Further, data must also be cleaned to delete cases and values that are not just outliers but are deliberately incorrect (i.e., timestamps with impossible values, teacher check accounts for learning system results). Microsoft Excel, Google Sheets, and EDM Workbench are widely used to store, clean, and format data and data creation and feature engineering. We will also address Python and database queries play a vital role in this specific mission.

The next question an EDM or LA researchers will ask after data cleaning, transformation in a more workable format, and function engineering is: What experiments can be carried out, what models can be built, what relationships can be mapped and explored, and how can we validate our findings? We mention various resources for this task: RapidMiner, Weka, KEEL, KNIME, Orange, and SPSS. We also define many Python packages that are suitable for testing, analysis, and modeling.

The tools listed so far apply to a variety of data and analysis types. However, some types of data can be analyzed more efficiently with specialized tools adapted to these fields. We will address the most widely used methods for these kinds of specialized data in educational data mining, including information tracing algorithms, text mining, social network analysis, sequence mining, and process mining.

When a researcher has examined and has a validated, functional model, the work is also shared with other researchers, observers, and practitioners at schools and universities or developing curricula. A vital component of the delivery of research is legible and informative visualizations, and we will cover a range of resources in the final section of our debate that enables data scientists to create high quality and informative graphs, maps, models, networks, diagrams, and other types of information visualized. Tableau, d3js, and InfoVis are three visualization tools, and we explore visualization possibilities with a handful of standard Python packages.

The PSLC DataShop is a unique tool to combine data collection, development, analysis, and visualization. DataShop enables researchers to collect popular analyses with cognitive scientists and EDM researchers with one tool.

2.4.2.1 Manipulation of Data and Feature Engineering

Data sets must first be cleaned and processed in their raw state before data mining. Data miners generally work with messier data rather than statistics and psychometricians, although this issue usually exists with any data. Instead of meaningfully collected research or survey data, data mining companies frequently work with log data or learning management systems data reported on formats that cannot be analyzed immediately. Readers with experience dealing with such educational data know that it is unpredictable, often incomplete, often in many parts, and often indifferent or uncomfortable formats. A researcher might be involved in evaluating students, but its data must be systematically tracked behavior. Researchers may wish to use durations between actions to distinguish off-task students (Baker, 2007;

Cetintas, Si, Xin, & Hord, 2010). However, only raw timestamps can be obtained. In this case, a method known as feature engineering must be established to carry out the required analyses (Veeramachaneni, O'Reilly, & Adl, 2015). We present the following tools to clean, organize, and build data. We address the merits of and method, modify and restructure large datasets, and produce new and more useful variables from existing variables.

1. Microsoft Excel/Google Sheets. Microsoft Excel is the most straightforward resource for data scientists interested in analyzing or engineering data and makes it easily accessible when edited. It can be paired with a related web-based application, Google Sheets. These methods are not useful in producing variables in extensive data sets, approximately one million rows and above, but are ideal instruments for developing small features and prototyping new variables in a larger data set subset. One of the main reasons they help evaluate new data (variables) first stage and prototype data is that Excel and Sheets are excellent at clearly displaying data within a completely visual interface. This enables detecting structural or semantic concerns, such as irregular or incomplete values or duplicate entries. These tools also make it simple to create new features, apply these features easily to the entire layer, and visually test the features for proper functionality across various data. Student summaries, problem sets, and other aggregations can be easily determined by filtering and summing or pivot tables, with a feature for linking data sets or aggregation rates. Excel and sheets are not appropriate for all forms of feature design at the same time. Creating applications that require various database aggregations may entail sorting and resorting the data several times, making it difficult to document what has been done and making it easy to alter function semantics by chance. More significantly, the quantity of information that can be prepared, manipulated, and preserved is restricted by Excel and Sheets. Several Excel and Sheets common operators will further reduce efficiency.
2. EDM workbench. The EDM Workbench is an automated distillation and data labeling method (Rodrigo, Ryan, McLaren, Jayme, & Dy, 2012). Many EDM Workbench's automated feature distillation features fix specific Excel and Sheets deficiencies in specific data scientists-relevant tasks, such as generating complex sequential features, sampling and marking data, and aggregating data the subsets of student-tutor transactions, based on user-specified parameters (known as 'clips'). The EDM Workbench helps researchers build features using XML-based authoring and construct a collection of 26 features used in current literature and intelligent tutoring systems. Attributes include (but they are not limited to) the students time spent on the problem (in absolute and relative terms, for example, how much quicker or slower the student was in the same problem phase than other students) as well as the forms, number and amount of acts correctly, wrongly or helpfully for current ability during the final stages, for qualifications and the student. The EDM Workbench has the capability of generating text-replays in data labeling (Baker, Corbett, & Wagner, 2006), pretty print human behavior segments which are labeled in categories of conduct or other labels of interest by researchers or other domain experts. The EDM Workbench

supports the sampling, reliability monitoring, and synchronization of labels and distilled features.
3. Python and Jupyter Notebook. For data scientists with programming skills, a handful of languages are particularly suitable for data processing and functional engineering. For these reasons, Python is regarded by many as an incredibly useful language. In particular, in Python, it is easier to construct context-based or temporal features than in Excel or Google Sheets. Jupyter's Notebook – a server-client app to build and modify the Python code and rich text objects, such as graphs and tables inside a web browser, is another useful Python function. Jupyter Notebook is a tool for preserving order in-user behavior and its outcome, recording analyses performed, and interim results. Despite this benefit, however, data and features generated in Excel or Google Sheets can still be visually reviewed. In particular, data sets can difficult to identify missing details, same cases, or exceptional values, and it can take more time to validate engineered features, especially for inexperienced programmers. Python can also handle other types of uncommon or unique data formats, such as the JavaScript Object Notation (JSON) files provided by various MOOC and online learning platforms. Although Python is computationally stronger than previously covered spreadsheet tools, its capabilities in these areas are not limitless. Although Python can handle larger datasets than previous tools, it remains subject to size limitations, which for these researchers are slower for the range of about ten million rows of data. It should be noted that certain types of programs (for example, those with nested loops) are considerably slower to use the notebook than in standard Python.
4. SQL. SQL (Structured Query Language) is used to organize databases. SQL queries can be a powerful way to retrieve the desired information exactly and sometimes combine ("join") across multiple database tables. Many simple filtering tasks such as selecting a specific student subset or extracting data from a certain date range are significantly quicker than in any of the tools listed above in the database languages such as SQL. SQL can, however, be a very clunky language for constructing complex functions in the system engineering process. In conjunction with other tools listed above, SQL can work effectively: SQL excels at large size sorting and filtering tasks, which in Excel or Python are very slow, while the tools perform better on the kind of small datasets that can be generated by SQL.

2.4.2.2 Algorithmic Analysis

Once features are created, results and ground truth variables have been identified, data collected and organized adequately for analysis, the next step is to initiate data analysis and modeling and validate the resulting models. The tools mentioned in the following section provide a broad range of algorithms and frameworks for modeling and predicting educational data processes and relationships.
1. RapidMiner. RapidMiner is a program to analyze and construct models for data mining. It has restricted flexibility to develop new features from existing features

(for example, multiple interactions) and pick features (based on user interconnections and results measures). RapidMiner, however, has an incredibly wide variety of classification and regression algorithms and clustering algorithms, association rule mining, and other applications. Other algorithms may typically be composed of RapidMiner operators, e.g., for set selection or model bagging. However, support for resampling processes such as bootstrapping is more restricted than in other data mining packages. The graphical programming language of RapidMiner is comparatively more powerful than most other data mining software with comprehensive user specification functions. For example, RapidMiner can be used to perform multi-level cross-validation with the BatchCrossValidation Operator. This support can benefit generalizability analysis and benefit most other data mining packages over the graphics languages. RapidMiner also has a wide range of metrics for model evaluations that can show views such as Receiver-Operating Curves to help users determine a model's fitness. Models can either be generated in terms of the current math models or XML files, running the model using RapidMiner code on new data. The Application Program Interface (API), which can be incorporated into programs written in Java or Python, can perform various tasks that are not possible with RapidMiner's graphical programming language. RapidMiner contains all Weka algorithms discussed below. RapidMiner also features crowd-sourced algorithms and parameter suggestions. RapidMiner has a wide variety of tutorials to learn the graphic programming language easily.
2. WEKA. Waikato Environment for Knowledge Analysis (Weka) is a free, open-source software package that assembles various data mining and model-building algorithms. It does not allow the creation of new features but allows automatic selection of features. Weka has a wide range of algorithms for classification, clustering, and association mining that can be used in isolation or combination with methods such as bagging, boosting, and stacking. Users can invoke command-line data mining algorithms, a GUI, or a Javan API. Command-line Interface and APIs are more comfortable than the Software that does not allow users to access any advanced functions. Weka can create the models that it produces either in terms of the actual mathematical model or in PMML files used to run the model on new data with the Weka scoring plugin to run the model.
3. SPSS. Like Excel, SPSS is not only familiar with the world of data science. It provides various statistical measures, regression models, correlations, and factor analyses, mainly a statistical package. IBM SPSS Modeler Premium complements SPSS, a relatively new data mining software that combines previous analytics and text mining packages. SPSS Modeler can specifically build new features from existing features, filter data, select features, and reduce function space. The tools for transforming the data, selecting features, and the space available in data mining packages with fewer selection methods. There is also an option in the product range to use the target class, which is not included in many other packages. Although SPSS is a comprehensive statistical analysis tool, modeling support is slightly worse than the other tools in this section. SPSS is less versatile, more comfortable to configure, and less documented than other

2.4 Educational Data Mining & Learning Analytics Applications

devices. Procedures that are seen as important by researchers in educational data mining, such as cross-validation, are also lacking in comparison with more data mining-focused tools.

4. KNIME. KNIME is a data clearing and analysis package similar to RapidMiner and Weka ("Naim", KoNstanz Information MinEr, www.knime.org), formerly Hades. It provides many of the same functions as these tools and includes all Weka's algorithms, including RapidMiner. It also provides several advanced algorithms, such as sentiment analysis and social network analysis. KNIME's capacity to incorporate data from many sources (e.g., a .csv of engineered features, word document for answers, and a student demographic database) within the same study is particularly strong. KNIME also provides extensions to Interface with R, Python, Java, and SQL.

5. Orange. Orange is a program for data visualization and analysis. Although the Interface is considerably less algorithmic and more comfortable to understand than RapidMiner, Weka, or KNIME, color-coded widgets differentiate between data entry and cleaning, visualization, regression, and clustering. It provides a wide range of common algorithms, including k-nearest neighbors, random forests, naïve Bayes classification, and supporting vector machines. Orange also has customizable display modules with reasonable documentation for presenting model results. Orange is, however, somewhat limited to Excel in the amount of data it can process. Orange can be better suited as a tool for smaller projects or more advanced researchers based on its easily understood Interface and menu layout.

6. KEEL. KEEL is a tool for data mining used by many EDM researchers. In contrast to some of the tools mentioned above that seek to survey various methods in general, KEEL supports some algorithms and tasks extensively but restricts the support of other algorithms and tasks. For example, KEEL supports discretization algorithms very extensively but has limited support for other techniques for creating new features from existing features. It provides outstanding feature selection support with a wider variety of algorithms than any other method. It also encourages the imputation of missing data and provides substantial support for resampling data. KEEL has a broad collection of classification and regression algorithms for modeling, emphasizing evolutionary algorithms. Its support is more limited than other packages for other types of data mining algorithms like clustering and factor analysis. Association rule mining support is decent but not as comprehensive as some other packages. Although there are help features and a user manual, KEEL has relatively less support for new users than most other data mining packages.

7. Spark. MLLib Spark is a framework for large-scale data processing in a distributed fashion across multiple computer processors. Spark can connect via an API to several programming languages, including Java, Python, and SQL, for distributed processing. The MLLib machine learning platform from Spark offers several popular machine learning and data mining algorithms for implementation. While the functionality of MLLib is still somewhat limited and a purely programmatic tool, its distributed nature makes it a fast and efficient choice.

2.4.2.3 Visualizations

Beyond just mining data, there is a growing awareness that both analysts and practitioners can support useful visualization methods with data meaning (Baker & Siemens, 2014; Duval, 2011; Tervakari, Silius, Koro, Paukkeri, & Pirttilä, 2014; Verbert, Duval, Klerkx, Govaerts, & Santos, 2013). In the next section, we discuss specialized tools for social network analysis applications that can provide sophisticated viewing (e.g., Gephi, SNAPP). Specifically, we want to introduce some general tools and methods for visual analysis, which enable students and instructors to build interactive visual interfaces to acquire data knowledge and insight.

1. Tableau. Tableau presents an interactive data analysis and visualization, product family. Although support for enterprise intelligence is the main focus of the Tableau toolkit, it is commonly used in educational settings to analyze student data, provide actionable insights, increase teaching practices, and streamline educational reporting. Tableau's main advantage is that it needs no programming knowledge to analyze large numbers of data from different sources and make a range of visualizations easily accessible to a broader community. Tableau offers functionality for connecting or importing data from several standardized data storage formats (e.g., databases, warehouses of data, log data). Tableau also provides functionality to build rich and interactive dashboards that allow end-users to display dynamic real-time visualizations. However, Tableau's functionality is limited to this; it does not support predictive analytics or relational data extraction. Also, Tableau is not extendable as a commercial tool and does not support integration with other software platforms.
2. D3js. D3.js (Data-Driven Documents) is a JavaScript library that enables data-driven document manipulation, enabling researchers and practitioners to create complex, interactive visualizations that need the data management and are designed for the modern web browsers. D3.js offers several advantages; it offers considerable flexibility in building a range of data visualization types, requires no installation, supports code reuse, and is open and free. However, the broader adoption of educational research purposes is challenged. D3.js requires extensive knowledge of programming and has problems with compatibility and certain performance limitations for larger data sets. Finally, it provides no way to hide data from visualization users, requiring preprocessing information to ensure data protection and security. In addition to D3.js, many other programmatic data visualization tools offer various visual presentations and interactive dashboards. Chart.js, Raw, JavaScript InfoVis Toolkit, jpGraph, and Google Visualization API are among the most common tools. These tools offer similar to D3.js but are less frequently used by EDM and LA researchers.

2.4.2.4 Specialized EDM and LA Applications

We addressed general-purpose tools for EDM modeling and analysis in the previous section. However, specific data types and particular research purposes also require more complex algorithms not included in these tools. Researchers and practitioners typically use more advanced tools for these cases.

Tools for Bayesian Knowledge Tracing

Bayesian Knowledge Tracing (Corbett & Anderson, 1995) is a standard method for latent knowledge evaluation in which the knowledge of a student is assessed in online learning. This is different from the type of educational assessment typical in tests in that information changes through online education. Bayesian Knowledge Tracing is a Hidden Markov Model and, at the same time, is a simple Bayesian Network (Reye, 2004) that predicts whether or not a student has mastered a special knowledge within an intelligent tutoring system or similar software. BKT models are generally suitable for two algorithms: brute force grid search or expectation maximization (EM). The two algorithms differ in predictive analysis comparably. BKT's tools are BKT-BF, BNT-SM (also Matlab needs to run) and, hmmsclbl.

Text Mining

Text mining is an increasingly growing field of data mining, and there is a broad range of tagging, processing, and recognition systems, applications, and APIs for text data. Text analysis software may analyze text parts of speech, phrase form, and the context of semantical terms. Also, some tools may define symbolic relationships between various words and phrases. Several tools for text mining and corpus analysis are available more than any other set of tools mentioned so far. This is mainly for two reasons: text mining's complexity and the English language are complicated. Developing a full suite of resources for various text bodies and media types is an exceedingly difficult task. The variety of lexical analytical methods represents the nature and sophistication of the language to be analyzed and evaluated. The second explanation is that various linguistic groups often have varying approaches to text definition and analysis and the wide variety of tools available for text mining is a result of many different areas of researchers developing their tools. We consider that the following methods constitute tools that cross the many dimensions of textual processing and analysis and are appropriate for general approaches to text mining and the study of particular structures within text and discourse.

1. LIWC. The Linguistic Inquiry and Word Count (LIWC) tool (Tausczik & Pennebaker, 2010) is a computerized graphical and user-friendly tool for studying vocabulary used to calculate the latent characteristics of a text. LIWC offers more than 80 metrics for various psychological vocabulary categories (e.g., cognitive words, affective words, functional words, analytical words).
2. WMatrix. WMatrix is an online graphical tool for word frequency analysis and visualization for text corpora. While it can be used to complete the study, it is most useful in the function engineering process for extracting linguistic characteristics such as word n-grams and multi-word sentences, such as idioms and similar, part-of-speech tags and semantic word categories. It also allows the text corpora to be visualized in word clouds and simultaneously offers an interface to compare multiple text corpora.
3. Coh-Metrix. The Coh-Metrix (Graesser, McNamara, Louwerse, & Cai, 2004; Graesser, McNamara, & Kulikowich, 2011) a common tool for text analysis,

offers over 100 text measurements in 11 categories. CohMetrix provides a more detailed interpretation and examination of text characteristics and relationships in the data than the WMatrix. Although WMatrix semantically tags terms and multi-word units, CohMetrix has many tags for evaluating deep cohesion text such as narrative steps and/or referential cohesion. With these increases in the research's profound significance, larger data sets are required – CohMetrix essentially appears to need a larger body of text than semantic taggers.

4. Latent semantic analysis (LSA). Latent semantic analysis is another tool frequently used to extract subjects from text corpora (Landauer, Foltz, & Laham, 1998). While LDA and similar probabilistic methods use word co-occurrence to estimate the words which constitute a field, LSA uses a linear algebra technique of matrix decomposition to find words representing various themes. It can also be used by comparing their vectors in the topic space to calculate the semantic similarity of two documents or sections of documents. LSA has been implemented in many programming languages, with one of the most common LSA implementations being a java-based text mining library and the lsa R package (Alves dos Santos & Favero, 2015).

5. NLP toolkits (***Stanford CoreNLP, Python NLTK, Apache OpenNLP***). Text mining systems usually require natural language text analysis, the toolkits for natural language processing (NLP) form a significant part of the text mining toolbox. These methods are usually used in the analytical preprocessing step, for example, (a) split paragraphs into individual phrases, utterances, or words, (b) extraction of syntactic dependency between words (c) assign parts-of-speech categories (word grammatical class) to each word, (d) reduction of derived words (i.e., stemming and lemmatization), (e) named-entity extraction, and (f) co-reference resolution. Several NLP toolkits provide common programming languages (e.g., Java or Python) with programmable APIs. One famous example is the Apache OpenNLP toolkit, which supported most basic NLP activities. Similarly, Python NLTK (Bird, 2006) is an NLP library with somewhat similar python programming language capabilities. The NLP toolkit offers a Java API and standalone GUI on the command line and a collection of wrappers for other programming languages, including C #, Python, R, Ruby, Scala, and JavaScript.

6. ConceptNet. ConceptNet. One of the key reasons why natural language comprehension is a complicated issue is that each statement depends on the listener's meaning and background knowledge. The method adopted by ConceptNet (Liu & Singh, 2004) is to create a vast graph of "common-sense" knowledge and then to be used to understand and process natural text. ConceptNet can use a broad knowledge base to categorize textual articles, extract topical information from corpora, sentiment analysis, and text summarization.

7. TAGME. TAGME is a text annotation tool explicitly developed for short, unstructured, or semi-structured text segments, such as text collected from snippets, tweets, and news feeds (Ferragina & Scaiella, 2010). The text annotation method defines and annotates a series of words with appropriate links to Wikipedia sites. In other words, TAGME assigns each sequence in the analyzed text to a Wikipedia concept. An experimental TAGME (Ferragina & Scaiella,

2010) evaluation demonstrated better performance over short text segments and similar accuracy/recall outcomes for longer text than other solutions. The tool offers an API for text processing and integration with other applications on-the-fly.
8. Apache Stanbol. Apache Stanbol is an open-source text analysis software tool. It is intended primarily to combine semantic technology with existing content management systems and extract text and functions. Like TAGME, it binds keywords extracted from text to concepts from Wikipedia. Apache Stanbol is easy to configure and run in a small set of instances. However, the tool also enables a domain-specific ontology to be integrated into the annotation process. This is particularly useful when dealing with local ideas that are unique to a particular educational setting. Finally, Apache Stanbol supports multi-language text annotation. Multiple content management systems have been built into the application.

Social network analysis

Social network analysis attempts to explain the interactions and relationships most frequently represented as nodes and edge diagrams between individuals and/or societies. SNA is widely used to evaluate interactive social networks, such as social media or student engagement in MOOCs or online courses.
1. Gephi. Gephi is a common and widely used interactive tool to analyze and visualize various social networks. Gephi is commonly used in learning analytics research and supports social networks defined in a broad range of data input formats, which are both direct and undirected. It has various charts for a simple view of social networks and provides the ability, often used as a tool for exploratory research, to color nodes and edges, based on the characteristics of their location in the network. The tool also offers a Java API for manipulating social network graphs, measuring multiple measures (for example, density, average trajectory, and betweenness centrality), and execution algorithms widely used in social network analyses (for example, graph clustering and giant interconnected component extraction). It is licensed under the GPL license and is available on Microsoft platforms such as Windows, Linux, and Mac OSX.
2. EgoNet. EgoNet is a free social network analysis tool that focuses on analyzing egocentric networks that are, in general, social networks developed from particular network actors' viewpoint, usually using survey instruments. Via EgoNet, a researcher specifies the number of network members and gives them a small survey of their relationships with other network members. As participants provide information from their viewpoints about the network structure, EgoNet visualizes the entire network structure and offers various analytical instruments better to understand the network's overall nature and opportunities to ask a network member for further questions.
3. NodeXL. NodeXL, Network Overview Discovery Exploration for Excel, a Microsoft Excel extension that makes it easy to display network data from various data input formats in Microsoft Excel. It is also used for the estimation of the primary network properties (e.g., radius, diameter, density), node properties

(e.g., degree centrality, betweenness centrality, eigenvector centrality), and other network analytics approaches (e.g., cluster analysis for community mining). There are currently two versions, NodeXL Basic and NodeXL Pro. Beyond the primary social network analysis support, NodeXL Pro provides data aggregation functionalities from different social media sites (e.g., Twitter, YouTube, Flickr) and social media text and sentiment analysis.

4. Pajek. Pajek is a free desktop tool for complex analysis of many large networks (thousands and hundreds of thousands of nodes), including social media networks. Pajek is widely used for social network analysis and LA research in academia for network partitioning, group identification, large-scale network visualization, and information flow analysis. There is also a Pajek-XXL version, a specifically built Pajek version for the efficient operation of vast networks (with millions of nodes).

5. NetMiner. NetMiner is a popular graphic tool for the study and visualization of networks. It supports network data import in various formats, network views, and the measurement of standard graphic and node-based statistics, similar to Gephi and NodeXL. NetMiner has a built-in data mining module supporting various data mining tasks such as classification, clustering, reduction, and recommendation) which is also suited for advanced NetMiner network analysis. It also has a Python integrated scripting engine for more complex and personalized analytical forms. It also supports a scripting interface and the graphical user interface, making it ideal for module integration in other software systems. It also facilitates 3D network viewing and network exploration video recording (e.g., for inclusion). Currently, NetMiner is available on Microsoft Windows OS only.

6. Cytoscape. Cytoscape is another open-source framework for the visualization of molecular interaction networks, which is now a fully-functional package for studying different network types, including social networks. Cytoscape consists of a core distribution that uses several user-contributing modules to analyze and view basic network capabilities. Cytoscape is developed and can be used in various operating systems on the Java platform.

7. SoNIA. SoNIA is an open-source framework for longitudinal network data analysis. For the longitudinal network data, in addition to information on relationships (i.e., edges) between network members (i.e., nodes), the time of these relationships occurred, or the order in which they formed is also available. SoNIA can display network change over time, allowing various network architecture algorithms to be defined in multiple timeframes to better visualize network structure changes. The effect is a good, 'smooth' animation of structural changes exported in QuickTime video format over time. SoNIA is developed by Stanford University and can be used in all critical operating systems in the Java programming language.

8. SocNetV. Social Networks Visualizer (SocNetV) is an open-source tool for analyzing and manipulating social networks. This facilitates the loading of data of different network formats, computing traditional graph and node characteristics, and versatile network data visualization (e.g., filtering, coloring, and resiz-

ing nodes based on their characteristics). One of SocNetV's exciting and unique features is the embedded web crawler, which automatically extracts a link structure from a set of HTML documents. It is licensed under GPL and available on Microsoft Windows, Linux, and Mac OSX.

9. NetworkX. NetworkX is a Python Open Source software library for complex network functions, architectures, and dynamics. It is commonly used in academia and has a wide range of advanced features in networked data, including the reduction of graphs through block modeling, group clustering, group detection, link prediction (finding missing links, for example, missing Facebook connections between two friends), analysis of network triads, and others.

10. ***R packages: statnet (network, sna, ergm) and igraph***. In addition to the graphical tools for analyzing social networks, other social network research packages are available in the R programming language. The network package is used to construct and change network objects, extract basic network metrics, and visualize network graphs. Often used together with the network package, the sna package provides a set of features commonly required for social network analysis, including network and node metric measurement, block-modeling graph reductions, network regression, network visualization, and others. The igraph software is another package that is mostly used for social network analysis. It is a library written in C programming language with additional language bindings in R and Python's languages. It can be used to construct and change social networks from a broad range of input formats (e.g., Pajek, Gephi, GraphML, edge list, an adjacency matrix), measurement of network and node properties, visualization of graphs, and various network analysis, including group identification, graph clusters, block modeling, unified blocks measurement, and others. The stat network package focuses on statistical network simulations using exponential random graph models, latent space, and latent cluster models. Another vital package for social network analysis is the stat network package. The statnet package contains network model estimation methods, network model validation, model-based network simulations, and network visualization. It also contains and uses several of the other packages, such as network, sna, and ergm.

11. SNAPP. The Social networks Adapting Pedagogical Practice is a bookmarklet, developed by Bakharia and Dawson (2011), to evaluate student social networks created under popular learning management systems-LMSs (e.g., blackboard, Desire2learn, and moodle)-which is designed to be a bookmark button for the browser bookmark bar. SNAPP extracts a student social network from HTML pages of LMS discussions (formed through student posting and response interactions). The data can then be exported or displayed with a range of graph layout algorithms via SNAPP, or further analysis can be done with other above listed SNA tools. SNAPP can also investigate student social networking trends over time, evaluate extremely active/inactive users, find systemic gaps, and compare analysis for multiple discussion forums.

Process and sequence mining

In addition to more conventional approaches to analyzing education data, such as forecasting learning outcomes or continuing learning, research engaged in monitoring learning sequences to understand learning strategies and processes (Bogarín, Romero, Cerezo, & Sánchez-Santillán, 2014). For this form of application, a distinctive collection of resources has evolved. We will present in this section the process and sequence mining tools ProM and TraMineR that are widely used to support EDM and LA research. These tools are generally used for analyzes, although they often allow some preprocessing levels of data.

1. ProM. ProM is an autonomous, scalable, and open-source Java-based framework supporting several process mining techniques (Van Der Aalst et al., 2009). The new version, ProM 6, supports process mining in a distributed environment or batch processing. ProM supports chaining many process mining algorithms to explicitly define the predicted inputs and outputs for each of the implementations supported. Also, new plugins can be introduced at runtime to allow fast integration into the analysis process. Finally, ProM allows quick integration without programming with current information systems.
2. TraMineR. TraMineR is a free, open-source R package that supports state or event sequences mining and visualization. For analysis and visualizing status sequence data, TraMineR has a variety of primary features: (i) processing various state sequence formats and converting them to and from different representations; (ii) defining longitudinal (i.e., length, complexity, time in each state) and other aggregate sequence characteristics; (iii) accessing a wide range of plotting capabilities (i.e., frequency or density plots, index plot), and (iv) a broad set of metrics for evaluating distances between sequences.

PSLC DataShop

A multifunctional platform is PSLC DataShop (Koedinger et al., 2010). The PSLC DataShop comprises several data sets that can be downloaded and analyzed, and resources to enable exploratory analysis and models. DataShop has a domain structure (knowledge component) comparison functionality on a dataset like q-matrices (Tatsuoka, 1983). It also can visualize student performance over time in terms of correctness, hint use, latent knowledge, response times, and other variables of interest. It also includes visualizations of student performance regularly. The PSLC DataShop is a free, though not open-source, web-based application.

2.5 Conclusion

Two communities have evolved in recent years around the concept of using large-scale educational data to change education research practice. As this field evolves from relatively small and obscure conferences to a subject known across educational research and affects schools worldwide, the above approaches are available to achieve several goals. Every year, researchers and practitioners use these methods to analyze new constructions and address new research questions, making the application of these methods more understood.

The methods and applications of educational data mining and learning analytics are discussed in this chapter. These approaches can be useful for researchers, teachers, administrators, and ultimately students by evaluating students' attitudes and results. We also discussed variations and similarities between these two methods.

2.6 Review Questions

Reflect on the concepts of this chapter guided by the following questions.

1. Define Educational Data Mining. Illustrate the similarities and differences of Educational Data Mining with Learning Analytics.
2. Trace out the similarities between Data Mining, Educational Data Mining, and Learning Analytics.
3. List the key events that occurred in the formation of the EDM community.
4. Define Educational Data Mining. Identify the goals of Educational Data Mining.
5. Describe the phases involved in Educational Data Mining.
6. Explain the methods of Educational Data Mining with suitable examples.
7. Explain the standard methods used both for Educational Data Mining and Learning Analytics.
8. Describe the broad categories of typical applications of both Educational Data Mining and Learning Analytics.
9. Which are the primary tools for Educational Data Mining and/or Learning Analytics?
10. How Educational Data Mining brings real change in the education system?
11. What are the current trends in educational data mining?

References

Alani, M. M., Tawfik, H., Saeed, M., & Anya, O. (2018). *Applications of big data analytics: Trends, issues, and challenges* (pp. 1–214). https://doi.org/10.1007/978-3-319-76472-6.

Alves dos Santos, J. C., & Favero, E. L. (2015). Practical use of a latent semantic analysis (LSA) model for automatic evaluation of written answers. *Journal of the Brazilian Computer Society, 21*(1), 1–8. https://doi.org/10.1186/s13173-015-0039-7

Baker, R., & Siemens, G. (2014). Educational data mining and learning analytics. *Learning Analytics: From Research to Practice*, 61–75. https://doi.org/10.1007/978-1-4614-3305-7_4.

Baker, R. S. (2015). *Big data and education* (2nd ed.). New York: Teachers College, Columbia University.

Baker, R. S., & Inventado, P. S. (2014). Educational data mining and learning analytics. In *Learning analytics: From research to practice*. https://doi.org/10.1007/978-1-4614-3305-7_4.

Baker, R. S. J. (2010). Data mining for education. *International Encyclopedia of Education (3rd Edition)*, 7, 112–118. https://doi.org/10.4018/978-1-59140-557-3.

Baker, R. S. J. D. (2007). Modeling and understanding students' off-task behavior in intelligent tutoring systems. *Conference on Human Factors in Computing Systems – Proceedings*, 1059–1068. https://doi.org/10.1145/1240624.1240785.

Baker, R. S. J. D, Corbett, A. T., & Wagner, A. Z. (2006). Human classification of low-fidelity replays of student actions. In *Proceedings of the educational data mining workshop at the 8th international conference on intelligent tutoring systems, 2002* (pp. 29–36).

Baker, R. S. J. D., & Yacef, K. (2009). The state of educational data mining in 2009: A review and future visions. *Journal of Educational Data Mining*, 1(1), 3–16. https://doi.org/http://doi.ieeecomputersociety.org/10.1109/ASE.2003.1240314.

Bakharia, A., & Dawson, S. (2011). SNAPP: A bird's-eye view of temporal participant interaction. *ACM International Conference Proceeding Series*, 168–173. https://doi.org/10.1145/2090116.2090144.

Bakhshinategh, B., Zaiane, O. R., ElAtia, S., & Ipperciel, D. (2018). Educational data mining applications and tasks: A survey of the last 10 years. *Education and Information Technologies*, 23(1), 537–553. https://doi.org/10.1007/s10639-017-9616-z

Bienkowski, M., Feng, M., & Means, B. (2014). Enhancing teaching and learning through educational data mining and learning analytics: An issue brief. In *Educational improvement through data mining and analytics* (pp. 1–60). U.S. Department of Education, Office of Educational Technology: Washington, D.C., USA.

Bird, S. (2006). NLTK: The natural language toolkit. In *Proceedings of the COLING/ACL on interactive presentation sessions* (pp. 69–72). https://doi.org/10.1017/9781108642408.013.

Bogarín, A., Romero, C., Cerezo, R., & Sánchez-Santillán, M. (2014). Clustering for improving educational process mining. *ACM International Conference Proceeding Series*, 11–15. https://doi.org/10.1145/2567574.2567604.

Bousbia, N., & Belamri, I. (2014). Which contribution does EDM provide to computer-based learning environments? *Studies in Computational Intelligence*, 524, 3–28. https://doi.org/10.1007/978-3-319-02738-8

Buckingham Shum, S. (2012). *Learning analytics: Policy briefing.* pp. 1–12. http://iite.unesco.org/files/policy_briefs/pdf/en/learning_analytics.pdf

Calvet Liñán, L., & Juan Pérez, Á. A. (2015). Educational data mining and learning analytics: Differences, similarities, and time evolution. *RUSC. Universities and Knowledge Society Journal*, 12(3), 98. https://doi.org/10.7238/rusc.v12i3.2515

Cetintas, S., Si, L., Xin, Y. P., & Hord, C. (2010). Automatic detection of off-task behaviors in intelligent tutoring systems with machine learning techniques. *IEEE Transactions on Learning Technologies*, 3(3), 228–236. https://doi.org/10.1109/TLT.2009.44

Corbett, A. T., & Anderson, J. R. (1995). Knowledge tracing: Modeling the acquisition of procedural knowledge. In *User modeling and user-adapted interaction* (Vol. 4, Issue 4, pp. 253–278). http://www.springerlink.com/index/M50H664760426738.pdf%5Cnpapers3://publication/livfe/id/110900

Duval, E. (2011). Attention please! Learning analytics for visualization and recommendation. *ACM International Conference Proceeding Series*, 9–17. https://doi.org/10.1145/2090116.2090118.

Ferragina, P., & Scaiella, U. (2010). TAGME: On-the-fly annotation of short text fragments (by Wikipedia entities). *International Conference on Information and Knowledge Management, Proceedings*, April 2015, 1625–1628. https://doi.org/10.1145/1871437.1871689.

Graesser, A. C., McNamara, D. S., & Kulikowich, J. M. (2011). Coh-metrix: Providing multilevel analyses of text characteristics. *Educational Researcher*, 40(5), 223–234. https://doi.org/10.3102/0013189X11413260

Graesser, A. C., McNamara, D. S., Louwerse, M. M., & Cai, Z. (2004). Coh-metrix: Analysis of text on cohesion and language. *Behavior Research Methods, Instruments, and Computers*, 36(2), 193–202. https://doi.org/10.3758/BF03195564

References

Greller, W., & Drachsler, H. (2012). Translating learning into numbers: A generic framework for learning analytics. *Educational Technology and Society, 15*(3), 42–57.

He, W. (2013). Examining students' online interaction in a live video streaming environment using data mining and text mining. *Computers in Human Behavior, 29*(1), 90–102. https://doi.org/10.1016/j.chb.2012.07.020

Johnson, L., Smith, R., Willis, H., Levine, A., & Haywood, K. (2011). *The Horizon report*.

Koedinger, K., Baker, R., Cunningham, K., Skogsholm, A., Leber, B., & Stamper, J. (2010). A data repository for the EDM community. April 2016, 43–55. https://doi.org/10.1201/b10274-6.

Landauer, T. K., Foltz, P. W., & Laham, D. (1998). An introduction to Latent SEmantic Analysis. *Behavior Research Methods, 25*(2–3), 259–284. https://doi.org/10.3758/BRM.41.3.944

Lang, C. (2017). *Handbook of learning analytics*. https://doi.org/10.18608/hla17.

Liu, H., & Singh, P. (2004). ConceptNet – A practical commonsense reasoning tool-kit. *BT Technology Journal, 22*(4), 211–226. https://doi.org/10.1023/B:BTTJ.0000047600.45421.6d

NMC Horizon Report > 2012 Higher Education Edition. (2012).

Papamitsiou, Z., & Economides, A. A. (2014). Learning analytics and educational data mining in practice: A systemic literature review of empirical evidence. *Educational Technology and Society, 17*(4), 49–64.

Reye, J. (2004). *Student modelling based on belief networks to cite this version: HAL Id: hal-00197306*. pp. 63–96.

Rodrigo, M. M. T., Ryan, R. S. J., McLaren, B. M., Jayme, A., & Dy, T. T. (2012). Development of a workbench to address the educational data mining bottleneck. *Proceedings of the 5th International conference on educational data mining, EDM 2012*, 152–155.

Romero, C., & Ventura, S. (2010). Educational data mining: A review of the state of the art. *IEEE Transactions on Systems, Man and Cybernetics Part C: Applications and Reviews, 40*(6), 601–618. https://doi.org/10.1109/TSMCC.2010.2053532

Romero, C., & Ventura, S. (2013). Data mining in education. *Wiley Interdisciplinary Reviews: Data Mining and Knowledge Discovery, 3*(1), 12–27. https://doi.org/10.1002/widm.1075

Romero, C., & Ventura, S. (2017). Educational data science in massive open online courses. *Wiley Interdisciplinary Reviews: Data Mining and Knowledge Discovery, 7*(1). https://doi.org/10.1002/widm.1187.

Romero, C., & Ventura, S. (2020). Educational data mining and learning analytics: An updated survey. *Wiley Interdisciplinary Reviews: Data Mining and Knowledge Discovery, 10*(3), 1–21. https://doi.org/10.1002/widm.1355

Schroeder, U., Thüs, H., & Technologies, I. L. (2012). A reference model for learning analytics Mohamed Amine Chatti*, Anna Lea Dyckhoff. *Int. J. Technology Enhanced Learning, 4*(CiL), 318–331.

Siemens, G. (2012). Learning analytics: Envisioning a research discipline and a domain of practice. *ACM International Conference Proceeding Series*, May, 4–8. https://doi.org/10.1145/2330601.2330605.

Siemens, G., & Baker, R. S. J. D. (2012). Learning analytics and educational data mining: Towards communication and collaboration. *ACM International Conference Proceeding Series*, April 2012, 252–254. https://doi.org/10.1145/2330601.2330661.

Slater, S., Joksimović, S., Kovanovic, V., Baker, R. S., & Gasevic, D. (2017). Tools for educational data mining: A review. *Journal of Educational and Behavioral Statistics, 42*(1), 85–106. https://doi.org/10.3102/1076998616666808

Tatsuoka, K. K. (1983). Rule space: An approach for dealing with misconceptions based on item response theory. *Journal of Educational Measurement, 20*(4), 345–354. https://doi.org/10.1111/j.1745-3984.1983.tb00212.x

Tauszcik, Y. R., & Pennebaker, J. W. (2010). The psychological meaning of words: LIWC and computerized text analysis methods. *Journal of Language and Social Psychology, 29*(1), 24–54. https://doi.org/10.1177/0261927X09351676

Tervakari, A. M., Silius, K., Koro, J., Paukkeri, J., & Pirttilä, O. (2014). Usefulness of information visualizations based on educational data. *IEEE Global Engineering Education Conference, EDUCON*, April, 142–151. https://doi.org/10.1109/EDUCON.2014.6826081.

Vahdat, M., Ghio, A., Oneto, L., Anguita, D., Funk, M., & Rauterberg, M. (2015). Advances in learning analytics and educational data mining. *23rd European symposium on artificial neural networks, computational intelligence and machine learning, ESANN 2015 – Proceedings*, April, 297–306.

Van Der Aalst, W. M. P., Van Dongen, B. F., Günther, C., Rozinat, A., Verbeek, H. M. W., & Weijters, A. J. M. M. (2009). Prom: The process mining toolkit. *CEUR Workshop Proceedings, 489*(May 2014).

Veeramachaneni, K., O'Reilly, U. M., & Adl, K. (2015). Feature factory: Crowd-sourced feature discovery. *L@S 2015 – 2nd ACM Conference on Learning at Scale*, 373–376. https://doi.org/10.1145/2724660.2728696.

Verbert, K., Duval, E., Klerkx, J., Govaerts, S., & Santos, J. L. (2013). Learning analytics dashboard applications. *American Behavioral Scientist, 57*(10), 1500–1509. https://doi.org/10.1177/0002764213479363

Verbert, K., Manouselis, N., Drachsler, H., & Duval, E. (2012). Dataset-driven research to support learning and knowledge analytics. *Educational Technology and Society, 15*(3), 133–148.

Wikipedia.(2019).*Educationaldatamining*.Wikipedia.https://doi.org/10.4324/9781351044677-18.

Chapter 3
Preparing for Learning Analytics

3.1 Introduction

In the education sector, learning analytics has become a famous slogan. Learning Analytics will undoubtedly be a powerful tool for organizations to promote retention and demonstrate that institutions deserve federal funding in the future. Nonetheless, steps are necessary before it can be introduced (Weitzel, 2019). Just because organizations have software that gathers student data does not mean that they can turn a key and unexpectedly use learning analytics. It is an effort for which organizations have to plan and develop.

They have to determine what they want to know from their data before creating a learning analytics initiative. Institutions should collect data to understand the student's results and/or institutional policies and operations effectiveness. Before developing their learning analytic processes, organizations must determine what they want to know so that staff will analyze data that correspond to the organization's objectives.

The most significant step must be taken by institutions to ensure standardization on all campuses. Institutes must improve standardization at all levels, including departmental policies and teacher actions, to monitor student outcomes' reliable data. Many higher education institutions give teachers flexibility across their classes, making it almost impossible to equate learning data with different teaching styles. Institutions need to reduce discrepancies for data to tell a good story to use learning analytics. For standard practices, students ideally follow the same educational process irrespective of the curriculum. Add standard policies into the mix that decide how data are gathered and what information is gathered, and school staff can compare accurate student data and obtain relevant insights.

In the future, private institutions are well-positioned to incorporate learning analytics because, as an industry, they tend to write standard training practices from attendance tracking and content delivery to technology. Additionally, private institutions are not as diverse in teachers' teaching styles and can make changes quicker than non-profit institutions.

In addition to university-wide standardization, universities will invest in analytical tools and software. Institutions cannot rely on manually entered data to use learning analytics since it will likely contain prejudices and allow room for human error. Technology is essential for the accurate and rich collection of data to produce more reliable forecasts. Nevertheless, technology data collection sheds much light on student behavior. Institutions will identify behavioral trends with more informative data.

In addition to investing in technology for effective learning analytics, organizations may recruit or reassign personnel to track the data, report relevant insights and assess where and how the data should be stored and handled before and after review.

As the education sector modernizes and new technologies become prevalent in the classroom, Learning Analytics is a valuable opportunity for higher education institutions soon. To prepare for learning analytics, organizations now need to lay the foundation for updating policies to include data collection. Students must also be mindful that staff and teachers regularly follow these procedures to ensure that the data collected accurately reflects their behavior and results. When standardizations are met, universities may start learning analytics to improve students' performance, increase retention, and reduce the average time it takes for students to graduate. They have to define; until then, the measures are needed to prepare for effective learning analytics!

3.2 Role of Psychology in Learning Analytics

The role influential peers play in setting a norm or pattern others would like to emit important for self-efficiency and self-regulated learning (Zimmerman, Bandura, & Martinez-Pons, 1992). While self-regulated learning theories vary from behavioral to socially cognitive to constructivist, lead proponent Barry Zimmerman demonstrated that the social context is central to building one's self-regulation capacity. In short, we gain initial knowledge and reflection when matched with a good mentor or model that usually takes four steps (Fritz & Whitmer, 2017):

- *Observational*: Students learn to differentiate between the main elements of the skills or technique of a student.
- *Emulative*: The performance of a learner approximates the overall type of skill or technique of a student.
- *Self-control*: students may exercise skills or techniques based on a successful model's mental representation.
- *Self-regulation*: Learners should regularly adapt their skills and strategies as circumstances change.

The faculty will look for an improvement in the design of courses focused on Learning Analytics, but only if they have a minimum number of people with a more successful method. That is why and how learning analytics will help recognize, encourage, assess and facilitate significant activities and practice by acting as a benchmark against which the faculty not only tests itself but also points to a path forward, against encouraging students to accept responsibility for learning. Sure, technology could help, but only if the teachers first believe it would, sufficiently try it or look for people who did. Thus, the students responsible for their learning are the only flexible way to learn, and the teachers must, therefore, take care of "teaching failures" by being open to particular pedagogical examples and working hard to understand and execute them.

Such pedagogical and psychological contexts that motivate and persuade people may start to have important implications for successful learning analytics, be they nudges, visualizations, or messages directed at students (or faculty), incorporated into academic technology. In short, it is not enough simply to present what we believe is straightforward and reliable quantitative data. Further research must clarify how we can identify and share stories in data that shift our hearts and minds. To increase student self-regulation or increase professional consciousness about their education, we need to define, express, and present quantitative findings. To illustrate, consider a few examples.

Normally, it was a more challenging task to find the right messages for students. It could be demotivating to submit a message like "You are in the bottom five percent of your class in LMS activity," but to create the right message was harder and something the data science team might poorly construct. Designers and text-on-page experts will do this. A language that uses a "concerned friend" tone motivates students to provide conference messages that catch students' attention and include information on activities that cause the notification.

These psychologically influenced messages can support radical educational innovation through learning analytics. On the other hand, people with experience in data analysis and quantitative techniques are as rarely (and almost as expensive) as scientists, though the value of effective communication has been recognized in other industries. Maybe it is time to introduce new data science initiatives for people with lower interest in numbers and algorithmic solutions through data visualization or design thinking tracks.

Truly functional approaches are designed to promote and harness students' or teachers' encouragement in an evidence-based intervention that increases their consciousness to try (or accept) institutional help. However, this will probably take more than a quantitative approach to the identification and dissemination of evidence.

For systemic transformation and improvement, we need data and research with specific forecasts, but, as suggested in (Macfadyen & Dawson, 2012), we need to go beyond the forecasts to enable us to find and say stories about successful practices and practitioners whose examples may be much better by example.

Ultimately, we cannot use theoretical approaches to punish others, but as enlightenments for education and educate people about what is possible. Showing people how they can function constructively without humiliating them will enable them to take the next steps forward. With the right stories that touch people's hearts about the importance of learning analytics and reliable results, everyone will consent to the possible uncomfortable pursuit of excellence.

3.3 Architecting the Learning Analytics Environment

Learning analytics is an area that has been taking shape since 2010, and over the years, has frequently been featured in studies on the future of learning technology. This focuses on the integration of learning (learning, educational studies, learning/assessment sciences), analytics (statistics, simulation, computer science, and artificial intelligence), and interaction of humans and computers (participatory design, behavioral science, social-technical system design, usability assessment). For some colleges and universities investing substantially in their analytical infrastructures, how does an institution develop itself to evolve pedagogically and analytically in this academic crossroads to meet significant, strategically relevant educational and learning challenges? Briefly, how does an organization evolve to have a sustainable impact?

Learning analytics focuses on using analytical methods to gain insights into educational data to improve teaching and learning. Whether this offers new "power tools" for academic researchers who have been researching teaching and learning data nondigitally for decades, Learning Analytics would, without a doubt, be a step forward. This work is the first step essential to validate the approaches. However, as we move from research to development, the real potential of learning analytics will be realized, and human-computer systems will be generated to automate this analysis process from data collection to visualization and recommendations, which provide more timely, reliable, and actionable input to students, educators, instructional designers and other stakeholders who are the participants (Lang, 2017).

The term automation evokes many significances. It is important to note that automation does not automatically mean the full automation of assessments, decisions, and behavior, putting educators "out of the loop." Automation may only turn the data collection, cleaning, review, and visualization phase into a commodity service that previously needed qualified, but limited, researchers or analysts. The responsibility for making sense of and acting on that input may be shared entirely with a human student, instructor, or analyst (e.g., The analytics system can suggest areas of concern that encourage users to prioritize attention or recommend courses). Feedback and guidance can also be entirely collected by professional teachers but customized through custom contact (Huberth, Chen, Tritz, & McKay, 2015).

In conclusion, the data revolution's potential in teaching and learning consists of creating much more timely feedback loops to monitor a complex system's efficiency. In a field where feedback has already been identified as a critical tool for students and educators, the question is how effective human-computer systems can realize this potential.

3.3.1 The Problems

While some of the best scholars in data science, analytics, user interface design, and organizational creativity are located there, a school or university is unwilling to innovate in monitoring, reviewing, and feeding knowledge to enhance teaching and learning on those fronts. While paradoxical to an outsider, the inherent chaos is all too common for the insider: Academics do not have opportunities to focus on strategic planning and learning challenges in their organization. As a result, research-active analytical groups do not necessarily respond to the analytical needs of their institutions. Academics do not want to be identified with the hated logo of the service center that has not research-worthy connotations. There will be some issues (Shum & Mckay, 2018).

1. **Academics are under pressure to perform new research**. They need to make an empirical breakthrough worthy of publications and grants checked by peers as they make proof-based statements on data based on robust analysis and sometimes use state-of-the-art technology well beyond what is available in existing products. They respect their intellectual independence, and they prefer to perform work on learning analytics that interests them. Academics reserve the right not to solve the "boring" (though serious) data issues in the organization because they see the problems as repetitive and/or because they do not want their study story dictated. Scientists, distribution, and resources are spent on procurement. There is time to compose, train PhDs, and submit and review articles.
2. **There is no praise for academics for developing scalable applications**. Any competent academic group can develop fresh, well-founded, and small-scale analytics, but it reserves the right to take on future challenges. Researchers have no incentive for more widely validating or moving progress into mainstream implementation. You definitely do not think it is your job to repair the institution's dysfunctional data structures; it is an IT or business intelligence (BI) job. Crossing the gap between innovation and technology often includes several competencies that are not common in research communities, technical software development, user interfaces, interface design, behavioral science, and innovation advocacy. This also includes an ongoing emphasis on the user community's needs. The key deployment of analytical instruments often includes comprehensive cross-campus collaboration with other academics and units to develop their commitment. It is a long-standing challenge for research and development of learning technology.
3. **Universities and colleges want students to have an impact**. This effect takes several forms. It increases student engagement, offers more effective education, tackles inequality in student results, protects budgets, and enhances retention and graduation rates. Such realistic findings are often seen as counter-incentives by academics. Academics should be careful when alleging causal ties or being pressured to justify their research financially. Unless the mainstream application of analytics involves scalable infrastructure that academics cannot provide, commercial products are created. We can include simplistic dashboards which give analytics a lousy reputation and which academics, as end-users or researchers, are reluctant to associate with. Things tend to reach the broader traditional mass markets rather than the future-oriented cutting edge of teaching and learning.

3.3.2 Organizational Architectures for Learning Analytics

Shum and Mckay (2018) suggested three learning analysis organizational models that can be considered by the college or university leadership to facilitate advanced analytics to accomplish their own goals and context.

The three main organizational models used to provide learning analysis are:

- IT Service Center model
- Faculty Academics Model
- Hybrid Innovation Center Model

1. ***The IT Service Center Model***: Under this model (Fig. 3.1), an IT service center offers analytics from an enterprise platform. For example, the following are:

    - The LMS team leads to the provision of analytics by using/configuring the product dashboards for academics (and perhaps students).
    - The enterprise data warehouse, BI, or institutional research (IR) team offers analytical information by combining LMS data and other data sources.
    - A team in the Center for teaching and learning works with these units to help academics use analytical technology.

   Advantages:

    - The center is designed to provide a production-grade analytics service near 24/7 uptime and system support accessible to all students and employees as a central integrated network for other institutional systems. The research typically involves "academic analytics" (conventional demographics, enrollment, and grades of students) and different types of learning analytics (finer-graining, mid-course progression, and activity data).
    - Staff will innovate what products can do and how they can integrate with current infrastructure.

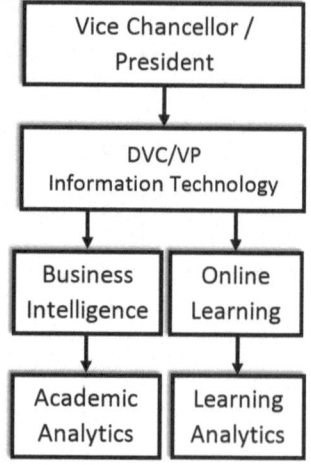

Fig. 3.1 Archetypal Organization Chart, IT Service Center Model. (Shum & Mckay, 2018)

- End-users are typically academics because, to date, most LMS and other items have dashboards to help educators monitor students' progress.
- However, generic LMS products continue to supply student dashboards (but poorly grounded in learning sciences), and when specialized products are used (such as an adaptive tutor on a specific topic), they can also deliver feedback to students since a model of the curriculum and the level of student masters is such a rich one.
- If products permit the customization of report/dashboards or facilitate the export of data, and if the center provides the capability for coding and analysis for subsequent analysis or visualization, user experiences can be provided.

Disadvantages:

- The staff typically only deal with data that products can supply by predefined user interfaces. It is highly doubtful that a participatory design model has helped end-users shape a product with the possibility of getting analytical services accessed on a limited basis and instead of obtaining them poorly.
- Staff seldom know the fields of data science, user interface, learning design, or advanced analytics techniques, thereby restricting the reach of the center's analytics innovation. Such expertise must come from other groups, and most IT services centers have little heritage of widespread collaboration.

2. **The Faculty Academics Model.** Faculty academics (possibly in collaboration with an IT service center) (Fig. 3.2) conduct applied research in the model. Examples are as follows:

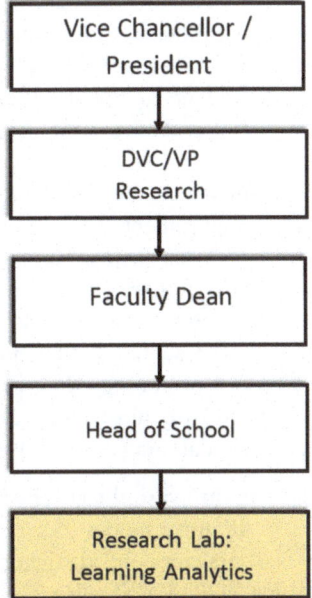

Fig. 3.2 Archetypal Organization Chart, Faculty Academics Model. (Shum & Mckay, 2018)

- Faculty academics develop creative (often externally funded) learning tools to facilitate unique LMS-supported modes of learning. This produces much richer data than generic (i.e., discipline-agnostic) LMS products usually provide. This can be used as research data on learning sciences and input to educators and students.
- Approval of research provided by their institutional LMS and/or BI teams examined by faculty academics. We recruit academics who want to test these analytics, research student reactions, and maybe include other groups such as student support teams.

Advantages

- This model offers sufficient room for revolutionary innovation for academics who can explore beyond existing products with unconventional sensors and advanced analytical techniques.
- Empirical evidence for adopting vendor products is gathered, which typically identifies obstacles to employee readiness, instructional activities that are incompatible with analytics or other organizational factors.
- Evidence-based statements are likely to be submitted with a high rigor, consistent with the Board of Human Research Ethics guidelines and peer-reviewed studies when published.

Disadvantages

- The work is advanced but requires sufficient research skills in design, implementation, and maintenance. This is also a limited knowledge, only briefly available.
- Because analytics become advanced, early adopters attract pilot students, but if these students move away from a subject's theory, the studies are over.
- The experiments are typically fairly limited and/or use different cohorts of students and/or short-term (e.g., only before external funding expires).
- Researchers are less likely to take user's design ("customer discovery") needs into account, and while prototyping analytics are conceptually involved, they may either be unusable or fail to answer widely understood requirements.
- After the lead researcher or key project staff leaves, nobody will drive the analytics service vision. Vision is required so that creativity can be continued through resource codes management, additional grants, strategic exposure, and essential partnerships.
- Developing a hybrid software/pedagogical concept to an enterprise-wide infrastructure is a process of growth that is frequently not compensated for re-searching and involves skills lacking in research groups.

3. **The Innovation Center Model**. A hybrid, autonomous innovation center is built in the third model to serve the entire organization. However, such innovation centers work outside the organization in close partnerships with faculty academics, IT/BI/LMS college/University teams, etc. This model appears to be dealing with fewer organizations, which we now turn into two examples:

3.3 Architecting the Learning Analytics Environment

- Research-active academics and data scientists sponsored by practitioners have a Core of innovation beyond the faculties and independent from institutional IT/Analytics. (For example, Connected Intelligence Centre, University of Technology Sydney)
- A center for innovation outside Universities, separate from the IT/analytics agency, is committed to the maturation and mainstreaming of the popular analytics technologies that academics create and the invention of their analytical services. (For example, Digital Innovation Greenhouse, University of Michigan)

(i) *Connected Intelligence Centre, University of Technology, Sydney.* The University of Technology Sydney (UTS) Connected Intelligence Centre (CIC) (Fig. 3.3) is an Innovation Center built to develop the capacity of the University to gain insights into analytical instruments and techniques — the teaching and learning cycle, testing, and operating units (Ferguson et al., 2014, 2016).

Staffing CIC is a small center with about 20 staff (not all full time). It looks in several respects like a University community of researchers at all levels, PhDs, faculty, and professionals.

While CIC can appear as an academic research group — because it has the mission to create research-driven, sustainable innovation within the UTS — academics are recruited for their research skills and their teamwork, transdisciplinary perspective, and communication skills. CIC has developed and launched the Master of Data Science and Innovation (MDSI) program coordinated and taught mainly by CIC's

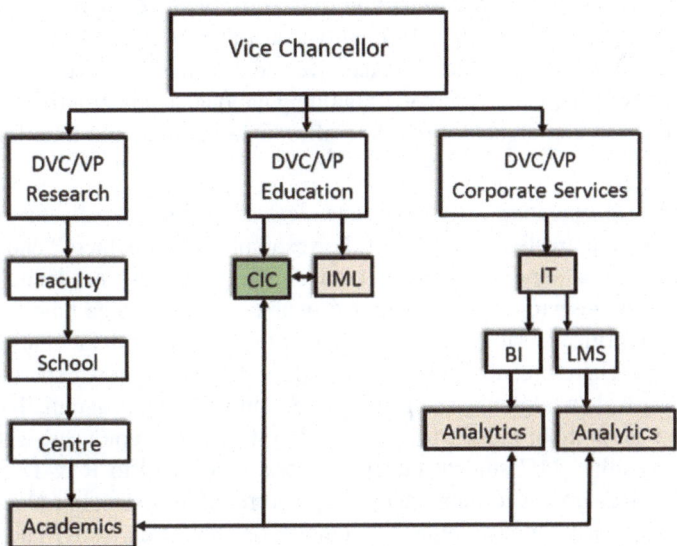

Fig. 3.3 Connected Intelligence Centre, University of Technology Sydney. (Shum & Mckay, 2018)

academics in 2015. It was the only degree program at UTS to take place outside a department until 2017 when UTS launched its Faculty of Transdisciplinary Innovation. The staff will oversee the MDSI program in 2018, but the same personnel will continue to teach it.

CIC has thus operated as a mini-faculty, running MDSI and an optional subject in quantitative literacy and critical thinking ("Arguments, Evidence & Intuition"). CIC's Academic Board of Studies reflects its transdisciplinary nature across UTS. These teaching programs created revenue that allowed CIC to expand beyond the University's baseline funding.

CIC reports to the Deputy Vice-Chancellor of Education. The Director of CIC has the opportunity to address the obstacles to accessing data, operating servers, coordinating meetings, and more with IT administrators, Teaching & Learning Innovation, Student Support, and libraries. This opens up strategic possibilities that would usually not be available to a faculty team.

Critical transitions for CIC will occur from the prototype to small-scale pilots, pilots with several hundred students, and the mainstream implementation to thousands of students. Also, students start expecting certain services and complain about downtime. In general, CIC is pushing a digital technology frontier (e.g., Amazon Web Services), facilitated by and in collaboration with the IT Division (ITD). However, this form of research needs to be secure and involves a positive and respectful relationship with ITD staff, who feel that fulfilling CIC specifications prepare them for what faculty members are likely to request in the future. For example, CIC and ITD co-funded a cloud specialist to assist MDSI students, hoping that other degree programs will call on this cloud services specialist in a limited period.

Cultivating Research-Grade Innovation in a Non-Faculty Center In this work, it is essential to attract and retain high-quality researchers who build an academically stimulating culture that provides the incentive and direction that researchers need in various stages their careers. It involves building national and international exposure through research conferences, providing affordable funding, and time for thought and writing.

Nonetheless, operating a hybrid academic/service process calls for managing conflicts between creativity and effect. For example, when is there "enough" evidence for scaling a prototype with compelling interest by academic research standards? CIC researchers recognize that their work needs to be tailored to bring UTS value as critical customers while collaborating closely with faculties and other client groups. Therefore, all PhDs work together with one or more experts, offering credible test beds while integrating risk factors into a Ph.D. program. Technology breaks new ground but is built in collaboration with ITD employees, who are not used by any other 24/7 student-facing network. Compared to R & D centers in industries, CIC's goal is to improve existing and future programs' productivity but does not necessarily pursue "blue sky" innovations out of curiosity. The CIC was built to create a sustainable capacity for data science and data analytics resources in UTS staff and students.

(ii) *Digital Innovation Greenhouse, University of Michigan.* Learning Analytics at the University of Michigan (UM) began in 2011 (Fig. 3.4) with SLAM Student Learning and Analytics in Michigan as a coherent work topic. This series of seminars combined a forum to share ideas and knowledge between faculty and staff on the campus with an opportunity to connect with external speakers. The UM project was inspired by the interest in SLAM in 2012 to launch a three-year, faculty-led Learning Analytics Task Force (LATF) that would encourage increased use of campus data and finance various Learning Analytics projects. Such programs took two forms: data collection to inform policy and practice; development of methods to use data to facilitate teaching and learning. Many of these methods were used as pilot projects in the classroom and received funding from external research (Lonn et al. 2017).

In 2014, the Digital Innovation Greenhouse (DIG) was introduced to address a common issue faced by LATF ventures. Innovators from the Faculty and their research teams have planned, built, and tested analytical methods to enhance education and campus learning. These technologies have usually been studied in academics' home environments, mostly in classes to be taught. When news of their existence and impact on the campus became known, interest in expansion to other areas came to light. While often involved in this development, the founding research groups lacked the requisite tools, expertise, and/or incentive mechanisms to develop a seedling invention into an aspect of the campus infrastructure.

Many of these initiatives have sought to scale up by distributing their resources to the campus's ITS unit. In setting up and maintaining mature software

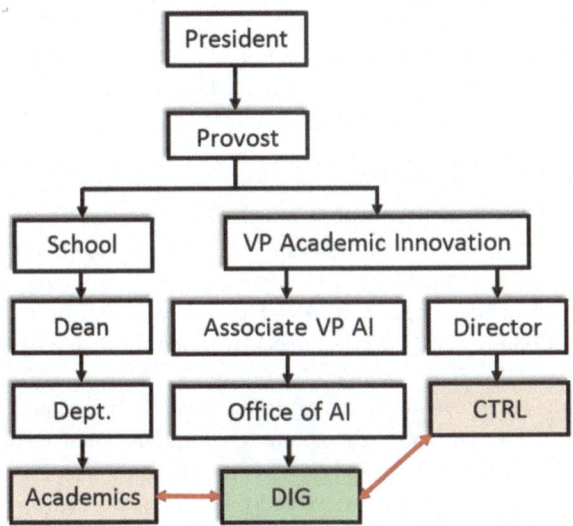

Fig. 3.4 Digital Innovation Greenhouse, University of Michigan. (Shum & Mckay, 2018)

systems, ITS as an enterprise is very successful. Unfortunately, the unit's skills and organizational strategies are not compatible with the researchers' loose, rapid "duct tape and chewing gum" methods. Eventually, DIG was founded as a pilot in 2015 to take advantage of the dynamic innovation culture on campus. They aimed was to adopt a series of existing digitally engaged innovations from research laboratories they had grown out of, take them through the "Valley of Death" innovation, and provide them to ITS as a campus-wide infrastructural tool. By doing so, DIG has accomplished the immediate aim of increasing current research resources' availability and the long-term objective of demonstrating the importance of this greenhouse strategy to create digital communication tools of the twenty-first century.

The University turned to the Office of Digital Education and Innovation to build a home for DIG. In 2013, this unit was initially set up to support UM's newly growing involvement in MOOCs and is reporting on the Vice Provost for Academic Innovation. It has become the focus of campus educational research and development activities and was renamed the Office of Academic Innovation (OAI) in 2016. OAI is currently home to teams working on three main subjects: designing, developing, delivering, and experimenting with online and hybrid education; growing analytics-driven educational innovations to scale; and promoting the gameful design of educational experiences. Both teams also work together with the long-standing Center for Research on Learning and Teaching (CRLT), particularly on residential learners' initiatives.

Staffing In a highly collaborative environment, DIG projects proceed, including at least four elements:

1. *Faculty champions and their research teams.* DIG carried out each project with a principal advocate from the faculty, usually assisted by research team members. DIG is now also investigating how technologies funded by students and staff can be funded. Innovators help drive each project's vision. Also, they regularly contribute to the design and impact of innovation research, often with external support.
2. *The DIG team of software developers, user experience and interface designers, behavioral scientists, and innovation advocates.* The group provides the professional credentials and award program required for technologically mature inventions in close contact with the increasing user community. A wide variety of graduate and undergraduate student fellows assist full-time DIG staff who provide additional effort, a fresh perspective, and close interaction with DIG resources.
3. *An expanding campus community of users, from early adopters to those who intend to use DIG tools as infrastructure.* Continuous, intense contact with this faculty, staff, and students' group is key to the DIG tools' success. The DIG team connects between faculty innovators and this group by ensuring that deep and mutually beneficial ties can be established and maintained.

4. *The UM ITS organization.* The DIG team works with ITS to achieve the technical support needed (servers, single sign-in authentication, data access) and ensure that the DIG tool implementation process stays within ITS systems on campuses.

Also, the main DIG team of these four classes is officially working in the OAI. The DIG team was initially formed as a team of three leading software developers and included a constantly expanding, full-time personnel. Support for the employee comes from three sources: UM Third Century Initiative grants for DIG launch, additional university contributions through the OAI budget, and project funds from various sources (NSF and other grants). OAI provides excellent administrative support and has proved essential to build and maintain a smooth, responsive organization within a sometimes peaceful and conservative campus community.

Engaging Faculty in Academic Innovation DIG was formed as an employee unit within the OAI, without official appointments for any faculty members. The model is focused on strong cooperation between faculty champions, their research groups, DIG staff, and the broader education community across the campus. Although this model has worked well, there have been significant tensions for some faculty members, particularly those who do not concentrate on education. They carry out this work in addition to their current research, teaching, and service responsibilities. To advocate an empirical breakthrough as it spreads on campus is not a simple challenge, mainly though the DIG team provides comprehensive professional support. In reality, the rapid growth and expansion that the DIG team can offer make the professorship champion more demanding. For this purpose, the DIG compares educational R&D – applied research aimed at reinventing higher education at an information age – to the activities taking place in the OAI. With this lens, DIG and OAI can be considered a research institution, similar to UM's former Institute for Social Research or its Life Sciences Institute. All units include faculty members with different positions, from 100% working to 0% affiliated faculty status. In 2018, OAI explored such appointments to ensure professional champions have the support they need to expedite innovation.

Reflections on the Innovation Center Model CIC and DIG have begun at various points and respond to various drivers. Since the launch of CIC, research-active scholars have been running their own Master's and Ph.D. programs, but now they have to build developers' capacity as demand for their analytics tools increases. DIG has also introduced projects from established academics with technology staff but is now looking at new models that include academics. Today the DIG and the CIC appear to shift towards a similar position: they are independent centers reporting to a VP/DVC with advanced data and analytical resources to address strategic teaching and learning issues while collaborating with facilities, professional development, and IT services in collaboration.

At this point, we can summarize the hallmarks of CIC and DIG:

- Reporting the center directly to a VP / DVC senior leader provides the strategic leadership required to improve data access and campus-wide analytical or innovation services.
- The center either integrates or operates very closely with their faculties (DIG) academics and research students (CIC). This helps the center innovate based on the study, which focuses on teachers' and students' needs, contributes to proof-based arguments, and meets ethical standards.
- The center has a central function and can translate these creative concepts into reliable analytical services incorporated with the institution's infrastructure and are subject to IT-approved requirements (e. g. security, architecture). When the prototypes of CIC begin the transition to more wide-ranging internal "products," the value of the DIG software design, development, assessment, and communication team is recognized.
- The center may add additional revenues to its institutional support, including internationally funded faculty collaborative ventures, domestic strategic grants, student fees from formal educational programs, and faculty purchases from academics.
- The Center will generate substantial design efficiencies and organizational synergies by providing a campus-wide focal point for creating analytical resources. For example, the DIG team has built a common, expandable framework for access to campus data that can be used by all tools to eliminate the need to replicate this framework with each tool. It has also coordinated a toolkit of products commonly useful for education in comprehensive introductory courses to improve the use of the entire array of resources. Similarly, CIC has re-archived the written feedback method to improve the range of services it can provide a better understanding of academics' various needs.
- If the center (like CIC) is home to its scholars and Ph.D. students, it looks like faculty study groups. The center must also be particular in stating that it is doing "business-as-usual" research and focuses on data issues facing the institution and generic/customized analytical services for academicians, students, and professional business units around the campus value. The developments of the center must be carried out with the support of institutional "clients."
- In cases where (as DIG) the center only has the personnel and cooperates with faculty who are not given a formal position in the organization, a significant burden may be imposed upon both the faculty's innovators and early adopters from its practice group. The incentive programs for research university faculty members are carefully designed such that new modes of practice are little known. If faculty members' home departments approve these creative activities as either study or service, the faculty can contribute easily.
- The center complements but does not duplicate a campus division's work, which leads to academic and educational professional development. These well-established centers provide pedagogy and student development expertise, but they cannot enhance learning analytics at the college or the university. For example,

3.3 Architecting the Learning Analytics Environment

CIC has collaborated very successfully with the UTS Institute of Interactive Media in Learning, whose academic learning and literacy specialists have advised and co-authored research papers on the CIC automatic writing-feedback. DIG and its representatives are working closely on the launch of the Fundamental Course initiative (FCIP) with the UM's Center for Research on Learning and Teaching and the Sweetland Center for Writingin the M-Write project.

- The center supports the function of the IT section but does not replace it. While colleges and universities already have an existing LMS and BI network, the center's focus is not on learning modes, data forms, and analytical user groups. The center will work closely with other departments and divisions involved in data management and create new test system services. Similarly, the center may be the first non-IT organization that supplies software applications for students or staff 24/7, which needs solid IT collaborations to provide security, network infrastructure, sensitive maintenance, etc. The partnership in IT will be mutually beneficial. For example, CIC and DIG have provided IT workers with secondment opportunities to work in a more start-up-like environment, learning new skills in various projects.
- The center continues to build resources to facilitate the work of skilled researchers in fields beyond education. The DIG ECoach method, for example, was used as an experimental framework for social psychology, online interaction, and the visual representation of quantitative knowledge. Similarly, CIC's framework for text analytics, social networks, and multimodal communication research can be widespread in non-educational contexts to support other UTS students.

Finally, it might not be a coincidence that both CIC and DIG have converged separately on the common strategically relevant problems of education and learning; it is about working together on the role that analytics can play:

- *Personalized messaging enabling feedback at scale.* Although all education evidence points to the value of timely, realistic, and personalized feedback for successful learning, it is incredibly challenging to provide this feedback in large classes. Both universities have built systems that allow students to generate coaching messages (e.g., over a week): UM has built the noted ECoach platform, while UTS has been running its own customized message platform for a decade and a collaborator of the Australian National OnTask project to create an open-source tool. The research task is to evaluate students' behavior profiles from multiple sources and compile feedback into a personalized e-mail, with the evidence that students interpret this feedback well and enhance the results (Huberth et al., 2015; Wright, McKay, Hershock, Miller, & Tritz, 2014).
- *Text analytics to send reviews to students.* Critical, compelling, reflective, scholarly writing is challenging to read, challenging to teach, and challenging to receive quick feedback. Both universities design natural language processing software to provide immediate formative input on student drafting (not summative grades) to promote revision and reflection. Scalable text analytics platforms are needed to adapt to the different writing features that allow usable feedback. According to curriculums, assignment tasks, and grading rubrics, the acknowledgment that

these instruments are most successful if they are matched with the right "learning style," is common to both efforts (the UTS Academic Writing Analytics tool and the research program and UM M-Write initiative).
- *Human-centered analytics.* Software design has slowly changed from technology-driven to human-centric, and it is no accident that both universities have academic professionals from the relationship of human computers on their teams and user interface designers. The Learning Analytics' human aspects range from assessing users' general needs to designing the user interface and analyzing users' participation by studying data ethics, algorithms, and visualizations. In order to achieve, these goals it is essential to find ways to engage stakeholders early on through participatory design approaches (Brown, Demonbrun, & Teasley, 2017; Knight, Buckingham Shum, Ryan, Sándor, & Wang, 2018; Lonn, Aguilar, & Teasley, 2015).

3.4 Major Barriers to Adopting Learning Analytics

3.4.1 Barriers

Learning Analytics Community Exchange (LACE, 2020) reports that the key challenges in using learning analytics are as follows.

1. **Data availability**: The data generated by students in institutional systems are frequently pointed out that it is not 'big' data and that 'small' data techniques may be better suited to education. However, for some instances, the obstacle is not so much that educational data are low, but they are not accessible.
2. **Data accessibility**: When data are available (as is increasingly the case), analytical applications are not automatically usable. Institutions and/or their employees may have ethical concerns that prevent their involvement. The laws governing the collection and storage of data generated by users (and children in particular) are also different in countries, so that effective solutions in one context may not be replicable elsewhere.
3. **Interoperability**: The diversity of IT systems presents the challenges of analyzing data stored at multiple locations in different formats. This problem can be solved by restricting the scope to a single form of data collection (which can mean a single system), but this cannot be done in all situations.
4. **User resistance**: The intended users of apps to learning analytics, especially teachers and parents, may have personal concerns regarding privacy and political concerns regarding surveillance. This can lead to boycotts or campaigns.
5. **Incidence of professional roles**: Initiatives of learning analytics have long been explicitly linked to data-driven management technologies. The high-level leader (except institutional managers) should have access to institutional performance data to promote assistance, incentives, and consequences decisions. Professionals who fear expanding managerial power and responsibility and a symmetrical

restriction of their professional autonomy could be limited, and support their concerns should be supported. Such issues contribute to obstacles ranging from widespread distrust of advances in learning research to well-developed criticism and active resistance.

6. *Hype*: It is evident that empirical approaches have tremendous potential to transform science, pedagogy, and management of education and create significant business opportunities. Most learning analytics applications aim to provide evidence-based, actionable insights, which would lead users to plan their use of learning analytics with plenty of evidence. However, as with other emerging innovations, implementation studies have also been driven by highlighting the enticing prospects while skirting the possible obstacles. Although the chances can be real, inflated expectations will lead to excessive cynicism if the benefits offered do not materialize, putting up further deployment barriers.

3.4.2 Steps to Successfully Adopt Learning Analytics

You will need to incorporate learning analytics within your organization to get the most out of your learning management system. However, it is easier to say than to do. Organizations would undoubtedly resist change, and obstacles to the implementation of learning analytics can be predicted (Ifenthaler, 2020).

However, you can significantly improve the chances of effectively applying learning analytics by taking a systematic approach. The Rapid Outcome Mapping Approach (ROMA) offers a valuable seven-stage approach to LA implementation that can be applied to an organization, regardless of its aspect, culture, or industry (Leah, Clow, Tynan, & Dawson, 2015). ROMA is a policy management model focused on evidence to help you understand your organization, assess its resistance to changes, and recognize the tools and stakeholders which can contribute to your success.

Make sure your Learning analytics is successful; follow the seven steps (Leah et al., 2015) to implement your organization's learning analytics.

1. *Defining your policy objectives precisely*: The most critical prerequisite to successfully making a policy change is that the justification for it should be communicated. Your goals will reflect the organization's overarching purpose and match it with its core values, mission, and culture. Specify your goals very clearly, and the improvements you want to make to incorporate learning analytics. Remember also the sort of improvements that you intend to introduce. Several instances are:
   - Patterns of communication
   - Procedures
   - Recording
   - Perceptions and attitudes
   - Behaviors and habits

While procedures, records, and communication require careful preparation, investment in considerable time, attitudes, and behaviors present the most significant challenges as these changes allow the employees to change themselves. Expect resistance to some extent.

2. *Map the Context*: Mapping your project context is essential because it allows you to recognize economic, political, cultural, and other factors that will influence the outcomes of your implementation efforts. Knowing the organization's history will help you predict obstacles you will have to resolve and encourage partners to succeed.

   Mapping the context involves analyzing the following:

   - *Context*: Individuals, organizations, and structures that may lead to or discourage change.
   - *The evidence*: How can you convince skeptics that reform is essential, and how do you present your case?
   - *Links*: People and processes that provide you with access to meaningful connections. This is the set of networks that you can use to support the implementation of Learning analytics.

3. *Identify key stakeholders*: The primary stakeholders are more than the individuals in the organization who apply Learning analytics. They are the ones that are better served by Learning analytics. Several stakeholders should be identified. When you know who is most advantageous by using learning analytics, consider which stakeholders exert the most influence. This may be individuals or stakeholders, such as the heads of your organization. Once you recognize the top players, you will also begin to gain insight into your strategic plans and the approach to involving, advising, supporting, and preparing key staff.

4. *Identify the goals of Learning analytics*: It depends on your clear understanding of your organization's purposes for Learning Analytics to implement Learning Analytics in your organization successfully. Learning Analytics can serve a wide variety of purposes, and many do not apply to your organization. You may, however, have several valid purposes for your organization to use Learning analytics.

   Types of purposes for Learning analytics may include the following:

   - Awareness of learners
   - Tracking and monitoring
   - Research
   - Assessment and planning.
   - Communication and reporting

   Think about the goals and interests the organization is concerned with – not all interests have the same needs or priorities. Remember which goals and stakeholders are your top priorities to direct your plan.

5. *Develop a plan*: A strategic plan ensures that the execution is consistent and regulated. Your implementation is much more likely to go off track without a plan. Your strategic plan should identify everything you need to do to achieve your

objectives. The previous steps you have taken should be informed until now and involve the stakeholders. Create plans, review, and update the plan as appropriate.

6. ***Analyze the potential of your resource***: You are facing a long uphill battle if you do not have the money, expertise, or staff to incorporate learning analytics in your organization.
   Most organizations will require expertise in areas like:
   - Data Science and qualitative analysis
   - Project implementation and assessment
   - Development of the database
   - Management of learning technologies
   - IT support and interface development.
   - Design and development of analytics
   - Reporting on learning analytics
   - Business intelligence and strategic analysis

7. ***Creation of a Monitoring Control and Learning System***. By implementing learning analytics in your organization, you continuously monitor your progress and make the necessary adjustments. The continuous assessment helps you understand your current initiative and provides valuable insight into the future. Review your first principles, the initial policy priorities, and vision — in this phase, to ensure they are still valid, and you keep going in the right direction. At the end of implementation, review the overall process and report on future efforts. Implementing change in your organization can be a risky move, especially if you do not take the time to consider the challenges you are likely to face. However, even in the most resistant organizations, you can effectively execute Learning Analytics if you prepare correctly and use the people and tools at your disposal. Follow these seven steps to ensure your project is successful.

3.4.3 Recommendations and Opportunities for Policymakers and Education Leaders

Wolf, Jones, Hall, and Wise (2014) and the Alliance for Excellent Education formulated several recommendations aiming mainly at capacity building and ensuring that policies enable innovation in learning analytics instead of hindering it. Policymakers and educational leaders should do the following.

1. ***Develop a good understanding of learning analytics ability and rationale***: Learning analytics can help ensure equity for all students through the provision of useful information and information to educators, parents, and students to satisfy the requirements of each student. Although data usage also poses issues about privacy and security or the notion of a vast amount of information, Learning Analytics can be applied carefully and systematically that addresses security, safety, and feasibility.

Education leaders need to unlock the value of learning analytics by

- Encourage support for the importance of individual and equitable learning.
- Ensure that community leaders, board members, staff, parents, instructors, and students recognize teaching and learning advancement through learning analytics.

2. ***Build ability for learning analytics implementation***: While more comprehensive data systems have been developed in recent years, especially for longitudinal data systems and learning management systems, most students cannot still regularly, even daily, use data to inform educational and learning decision making. Capacity includes establishing infrastructures and data and evaluation systems and developing the human resources needed for an environment where evidence-based decision making is the standard. Education leaders need to develop the capacity needed for learning analytics for impact training:

   - To create an informed decision-making culture in which data is seen as a tool to make teaching and learning decisions and critical aspects.
   - Define new positions and school environments required to optimize learning analytics, including data scientist and instructional coaches who can help bridge pedagogy and data discussion
   - Develop human capital through professional learning possibilities at different embedded, permanent, and sustainable employment levels.
   - Build infrastructure and technologies to ensure bandwidth is readily available for data processing, evaluation, and access to synthesized data for educators and administrators, as well as meeting privacy and security needs

3. ***Identify and develop policies to support and facilitate Learning analytics***: Policies and guidelines at the level of policymakers/government have a significant effect on the future implementation and use of learning analytics.

   (a) To ensure that policies make it possible to personalize learning instead of hindering the use of data, education leaders must

   - continue to clarify what is and is not acceptable and to provide technical assistance;
   - increase funding to expand broadband access to allow efficient and effective use of data systems, online evaluations, and other digital content;
   - Add opportunities that promote learning analytics to ensure a holistic approach to the acquisition of technology and data in line with curriculum and instruction, data, and assessment decisions.

   (b) Education leaders must ensure that policies allow and not hinder the use of data to personalize learning.

3.4 Major Barriers to Adopting Learning Analytics

- recognizing and directing the use of student data to enhance education;
- Create policies to ensure compatibility between longitudinal data systems (interoperability) with data systems;
- ensure enforcement with policies and processes with elements with data quality and action steps;
- find policies to support, facilitate and promote the adoption and successful use of learning analytics by incorporating standards and modern online assessments;
- make the use of data and Learning Analytics as to the required component of education, teacher preparation, and teacher evaluation programs;
- recommend policies that address the connection between learning analytics and competency-based learning.

(c) For policies to make the use of knowledge to personalize learning to be hindered, educational leaders must

- to explain how privacy is important to the use of student data and to provide administrators, teachers, and parents with a concise overview of how the privacy and protection of a student is per the laws;
- consider introducing responsibilities policies to increase access to, and accept responsibility of schools, students and parents with data, content, and curricula;
- Elevate data use and research analytics as a key component for technical learning opportunities.

4. ***Create models of funding to promote Learning Analytics***: There are several different funding sources and services related to the analytical field. It is also important to understand how the variety of sources of funding will contribute to the overall effort to personalize learning, including:

   - use current data and evaluation tools, broad-based networks, and cloud computing to incorporate learning analytics;
   - investigate and leverage alternative sources of financing not traditionally used in data and digital content systems;
   - Build plan opportunities and guidance

5. ***Conduct research supporting capacity building and policies critical to the Learning analytics:*** The identification and development of case studies that illustrate how capacities and strategies can be built will provide concrete examples for others to adopt. In this way, the scope of learning analytics can be expanded in more schools by knowledge obtained from early adopters and implementers.

The research will cover the following:

- a series of in-depth case studies that make significant progress with customized learning analytics;
- a review to better identify such capability-building approaches and resources, including an educated decision-making culture, appropriate infrastructure, human capital, and technical learning opportunities;
- analyzes to identify specific policies that allow analytical learning;
- Design a range of methods, techniques, resources, and sample policies to distribute Learning Analytics broadly.

3.5 Case Studies: Adopting/Implementing Learning Analytics at Institutions

3.5.1 The Open University, UK: Data Wranglers

The Open University (OU) is a distance education institution with more than 200,000 students and 10,000 academic and non-academic personnel engaged in educational assessment and learning analytics over 40 years ago. It has carried out two important activity programs, both explicitly rooted in learning analytics. This case study concerns Data Wranglers development.

Data Wranglers are academic staff who analyze various student learning information and make valuable suggestions to their University faculties'. Their position as interpreters of human data who help closure the feedback loop is described elsewhere in-depth (Clow, 2014).

The University has acknowledged that increased amounts of educational data are available but not effectively utilized (student input, activities in Moodle VLE / LMS, mode of delivery data, and quantitative demographics and findings). No integrated, systemic view to informing and improve teaching and learning practice was developed. Pilot testing was undertaken in 2010 and 2011, and the Data Wrangling project was released in 2012. The operation was not initially established with an apparent reference to the ROMA context but should be evaluated in those terms.

Step 1: Defining your policy objectives clearly: The project's goals were strongly incorporated into the current University policy and planning system. Initially, (1) a group of staff with expertise in the various faculty contexts should also be developed, (2) a system to collect, synthesize and report the available data should be created, (3) reports should be generated at regular intervals, and (4) good relations should be developed with the faculties. The primary types of improvement as per Young et al. (Young and Mendizabal 2009) were discursive changes to how data is exchanged and transmitted and structural changes to decision-making in curriculum development and support for students.

Step 2: Map the Context: The project leaders understood the dynamic organizational climate. In an established entity, the Institute for Educational Technology (IET), data confrontation was conducted to examine and impact teaching and learning. IET was already responsible for curating and sending some of the data involved. Many Data Wranglers already had connections to different faculties, and the unit had clear access to the management. There was already a considerable interest and commitment in learning analytics and data at the senior level, and a crucial relationship was identified in the early stage between the Data Wrangling project and the development of a broader analytical strategy.

Step 3: Identify Key Stakeholders: Because of the results' nature, all university members were regarded as stakeholders. The project focused in particular on providing insight into the development of curricula and quality improvement processes. The unit responsible for this work was also involved in implementing learning design across the faculties so that design work could be based on evidence from Learning analytics. In both cases, several key contacts were the same. The unit also conducted programs that concentrated on other facets of the learning cycle. Thus, each faculty responsible for learning and teaching and/or curriculum development was the key stakeholder. The curriculum at the OU is built by module teams that have also been designated as stakeholders. Certain primary players included senior management and data collection and curation managers.

Step 4: Identify the goals of Learning analytics: The project focused on designing curricula and improving quality. In addition to the above drivers, this focus was influenced by data-related considerations. Twice a year, student feedback and final results data (completion and exit rates) are published. The development of the curriculum and improved quality processes at the OU follow a similar cycle. It offers two points per year, where the project Data Wrangling will incorporate data from the university's interactive learning environment Moodle. Moodle systems do not yet embrace real-time monitoring, and therefore adjustments in real-time are outside the project's reach.

Step 5: Develop a Plan. Extensive consultation and feedback culminated in an implementation plan being developed. Early pilot work led to informing the shape of the Data Wrangling project. The Host Unit had a comprehensive project management program, and documentation was created that included both an implementation plan and review dates.

Step 6: Analyze your resource's potential: A vital aspect of the project preparation was capacity review. The Data Wranglers themselves were among the original targets to establish a thorough understanding of the teaching and teaching background. Education was planned for the Wranglers in the advanced use of Microsoft Excel. There has been a significant amount of time researching and learning the knowledge, including liaison with those who collect and cure it. New technical tools (including Tableau workbooks and SAS stored procedures containing data from the Data Warehouse that Intranet) have been deployed and developed, requiring further personnel development. On the "client" side, one goal of the project was to gain an understanding and understanding of what the data could show and to be aware of how you would access it without a Data Wrangler intermediary. It was a method that was iterative. It was not easy for Data Wranglers to understand and interpret some of the data. Some of the challenges they faced have been solved, some have been established as challenging to address data quality issues, and some remain puzzled.

Step 7: Creation of a Monitoring Control and Learning System: Feedback from stakeholders was integrated into the reporting process. In July 2013, an explicit evaluation exercise gathered input from key stakeholders and informed further growth.

The project was highly time-intensive in terms of both employee time and the delay between completing the course and the Data Wrangler study. Reports were also very different from each other in terms of coverage and quality. To a certain degree, this was a positive aspect as each Wrangler negotiated and established a mutual understanding with client stakeholders. Many faculties were optimistic that they could read various data visualizations; others were interested in qualitative research, which would allow them to understand what was happening and why. Some broad faculties wanted their data to be broken down in various ways, while smaller faculties wanted to see the whole picture.

Much was learned, and a further analysis was carried out in the summer of 2014 to simplify the operation. The initiative has made it possible for the data used by training and quality assurance processes to be better understood. Tools were built that can rapidly and accurately produce data reports to high standards with minimal manual intervention. This reduces the time requirements for Data Wranglers, enabling them to explore data further to answer faculty clients' urgent questions.

This section discussed several ways of ensuring a degree of success in promoting adoption on a scale for the Data Wrangler project. The secret to this success is that it has been incorporated from the outset with existing systems, processes, and networks. The involvement of stakeholders at all levels was critical. The project required a substantial allocation of staff resources, including resources from stakeholders of the faculty "client." This account of the Data Wrangler project has been coordinated with the ROMA system to provide an excellent example of the process.

3.5.2 The University of Technology, Sydney, Australia

The University of Technology of Sydney (UTS) is an inner-city university with a dream of being a world-class technology university. It began in 2011 as a "data-intensive university" (DIU) in line with this dream. This case study focuses on the technique used and the progress achieved so far. As mentioned above in the OU case study, the UTS strategy was not initially designed directly for the ROMA process, but reviewing recent trends and achievements indicates that the UTS approach is well incorporated into this strategic planning structure.

The UTS project was launched to believe that access to data can improve all aspects of the University and provide a springboard to create and innovate. UTS first created an organizational concept that defines the value of data analytics for contemporary university practice: "A university where staff and students understand data and, regardless of its volume and diversity, can use and reuse it, store and curate it, apply and develop the analytical tools to interpret it."

Based on this concept, DIU was created to make better use of the data to enable students, staff, alumni, and partners in the industry to explore and flourish, to understand their climate, to solve problems and challenges, to lead their fields, and to provide opportunities for the creation of knowledge.

Step 1-Defining your policy objectives specifically: The UTS project is driven by a broad methodological approach, which aims to cover all aspects of the university's work: teaching and education, research, and management.

UTS seeks to use learning analytics to enhance student performance and develop student experience in universities. The aim is to ensure that all stakeholders can understand and interpret today's data-rich environments.

The study's goals are to provide researchers with an atmosphere that makes it easier and more effective to access and manipulate data, allowing them to think and behave differently as they develop their investigative methodologies and practices.

The administration's main objective is to identify opportunities for data and analysis to be obtained, generated, visualized, and communicated to improve decision-making capabilities and improve core business outcomes.

At the University level, the approach focuses on the value of mining existing institutional data to find areas that can provide staff and students clear evidence or help. For example, data and analysis may be provided for employees to promote a collection of intervention approaches for students at risk of withdrawal before completing a course of study.

Step 2: Map the Context: The project was initiated and directed by a member of the University's Senior Executive, Deputy Chancellor, and Vice President (teaching and learning). Initially, it obtained pilot funding and secured ongoing funding after completing several pilot projects. The ongoing project funding has made it possible to create a Connected Intelligence Centre. As its first director, an internationally renowned professor of research analytics has been recruited. The presence of an Established Analytical Institute was crucial to the initial pilot projects' success with globally known experts in Big Data, Data Science, and Analytics.

Step 3: Identify Key Stakeholders: To obtain the level of continuous funding necessary to ensure the initiative's longevity, a broad level of support throughout the University, particularly by the senior management, deans, and directors of the appropriate units, was vital. The idea of becoming a "Data-Intensive university" was first proposed during a retreat in early 2011, and a scoping project was sponsored.

Around 190 UTS (150 present and 40 online) staff attended a one-day "Data-Intensive University Conference" during the latter part of 2011, thus opening a university-wide discussion. Although the project's premise was almost universal, the naming of the program was significant controversy. Although the phrase "data-intensive" is well established in several science areas, it was thought to create obstacles for many people to alienate academics in other fields of study. Therefore, the name "data-intensive university project" was replaced by the word "connected intelligence project."

The Deputy Vice-Chancellor (Teaching and Learning), Deputy Vice-Chancellors (Research, Corporate Services), and Deputy Chairs set up a working group. A senior library employee was appointed as the senior manager of the project. Each faculty was included in the working group, as was each of the administrative fields with relevant expertise. The success of the project was crucial to the achievement of stakeholder buy-in and continuing involvement.

Step 4: Identify the goals of learning analytics: Learning analytics are used or used for:

- Include information to decrease the attrition of students;
- Offering a more detailed explanation of the factors that influence low passes in subjects with very high failure rates over time, known as 'monster subjects';
- Offering a customized guide to students with more knowledge about their study and interaction patterns.
- Allowing a more comprehensive understanding of the effects of several potential interventions on pass rates and completion, for example, the impact on pass levels and retention overtime of the peer-assisted study scheme;
- Provide valuable input to future learning projects that include adapting and intervening to personalize learning.

Step 5: Develop a Plan: Elements of strategy have been planned from the beginning of the project to:

- Give attention to institutional culture — ensuring the engagement and dedication through effective communication and governance of key stakeholders;
- Participation in university-significant pilot projects and recording of results;
- Technology investment: — tools, software, services;
- Investment in expertise: — vital staff recruitment;
- Leadership and strategic leadership engagement.

Step 6: Analyze the potential of your resource: As UTS becomes a more data-intensive organization, one of the most critical elements in its success is to ensure that analytical actors can interpret data, judge their value, and then engage in decision making based on facts. There is no point in investing so much if students and staff are not adequately numbered and trained to use the analysis generated by analytical projects.

For this reason, a subject has been developed and studied to develop the "ability to engage with complex, extended arguments underpinned by numerical data as a key to participate as informed citizens in issues of significance to our culture and society." The goal is to continue this activity to increase employees' numeracy.

Step 7: Creation of a Monitoring Control and Learning System: Some of the early pilot projects have already been studied. For example, the Outreach program includes as many students as possible by telephone contact. Early findings showed a large decrease in attrition in the communication group. Without funds to reach each student, empirical approaches have been used to identify these students deemed most at risk.

Also, the project "Killer subject" defined many areas to be tackled by the course coordinator. Such concerns have now been solved, and the failure rate has decreased substantially. To date, UTS has participated in a range of Learning analytics projects under the auspices of the larger DIU project to assess scale and effect. Although this project remains a multidimensional project, the degree of institutional buy-in and funding commitment shows that the structural, strategic plan strategy used leads to the project's success and the inclusion of analytics in the institutional culture.

3.5.3 The OU Strategic Analytics Investment Program

Through extensive data sets and a willingness to enhance learner performance, the OU has launched an eight-strand research plan to encourage Learning Analytics to benefit students. Pro-Vice-Chancellor Learning and Teaching is funded by the institution and considers the interests of various stakeholders' interests, including university administrators, students, and educators.

The Strategic Analytics Investment Program was launched in 2012 and put together various groups around the university under one vision: strategically (by indicators) use and apply knowledge to sustain students and encourage them to develop and reach their study objectives. The goal was to focus on this on two levels:

- Macro-level work adds information from institutional learning experiences to inform strategic priorities to improve the retention and progression of students;
- Micro-level work uses analytics to conduct short, medium, and long-term interventions.

To achieve the vision of the program, three key areas are mutually dependent and underpin the work. These include (1) analysis and insight development, (2) data availability, and (3) processes with an impact on the success of the students.

The vision and associated action are informed by understanding data in action, data on the action, and data for action. Multiple stakeholders use data in action via a live portal to understand their learner behavior and make changes and interventions with immediate positive effects. Data on the action is a more reflective process following adjustment or intervention. Data for action benefits from statistical modeling and creativity to identify different variables and alter them using a range of analytical methods.

This student performance strategy allows for versatility and a continuous assessment of all behavior. The four steps of recruitment, retention, advancement, and completion are identified as key performance outcomes and lead indicators. Many stakeholders have programs focused on "learning and teaching" and "student support activities." Stakeholders use advanced analytics to advise programs to boost performance.

Such approaches are analyzed and then the basis for factors affecting student progress. For example, a "module pass rate model" is used as part of university quality assurance processes to equate real module pass rates with those predicted based on the statistical analysis of the previous student's achievement over the last 5 years. The use of the model has strengthened the university's comprehension of students' nature and behavior, who are more likely to fight for their studies. The Model for pass rates ensures that key stakeholders can introduce effective short- and long-term support interventions.

Another strategic move was the launch in 2014, the latest OU Student Support Strategy, along with a new data platform that allows subject-specific student support teams to facilitate involvement in their progress assessments, using demographic data, task submissions, and online activities.

The job plan promoting the progress of students has seven branches. They offer professionals opportunities to enhance their performance by designing and implementing tailored and evidence-based approaches in critical market cycles.

This strategy has built a group of stakeholders that rely on each other to their full advantage, led by a senior executive. Data are handled from a single database holistically to ensure the best standard and reporting standards are accepted in the work program. It has ensured a cohesive approach to how the University uses analytics.

The seven program standards are:

1. Intervention and Assessment

    - A student success review is used to define priority focus areas in terms of curriculum improvement and learning design and strategies for the students most at risk of not going forward with studies.
    - A common methodology for assessing the relative value of interventions is to measure student behaviors and performance, informing potential improvements to the student experience.

2. Usability of data

    - Clear data visualizations around key performance metrics are being created. This will be available to key stakeholders in almost real-time to track student success.
    - A new self-service analytics platform triangulates various data sources, allowing academics and support staff to recognize trends and the variables that affect their performance.

3. Ethics Framework

    - A Learning Analytics ethics policy outlines the data gathered and its ethical use to enhance education and help individual students.

4. Predictive Modeling

    - Predictive machine-learning models are now present in many subject areas at university and include a weekly forecast of the probability of each student's next assignment based on the analysis of key variables, including online behavior.

5. Learning Experience Data

- In the future, the University will gather input during modules instead of depending on surveys at the end of each study session. It helps educators and student support staff to respond to all student issues more rapidly.
- The University should investigate how these designs affect its diverse student base's performance through the systematic correlation between learning design data of study modules and student activity data.

6. Career growth

- A professional research group based on retention and success in the first year uses the evidence to exchange best practice across faculty borders.

7. Student Tools "Small Data"

- Small data provides citizens with relevant, practical information (big data and/or "local" sources), arranged and packaged – mostly visually – to be usable and comprehensible, and feasible for day-to-day activities. Tools to provide actionable analytically validated knowledge, help students monitor their progress, and make the correct study decisions as they progress through their studies.

Strategic Analytics at the OU and the ROMA Framework This high-level account of the OU method is an example of how institution-wide analytics are applied. This also provides the ability to show how pre-existing research in ROMA steps can be interpreted.

In Step 1, the OU's overarching policy objectives include discursive changes in the communication of the institution's data and analytics, procedural changes in the way the students are supported, and behavioral changes in support for sustainable change. At Step 2, the context mapping was done in several ways. University leaders, students, and educators are identified as main stakeholders (Step 3). This also split down such stakeholder groups.

The goal of learning analytics (step 4) is clearly defined in terms of the strategic use and implementation of information to retain and support students in achieving their study goals. It is done by a carefully thought-out approach (Step 5), which is implemented at the macro and micro levels and is organized around data in action, data on the action, and data for action.

Step 6 of capacity analysis and human resources growth is structural and thus not included in the overview mentioned above but includes training, capacity building, and establishing an ethical structure for Learning Analytics. Finally, the monitoring (step 7) is carried out through a continuous evaluation process that focuses on specific results and leading indicators.

In this scenario, an overview of the ROMA implementation system reveals that each move was taken. For other situations, the system may recognize missing steps and then propose potential interventions to improve current research.

3.6 Conclusion

We have laid down the psychological dimensions, challenges, and dilemmas that higher education institutions face: How can they organize themselves to advance learning analytics and see the sustainable impacts of learning analytics across traditional services. Three case studies on how businesses incorporate learning research through challenges to involve students and teachers in exploring and uncovering new insights into student learning and transforming institutions' attitudes towards continuous enhancement in education and learning processes have been presented.

3.7 Review Questions

Reflect on the concepts of this chapter guided by the following questions.

1. What are the psychological aspects of students, administrators, and institutions face in implementing leering analytics? How to overcome them.
2. Does the personality of an individual influence the use of Learning Analytics? How?
3. Illustrate, with an example the, three organization architectures/models for learning analytics.
4. Explain the advantages and disadvantages of each organization's architecture/model for learning analytics.
5. What are the major barriers to making use of Learning Analytics?
6. List and explain the steps to successfully implement learning analytics in an organization.
7. What are the recommendations made for policymakers and education leaders for building capacity and ensuring learning analytics innovation?

References

Brown, M. G., Demonbrun, R. M., & Teasley, S. D. (2017). Don't call it a comeback: Academic recovery and the timing of educational technology adoption. *ACM International Conference Proceeding Series*, 489–493. https://doi.org/10.1145/3027385.3027393.

Clow, D. (2014). Data wranglers: Human interpreters to help close the feedback loop. *ACM International Conference Proceeding Series*, 49–53. https://doi.org/10.1145/2567574.2567603.

Ferguson, R., Brasher, A., Clow, D., Cooper, A., Hillaire, G., Mittelmeier, J., Rienties, B., & Vuorikari, R. (2016). Research evidence on the use of learning analytics. In *A European framework for action on learning analytics* (Issue 2016). https://doi.org/10.2791/955210.

Ferguson, R., Macfadyen, L. P., Clow, D., Tynan, B., Alexander, S., & Dawson, S. (2014). Setting learning analytics in context: Overcoming the barriers to large-scale adoption. *Journal of Learning Analytics*, *1*(3), 120–144. https://doi.org/10.18608/jla.2014.13.7

References

Fritz, J., & Whitmer, J. (2017). *Moving the heart and head: Implications for learning analytics early adopters are rare for a reason.* https://er.educause.edu/articles/2017/7/moving-the-heart-and-head-implications-for-learning-analytics-research

Huberth, M., Chen, P., Tritz, J., & McKay, T. A. (2015). Computer-tailored student support in introductory physics. *PLoS One, 10*(9), 1–17. https://doi.org/10.1371/journal.pone.0137001

Ifenthaler, D. (2020). Change management for learning analytics. In N. Pinkwart & S. Liu (Eds.), *Artificial intelligence supported educational technologies* (pp. 261–272). Cham, Switzerland: Springer.

Knight, S., Buckingham Shum, S., Ryan, P., Sándor, Á., & Wang, X. (2018). Designing academic writing analytics for civil law student self-assessment. *International Journal of Artificial Intelligence in Education, 28*(1), 1–28. https://doi.org/10.1007/s40593-016-0121-0

LACE. (2020). *What are the main barriers in making use of learning analytics? Most commonly discussed issues grouped in 6 barriers.* http://www.laceproject.eu/faqs/barriers-to-learning-analytics/

Lang, C. (2017). *Handbook of learning analytics.* https://doi.org/10.18608/hla17.

Leah, P., Clow, D., Tynan, B., & Dawson, S. (2015). Setting learning analytics in context: overcoming the barriers to large-scale adoption. *Journal of Learning Analytics, 1*(3), 120–144.

Lonn, S., Aguilar, S. J., & Teasley, S. D. (2015). Investigating student motivation in the context of a learning analytics intervention during a summer bridge program. *Computers in Human Behavior, 47*, 90–97. https://doi.org/10.1016/j.chb.2014.07.013

Lonn, S., McKay, T. A., & Teasley, S. D. (2017). Cultivating institutional capacities for learning analytics. In *new directions for higher education* (Vol. 2017, Issue 179, pp. 53–63). https://doi.org/10.1002/he.20243

Macfadyen, L. P., & Dawson, S. (2012). International Forum of Educational Technology & Society Numbers are not enough. Why e-learning analytics failed to inform an institutional strategic plan. *Source: Journal of Educational Technology & Society, 15*(3), 149–163. https://doi.org/10.2307/jeductechsoci.15.3.149

Shum, S. J. B., & Mckay, T. A. (2018). Architecting for learning analytics: innovating for sustainable impact. *Educause Review*, March/April, 25–37. https://er.educause.edu/-/media/files/articles/2018/3/er182101.pdf

Weitzel, A. (2019). *How to prepare your school for learning analytics.* https://coursekey.com/preparing-for-learning-analytics/

Wolf, M. A., Jones, R., Hall, S., & Wise, B. (2014). *Capacity enablers and barriers for learning analytics: Implications for policy and practice table of contents capacity enablers and barriers for learning analytics: Implications for policy and practice All4Ed.Org.* June. www.all4ed.org

Wright, M. C., McKay, T., Hershock, C., Miller, K., & Tritz, J. (2014). Better than expected: Using learning analytics to promote student success in gateway science. *Change: The Magazine of Higher Learning, 46*(1), 28–34. https://doi.org/10.1080/00091383.2014.867209

Young, J., & Mendizabal, E. (2009). Helping researchers become policy entrepreneurs. *Overseas Development Institute, 53*(September), 1–4. https://doi.org/10.1063/1.1671652

Zimmerman, B. J., Bandura, A., & Martinez-Pons, M. (1992). Self-motivation for academic attainment: The role of self-efficacy beliefs and personal goal setting. *American Educational Research Journal, 29*(3), 663–676. https://doi.org/10.3102/00028312029003663

Chapter 4
Data Requirements for Learning Analytics

4.1 Introduction

As an evolving field, learning analytics has many definitions. When one explores these meanings more closely, we will find that the meanings have variations. You may also note that these concepts emphasize translating educational data into useful learning activities. It is also evident that these concepts are not limited to an automated data analysis by Learning Analytics. So far, Learning Analytics is a data-driven methodology that uses various educational data sources. It can come from central school systems, online learning environments, open data sets, personal learning environments, adaptive systems/ITS courses, student information systems, social media, mobile devices, etc. Such data sources have centralized education systems in the background. They are learning management systems like Blackboard, Moodle, etc. Such learning management systems collect comprehensive student behavior reports and interaction data. These programs are also used to enhance conventional face-to-face learning or facilitate distance learning in structured learning settings. The content created by users, made possible with all kinds of technology, has resulted in huge amounts of data provided by students in various learning environments and systems (Chatti, Dyckhoff, Schroeder, & Thüs, 2012).

In short, learning data can and should come from both formal and informal channels since learning and development of information are often spread through various media and sites in networked environments (Suthers & Rosen, 2011).

4.2 Types of Data Used for Learning Analytics

4.2.1 Sources of Data You Should Be Collecting

You might ask what data are the appropriate data to track when you have not previously used Learning Analytics. Which are the best sources of learning analytics in your LMS, and how do you decide the ones to use? With the overwhelming amount of data available, the prospect of learning analytics is easy to overwhelm. However, if you start small, you can establish a base to build on as you become more familiar with the available learning analytics data. The aim is, to begin with, the appropriate learning analytics data.

This section presents you with the best Learning Analytics sources and allows you to think about what makes sense for you.

4.2.1.1 Why Are You Collecting Learning Analytics Data?

There are several reasons for collecting data for learning analytics (Yupangco, 2018). For a wide range of purposes, companies use learning analytics, including:

- *Prediction* — Identify students at risk of drop-out or failure of course.
- *Customization and adaptation* — Give students custom pathways or materials for assessment.
- *Intervention* — provision of information to teachers to support students.
- *Visualization of information* — Dashboards that show summary data.

You should understand what you are collecting and why you collect it before you begin analyzing your results. Just like your courses have unique goals and outcomes, so does your data set.

You will only generate problems for yourself if you try to collect all the data you can find and try to solve it later — and probably you end up overwhelmed by chaotic events. Nonetheless, a pragmatic, goal-driven approach can direct your choice of data sources and help you retain management ease.

Learning analytics typically helps you understand the effectiveness of three levels of your learning modules (Yupangco, 2018). You need to consider which of these rates you want to learn before you choose the data you want to use:

- *Learner Impact*: Individual success about other classmates' learning goals, learning resources, and study habits.
- *Course Impact*: This includes social networks, intellectual growth, disclosure analysis, and "Intelligent Curriculum."
- *Organizational Impact*: Predictive modeling, and performance and failure trends.

You will use Learning Analytics to consider the progress of every stage of your online learning programs. Fulfilled, you may want to answer questions like these (Yupangco, 2018):

4.2 Types of Data Used for Learning Analytics

- What are the areas for change in the course?
- How do we find students in trouble early on?
- What is the rate of adoption of learning modules?
- Is the course content suitable for the level of skills of students?
- Are we raising the efficiency of the organization?
- Are we conforming?
- How do online courses lead to cost savings or revenue increase?

Understand your goals and map your objectives to the type of data available. The data you interpret will be dictated by the results you want. So, stop the illusion of the shiny object — do not collect data you will not use.

4.2.1.2 Top Learning Analytics Sources

You will select the most relevant data sources once you understand why you are collecting data. Your most important data will be obtained from either one or a combination of the following contexts depending on your priorities (Yupangco, 2018).

1. ***Statistics of engagement***. Data relating to engagement will help you determine learner interaction with the module. If you have to assess a user-based learning program's progress, this is a perfect starting point. Look at these sources for insights into engagement:

    - Statistics of site and logs, location/IP, statistics on quiz/course activity (question evaluation)
    - Logins
    - Access to the course, "learning" time spent
    - Session – metrics of the session, accessed resources and information, frequency.
    - Registration.
    - Learner access origin – home, school, etc.
    - Access to the computer – desktop or mobile.
    - Correlation between exposure to course tools and assessment outcomes.

2. ***Statistics on performance***. Such statistics relate to performance. You will assess the consistency of your courses and the performance of your training modules. You will not all need them in your evaluations. Just use the data that is most useful for your goal — what you want to understand.

    - Involvement in debates.
    - Involvement in the course.
    - Gradebook ratings – questionnaires, tests, homework submissions.
    - Self-evaluations (graded and ungraded).
    - Journals
    - Supplementary course events – webinars, library, lessons in collaboration.
    - Resource use (video, PDF, etc.).

- Progress in a course.
- Position in Leaderboards.
- Access frequency – how often and how long a resource or activity is accessed.
- Online feedback from students on the course, the professor, etc.

3. **Course or web Helpdesk**. Although this knowledge is external to your LMS, it can be useful. Helpdesk data is usually quite rudimentary, but it can be a valuable source of knowledge for identifying patterns and commonly asked questions or concerns.

4.2.1.3 Examples of Learning Analytics in Action

Imagine defining specific areas for change. Online learner success reports, learner feedback, and completion levels will help you to recognize the problem. Seek patterns that may lead to flaws in the course design — perhaps particular tasks or course components that are quite incomplete. For instance, students can consistently fail a test because they miss a specific content resource — a video, a pdf, or a lesson. You can solve the issue by limiting access to the questionnaire before the student has read it. When you want to get a sense of your learners' learning environment during the course, gather student feedback asking about e-learning, the course, and even the teacher. Using LMS metrics to test the theory-to-practice implementation to assess how training modules impact results successfully. Interactive test outcomes from simulations can also be monitored.

4.2.1.4 Making Learning Analytics Manageable

Learning Analytics is widely discussed in educational design, but it is unusual to hear how empirical sources are best gathered. A proactive strategy will help to handle a considerable challenge. Understand your goals, map your goals to the type of data you have, and then gather the data you need.

4.2.2 Types of Data

This section discusses what data can be defined regarding learners (Klašnja-Milićević, Ivanović, & Budimac, 2017). Educational data can be classified into five types: four sets of data on learner behaviors, one on learner identification, and invasion. Such data forms are derived from the LMS/CMS/tutoring systems:

1. **Data about personality**. These data include essential identification and descriptive learner detail, such as:
   - name
   - surname
   - demographic details

- user approval
- admin rights, etc.

Such data definitions follow the answers to the following questions:

- Who are you?
- Are you allowed to use this application?
- What are your administration rights?
- In what region are you?
- How about demographic information?

2. **System-wide data**. These data include:

   - schedules
   - grades
   - disciplinary documents, and
   - attending information

   Teachers or principals can quickly obtain in a classroom or school. This is not very useful on a small scale based on little knowledge per student. On a vast scale, it is more valuable and may help inform system-wide recommendations.

3. **Conditional content data**. Such data clarify whether a group of students can do part of the content. These data are also useful for defining the quantifiable progress in learner comprehension if a specific learner covers a certain part of the content. So well, does a query determine what it wants to do? Information on instructional materials requires uniform calculations algorithmically. Consequently, generating these data is not easy.

4. **Data on user interaction**. These data contain metrics

   - engagement
   - page views
   - click rate
   - bounce rate, etc.

   Such indicators will enhance user experience and maintenance for customer web companies based on Internet optimization. This kind of data is straightforward to obtain.

5. **Inferred learner data**. These data display the level of awareness of learners about their concepts and the percentile of their skills. Such data types often determine whether an incorrect learner's response is due to a lack of expertise, a poorly constructed query, a bad memory, lack of concentration, or something else. The answers to the question, how the student should perform the test next week, and how to increase their willingness to do so, can be included in this sort's data. Diverse content and many learners, curriculum designers, developers, and data researchers are needed to create such data. It also includes functional database design, tagging structure, creative machine learning for algorithms, and multifaceted taxonomic systems.

   It is challenging for most educational institutions to build functionalities that achieve all five of the data sets mentioned above. Nonetheless, every institution needs to have an answer to all five. The approach would be to incorporate a general framework with suitable solutions for each broad data collection. They must also be combined with data from the faculty information systems, learners' experiences outside the LMS, and the expertise of professors, knowledge, and insights that can be used to develop effective action plans and procedures.

4.2.3 LMS Data Tracking Methods

Because your Learning Management System (LMS) is rich in content, you may well not know if it successfully helps you achieve your learning objectives. It can prove difficult to express the importance of your L&D program and how your training programs affect performance without knowing the effect of your formal and informal learning initiatives. That is why it is essential to help any LMS by data tracking and assessment methods, which will assess if learning and development goals have been achieved.

Why are we doing that? For data, a lot, and many data, you can obtain them in several ways, depending on the findings you want to report. There are ways to track the data (eThink, 2019) and use the most relevant knowledge about LMS students and learning programs.

1. ***Internal reporting***. At least some simple reporting tools should be given for any LMS, which allows you to initially understand the actions being taken in your LMS. For example, out-of-box Moodle and Totara provide reports quickly and efficiently when your LMS is logged in and which programs are being used. It can be at the level of the site up to and including the level of activity.
   Event reports are beneficial for LMS instructors. Such clear reports may contribute to greater engagement and lead to discussions on addressing common challenges, such as access to the course and time to complete all assigned tasks.
2. ***Custom reports***. The above reports provide input on general training details such as whether the user has signed in or completed the operation x or y.
   But, what about details like?

   - How long has the test been taken to determine users' incomprehension of the learning materials? And
   - In what order were a variety of operations carried out?

   Also, for these types of things, Moodle and Totara provide simple reporting. Both Moodle and Totara allow you to add personalized reporting tools by default.
3. ***Course evaluations***. One field frequently addressed when it comes to analytics is the push to find areas for improvement. This is where the LMS data can be robust. When analyzing how people answered questions in a questionnaire or a SCORM kit, the program can be designed, and new learning pathways can be automatically activated for students based on their grades. Such details are also accessible to teachers instantaneously to ensure that the initial materials and services meet the course requirements.

4.2 Types of Data Used for Learning Analytics

4. ***Scheduled reports***. It is nice to have access to all these reports, but what about activating them at times? Moreover, sent to the right people? The answer is scheduled reports.
For example, Totara provides easy-to-use planning options for almost any report you make. It enables decision-makers to access relevant details without even connecting to the LMS platform. Some plugins can also be used to ease reporting within Moodle, such as one that sends reporting data for processing on an SFTP server. After the initial set-up and process testing, an automated process may be feasible, meaning that the file never needs to be accessed. It is generated and saved to the server where the vendor system consumes it.
5. ***Tools for third-party reporting***. Whether these are features already included in Moodle or Totara – or can be extended using plugins. To continue to monitor your LMS data, eThink (eThink, 2019), for example, has a comprehensive list of partners to help satisfy your needs when it comes to reporting, analytics, and other solutions to track your LMS training efficiently. Intelliboard will be a perfect example of this. With this product, you can immerse yourself in a world of real-time portfolios, dashboards, graphs, and KPIs powered by the LMS data.
Tracking and making data-driven decisions on your LMS training data is important for your organization to offer engaging and forward-looking learning programs.

4.2.4 What Data Is Available to Institutions?

The section includes an overview of many of the data sources available for use by institutions in the LA strategy (National Forum for the Enhancement of Teaching and Learning in Higher Education, 2018). It is a comprehensive but not exhaustive list because almost every way students interact with their school offers invaluable insights. This is the organization's responsibility to ensure that all usage is carried out in full compliance with the provisions of the GDPR.

Their data source distinguishes different data items, and all VLE data items are in unity, and all the Student Information System data items are in the union, and so forth.

1. ***At-Risk Students (AR)***. This flag can be used to identify students who may be at risk of under-performance and/or withdrawal from their studies to ensure that preventive support is given. Predictive identification can be accomplished by searching for trends in previous students' data whose findings would classify current students' data associations.
2. ***Learning Design (LD)***. Data items with this flag can allow teachers to understand their students' learning actions better. This incomprehension will inform successful module design and allow the identification of student-compatible learning resources.

3. ***Student Engagement (SE)***. Such data items may be used for recognizing students whose behavior indicates they are less interested than their peers. The recognition of these students at the beginning of the semester will allow targeted support to enable students to reengage.
4. ***Student Welfare (SW)***. Low commitment or abrupt behavioral changes may indicate student problems, such as medical, social, financial, or personal, with non-academic challenges. Data items with this flag can help student support staff identify students who may need extra, specialized support.

The Tables (4.1, 4.2, 4.3, 4.4, 4.5, 4.6, 4.7, 4.8, 4.9, 4.10, and 4.11) below (National Forum for the Enhancement of Teaching and Learning in Higher Education, 2018) show which of the questions below can be explored. It serves as a reference rather than a static set of rules as they can tackle almost unlimited combinations of data items and Learning analytics issues.

4.3 Data Models Used to Represent Usage Data for Learning Analytics

Learning analytics data is the compilation of information on the student, the learning environment, the connections between learning, and the learning outcomes. This knowledge is usually obtained during the learning process (Snola, 2018).

Learning analytics is a data-driven methodology that uses various educational sources (Soltanpoor, 2018). The data can be extracted (but not limited to) from: structured education structures, interactive learning environments, open-ended data sets, personal learning settings, adaptive programs, and STIs, web-based courses,

Table 4.1 Virtual learning environments

Data item	Description	AR	LD	SE	SW
Student hits	List of interactions between students and VLE	X		X	X
Peer average hits	Average VLE interactions among peer groups of students	X		X	X
Timing of activity	At what point students use the various learning resources in the VLE	X	X	X	X
Duration of activity	How long students use per VLE learning tool	X	X	X	
Type of activity	What resources students use to learn	X	X	X	
Assignment submissions	Identify if students have met their required deadlines for submission	X	X	X	X
Discussion groups	How actively students participating in online discussion groups	X	X	X	X
Assignment/ CA grades	Grades for 'for-credit' tasks for students	X	X	X	X
Online test grades	Engagement of students and grades informative, "not-for-credit" occupations	X	X	X	X

4.3 Data Models Used to Represent Usage Data for Learning Analytics

Table 4.2 Student information system

Data item	Description	AR	LD	SE	SW
Peer group data	The recognition of peer groups of students such as curriculum, major, year, and status to make comparisons possible	X		X	
Demographic data	Population factors like gender, age, nationality, etc.	X			
Registration/Workload	Registration and overall workload of students' module (i.e., how many credits they receive)	X	X		X
Fee compliance	Identifies that their minimum fee requirements have been met	X		X	X
Grades	Identify how students learn	X	X	X	X
Entry points	Incoming CAO points for students	X			
Leaving cert subjects/grades	Identifies which subjects' students studied for Leaving Cert and their performance in them	X	X		
CAO Preferences	Identifies the level of the current student's CAO application	X			X
Student logins	How involved students are in online record management for things such as registration and payment of fees	X		X	X
Online activity	What parts of their record students handled online	X		X	
Length of commute	Through using the student's term address/Eircode, you will estimate the duration of their journey from/to the institution	X			X
Family support	Identifies whether students stay at home or are leased.	X			X

Table 4.3 Timetabling system

Data item	Description	AR	LD	SE	SW
Anticipated schedule & location	These two flags show where a student is expected to be during class times.	X	X	X	X

Table 4.4 Swipe card logs (for enabling building access)

Data item	Description	AR	LD	SE	SW
Existence of records	Identifies students on campus	X	X	X	X
Deviation from schedule	Identifies the place of students at the time of a scheduled event (e.g., library, fitness center, etc.)	X	X	X	X
Use of learning resources (e.g., library)	Use swipe cards for library access etc.	X	X	X	X
Use of campus resources	Use of swipe cards for other campus facilities like fitness, student center	X	X	X	X

Table 4.5 Swipe card logs (for enabling on-campus purchases)

Data item	Description	AR	LD	SE	SW
Presence on campus	Identifies students on the campus by recognizing shopping by using an educational swipe card	X	X	X	X
Location/Timing of purchases	Identifies the location of students at a given time (e.g., store, gum, etc.).	X	X	X	X
Use of learning resources	Use of swipe cards to print, photocopy, etc.	X	X	X	X
Co-academic behavior	Application of swipe cards for non-university campus services such as the gymnasium and student lounge.	X	X	X	X

Table 4.6 Library system

Data item	Description	AR	LD	SE	SW
Borrowings/ Borrowing history	Which books, etc., did students borrow?		X	X	
Searches	Identifies the logged-in student search patterns		X		
Group study bookings	Personal room allocation for joint ventures or research groups		X	X	
Equipment borrowing/hire	Local equipment/resources borrowing		X		
Librarian consultation	Having students arrange and/or engage in one-to-one or community meetings to develop their study skills or literacy.	X	X	X	X
Library guides	Curated services offered by librarians in support of their fields or relevant faculties		X		

Table 4.7 Attendee system

Data item	Description	AR	LD	SE	SW
Presence/ Absence	Identifies, in conjunction with timetable, whether students attended their lectures/tutorials/labs, etc	X	X	X	X

Table 4.8 Wi-Fi Logs

Data item	Description	AR	LD	SE	SW
Presence on campus	Through analyzing the Wi-Fi logs, the approximate location of students on campus with intelligent devices can be identified	X	X	X	X
Deviation from schedule	Identifies the location of students at a particular time (e.g., library, gym, etc.);	X	X	X	X
Identification of peer groups	Identify groups of students by identifying smart devices outside formal meetings (e.g., lectures)	X		X	X
Socialization/membership of the institutional community	Using Wi-Fi logs as mentioned above to recognize students without a social network within the institution	X			X

4.3 Data Models Used to Represent Usage Data for Learning Analytics

Table 4.9 Self-declared data (For example Student Surveys)

Data item	Description	AR	LD	SE	SW
Psychometric factors	Implementation of personality assessments, motivation, and learning approaches	X	X	X	X
Socio-economic	Survey of new socio-economic community students	X			X
Goal-setting	Surveying new students on their higher education priorities	X			X
Family HE history	Using surveys, students who are first in their higher education entrants will be listed	X			X
Satisfaction surveys	Satisfaction surveys are issued to students at critical points in their lifetime.	X	X	X	X

Table 4.10 Customer relationship management system (CRM)

Data item	Description	AR	LD	SE	SW
Interactions with academic staff	CRM tools can be used to track student interactions with university staff.	X	X	X	X
Interactions with the pastoral staff	CRM software can be used with confidence to monitor interactions between students and support staff (such as student counselors, advisors, etc.).	X		X	X
Interactions with administrative staff	CRM software may be used to monitor student interactions with the support staff (e.g., fees office, test office, etc.).	X		X	X
Issue categories	Broad categories that show the kind of issues students are presenting with	X	X		X
Agreed actions	Actions decided between a student and a consultant/academic can be reported	X		X	X

Table 4.11 Other sources

Data item	Description	AR	LD	SE	SW
Authentication logs, lecture capture, e-portfolios, Office 365, Google Apps, Club/Society membership, School systems (for example, ARC, APPEL, GIS/Geospatial data, Network logs	Various logs of student activity	X	X	X	X

social media, and mobile structures (Lukarov et al., 2014). Such data sources have structured education systems in the past. These are essentially learning management systems like Blackboard, Moodle, L2P, Ilias, etc. (Lukarov et al., 2014).

These learning management systems collect detailed logs of student behaviors and data on experiences. Furthermore, these systems are often used in formal learning environments to improve traditional face-to-face teaching methods or support remote learning. The user-generated content, enabled by ubiquitous technology, led to vast quantities of data provided by students through learning environments and systems (Chatti et al., 2012).

In short, learning data can and should be formal and informal, as learning and the development of information is often spread across multiple media and websites in networked environments (Suthers & Rosen, 2011). The challenge is how raw data from various and heterogeneous sources, often in different formats, are aggregated and incorporated to create a useful educational data set representing the learner's activities to deliver better learning analytics results.

4.3.1 Data Models

"The user activities and their usage of data objects are different applications are called Usage Metadata (Lukarov et al., 2014)." There are today a growing number of formats for data representation for data use. There are not only essential logging files but also user activities. This section first discusses the four most widely used data representations, namely Contextualized Attention Metadata, Activity Streams, Learning Registry Paradata, and NSDL (Lukarov et al., 2014).

It then gives IMS specifications for capturing and sharing data about learning experiences in the learning systems.

1. ***Contextualized Attention Metadata (CAM)***. Contextualized Attention Metadata (CAM) allows user experiences with learning environments to be tracked. The emphasis has shifted to the event itself from the user and the data set. Events may also have versatile attributes.

   Figure 4.1 displays the modified CAM scheme version. This scheme stores the necessary event details. Additional information is stored as entities for each event. Due to the abstract and straightforward scheme, the position attribute has been removed from much detail. It must be established from the outset. For example, the sender, receiver, context, writer, forum, and thread can be sample role values. It also includes rules for instances of role attributes to be followed. This ensures that if the role attribute is "forum," there must be only one associated person with the role character attribute "writer" and at least one with the message value. The scheme determines the length of the operation. This scheme

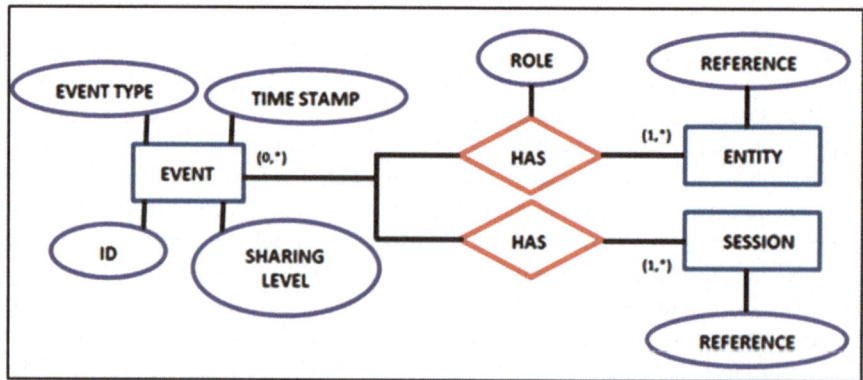

Fig. 4.1 The CAM scheme (Lukarov et al., 2014)

4.3 Data Models Used to Represent Usage Data for Learning Analytics   105

can be modeled for various learning platforms with versatile and straightforward representation, but it needs specifying rules and constraints to make this model simpler and stronger. The data can be stored in different formats such as JSON, XML, RDF, or reference databases.

2. **Activity Streams**. An Activity Stream (Fig. 4.2) is a series of one or more user behaviors. There are specific requirements for each operation. Figure 4.2 demonstrates the scheme for operation sources. There are three properties in action, such as actor, object, and target. Every property is an object in an activity stream format. The verb attribute plays the same function in the CAM scheme as the event form. It defines an event in the learning activity. Furthermore, every object within an Activity Stream can be expanded to include properties not defined by the core definition and specification, thus providing much flexibility.

3. **Learning Registry Paradata**. Learning Registry Paradata (Fig. 4.3) is an extended version of Activity Streams to store aggregate resource information. Paradata's three main elements are actor, verb, and object. The verb refers to a learning action, and it is possible to store detailed information.

4. **NSDL Paradata**. This data format (Fig. 4.4) gathers aggregate data of resources such as downloaded or rated resources. This format is object-centered, given the fact that many usage data formats are event-centered. The primary item is the usageDataSummary, which includes all available resource statistics and data using five different value types: integer/float, string, rating type, vote type, and rank type.

Integer/float shows the number where the resource performs specific actions, such as "downloaded" or "rated." A String can be a textual meaning like a statement. A rating type form is an average rating value for some parameters; for example, the usability of Fig. 4.3: Learning Registry Paradata scheme Fig. 4.4: NSDL Paradata scheme the resource. The vote type and rank type are the interest rate on a particular resource.

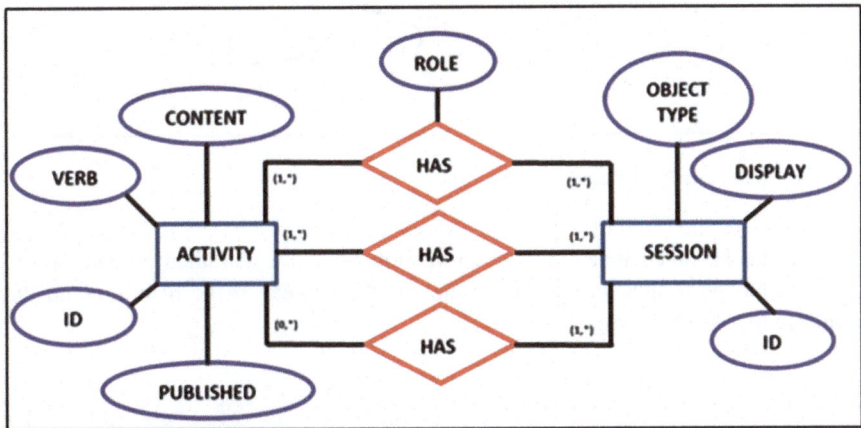

Fig. 4.2 Activity streams scheme (Lukarov et al., 2014)

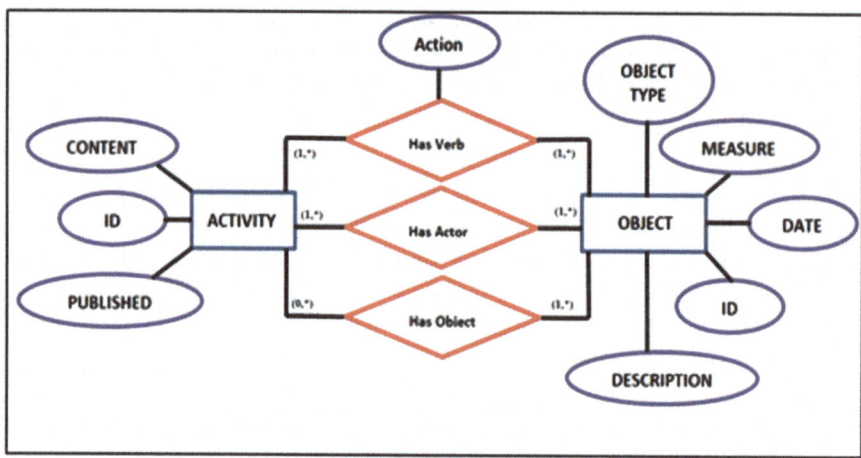

Fig. 4.3 Learning registry paradata (Lukarov et al., 2014)

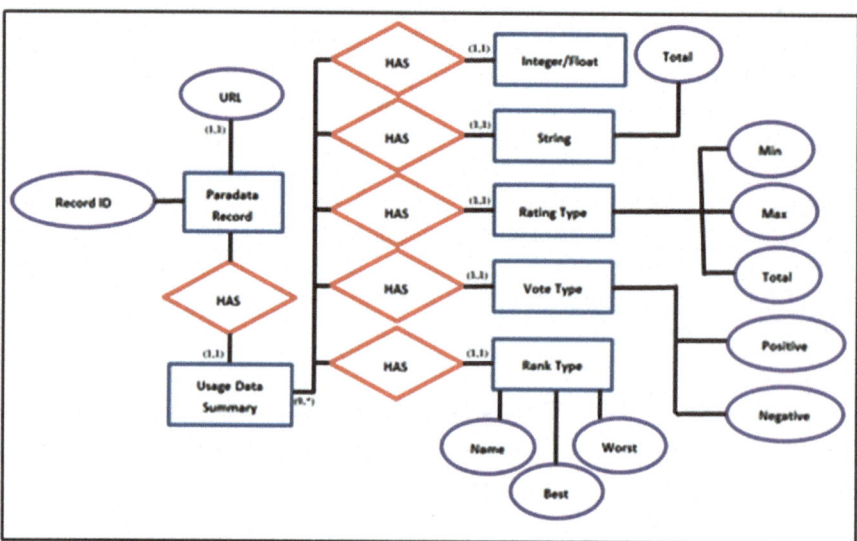

Fig. 4.4 NSDL Paradata scheme (Lukarov et al., 2014)

It should be noted that the detailed version of NSDL Paradata contains more detail about the usageDataSummary, such as the subject of the resource and the audience of a used resource.

4.3 Data Models Used to Represent Usage Data for Learning Analytics

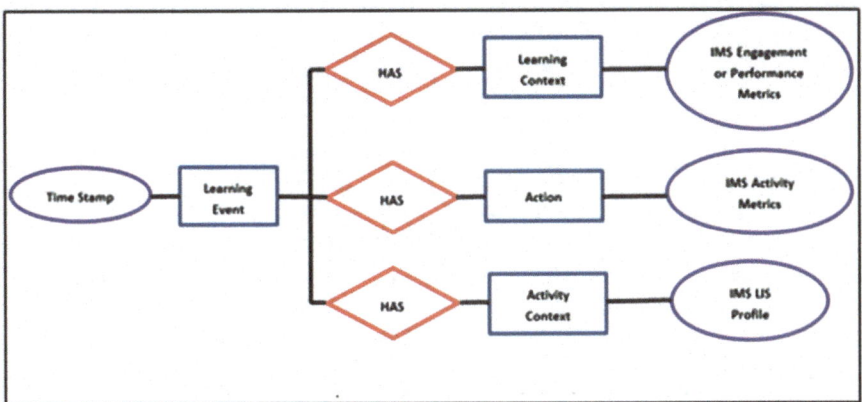

Fig. 4.5 LMS Calipher Scheme (Lukarov et al., 2014)

5. ***IMS Specifications of Learning Measurement for Analytics (IMS Caliper)***. IMS defines a framework for learning measurement, Caliper. IMS Caliper consists of IMS Learning Metric Profiles, IMS Learning Sensor APIs, and Learning Events IMS LTITM / LIS / QTITM leverage and extension. The idea behind the learning metric profile is defining the structured collection of learning activity metrics that represent measurements specific to actions within each activity genre. Most learning activities can be grouped into one or more classes, for example, reading, evaluation, media, etc. Furthermore, basic metrics such as engagement and performance are available. The IMS Caliper scheme connected to various IMS metric profiles is shown in Fig. 4.5.

6. ***Learning Context Data Model***. The new L²P follows an approach focused on students and focuses on personalization, extensibility, and versatility. There are also various distribution learning environments, and the data model must be established to gather all the information needed and be independent of each learning platform. CAM representation is the basis of the learning context data model. To answer, "Which level of abstraction is suitable for this data model," two points must be considered. First of all, we need to think about what kind of learning practices should be filtered. Furthermore, background knowledge's meanings should be recognized when they come from different sources, such as smartphones or sites. Figure 4.6 displays the proposed data model.

All the data models for analytics (recommenders, data mining, learning analytics) are developed. While using them to control and represent usage data in their respective applications, researchers, developers, and device engineers must know their strengths and weaknesses. One should define the intent of his learning analytics tool and choose the data model accordingly. Nevertheless, these data models should not be taken as given and supplemental, but rather additional elements that can help organize the data, making analytics more reliable.

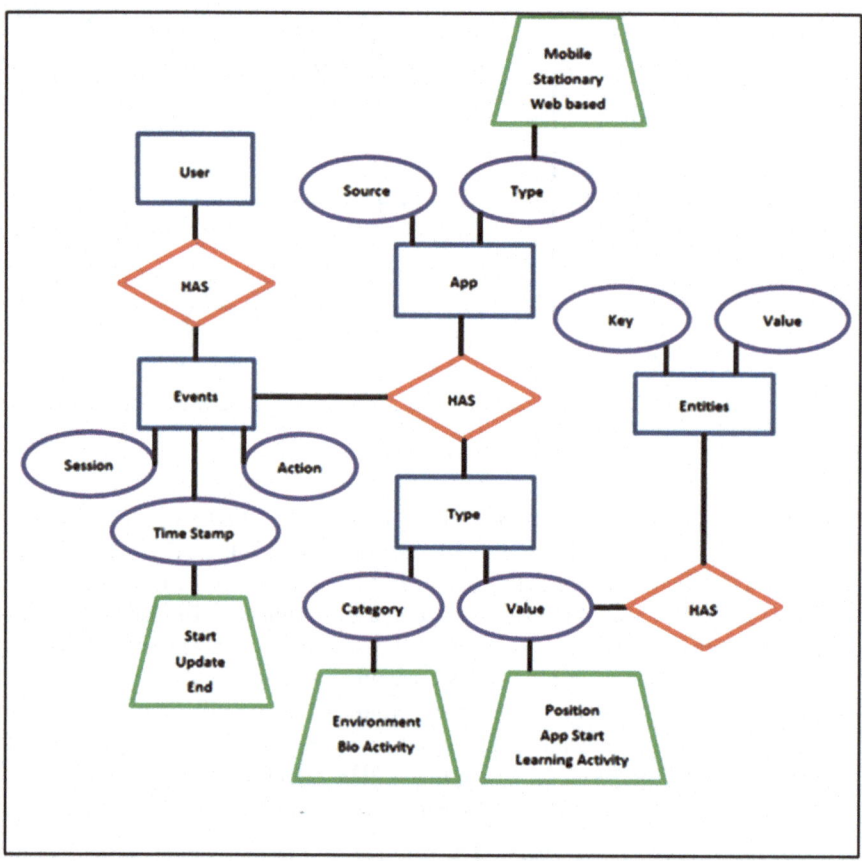

Fig. 4.6 Learning context data model scheme (Lukarov et al., 2014)

4.4 Data Privacy Maintenance in Learning Analytics

4.4.1 Student Data Privacy

While it is essential to collect and evaluate student data for education and learning, this must be done in the sense of criteria that protect the students' privacy and ensure that their data are used only for valid educational purposes (Ifenthaler & Schumacher, 2016). The Family Educational Rights and Privacy Act (FERPA), passed in 1974, usually forbids the release of personal information by schools without permission in students' educational records. There are exceptions to the requirement for consent, which allows such information to be disclosed to "school officials" for educational purposes. In 2008, this specific rule was extended when the United States Department of Education adopted new regulations to clarify that third-party vendors may be included under a school official exemption (such as those who help maintain school databases or have digital curricula). Also, the protection of the pupil rights amendment requires school districts to notify the parents if personally identifiable information is being used for marketing purposes; and before collecting, using, or distributing personal information from children under the age of 13, the Children's Online Privacy Protection legislation requires parental consent. While third parties must be under the school's strict supervision about the use and preservation of records and only use the records for the purposes they have been shared, and there is still some concern that student data security remains unclear. While overall, the importance of data collection for enhancing education quality is understandable by most policymakers and educators, there is some concern that both FERPA and the corresponding regulations are now obsolete in the modern digital age (NASSP, 2018).

In 2014, a convention was held to discuss issues concerning the students' privacy, and a bill was introduced by the Senate to update FERPA and make it clear that it is forbidden for third parties to use student information for marketing and advertising purposes. The National Conference of State Legislatures has announced that more than 100 student privacy bills have been introduced in more than 36 states. Each director is entirely unaware of and familiar with federal, state, and district data collection policies and student privacy requirements.

The National Association of Secondary Schools Principals (NASSP) has proposed legislation to ensure student privacy and the use of student knowledge to improve education and learning (NASSP, 2018).

1. ***Recommendations for Federal Policymakers***

    - Review student data usage policies to ensure they align privacy with the need to improve education and learning
    - Require all organizations to gather and/or store sensitive data from students to implement a robust security system designed to protect the health, privacy, confidentiality, and integrity of personal information from harm.
    - Provide advice to states on the collection, storage, protection, and student data destruction
    - Provision of funding to states and districts for addressing student data protection concerns, including educators' training and professional development, technological resources, and technical funding
    - Ensure that personal information and online learning are not used to manipulate student or family advertising related to non-education
    - Limit non-consensual access by staff members of schools, districts, or government educational agencies and authorized service providers to personally identifiable student data under their direct control for only authorized purposes.

2. ***Recommendations for State Policymakers***

    - Create a statewide data security strategy that covers administrative, physical, and technical guarantees for the processing of state data systems and other State data

- Develop notification of data infringements for districts and schools
- To designate a government official responsible for the privacy, data protection, and compliance with all federal and state laws and regulations on privacy
- Develop data collection, storage, and access policies to ensure that student data collected via statewide longitudinal data systems is not being shared or used improperly
- Provide instructions on gathering, processing, safeguarding, and deleting student data for districts and colleges.

3. *Recommendations for District Policymakers*

- To create specific policies about what information about students is collected, how this data is used, to whom the data is communicated, and the obligations of each party in the event of a violation of the data
- Ensure the correct data deletion and disposal practices include the elimination of electronic data, shredding of physical documents, and the destruction of all data on old electronic equipment where data has been stored
- Identifies a district data protection officer responsible for monitoring and compliance with federal, state, and district data privacy policies and guiding school leaders and teachers in their use and protection of information.
- To train all district personnel to ensure they recognize the fundamental legal standards, obligations, and relevant district policies relating to student data.
- Ensure that principals receive education on policies and procedures to support the prevention of data violation — and specify steps in cases of data violation. This will include protocols for notifying officials, parents, and other members of the group.
- Train district staff on online education (paid and free) and determine if they comply with FERPA and state and district regulations;
- Plan annual data security programs for all school and district employees requiring access to student data, acceptance of electronic educational resources or applications, or procurement and contracting with providers of services;
- Ensure that all third-party providers who obtain or have access to student data have written contracts that discuss the privacy and acceptable use of personal data so that any information is forbidden without parents' permission from being re-released.
- Contact parents directly about collecting and using student data and privacy measures to prevent confusion and misunderstanding.
- Ensure that the contracts or "service terms" include the relevant legal rules concerning the access, use, security, and destruction of student data before using online educational services.

- Ensure that the parents' agreements with external providers directly access personally identifiable information and support indirect parental access by the school to other student data.
- Ensure greater transparency by posting all policies governing the externalization of school functions and agreements with third party providers on district and school websites
- Make a list of online educational services or apps used in the district available.

4. *Recommendations for School Leaders*

- familiarize yourself with FERPA, state and regional rules on data privacy for students
- Communicate district policies for collecting and using student data for your teachers and parents
- Make sure that the teachers are informed on the use of online education resources and that they comply with FERPA and the state and district regulations
- Communicate the privacy, security, and infringement and indemnification policies of third-party vendors to parents personally identifiable information shared with such vendors.

4.4.2 Security and Privacy Balance for Optimal Data Protection

Privacy is about protecting individual rights and ensuring that institutions have control over their data. It includes identifying and developing policies and procedures that direct the collection, storage, and use of data and to whom it can be transmitted. Security means that information is protected against cyber-attacks and other types of data disasters using technological and physical strategies. This involves preventing and preserving unauthorized access or unintended data manipulation.

The security and privacy of data protection go hand in hand. Institutions cannot start creating strong privacy policies without security checks to protect their data from threats such as email breaches and infringements. These two concepts need to be balanced by institutions today. Through understanding how security and privacy work together and being clear on student data, colleges and Universities can implement best practices for data protection while taking the best interests of their students into account. Understanding how data security and privacy integrate into data protection will help universities and colleges manage student data correctly and ethically (Durand, 2020).

4.4.3 Learning Analytics Data Protection Checklist

The Office of the Data Protection Commissioner has published eight rules to emphasize data controllers' responsibilities in data management (https:/www.dataprotection.ie/docs/Data-Protection-Rules/y/21.htm). These rules are set out below, along with a checklist derived from the https:/www.dataprotection.ie/docs/Self-Assessment-Data-ProtectionChecklist/y/22.htm Data Protection Checklist. This checklist aims to make it possible for institutions and people to establish systems, policies, and Learning Analytics practices that comply with the 1988 and 2003 data protection Acts. Institutions should be able to say yes to all the following questions to comply.

4.4.3.1 Data Controller Responsibilities (e.g., Institutions)

Data Controllers have to:

- Acquisition and fair processing of student data
- Keep it for only one or more legally specified purposes
- Process it only in ways that are consistent with the purposes originally offered
- Maintain it secure and safe
- Keep it up-to-date and accurate
- Ensure reasonable, acceptable, and not excessive
- Do not maintain it longer than is required for the purpose or purposes stated
- Send a copy of his/her personal information on request to any student or graduate.

4.4.3.2 Data Protection Checklist

Rule 1 – *Obtain and process data lawfully:*

- Are they aware of the use of the information when the information is gathered about students?
- Are students notified of any disclosures to third parties of their data?
- Learning Analytics requires using personal information in a way that students cannot see. Have students been asked to use it in this way?
- Are data collection activities of the organization free, clear, and up-to-date?

Rule 2 – *Keep only for the purpose specified.*

- Has the organization specifically established what Learning Analytics is intended for?
- Were students aware of these goals?
- Is the organization responsible for maintaining a list of all data sets and the associated purposes?

4.4 Data Privacy Maintenance in Learning Analytics

Rule 3 – *Use and disclosure of Data*

- Does the use and disclosure of student information relevant to Learning Analytics have specified rules?
- Are all staff aware of the rules?
- Are students aware of their personal data uses and disclosures? Would they be shocked if they learned?

Rule 4 – *Security.*

- Is a list of protections available for each data set?
- Is anyone in charge of creating and updating these provisions?
- Are these provisions appropriate for personal data sensitivity?
- Are password-protected computers and databases and authenticated, if applicable?
- Are computers, servers, and archives secured safely from unauthorized individuals?

Rule 5 – *Data is adequate, appropriate, and not excessive.*

- Does this institution obtain all the information required to accomplish this goal efficiently and to deal equally and thoroughly with its students?
- Has the institution verified that all collected information is essential to the defined purpose(s) and not excessive?
- If a student asked the institution to explain any information kept about him or her, could it?
- Is there a policy in this respect?

Rule 6 – *Data is precise and up-to-date.*

- Does the institution verify the accuracy of the data?
- Does the organization know how vulnerable the personal data kept are, i.e., unreliable over time, unless it is updated?
- Should the institution take action to upgrade its databases?

Rule 7 – *Data preservation.*

- Is it clear how long data will be retained?
- Are there legally applicable data retention conditions for a certain period?
- Does the organization have a program which is more required to purge databases periodically?
- Are there rules on the deletion of personal data as soon as it has been finalized?

Rule 8 – *Right of access to personal data.*

- Is a designated individual responsible for managing access requests?
- Are appropriate procedures in place to deal with such requests?
- Would these measures guarantee that the provisions of the Act are complied with?

4.5 Case Studies

4.5.1 California University

The Learning Data Privacy Principles and Practices developed by the Educational Technology Leadership Committee (ETLC) and the University Committee on Academic Computing and Communications (UCACC) (Uc & Use, 2016) with assistance from the IT Leadership Committee (ITLC).

4.5.1.1 Data Privacy Principles

1. *Ownership*: Data ownership and subsequent computer transformations of the data produced by the University of California (UC), its faculty, and the students remain. Individual data owners are entitled to decide how their data is used. The UC acts on behalf of its faculty and students as data stewards.
2. *Ethical use*: Learning data collection, use, and computational transformation is governed by pedagogical and educational concerns aimed at the success of students by prescription, description, or prediction methodology. Like with grades and other sensitive data, the use of learning analytics on a "need to know" basis should be followed.
3. *Transparency*: Data owners have the rights to understand the specific methods and purpose to which their data is collected, used, and transformed, including the transmission of data to third-party service providers (and their affiliates), and how these form summaries, in particular outputs and visualizations, are used by algorithms.
4. *Freedom of expression*: The faculty and students retain the right to communicate and engage each other in the learning process without worrying about unintended or unknown data mining.
5. *Protection*: Stewards ensure that learning data are secure and secured in compliance with all federal, state, and university regulations relating to safe storage on behalf of data owners.
6. *Access and control*: Information owners are entitled to access their details. Given that teachers and students possess and share their learning data, access and ultimate control of data is the responsibility of teachers, student owners, and the data managers acting on their behalf. Access to data retention and control practices will be governed by UC policies and contractual agreements between suppliers.

4.5.1.2 Practices in Information Protection

1. *Ownership*: Service providers accept the possession and use of learning data as teachers and students' rights.
2. *Usage Right*: Users can control the use of intellectual property through the user's profile setting. The consumer is therefore entitled to grant terms like

4.5 Case Studies

"a royalty-free, transferable, perpetual, irrevocable, non-exclusive, worldwide license to reproduce, modify, publish, publicly display, do derivative works."

3. **Opt-in**: Apart from the data elements distinctly needed for education, students would have the option to use the learning data obtained by faculty and service providers in an "opt-in" approach instead of "opt-out."
4. **Interoperable data**: Service providers will provide the institution with learning data in recognized standard interoperability formats to minimize integration costs, to support cross-platform and multi-application use, and to encourage institutional and university analysis and research.
5. **Data without Fees**: Service providers shall not charge professors, students, or other university data controllers for the right of access, including the transfer to the University of these data.
6. **Transparency**: Service providers will inform the UC of the data they collect and how they are used, based on pedagogical considerations and curricular improvements in the academic term.
7. **Service Provider Security**: All the service provider platforms on which student learning data are stored conform to UC and the state-mandated security procedures governing the reporting and correction of unintended incidents.
8. **Campus Safety**: UC data managers ensure that all faculty and student data are safely stored in line with the University data security policy. Learning data stewards shall report any incidents relating to the security of learning data to faculty and students and provide information on their remedies.

4.5.2 Gloucestershire University

The University of Gloucestershire, to fulfill its corporate and organizational functions, gathers, retains, and manages data on students, staff, candidates, alumni, donors, contractors, and other individuals. The law on data security describes personal data as any information relating to a person ('data subject') or an identifiable natural person. The natural person can be identified directly or indirectly by reference, in particular, to an identifier such as name, identifier number, location data, online identifier, or to one or more factors specific to that natural person's physiological, physical, genetic, mental, economic, cultural or social identity. Personal data also includes an opinion on and intended for the data subject. The University is committed to defending people's rights and freedoms regarding collecting their personal data (University of Gloucestershire, 2018).

4.5.2.1 Principles of Data Protection

1. Data privacy law includes compliance with the university's data security concept, its employees, and those who store or use personal information.
2. The principles of data protection state that personal data should be:

- lawfully, reasonably and transparently processed;
- collected for purposes specified, explicit and legitimate;
- sufficient, acceptable, and restricted to what is required;
- correct and up-to-date, where necessary;
- maintained in a form that allows data subjects not to be identified more than is necessary for the purposes for which data are processed;
- processed in a way that guarantees adequate personal data security.

3. Accountability is critical in data protection legislation, and it is up to the data controller to comply with these principles, and the UK regulator, the ICO, to demonstrate this.

4.5.3 The University of Leeds

Leeds University uses learning analytics to improve the education of students and help registered students to achieve success. It uses learning analytics to:

(a) support individual learners through action intelligence for students, teachers, and professional staff;
(b) help to understand cohort behavior and results; and
(c) contribute to understanding and improving the learning environment.

This means that the student education data is collected, analyzed, and presented to the staff and students in appropriate formats to encourage student learning, progress, and well-being. The University recognizes that data on its own cannot be a complete photo of a student's progress, but provide an indicative picture of progress and chance of success.

4.5.3.1 Privacy

Applications to student information and learning analytics are limited to those who have a valid right to use them by the University. The learning analytics data held with the University will be accessed by the following groups (University of Leeds, 2019).

- Students – have access to their data on learning analytics;
- employees who need the data to support the students;
- Staff members who are responsible for student education;
- University Data Analysts;
- Other people or groups associated with students in their research at Leeds University.
- University technical staff and contract agents to ensure functioning systems.

If student support is provided for individual students (including academic and pastoral support), data on learning analytics should be presented where students can be identified. Such details will only be made accessible to students involved and to University staff who have the necessary permits to display them at a sufficient level of access. If learning analytical data are made available to individuals or organizations, such as supporting students who work with external organizations, only the necessary support can be provided at levels that could include identifying data. Therefore, anonymous or pseudonymized learning analytics data will be used.

Where anonymized student data is collected for or generated by learning analytics, the University ensures that individuals from metadata are not identified or that multifaceted data sources are not aggregated. Where data are to be used anonymously, special care is taken to ensure that:

- Identification of individuals from metadata;
- Re-identify people by aggregating various sources of information.

To share access to data from learning analytics with external persons and organizations, relevant contracts, data processing, and data sharing agreements will be in place, following university and GDPR policies. For cases where data and information may be exchanged publicly – such as requests from school administrators, security forces, or employers – staff and students must be made clear.

Under the General Data Protection Regulation, students can access and obtain copies of their data in portable digital formats all learning analytics conducted on their data in meaningful, accessible formats. Students can correct inaccurate personal information about themselves.

The University periodically carries out data security impact tests for the use of learning analytics in the organization.

4.5.4 Jisc's Privacy Guidelines

Access to student data and analytics should be limited to those who have a legitimate need to see them by the institution. Institutions should take particular care to avoid data being used anonymously (Bailey & Sclater, 2015):

- Identification of metadata individuals
- Re-identify individuals by adding multiple data sources

Additional protections are necessary for the use of "special category data" for learning analytics. Circumstances in which data and analytics may be shared externally-such as requests from educational authorities, security agencies, or employers-will be explicitly made available to staff and students and may require further consent.

Additional protections are necessary for the use of "special category data" for learning analytics. Institutions will ensure that students' data are covered when third parties are hired to store or analyze data. Institutions may have a statutory duty to intervene and therefore overcome certain privacy constraints when data or analytics show a student is at risk. The circumstances of this kind should be clearly stated.

4.5.5 Learning Analytics and Data Protection in Ireland

All collection and processing of personal data must comply with so-called principles or data protection principles. These are laid down in GDPR Article 5. It states that personal information must be provided (Lambert, 2016),

- legally, fairly and transparently processed concerning the data subject ("lawfulness, fairness and transparency");
- collected for a specified, explicit and legitimate purpose rather than further processed in ways incompatible with such purposes, further processing shall not, under Article 89(1), be considered incompatible for public interest archiving or for scientific or historical research or statistical purposes ("Purpose limitation")
- adequate, relevant, and limited to the purposes for which they are being processed ('data minimization');
- accurate and, where necessary, up-to-date; every reasonable step must be taken to ensure the immediate deletion or correction of personal information which is inaccurate, taking account of the purposes for which it is processed ("accuracy");
- maintained in a form to allow the identification of data subjects for the purpose for which the personal data are processed for no more than is necessary; personal data may be stored for more extended periods, so long as the personal data is solely processed for the public interest, scientific or historical research studies or for statistical research according to Article 89(1).
- processed in a manner that ensures proper personal data security, including protection from unauthorized or illegal processing and accidental loss, destruction or harm, through appropriate technological or organizational steps (integration and confidentiality").

4.6 Conclusion

The widespread use of digital technology has created an explosion of data in education. You leave a digital footprint of your activity every time you use digital technology. Moreover, in recent years, the collection, aggregation, analysis, categorization, and learning from all of these data has become possible. Education data provides useful knowledge to be gathered from learning analytics to provide new insights into improved education delivery. Educational institutions currently have access to a wide range of digital information on learners, such as records of performance, educational resources, attendance at classes, feedback on course materials, course evaluation, and social data on students and educators. The aim is to enrich further the types of information available to institutions in new educational environments, technologies, and regulations. Learning Analytics offers new insights into a better educational system with various data types and information sources.

While the collection, use, and exchange of educational data have apparent benefits, the data's sensitive nature poses legitimate privacy questions. Many initiatives and regulations safeguard the privacy of personal data. This chapter discussed different data types used for learning analytics, data models used to reflect data usage and data privacy issues, and some case studies.

4.7 Review Questions

Reflect on the concepts of this chapter guided by the following questions.

1. Review of various Data models used to represent usage data for learning analytics.
2. How can learner data help instructional designers improve course design?
3. How can data about education change public policy?
4. What are data sources appropriate for triggering interventions?
5. List and explain the various types of data used for learning analytics.
6. Describe the various methods used to track data in LMS.
7. How to ensure that the students' data only used for legitimate educational purposes. Explain.
8. List the data privacy principles followed by the University of California.
9. For the student or workplace learner, how can data about their behavior help them improve their performance?
10. How does data help L&D managers increase their impact across the organization?

References

Bailey, P., & Sclater, N. (2015). Code of practice for learning analytics. In *Jisc*. https://www.jisc.ac.uk/guides/code-of-practice-for-learning-analytics

Chatti, M. A., Dyckhoff, A. L., Schroeder, U., & Thüs, H. (2012). A reference model for learning analytics. *International Journal of Technology Enhanced Learning, 4*(5–6), 318–331. https://doi.org/10.1504/IJTEL.2012.051815

Durand, M. (2020). *To better protect student data, know the difference between security and privacy*. EdTech. https://edtechmagazine.com/higher/article/2020/02/better-protect-student-data-know-difference-between-security-and-privacy#:~:text=Privacy is concerned with protecting,it can be shared with.

eThink. (2019). *5 Effective ways to track training data in your LMS*. https://ethinkeducation.com/blog/5-ways-track-training-data-lms/

Ifenthaler, D., & Schumacher, C. (2016). Student perceptions of privacy principles for learning analytics. *Educational Technology Research and Development, 64*(5), 923–938. https://doi.org/10.1007/s11423-016-9477-y

Klašnja-Milićević, A., Ivanović, M., & Budimac, Z. (2017). Data science in education: Big data and learning analytics. *Computer Applications in Engineering Education, 25*(6), 1066–1078. https://doi.org/10.1002/cae.21844

Lambert, P. (2016). *Learning analytics and data protection in Ireland*.

Lukarov, V., Chatti, M. A., Thüs, H., Kia, F. S., Muslim, A., Greven, C., & Schroeder, U. (2014). Data models in learning analytics. *CEUR Workshop Proceedings, 1227*, 88–95.

NASSP. (2018). *Student data privacy statement* (Issue April). https://www.nassp.org/policy-advocacy-center/nassp-position-statements/student-data-privacy/

National Forum for the Enhancement of Teaching and Learning in Higher Education. (2018). *Data conceptual model*. https://www.teachingandlearning.ie/resource/data-conceptual-model/

Snola. (2018). *Learning analytics 2018 – An updated perspective*. https://snola.es/2018/02/21/learning-analytics-2018-updated-perspective/

Soltanpoor, R. (2018). *An integrated framework for learning analytics* (Issue October).

Suthers, D., & Rosen, D. (2011). A unified framework for multi-level analysis of distributed learning. *ACM International Conference Proceeding Series*, February, 64–74. https://doi.org/10.1145/2090116.2090124

Uc, T., & Use, E. (2016). *University of California learning data privacy principles and recommended practices*. 10–11.

University of Gloucestershire. (2018). *Data protection policy 1.1.1*.

University of Leeds. (2019). *Code of practice on learning analytics*. https://doi.org/10.1093/ilj/10.1.46.

Yupangco, J. (2018). The essential guide to learning analytics in the age of big data. *Lambda Solutions E-Book, 4*(5–6), 1–15.

Chapter 5
Tools for Learning Analytics

5.1 Introduction

The ultimate objective of training evaluation is to relate training directly to business impact: sales, efficiency, turnover, product quality. Data from a large sample can be challenging to collect and then interpret to isolate training. Fortunately, technology helps to assess the success of learning implementations through using Learning analytics tools.

Learning analytical tools take critically important business intelligence findings, connect them to training and training data, and provide business and training managers with the knowledge dashboard views required to manage corporate training and education efficiency. Specifically, learning analytics tools gather data from various sources and can pull data and construct a real-time component of an organization's training metrics by appropriate queries.

The systems can be connected in several combinations to build reporting, dashboards, and Management sites for learning and business professionals into business data (sale, production, inventory, and operations) and HR, financial, and training information.

Learning analytics is an enormous area in which various resources exist which perform specific tasks. They are also known as approaches for Learning Analytics. This chapter discusses different Learning Analytics tools and evidence on their use in institutions/organizations.

5.2 Popular Learning Analytics Tools

This section lists some popular Learning Analytics tools (Gautham, 2018) that can be used by L&D teams. Some organizations that already use LMS can use standalone Learning Analytics or link to such tools with an open-source LMS such as Moodle to support Learning Analytics, and some organizations that do not have an LMS in place will use standalone learning analysis tools. These two options were listed in this section. You may pick the one that fits your needs.

Categories:

- Learning Analytics as Moodle plugins
- Learning analytics as part of LMS

5.2.1 Learning Analytics as Moodle Plugins

1. **SmartKlass**. SmartKlass is a learning analytics plugin that can be incorporated with Moodle using a simple and easy dashboard, added directly as a new tab in the control panel. xAPI 1.0 is used to gather user interactions with the platform.
   Some of SmartKlass's advantages are:

   - Moodle 2.6, 2.7, 2.8, 2.9 and 3.0 are compatible. It supports the Tin Can API as well.
   - It highlights students with difficulties and provides information such as individual and collaborative work.
   - It can be used in business, school, and university learning.

2. **MOCLog Moodle Analytics**. MOCLog is a monitoring program to evaluate Moodle LMS log files more effectively and efficiently, thereby enhancing teaching and learning efficiency.
   This also provides benefits like:

   - Relevant log file analysis interpretation schemes
   - Easier and quicker log file review in Moodle online courses
   - Feedback from various stakeholders
   - Serving all primary LMS users
   - Monitor all log files status

3. **GISMO**. GISMO is an interactive graphical monitoring plugin that provides online visualization of student activity. This is a Moodle LMS plugin.
   You will try many things, like:

   - Student attendance
   - Content reading
   - Submission of documents

It also provides detailed views that offer an overview of the organization's entire learning pattern.
4. **Analytical Graph**. This plugin includes five separate graphs for the description of the learner profile. This is a plugin for Moodle LMS. This helps the administrative officer to send messages to users in a course based on their behavior. The diagrams show:

   - Grade chart
   - Content access chart
   - Number of active users chart
   - Assignment submissions chart
   - Hits distribution chart

5. **Heatmap**. The Heatmap plugin overlays a heatmap onto a course to show events with more or less activity to help teachers develop their course. It was inspired by a device called Moodle Activity Viewer (MAV), and it is a Moodle LMS plugin. It also provides information on the number of visits and unique users for each operation. It can even be turned off if it is not necessary.

5.2.2 Learning Analytics as a Part of LMS

1. **SumTotal Systems**. SumTotal Systems provides an interactive software kit focused on the technology of Microsoft Reporting & Analysis. SumTotal LMS provides regular reports that cover virtually all the daily reporting requirements. You may use these reports as the starting point for any further reports to be produced. Even you can create customized real-time dashboards to help your managers decide. Every report has its Amount Total LMS.
2. **Saba**. Saba has developed algorithms for machine learning that intelligently recommends appropriate course material based on user interests, expectations, and web-based activities. Saba has Saba analytics, which is meant to promote knowledge gathering and assessment in various learning systems. Reporting in Saba takes less time than the user's review. It gives you a full training summary with a button press.
3. **Docebo**. Docebo acts as a framework for managing abilities to improve employee efficiency. This offers an overall image of organizational learning, helping you understand more about learning habits and introducing tailored learning initiatives.
4. **Talent LMS**. It has a comprehensive reporting feature that reports on everything in the e-learning world. A timeline is documented for all device acts. Accurate reports are generated to obtain accurate details. You can also generate custom reports according to your requirements.
5. **Absorb LMS**. Absorb LMS assists you directly from the reports. You can conveniently register users directly from the report interface. You can also display or cover the corresponding columns and arrange them in any order. You can also

configure and save dynamic date filters. The Business Intelligence Module facilitates your team to gather valuable information from your LMS.
6. ***Cornerstone***. Cornerstone reports provide you with a variety of resources to increase the engagement and efficiency of employees. You should know what is going on in the company and maximize employee performance through objective decision-making—using Cornerstone Suite to build visually rich executive dashboards to complete data management and visibility for all reporting forms.
7. ***Litmos***. The "Reports" tab in Litmos gives you full access to real-time results that allow you to keep an easy track of individual trainee progress or compare team results within your company. You may also export the document as a PDF or a CSV file.

5.2.3 Top Learning Analytics Tools

We present the five top learning analytics tools (Nielson, 2019) that optimize the learner's learning experience and progress.

1. ***Wooclap***. Wooclap is an audience response tool that helps improve the engagement of in-class learners. It is a Belgian app that improves learning by a playful mechanism of in-class questionnaires. This app is also excellent learning analytics since it provides instructors with analytics. The instructors can assess who answered at what time and how long they needed to answer. The analytical software also has a feedback wall so that students can interact with their teachers and chat about their problems. Wooclap is also a good quality data provider.
2. ***YET Analytics***. YET analytics is one of the most extensive learning analytics and visualization tools used by freelance trainers and L&D professionals in firms. Built upon Xapi, YET analytics offers a wide range of visual analytics that improve the content of learning and the understanding of learners. It also provides valuable insights into role readiness, career path, talent development, and advanced engagement analytics on various learning ecosystems. It also provides precise predictive analytical solutions to meet the needs of various learners.
3. ***Bright Bytes***. Large organizations mostly use BrightBytes as it is built on a SaaS-based analytical tool focusing on four fundamental constructs that quantify technical effects in a learning environment. The analytics tool analyses how teachers and students use technology for learning, studies devices' availability and internet access, assess teachers' and learners' level of expertise through multimedia, and analyzes learning culture, professional development, and business-wide technology needs.
4. ***Knewton***. Knewton is an innovative US-based platform for personalized learning through data analysis. By analyzing student performance data in real-time, Knewton Alta, its higher-end version, allows teachers to adapt their learning and education content to every student and track their progress. The platform also has its online courses, which are checked and automatically adjusted to the

students' progress. Also, Knewton offers a full learning analytics solution for businesses, emphasizing the best knowledge that enables educators to develop and adapt their content efficiently.
5. **Clever.** Clever is now one of the fastest-growing U.S. learning analytics in Edtech. Clever released its advanced app, called Goals, providing teachers and students with a single sign-on platform for communicating between all software and learning resources. Firstly, the Goals Tool allows teachers to set targets for each learner, such as what to do, how to use, and so on. This then allows them to monitor the progress of the students accurately. The students are also able to track their progress. Clever is a handy analytical tool for students to learn and track their contribution to the learning environment.

5.2.4 Learning Analytics Apps

In pandemics like SARS-CoV-2 (COVID-19), thousands of schools around the world remain closed. Institute managers and teachers face the challenge of switching to electronic teaching within days. It involves searching for effective platforms and instruments to learn, discover, and/or develop digital content for learning, electronic communication tools, processes, and many other activities. Institutions will urgently search for free digital learning resources that could simplify their lives daily.

Go-Lab (https://www.golabz.eu/) allows both institutions and teachers to use the Go-Lab Platform to help institutions and teachers to deliver Online Education. Here is the most extensive collection of free online laboratories from leading providers to teach STEM subjects in the world, also, for any classroom session (the so-called "Inquiry Learning Spaces," containing online labs, inquiry apps, and any other digital learning material, you can easily create virtual learning scenarios. In many languages, over 1000 customized, ready-to-use spaces are available to save your time. The Go-Lab Ecosystem and its tools are free and expected to remain free after the COVID-19 pandemic. You will continue to use it free of charge as long as you want.

Apps are software tools that help students to develop hypotheses, design experiments, predict data, formulate interpretations, etc. for their study learning tasks. For example, other learning applications give students a quiz or allow students to view teacher feedback online. The applications can be combined with an online laboratory to create an Inquiry Learning Space. Learning Analytics tools provide teachers with an analysis of the success of students at the ILS.

Online laboratories allow your students to conduct scientific experiments in an online environment. Remote-operated laboratories (remote laboratories) provide the ability to experiment with real equipment from remote locations. Computer laboratories replicate scientific equipment. Data sets contain data from research studies already performed. Labs can be used to build Inquiry Learning Spaces (ILSs) along with different Applications.

Inquiry Learning Spaces (ILSs) are customized student learning facilities, including labs, software, and other media materials. ILSs follow a series of inquiries.

Survey cycles can differ, but the basic Go-Lab process of the introduction, conceptualization, inquiry, conclusion, and discussion phases is provided. The ILS aims to allow students to carry out scientific experiments, be directed through the investigation process, and assist at each level.

Below are applications (Table 5.1) that are appropriate for your class (https://www.golabz.eu/apps/category/learning-analytics)

5.3 Choosing a Tool

5.3.1 Checklist to Choose a Learning Analytics Tool

This section presents the checklist (Gautham, 2018) for your organization's choice of the right learning analysis tool.

1. *Needs Analysis*
   It is the first step in product choices. You will know here:

   - What data does the client want? Do you want to track learners, businesses, or do you want to track their performance according to the workflow or any tracking parameter?
   - What sort of learning programs do you analyze?
   - What is the foundation of the student, and what is the geographical distribution of the students?
   - Is the big tool data compatible?
   - Is it compatible with other ERP and LMS products and tools?
   - What is the data delivery mode?
   - Is it possible to export it to various formats, including PDF, Excel, or Word?
   - Does it provide management automated data sharing?

   Through understanding the answers to these questions, you can identify your needs and log them.

2. *Assess options*
   You should compare the resources available on the market according to the following parameters after you have met your requirements:

- To learn if the organization is a startup or well known.
- What is the seller's sort of technical support?
- Could it work efficiently with the current LMS?
- Can the tool be scaled?
- Can it perform data cleaning, data auditing, and data cross-validation?
- Is it a desktop tool or a cloud-based tool?
- Tool pros and cons
- What kind of protections does the data protection tool offer?

5.3 Choosing a Tool

Table 5.1 Learning analytics apps

S. No.	Learning analytics app	Description
1	Timeline	This software helps students to monitor and compare their job schedules with that of other students. It shows the periods in which students were involved in the different phases and applications of the ILS. The other students' names are anonymous. The feature also provides a teacher's view of the names of all students.
2	Time spent summary	This app displays a table with the time that all students spend in each step of inquiry learning. The time spent in real-time tracked. This app also provides a student's view of the anonymous names of the other students.
3	Time spent	The app will allow the student to focus on the time he has spent in the different phases of the ILS. The teacher can set a standard for each phase (as a percentage or in minutes). The app reveals the instructor norm and the time spent as a bar chart in the phases.
4	Time planner	The time planner software helps students to measure the time they spend in various phases of an ILS. This app is paired with the time checker that tells students how much time they spent on preparation. Usually, in the early stages of an ILS, the time checker is used at the end of an ILS. The most significant difference from the time the app is the person making the estimation (teacher for time and student for the time scheduler).
5	Time checker	Students can compare their actual spending time during the various phases of an ILS with their original schedule (as specified in the time planner app). The time checker is usually included in an ILS later stage, and the time planer is most likely included at the beginning of an ILS. A related feature is a time-spent app for students to measure their time spent on a teacher's schedule.
6	Ride dashboard	This tool lets teachers track the reflections of their students as created in the RIDE app. Typically, the device is put on the ILS Teacher Dashboard. The overall class and the distribution of the test outcomes, the outcomes of individual students, as well as how this is applied to the other students in the collaborative community and in the class, and the results of collaborative groups in comparison to other classes in the class can be seen here. Furthermore, time spent on assessing and setting objectives and the identified targets per community can be examined. Dates are visible on the dashboard once the students complete the first step of the RIDE app (assessment).
7	Quiz overview	This tool describes all the ILS contests by providing a graphical overview of all the students' responses and the students combined. Each response to each question can be given a ranking. For certain query forms, the score is determined automatically but can be adjusted manually later. The app automatically calculates each student's total score and the average score for each question.

(continued)

Table 5.1 (continued)

S. No.	Learning analytics app	Description
8	Phase transitions	The phase transitions app will allow the student to focus on the time and phase shift in an ILS. While the time spent on the app shows the average time for each point, this tool displays a graphic showing how long a student has been going in a process. Possible indications are (not) regular switching between phases (and so on), following the ILS order phases. In comparison to the tool spent time, no standard configuration is required
9	Online users visualization	This app displays every student currently participating in which step of the ILS. It can also be set to show the last activity of the students' app. The information on the operation is updated in real-time. The app also offers a student view of the names of the other teachers.
10	Concept mapper dashboard	This tool allows teachers to inspect the model maps created for an ILS by students. The device is usually mounted on the dashboard of the instructor. A summarized concept map of all students in an ILS is shown when the map icon is selected. The terms appear in a light color, and the names of the relationships are not shown. The thickness of the boxes and lines' border indicates how often all students use concepts and relations. To see who used it, click on a concept. Tap on a subject to illustrate the student's concepts. If the map icon is not chosen, the instructor will navigate through the individual student maps. In this respect, the names of relations and the path and the structure of the design map are maintained. If multiple concept map resources belong to an ILS, the concept map dashboard will retrieve each student from the latest updated concept map.
11	App overview	This tool tells the instructor what the students did in the other ILS settings. For every app, you can view the content generated by all students at once or individually. The device overview will display the content of the following applications: concept mapper, scratchpad hypothesis, scratchpad query, conclusion tool, data viewer, table tool, monitoring tool, and input box.
12	Aggregated concept map	This app helps students view a particular concept map created by combining all ILS students' concept maps. There is no need for configuration. There must, of course, be a design plan somewhere in the ILS, from which the overall project map can be built.
13	Activity plot	This app summarized the number of actions students perform in the various applications found in the ILS. Students may use it to equate their application practices with the average of other students. The other students' names are anonymous. The app also displays a teacher view where all students' names are shown.

- What is the technical know-how needed to incorporate the tool with your ERP or LMS systems?

  You may also shortlist the standard tools on the market that meet your requirements based on these criteria.

3. *Hands-on experience*

   Some tools provide a free trial or even request one. So, you can know the tool's usability, report production capabilities, etc. before you invest in a particular tool. You should also read reviews of the tool from independent blogs, take the opinions of both the internal IT experts and external consultants, and even get information from current customers.

   These are some of the things you have to note when selecting a tool for learning analytics.

5.3.2 Choosing a Learning Analytics Tool

The performance of the learning implementation can be calculated by using Learning analytics tools. Learning analytics tools provide institutional heads and teachers/trainers with an information dashboard for the successful management of education and training. In particular, Learning Analytical tools gather input from multiple repositories and can, in combination with appropriate queries, collect data and create a real-time portion of the organization's training metrics.

When organizations realize that analytical solutions give valuable insight into the learning programs' efficiency and efficacy, they will see that the right tool is essential to meet their needs.

The following are the key features (Ryann, 2020) that you need to test before selecting a Learning analytics tool.

5.3.2.1 Key Tools Features

1. *Easy UI*. One of the most critical aspects of buying of learning analytics tool is a quick user interface, commonly known as a dashboard or a scorecard. It is not always easy to find, unfortunately. Fortunately, a custom user interface can be created that is easy to use for non-technical people.
2. *Functions for data sharing*. To make your analysis even more powerful, your organization managers, executives, and directors will directly track your transaction from their inbox. Look for a solution that will allow you to prepare a saved analysis report that is automatically retrofitted and sent to a designated user set at a given time.

3. ***Scalable Architecture***. Since any analytics system's key benefits are the ability to distill vast volumes of data into usable information, a practical learning analytics system needs to be scalable at an enterprise level. It should be noted that this scalability should not be too costly.
4. ***Analysis and reports***. In addition to a straightforward user interface, please consider the tool's versatility to produce reports based on your organization's business processes. Some solutions offer out-of-box reports and give users integrated reports specific to their learning system software. Nevertheless, bear in mind that a one-size-fits-all solution cannot be an empirical method.

5.4 Strategies to Successfully Deploy a Tool

The deployment of a Learning Analytics tool in your organization benefits your students' engagement and success levels. However, you have to face a range of technical and human obstacles to succeed, as you may know.

This section presents 15 strategies (Omedes, 2017), which you can follow today to effectively deploy your Learning Analytics tool. You will discover from each technique what early adopters have experienced and how to benefit from their experience.

1. ***Take advantage of recording student experiences from the digital world***. Be mindful that not all relevant student experiences occur in a digital environment (LMS, online library catalogs, etc.) while gathering data for your learning analytical tool. The analytics engine cannot consider accounting for any factors affecting the learning process simply because they are not recorded.
   Such missing pieces of information can be obtained by:

   • create a simple web application in which teachers can document elements of interaction such as tutoring assistance, additional academic work, or class questions.
   • ensure that teachers applying for the application are recognized and thanked by the faculty for participating actively in the initiative to improve analytics.
   • Use the information obtained only when most teachers involved have used the application; otherwise, the data would be incomplete.

2. ***Consider the dashboard of students rich enough to grasp immediate behavior***. Small dashboards typically inform students, sometimes present in the LMS. Such dashboards should be sufficiently descriptive to give the students some thoughts and to suggest any immediate changes, if possible. For example, a red or green light can show the progress of the students in a course.
   Student dashboards should display:

   • the student's overall standing in a course or a semester (where the traffic light makes sense);

5.4 Strategies to Successfully Deploy a Tool

- the status of the students in the group, so that they have an apparent reference where comparing them with their peers;
- explains why others are doing better: "Students at the top of the class ... spend more time on LMS, take optional tests and go to tutoring sessions;"
- Ask for support for students if they believe it is time to lift their hands.

All this should be presented in a condensed way that is simple to understand.

3. ***Lead the project on the side of innovation learning, not IT***. IT is a vital player for any Learning Analytics project, but it should not take the lead position. Learning Analytics is about data, systems, and dashboards; it is about finding factors that contribute to the students' failures and successes and designing intervention strategies that work within your educational framework.
You have to:

    - list all relevant project stakeholders (leaders, teachers, students, IT, innovation learning, implementation teams, legal, etc.);
    - involve them in the core project team from the start to simplify things in the long-term;
    - Ensure that there are daily follow-up discussions with stakeholders other than the implementation team.

4. ***Remove from day one the legal issues***. When you use your learning analytics tool, people raise ethical concerns. It is entirely natural because they know that you can use their data to analyze how they learn and how they behave. In the end, knowledge is control. Transparency is your best strategy to strengthen your final learning analytics objective: to improve students' success.
You should: To clarify the ethical concerns:

    - Establish an ethical project committee for all stakeholders, in particular teachers and students;
    - Build a charter of ethical ventures together with the following elements:
        - Plan priorities,
        - Evidence to be obtained,
        - Data to be sent to teachers and students,
        - The code of conduct of the project or set of standards for data collection and use and
        - Student mechanisms to opt-out if they do not want to participate
    - Make sure that the charter of the ethical project is available to all.

5. ***Take advantage of multiple data sources***. The more data you use, the better your models of learning analytics are. It is not just about the quantity, but also about the quality of your results. Studies show, however, that certain well-defined predictive variables must be part of the collected data to be effective with the learning analytics tool.
The recommendations are as follows:

- collect demographic data, records of LMS activities, and historical academic data as a minimum;
- Collect the latest performance information (and past data) from students to complement what you already know about your student base;
- use certain data forms, such as financial data, if you firmly believe it would improve your models' consistency.

6. *Use several mathematical models to test your predictions.* Many mathematical models are used to classify the same set of learning analytics. Some of them are more accurate in your context and your data than others. Do not come up with single model insights. Explore many ways to process the data to obtain accurate research.
You have to:

- describe several mathematical models for measuring the measurement of learning analytics;
- Run the specified models over your existing data and accurately evaluate them (low volume of false positives) and recall them (low volume of false negatives);
- Choose the models that are best ranked in terms of precision and remember as the basis for your learning analytics tool (the balance between the two components is probably required because no model is 100% precise).

7. *Minimize your mistakes by tracking your analytics model's validity indefinitely.* Your learning analytics tool is focused on a variety of mathematical models. When those models were defined, they were identified as the best based on their precision and reminder. However, education is a living entity: changing the environment, developing students, and increasing the content of teachers. The quality of our theoretical models is affected.
You should be on the right track:

- Make sure that every model you deploy has a feedback component. In other words, the model should automatically assess and report its performance;
- check and evaluate the model in use regularly if the related deviations are not reported;
- Study other models that you have reviewed in the past if your model needs to be updated. They can now work but are only based on educational dynamics.

8. *Present analytical information in a format that all parties involved can understand.* Learning Analytics is about mathematical models applied to data relating to the population, academics, and student behavior, but if they have a full technological context, such models' sophistication should be kept away from the final consumers of the study information.
You have to:

- Try to present your analytics with the help of colors, symbols, other representation mechanisms necessary to summarize information visually;
- to use plain words rather than abstract principles about analytics;
- build a team to monitor your analytical data's end users to check your dashboards and make them easy to understand and run.

9. ***Boost the satisfaction of the students by carefully preparing communication.*** One of the primary goals of the analytical tool is to guide students to success. This involves regular communication with them, particularly with those who need your analysis for additional help. Communication must strike the right balance between making them know that they are behind them and not preventing them.
You should have a communication plan that sets out:
   - how much you will communicate with students (depending on the duration of the course);
   - Baseline content of each communication type. You should have scripts, but you should be personal if the number of students allows for it. Do not let your emails look like emails that are cut and pasted;
   - Communicate with those who need assistance, but also with those who have medium and sound results to sustain their level of involvement;
   - the experience and advice of your teachers. Learning analytical tools can help you decide who you are to contact, but your teachers know how to best address students at the end of the day.

10. ***Manage the students' "requiring vs. demanding" support needs appropriately.*** Some learning analytics projects include mechanisms for risky students to request extra assistance from the institution on demand. Such methods only operate as long as they are used. Research shows that a majority of students who need help do not demand it.
You have to:
   - recognize students who need extra support (your learning analytical tool for you will do so);
   - give all the risky students unsolicited help even though they have not demanded it.

11. ***Boost the efficacy of your interventions by establishing an intervention framework.*** The only goal of using analytical techniques is to cause improvements. Actions in the entire organization must be consistent. This is done by establishing an "intervention framework," which should be addressed pedagogically and defined by:
   - conditions that cause each intervention type;
   - types of interventions to be carried out;
   - the modes of communication involved in any intervention;
   - how measures are reported and returned to the analytics model;
   - how the efficacy of interventions is measured and reported.

12. ***Boost the level of comfort and encouragement of your learning analytics users***. To be successful, your Learning Analytics tool users should feel comfortable reading and act on your dashboards. This needs a training and support program to be developed. The scheme will define:

    - who should be educated (everyone uses dashboards actively);
    - how to read and view every dashboard's analytics;
    - types of interventions and conditions triggering under the defined intervention framework;
    - Plans for communications

13. ***Begin your institution's seed project***. Some organizations, in terms of Learning Analytics, are not very mature. This can be an invaluable opportunity to illustrate the potential of this technology to seek its acceptance. This can be done through a seed project. The scope of seed projects is minimal and is intended to explore the advantages of the technology. Seed projects ignore strict readiness requirements and follow the "lead-by-example" concept.

    - be limited in scope;
    - be limited in cost;
    - target easy wins;
    - include all the main stakeholders you would need in the long run from the beginning;
    - communicate successes effectively.

    It is important to note that overcoming readiness requirements does not mean ignoring two significant aspects:

    - The charter of an ethical enterprise
    - The application of several mathematical models and the constant obsession to validate their results

14. ***Profit from the instincts of your teachers and promote their freedom to act***. No matter how robust your learning research models are, they will never compile all of your students' dimensions. Students are much more than just a collection of data. Learning analytics is a powerful tool for forecasting dedication and results, but they must not banish your teachers' intuition.
    You have to:

    - Promote the use of the learning analytics tool as a required student follow-up method.
    - Foster a philosophy of 100% participation. All students at risk should be cared for.
    - Advise your teachers to obey your instincts, following the established intervention system.

15. ***Find not only fault causes but also success drivers***. Learning analytics are also used to perform risk assessments in education, leading to early steps that reduce or eliminate defined risks. Under this respect, they appear to concentrate on factors that negatively impact the students' engagement and success. Learning Analytics can also be used to research the "light side of the force."
That is what happens:

- ensure that your student performance models always predict how effective students will be;
- Mechanisms are in place to facilitate the success factors found.

5.5 Exploring Learning Analytics Tools

This section explores different Learning Analytics tools (Table 5.2) that can be used at various levels (Ferguson et al., 2016), e.g., school, higher education, workplace, etc.

5.6 Case Study: Initiation of Learning Analytics Tools Usage at Various Institutions/Organizations

This section offers details on using Learning Analytics tools in different institutions/organizations (Ferguson et al., 2016).

5.6.1 Institutional Pilots

5.6.1.1 Arizona State University

Arizona State University (ASU) partnered with the private Knewton Corporation in 2011 to use its online and mixed mathematics programs through the Knewton Math Readiness Program. For over 5000 students enrolled in the remedial mathematics modules, the software built personalized learning paths. The Knewton website points out that the system 'constantly assesses their mathematical abilities and adapts accordingly. After implementing the system, Knewton reports that the ASU retention program for remedial mathematics rose from 64% to 75%.

In 2015, ASU announced the launch of 'Active Adaptive' modules with Cengage Learning and Knewton Enterprises. Such programs will use technology similar to the Knewton Math Readiness program, which adapts students' learning pathways to their demonstrated skills. In combination, Cengage Learning provides tools for improving resources, such as note-taking and working with classmates.

Table 5.2 Learning analytics tools

S.No	Tool	Description	Tool providers website / Useful weblinks
1	ASSISTments	ASSISTments is an intelligent tutoring program developed by Neal Heffernan and his colleagues and studied by several universities and organizations in the United States at the Worcester Polytechnic Institute (WPI). To mimic the type of instantaneous feedback that a tutor can give, the core framework was designed to provide progressive tips to students who incorrectly answer the query. From this framework, several systems studies have focused on efficiently using the student log data generated from the system. For example, studies were conducted to see if such data might impact parent participation or predict high-stakes test results.	https://new.assistments.org/
2	Bettermarks	The Bettermarks program promotes adapted materials, linked to more than 100 books, for mathematics education. Teachers may either teach students online or delegate the program depending on the students' level of expertise. When students complete their lessons, Bettermarks analyzes their performance and behavior to detect knowledge gaps and offer lessons for improvement or other challenges. The program also includes a center for teachers where student performance data can be accessed. Teachers can view completion reports at a glance and pass rates across the module. We may also analyze individual student outcomes and development. This system uses any web browser, and no download software is needed.	https://bettermarks.com/

(continued)

Table 5.2 (continued)

S.No	Tool	Description	Tool providers website / Useful weblinks
3	Civitas learning	Civitas Learning is an American-based organization that partners directly with universities to develop tailor-made data science and research instruments that take advantage of the student data currently available. The data sources identified include virtual learning environments, social media, card swipes, libraries, and housing. The Student Insights Platform of Civitas Learning aggregates student data and utilizes a range of analysis and visualization tools. The Illume tool provides historical and predictive student data for institutional leaders and providers of student service. The Inspire for Faculty tool provides a real-time analysis of student involvement and behavior in specific modules, data visualization, and predictive modeling tools. The Inspire for Advisor tool simultaneously visualizes student performance and progress through modules and forecasts the course's completion. The Degree Map allows students and advisors to draw up individual graduation plans. The Hoot.me tool also lets teachers build module-specific Facebook Q&A pages. Finally, Civitas Learning offers a platform for module registration enrollment. Each of these wide varieties of tools is developed individually with partner institutions to meet their analytical needs. Civitas operates with more than 70 institutions in the USA.	https://www.civitaslearning.com/

(continued)

Table 5.2 (continued)

S.No	Tool	Description	Tool providers website / Useful weblinks
4	Cognitive Tutor software	Cognitive Tutor is a smart tutoring program developed by Carnegie Learning, an American organization. The web-based software is used mainly to teach mathematics to 9–12 grade students. The software offers personalized learning and guidance for various prepared mathematics courses, based on a context, tutoring, and student model. The 'Skillometer' and the instructor reports are two components of Learning analytics important to this software. The 'Skillometer' is a visual measure of students' mastering skills. This provides the student with a measure of skill mastery for each skill of a learning unit. The level of competence displayed by the tool represents the potential to demonstrate this skill once again in the future. The data for this visualization is based on the student's interaction with the software. A variety of software produced reports assists teachers. The class progress report indicates the number of successful students per class. The class skill report indicates the mastery level for each student for each skill. The detailed student report shows the number of skills learned, time spent, number of completed classes, parts, and problems for each student. The detailed by section report provide information on a unit by unit level for each student. Another report shows aggregated data per device. The student skill alert report indicates performance deficiencies. The class assessment reports compare pre-test results with post-test results by topic or issue at the class level. The student assessment reports display pre-test and post-test outcomes at the level of students by subject or question. Both reports are intended to assist teachers in their decision-making processes.	https://www.carnegielearning.com/

(continued)

5.6 Case Study: Initiation of Learning Analytics Tools Usage at Various...

Table 5.2 (continued)

S.No	Tool	Description	Tool providers website / Useful weblinks
5	FFT Aspire	The Fischer Family Trust, FFT, is a UK non-profit organization that provides educational services in the United Kingdom, such as the National Pupil Database for the Department for Education and school analysis. The FFT Aspire software is a school data collection and reporting tool. It provides numerous dashboards with school results, such as past accomplishments, growth, attendance, and potential performance projections. It aims at several user groups, including teachers, subject leaders, department heads, senior leaders, consultants, local authorities, and governors. The Dashboards include a comprehensive school dashboard, a department heads, subject leaders, and teachers' topic dashboard, a dashboard for the governor (helping schools to exchange knowledge with their government authorities), a dashboard for student explorers, a dashboard for collaboration (for comparing school results to other schools) and a dashboard for school performance. The tool also offers support for creating personalized reports and dashboards such as a three-year dashboard, a dashboard for children with special training criteria, and a dashboard with high attainers.	https://fftaspire.org/
6	Itslearning	Designed for K-12 schools, Itslearning is an LMS with a course management and implementation feature, curriculum management, monitoring, and review. Reporting and analytic features include functionality for mastery reporting standards (enabling teachers to see the percentage of students that have mastered each level of courses) and a content recommendation engine that 'provides remediation and enrichment activities based on student performance against learning objectives.' This allows the identification of students who strive to achieve learning goals and assigns them reinforcement activities. The engine for Itslearning can automate 'most' of the process of "identification of students who are struggling to meet learning objectives and assign them activities for reinforcement." The reporting features allow students, teachers, managers, mentors, and parents via their personalized dashboard to view student aspects of student progress. Teachers and administrators will filter views about how classes are performed by date or status regarding specific learning objectives (for example, only to show students who met one specific learning objective). A parent dashboard allows parents to see their child's progress on assignments, grades and learning goals, individual learning plans, behavior, and attendance.	https://itslearning.altitudelearning.com/

(continued)

Table 5.2 (continued)

S.No	Tool	Description	Tool providers website / Useful weblinks
7	Metacog	Metacog uses an interactive 'learning objects' content pool to individual students' content and pace. Students are asked to perform an actual task using the platform, and data relating to their use behaviors are collected, including click data, time-signs, and correct/false replies. The API of the platform examines student interactions to evaluate their comprehension. Metacog can be used in collaboration with existing resources. Students who use Metacog have access to details on whether they have done a task correctly. A leader board is also created to allow students to compare their success with their peers. To students, the success of platform color codes as green, yellow, or red shows an appreciation of the content on individual tasks or over time. The platform also helps teachers group students based on their current understanding, individualized assignments, or additional tools. Teachers can also examine which part of a task is a stumbling block for individual students or the entire classroom. On an administrative or publisher level, the macro platform can determine where additional resources can be invested by highlighting gaps in the under-represented classrooms.	https://metacog.com/
8	Schoolzilla	Schoolzilla offers a data warehouse and associated dashboard for the K-12 market in the United States. It provides 'connectors' to integrate data into the system through nightly updates from various sources, including evaluation, behavior, registration, ranking, observation, and student databases. Schoolzilla offers a dashboard library with multiple views of these integrated data. Representations are available for teachers, school leaders, school district leaders, and system administrators in the library, personalized by system administrators using Tableau's data visualization products. Teachers can use dashboards, such as the report on 'Early warning signs,' to identify students' risk. For example, this dashboard gathers attendance, actions, and grades data, allows users to view data for schools as a whole, compares schools (for local government officials), and drill down for viewing data on students. System administrators can track the system's data quality with dashboards displaying data audit reports, including automated inspections of incomplete or malformed data.	https://schoolzilla.com/

(continued)

5.6 Case Study: Initiation of Learning Analytics Tools Usage at Various... 141

Table 5.2 (continued)

S.No	Tool	Description	Tool providers website / Useful weblinks
9	SNAPP	The Social Networks Adapting Pedagogical Practice (SNAPP) tool conducts real-time social network analysis and data visualization for commercial and open-source learning system forum discussion. The explanations why such a method should be used include detecting individual students, facilitator-centered networking patterns, community breakdown, and users linking smaller networks. Much necessary, detailed information about users is available, including the total number of posts, the number of posts per user, and the number of posts and reaction rates per user. Research carried out with the tool comprises student networks monitoring, participant interactions over time, and broad-based admissions evaluation.	http://www.snappvis.org/
10	VitalSource CourseSmart	CourseSmart Analytics is available for teachers whose institutions integrate the LMS and CourseSmart's eTextbook. Integration is carried out using the Learning Tools Interoperability Framework (LTI) of IMS Global Learning Technologies. CourseSmart's analytics dashboard reveals the students' engagement with digital course content. A core piece of this dashboard is the CourseSmart Engagement Index Technology™, which is a proprietary algorithm for the evaluation of standard data – such as the number of pages read, the number of times a student has opened/interacted with the digital textbook, the number of days a student spends reading the textbook, the number of highlights, bookmarks, notes, and so on. The analytics are designed to give teachers insights into their students' behavior and how e-books are used so that teachers that male teachers intervene based on this data. VitalSource purchased CourseSmart early in 2014, and in October 2015, press releases revealed that the new analytics software would be rereleased. However, no further announcements have been made.	https://www.vitalsource.com/

(continued)

Table 5.2 (continued)

S.No	Tool	Description	Tool providers website / Useful weblinks
11	Degree Compass (Desire2Learn)	The selection of courses can be challenging for students. Desire2Learn quotes the Complete College America study, which reveals that students take 20% (on average) more classes than they need to graduate. Therefore, assisting with course selection will reduce the cost of tuition. Risky students not so likely to graduate could be the demographic that needs assistance in decision-making to improve retention rates and university graduation rates. Using information from other student enrolments, this system provides advice on which courses to complete and which courses to take the students most likely to complete. The Degree Compass application aims to increase student success by offering students academic advice when they start their school, monitoring progress, and making personalized courses and graduation path recommendations.	http://bit.ly/1PEQKMx http://bit.ly/1VUIMPz
12	Knewton	Knewton is a software company for adaptive learning that provides platforms for personalized training. The company was founded in 2008 and partnered with Pearson Education in 2011. More than ten million students have used their adaptive learning platforms at the primary, secondary, and university levels. Several services are available at different education levels, and Knewton often works with schools or colleges to create custom systems that address institutional needs. From a student's point of view, the software uses algorithms based on student success and attitudes to deliver lessons through differentiated instruction and remind about their progress. This provides immediate reviews, collaborative community forums, and gamification to promote involvement. From an educator's point of view, the software facilitates the summarization and visualization of data at class or individual student level. With a 'stoplight,' system students are marked as 'ahead of track,' 'on track,' 'off track' or 'very behind' for interventions.	https://www.knewton.com/

(continued)

5.6 Case Study: Initiation of Learning Analytics Tools Usage at Various... 143

Table 5.2 (continued)

S.No	Tool	Description	Tool providers website / Useful weblinks
13	Loop	Loop is an open-source analytics tool sponsored by the Australian Office for Learning and Teaching. The tool may be linked to Moodle or Blackboard to provide the teachers with a way to interpret student behavior. The dashboard portion displays student log data from the LMS, such as accessed class materials, discussion forums, and assessment results. Such data can be presented at the school level or the level of each student. Simultaneously, the tool integrates into its visualizations information on the course layout and the timetable. Through this sense, the tool aims to provide a 'pedagogical helper tool' that can help teachers understand important data through their context. In 2015, the tool was piloted across four courses administered by three Universities in Australia and planned for a wide release.	
14	Open Essayist	Open Essayist, created by Open University in Great Britain, is intended to provide students with automated draft essays. A computational analysis of the essential pieces and keywords in writing is the underlying idea to enable students to compare and adjust their written content with what they intend to convey. Learners are uploading their draft essay, which then generates different views based on text analysis, including the most effective terms and a graphical view through a document of their distributions; the critical phrases in the document with helpful reflection tips graphical view of the essay structure. The tool is intended instead of for summative evaluations as a formative, developmental tool.	http://oro.open.ac.uk/42041/1/lak15_submission_46.pdf
15	OU Analyse	OU Analyse – software that forecasts students at risk – has been developed by the Knowledge Media Institute (KMi) of Open University in Britain. OU Analyse is based on two previous projects (Retain and the OU-Microsoft Research Cambridge project). OU Analyse uses machine learning techniques to develop demographic and VLE data-based predictive models. The software offers a dashboard for all students of a module to display several models' aggregated prediction value. The tool shows the logic behind its prediction. Module chairs, module teams, and student support staff use OU Research forecasts to advise students and assist them.	https://analyse.kmi.open.ac.uk/

(continued)

Table 5.2 (continued)

S.No	Tool	Description	Tool providers website / Useful weblinks
16	Student Success Plan	The Student Success Plan (SSP) is a student support software: counseling, coaching, and pastoral care. This has a lightweight data collection focusing primarily on student support programs management and enhancement. This is adopted to help predictive research practice. SSP is designed to improve retention, academic success, attainment, graduation rates, and completion time. Students are recognized, assisted, and tracked by counseling, web-based support networks, and constructive intervention techniques. The software provides case management tools for communication, action planning, academic planning, alert, self-assessment, and monitoring progress. SSP is not a single 'out of the box' solution; it is a collection of configurable components that are opened to be incorporated into different device landscapes. An open-source software version, supervised by the Apereo Foundation, is available.	http://bit.ly/UniconSSP http://bit.ly/SSP-2011
17	Tribal's Student Insights	Tribal, headquartered in the UK, is a multinational software service provider specializing in products that support education management. Tribal's Student Insights is a software developed to predict student performance and 'at-risk' students from information systems available to students, including an academic performance at the entrance, demographics, and evaluation findings and activities, such as student interaction, VLE use, library use. The software provides predictive models of the probability of a student passing a module. The software offers dashboards to show this information at the level of students and modules. University educators and managers may use this information, for example, to provide support to individual students or to monitor modules concerning their predicted performance.	https://www.tribalgroup.com/

(continued)

5.6 Case Study: Initiation of Learning Analytics Tools Usage at Various... 145

Table 5.2 (continued)

S.No	Tool	Description	Tool providers website / Useful weblinks
18	X-Ray Analytics	Blackboard acquired x-Ray Analytics in 2015 as a predictive modeling tool, linked to Moodle and Moodlerooms. The dashboard offers teachers visualizations of past behavior in their teaching system at several levels: course, multiple courses, and intuition. The algorithms then forecast potential outcomes and activities such that 'at-risk' students are detected who may need an intervention. The tool also considers student engagement by evaluating responses to online collaborative tools, such as discussion boards, through social network analysis. Based on their time spent on the course, their grades, and their discussions forum activities, students may be categorized as at risk. X-Ray Analytics uses a cloud-based approach that analyzes the current data in the management system for learning.	http://bit.ly/1WXTRSF
19	Skillaware	Skillaware is an Italian company that designs learning and training environment software. The system is combined with current business software or procedures to assess worker productivity and areas in which training can be useful. Skillaware uses a range of tools to document user interactions and behaviors. The SkillEditor function records user activity and automatically recommends training to increase employees' productivity using various software types. The SkillAgent function offers suggestions for the next steps when a user appears to need help. The SkillAnalyzer tool also enables company analysts to monitor user activity in real-time and provide management personnel with data visualization.	http://skillaware.com/

(continued)

Table 5.2 (continued)

S.No	Tool	Description	Tool providers website / Useful weblinks
20	WATCHME Project	WATCHME is a European-funded project using educational analytics to improve feedback and professional development in the workplace. The acronym is the e-assessment system based on the workplace for higher multi-professional education based on competency. The project has developed an online portfolio system to provide trainees with views and input on their progress. The dashboard contains data from many sources, including self-reporting, online interaction, and qualitative narratives. A unique data model is used to aggregate data and deliver 'Just-in-Time" reviews to promote continued learning. The research team comprises a multidisciplinary history covering human medicine, veterinary, teacher training, and IT.	http://www.project-watchme.eu/
21	Claned	Claned offers a platform for e-learning in such diverse subjects as medical education and dance education. Claned aims to offer tools that make the learning process accessible to students and teachers, thereby incorporating the learning analytics components. E-learning materials or videos, documents, and slideshows may be inserted in the Claned environment. The system automatically provides keywords and topics and tracks all that a student does. It also provides a study of the mutual experiences between different learners. Claned provides teachers with data by finding student groups that behave in similar ways or have similar motivational trends. The aim is to show the teacher the learning process, so it is clear where supporting materials can be useful or where support is needed for challenging subjects. Claned also provides the learner with the data through a learning tracking tool. It may provide suggestions for individualized learning strategies and to help people reach their learning goals.	https://claned.com/

(continued)

Table 5.2 (continued)

S.No	Tool	Description	Tool providers website / Useful weblinks
22	Khan Academy analytics	Khan Academy is a collection of free online video-centric learning resources focused predominantly on declarative and procedural skills covering a broad range of subjects at school-age and adult learner levels. The Learning Analytics is presented in three ways: as the engine of services offered by the Khan Academy through its web pages, as access to data for third-party analytical processes, and as a means of continuous improvement of design. The Khan Academy provides teachers/coaches with information on individual and class results. This offers abstract estimates of effort, dedication, and material complexity. The learning materials are mapped to the number of qualified persons with different levels of mastery for each; the teacher/coach will train to this level and use success or difficulty information to suggest skills for follow-up and undertaking or encourage alternative learning activities (maybe outside the Khan Academy). The Khan Academy gives students a dashboard that shows progress against skills (as for the teacher/coach) and task trends in time and different skills. Third-party access to data is via the web-based API, which provides differentiated access depending on the data. Open access includes video, playlist, theme/skill charts, and exercise details. Activity at user level and progress logs are secured, requiring login and permission.	https://www.khanacade-my.org/

(continued)

Table 5.2 (continued)

S.No	Tool	Description	Tool providers website / Useful weblinks
23	Digital assess	Digital Assess supports workflow evaluation of coursework or other evidence-based evaluation scenarios. The method may be used for traditional assessor labeling or peer assessment. Learning analytics is used to conduct a process known as adaptive comparative judgment, which increases assessment reliability. Adaptive comparative judgment is an evaluation approach in which students' work pairs are compared using specific defined quality dimensions. Learning Analytics drives the adaptive dimension by automatically deciding which pairs of individuals perform assess to optimize the grading reliability in each round of comparison. Reliability statistics and statistics describing problematic student work are measured over many rounds of comparative judgment. The process can also support standardization year-on-year. The method applies particularly in cases where a comprehensive scheme of marking is unsuitable or time-consuming for assessment purposes – for example, for artistic subjects or 'soft-skills' – or where peer assessment has a pedagogical role. Work performed by academics and high stakeholders has shown that adaptive comparative judgment is a robust approach beyond the inter-relator reliability typical of traditional test labeling.	http://bit.ly/DA-AQA
24	Learning Analytics Processor (LAP)	The LAP is a program to handle workflow in learning analytics. This type of workflow is usually referred to as a pipeline and consists of three separate phases: input, model execution, and output. The pipeline is built using an open architecture that displays pipeline output through a set of web service APIs. The LAP is a general-use platform designed to meet the requirement to extend learning analytics from manually driven processes to routine technical tasks automation. The LAP's critical aim is to rationalize data preprocessing, predictive model usage, and post-processing outcomes to make this process more effective and accurate. It can be configured, not connected to particular sources of data, and agnostic as to the use of the predictive model results. LAP supports the Open Academic Analytics Initiative Early Alert and Risk Assessment model of Marist College and many other models.	https://www.apereo.org/projects/learning-analytics-processor/

(continued)

Table 5.2 (continued)

S.No	Tool	Description	Tool providers website / Useful weblinks
25	RAGE	RAGE (Realising an Applied Gaming Eco-system) is an Open University Netherlands European-funded project, in collaboration with gaming industry professionals and universities in ten European countries. The project aims to support the development of 'applied' or 'serious' games by using pilot tests and analytics in actual educational scenarios. The overall aim is to make serious games more comfortable, faster, and cheaper. Partnering participants belong to an 'Ecosystem,' a shared space built for partners to work together at all levels: commercial, educational, policies, research, and other fields. The project provides centralized access to software, resources, and data and provides development and educator training. The pilot test process during which developed games can be used in real-world educational scenarios and then tested for effectiveness with Learning Analytics and trace data is specific to this project.	http://rageproject.eu/

5.6.1.2 Progress and Engagement in Courses (RioPACE): Rio Salado College

Rio Salado College is a private university in Arizona, the USA, with over 40,000 students studying online. In 2010, the College launched the RioPACE program at the university. The program uses data mining and predictive analysis for low-performance interventions.

The program analyzes VLE (Virtual Learning Environment) behaviors and contrasts students with previously active students. Each week, a color-coded traffic lighting device similar to the one used for Purdue's Course Signals is supplied with individual labels. Teachers receive weekly progress reports and planned completion reports, allowing students to prioritize interventions if appropriate.

By accessing the RioPACE program inside the VLE, students can also display their warning labels. Students with a yellow or red symbol are encouraged to contact their module instructor for support.

5.6.1.3 PredictED: Dublin City University

In 2014, Dublin City University (DCU) unveiled a new predictED learning analytics system for ten modules. PredictED analyzes and compares student activities in the virtual learning environment (VLE) Moodle to previously active students in the same class.

Once a week, participating students receive an email that says they can pass or fail the module with a modified prediction. Those who seem to fail obtain advice and support for their study. The emails also provide information about how their VLE activities were relative to the previous week's VLE activities.

5.6.1.4 Dunchurch Infant School

Dunchurch Infant School is a UK Early Years Institution that teaches pre-school children during the first school year. During school, the play and students' interactions in the classroom are tracked and documented using the Development Matters program.

Development Matters are a non-statutory framework established with funding from the Education Department to help those engaged in early childhood education to meet the Early Foundation Stage Statutory Framework criteria. This contains instructions for seven learning factors, which are further divided into 17 subparagraphs.

Within a given year, approximately 8700 findings are made in the classroom, leading to learning analytics to process and analyze vast volumes of information on individual pupils.

The school has a dedicated data analyst who gathers information and provides classroom teachers with data visualization diagrams. Teachers will also use these assessments as a snapshot of the strengths and shortcomings of their students.

The school reports that the number of students who have achieved a reasonable development level since analytics has risen from 55% to 77%.

5.6.2 Institutional at Scale

5.6.2.1 Course Signals: Purdue University

Course Signals is a predictive system of learning analytics initially developed at Purdue University in the United States. The system uses student data to determine who may not complete a course successfully. The student is assigned a risk category, which is the color of a traffic signal (red, yellow, or green), using predictive analysis of student data and behaviors within the LMS.

5.6 Case Study: Initiation of Learning Analytics Tools Usage at Various... 151

To use the program, an instructor or teacher must manually use the model to collect the 'signals' from students, who will then provide personalized input or extra support for those at risk of poor results. Course Signals involves using intervention emails that can be written and sent to each instructor's risk group. Notifications can also be given on the LMS course page of a student.

Courses Signals allows educators to receive input in real-time as early as the second week of the school year and can be used at many points during the term. The research reported in LAK12 indicated a 21% retention rate increase in Purdue among students who took at least one-course using course signals than students who did not. Nevertheless, this has been disputed since then.

5.6.2.2 E²coach

Applied Learning Analytics for customized communications to students at the University of Michigan (UoM) High Enrollment Start Courses in science, technology, engineering, and mathematics (STEM). Typically, the grade point average (GPA) in other courses is the best forecaster of progress in one course in predicting student outcomes. The university has also asked students about their goals for the course and why they should take the course as extra information to interact. The project team interviewed faculty members to produce information about their recommendations to students who had diverse experiences, goals, and circumstances. The team also analyzed students who completed the course to obtain information on various students and suggestions about the courses. They interviewed students who performed better than expected and worse than expected to create testimonials for students relevant to the courses. Using all of this input from students and staff, they create a designed knowledge bank to provide students with various experiences, goals, and situations with personalized advice. E²Coach users have outperformed non-users. Occasionally, non-users reached 0.15 letter rates, while regular non-users surpassed 0.32 letter grades. At UoM, $1.4 million is invested in the Third Century Initiative to expand university programs like E²Coach.

5.6.2.3 Georgia State University

Predictive analytics is used at Georgia State University (GSU) to resolve the disparity in achievement between low-income and first-generation students. The University found that even though students had high-grade points averages and were close to graduation, they were removed from classes by non-payment. The graduation rate for GSU went from 32% in 2003 to 54% in 2014. The university reported that it had eliminated the performance difference between minority or lower socio-economic status students and their pairs with higher graduates. GSU notes that it systematically obtained these outcomes by collecting smaller winners. University has taken several steps to help students avoid being enrolled at university at the expense. The university employed former students as tutors, who were required to work as part of their financial support plan for the university. The university also helped students pick courses based on probability predictions.

5.6.2.4 Nottingham Trent University Student Dashboard

Nottingham Trent University (NTU) in Great Britain has created, tested, and implemented a Student Dashboard for all undergraduate students. The program obtains data from several sources: library use, attendance, online learning, ID card swipes into University buildings, and academic grades. They generated a composite engagement score and displayed this graphically along with the average for everyone and produce a high, decent, average, or low ranking. Automatic alerts are sent to a student's tutor for causes such as 'no quarter commitment' or 'academic failure.'

The students and their tutors are the primary users of a student's score; they are also accessible to other tutors, administrators, and student support personnel, but not to any other student.

5.6.3 National Level

5.6.3.1 Ceibal

Uruguay's school program has a 1:1 solution. The country explored the effect of the internet upgrade on complete learning activities using the software after delivering laptops to its students and offering adaptive math tutor applications.

The country supplied 450,000 XO laptops to students during the five-year project. In addition to placing computers in students' and teachers' hands, an intelligent mentor has been introduced. The goal was to reduce the digital divide between students with and without access to technology.

Several critics argued that this was an immense investment in access technologies and wondered if the pedagogy of successful use of technologies would have been given more importance. However, the project has been systematically implemented, taking distribution, Internet access, training, repair, and disposal into account. Internet connectivity is considered a civil right. The project's estimated cost was £159 per student, measured at £13 per student a year. Over the five-year project, the cost of education was less than 5% of the national budget.

5.6.3.2 Student Retention and Learning Analytics: An Outline of Australian Practices and An Advancement Framework

The Australian Government ordered a comprehensive analysis of the state of learning analytics in 2015. Study 1 defined two implementation categories:

1. Universities concentrated on assessing efficiency and retention procedures.
2. Universities focused primarily on learning to understand, which saw education as a significant agent for student engagement.

This highlighted contrasting views on using learning analytics to promote retention: a tool to help the university needs or as a tool to support education and social engagement for students. For this analysis, Cluster 1 had more uniformities than Cluster 2. The report emphasizes that policy on institutional learning analytics requires more than technological preparation, as universities still have significant driving forces for the benefits of learning analytics.

Study 2 outlined the primary performance factors.

The study states that most universities in Australia are in the early stages of successful learning analytics adoption. It emphasizes that Learning Analytics form a complex framework that includes creating six main areas: academic content, the conceptualization of the purpose of learning analytics, leadership, university strategy, feedback from stakeholders, technology, and an understanding of the unique context of the university.

5.6.3.3 Denmark: User Portal Initiative

A national User Portal Initiative was recently published by the Danish Ministry of Education to develop a standard learning management system and standardization to exchange data for all school students. The project aims to live during the academic year 2016–2017. These projects are being introduced in partnership with many technology-enhanced learning providers with the shared goal of ensuring data convergence across the country to establish and educate local or national projects.

All schools in Denmark are expected to implement technology to launch the large-scale Learning Analytics implementation by 2016. The Ministry contributes to the production and maintenance of many services and school programs. Many of these online platforms, including EMU, SkoDa, and Materialeplatformen, aggregate and sum up tools and proof for their usefulness. The establishment by the Ministry of specific educational goals, well-being priorities, and national testing also include the broader use of learning analytics tools and the exchange of knowledge. Secondary education is enrolled through an automated platform called Accession, allowing student demographic data to be conveniently obtained. The public has a data repository to compare student data between schools, districts, or regions.

5.6.3.4 Norway: Various National Initiatives

A variety of software tools with learning analytics capabilities are available in Norway in the commercial market. For example, Conexus, a Norwegian software company founded in 2000, provides data aggregation and visualization learning analytics tools. Conexus software provides tools for assessment, automated learning, and targeting. Another example is itslearning26. The research framework was created at Bergen University College in 1998. At the beginning of 2014, Gyldendal27, the largest Norwegian textbook firm, announced a collaboration with the adaptive learning software Knewton to build a multi-smart Øving28 system for adaptive learning textbooks schools that also includes resources for learning analytics. IKT-Norge29, an advocacy group for the Norwegian ICT industry, organizes an essential catalyst for these vendors and tool design.

To support and direct the development of learning analytics, the Center for ICT in Education (Senter for IKT i utdanningen) has arranged workshops and draw up policy recommendations on schools with a mandate to encourage ICTs in Norwegian schools. Morten Dahl's Learning Analytics Report (Laeringsanalyse) offers an introduction to the subject, written in Norwegian. It provides examples of usage in and around Norway. The report identifies potential learning analytics problems. This includes the lack of teacher training in the skills required in the successful use of analytics; risks to privacy and protection of information; the dynamic market for learning analytics where there are no clear standards or infrastructure, and an insufficient understanding of what data are essential to the promotion of learning quality. The report also addresses the privacy challenges of learning analytics and asks how far schools can go with collection, compilation, and data analysis on students without conflicting their right to privacy. In Norway, schools can use personal data only for empirical learning to find a legitimate legal justification for this use. When personal data is used, schools will be responsible for ensuring the accuracy of these data, ensure that it is used to promote learning, and ensure that pupils, teachers, parents, or guardians view, correct, and remove their data on request.

In 2015, 25 million Norwegian crowns (approximately € 2.7 million) were pledged by the Ministry of Education and Research to set up a research center for learning analytics. The Ministry accepted applications to assess the site of this new center. After a review process, the University of Bergen was chosen as a hosting institution, and the center was called the Centre for The Science of Learning and Technology (SLATE). Five million Norwegian Kroner (approximately 540,000 Euros) are donated to the center each year by the Ministry, and additional funding from the University of Bergen is given. Since the new contract for the center lasts for five years, it can be extended for another five years. SLATE should have a wide variety of lifelong learning and many study points of view and strategies. Understanding analytics was a part of the practices of SLATE.

Many improvements had taken place in 2016, in particular, the facilitation of the underlying infrastructure:

- Work is being pursued in Norway on digital infrastructure and interoperability. UNINETT, which builds and runs national research and educating network in Norway, establishes its service platform Dataporten (Norwegian for the "data gate"). This would eventually lead to better data sharing for learning analytics too.

- The Norway National Standards Body addressed three initiatives within the Norwegian Standards Body: Datasharing, vocabulary for activities descriptions, and guidelines on privacy and best practice, and all possible solutions underlying technologies such as learning analytics.

5.7 Developing a Learning Analytics Tool

This section briefly describes how to combine learning analytics and collective intelligence to develop a means to provide learners and teachers with support and feedback on self-initiated learning activities.

5.7.1 Introduction to this Section

The Danish university College sector began implementation of the Study Activity Model (SAM) (Fig. 5.1) in 2013. SAM would "provide for all programs a single academic tool that can shape the students' study expectations with study intensity." As shown in Fig. 5.1, the model is divided into four categories.

Based on the previous work (Fig. 5.2) (Ringtved, Wahl, Belle, & Clemmense, 2017) and Wahl, Bellè, Clemmensen, and Ringtved (2013) has built a platform that assists students in their research activities. Furthermore, allow teachers to become conscious of learning events related to studies and make them a part of specific SAM categories.

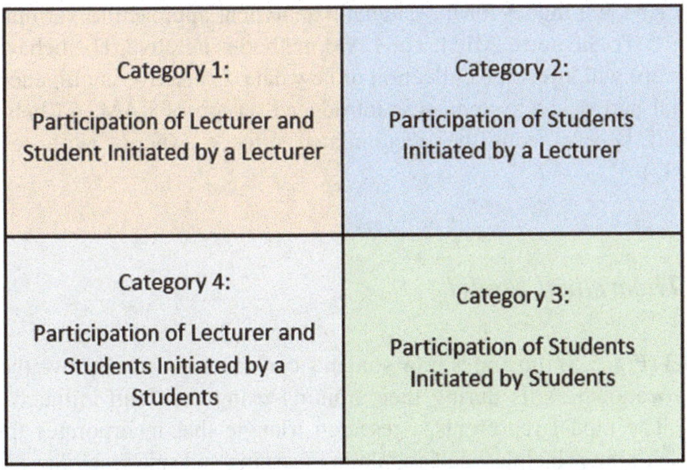

Category 1: Participation of Lecturer and Student Initiated by a Lecturer	Category 2: Participation of Students Initiated by a Lecturer
Category 4: Participation of Lecturer and Students Initiated by a Students	Category 3: Participation of Students Initiated by Students

Fig. 5.1 The four categories in the Study Activity Model (Absalon, 2014)

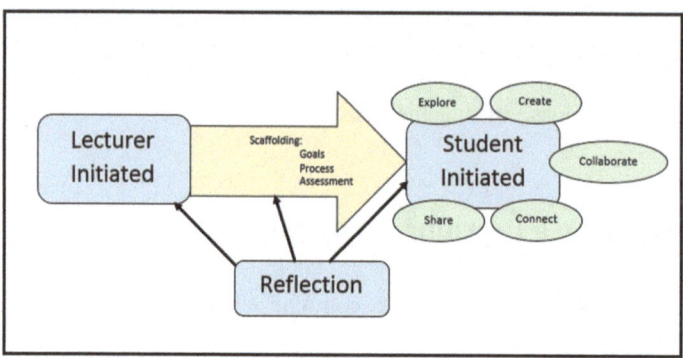

Fig. 5.2 Framework for enhanced use of students' self-initiated study activities. (Wahl et al., 2013)

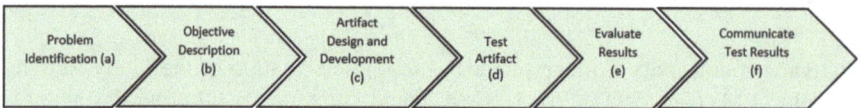

Fig. 5.3 DDR process (Ellis & Levy, 2010)

5.7.2 Methodology

Design & Development Research (DDR) is a tool for the production process. The research process for developing IT products or objects is defined by DDR (Ellis & Levy, 2010). The DDR method, as shown in Fig. 5.3, is divided into six stages.

The Learning Analytics Model (LAM) is one approach that can be used in this process. LAM is a model for a systematic analytical approach to various components (Fig. 5.4) (Siemens, 2013). The LAM method is iterative. The behavior at the end (last step) will affect the collection of new data. Collective intelligence (CI), as an essential part of the system, was introduced on top of LAM. CI believes that people will benefit from the accumulated effort's synergy with technology (Levy, 1997).

5.7.3 Theoretical Model

The model (Fig. 5.5) illustrates how students can develop and improve their learning and vocational skills during their training using their self-initiated research activities. The model represents a research triangle that incorporates three self-initiating learning principles: self-regulating learning and self-assessing learning in

5.7 Developing a Learning Analytics Tool

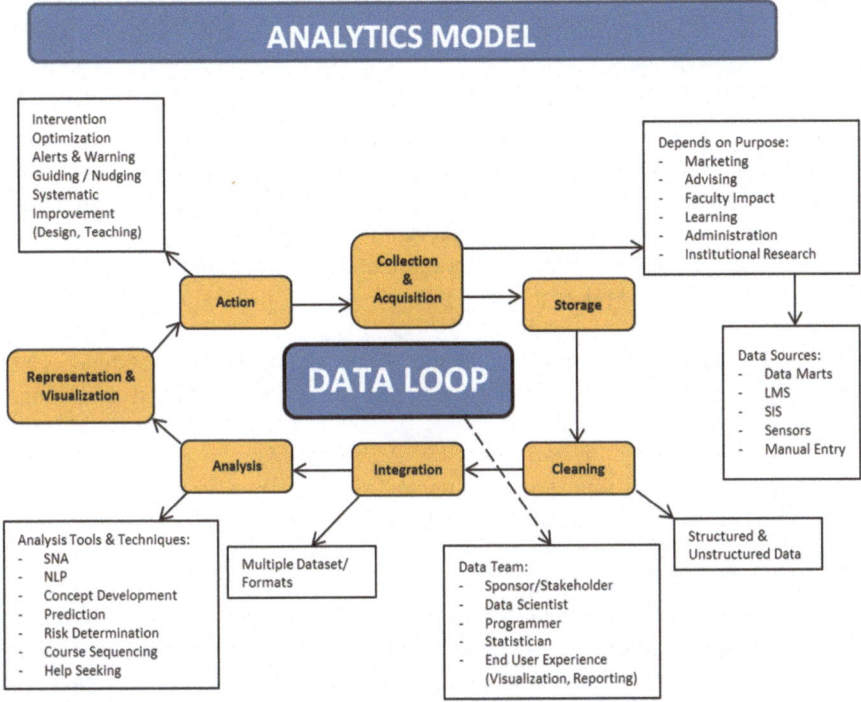

Fig. 5.4 Learning analytics model (Siemens, 2013)

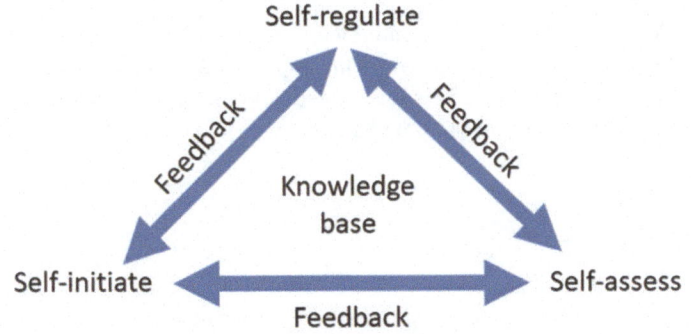

Fig. 5.5 Model for self-initiated, self-regulated, and self-assessed activities (Wahl et al., 2013)

every corner of the triangle. All three concepts are interdependent, and input is given and taken across all three concepts in a continuous cycle. Feedback is an essential component of the tool and is given back to the learner using learning analytical methods for keeping the learning analytics cycle as defined by Clow (Clow, 2012).

5.7.4 Analysis

LAM may be used to analyze the tool.

Collection & Acquisition The program facilitates its focus on study-related learning experiences from the viewpoint of a student. It is achieved by the recording or tracking and relation of learning experiences with learning objectives. Activities conducted by the instructor would be relevant in certain SAM categories. A former example may be students who report or represent an incident in the sense of home (category 2) or group work (category 1).

Integration SIS imported information about users and the user login (students and teachers), probably via the learning management system, is linked to a Single Sign-on System.

Analysis An impotent aspect of CI is the ability to link unconnected entities. The data can be direct as well as indirect. Such relationships (implicit and explicit feedback) will be provided to the users.

Representation & Visualization Student reflection on learning activities should be given to the student, along with the related learning aims. The management of these organizations and the formation of new partnerships are part of the reflection process. Recommendations give inspiration for future learning experiences. The recommendations are extracted from the CI's study of student metadata, linkages to learning activities, and goals.

Action Inform students of the potential learning activities they should participate in. It will improve mutual ability when the experience is documented in the tool. The resource will warn teachers of potential connections between SAM 3rd Category learning and teacher-initiated activities.

5.8 Conclusion

Learning analytics is an evolving and increasingly growing area of study. This profits from the past decade of e-learning in education, training, research, and development in educational data mining, web analytics, and statistics. Over recent years, the number of digital tools for education and training has grown to some degree in the context of learning analytics, and these have now been implemented at the early stages. This chapter contains an array of tools, case studies, and evidence to use learning analytics tools. This also presented guidelines for selecting Learning Analytics tools and the strategy to develop them.

5.9 Review Questions

Reflect on the concepts of this chapter guided by the following questions.

1. Explain the importance of Learning analytics tools
2. What are the most appropriate Learning Analytics apps available for free download?
3. Describe in brief some top learning analytics tools.
4. How to choose the right learning analytics tool for your organization.
5. What are the key features we need to check before going to choose a learning analytics tool?
6. By which properties can students be grouped?
7. List and explain various categories of learning analytics tools.
8. Describe various strategies that can be followed.
9. Explore some of the learning analytics tools currently in use in various prestigious institutions.

References

Absalon. (2014). *Expectations to students to be made clear.* http://danskeprofessionshøjskoler.dk/wp-content/uploads/2016/01/Expectations-to-study-model-1.pdf

Clow, D. (2012). The learning analytics cycle: Closing the loop effectively. *ACM International Conference Proceeding Series, 134*–138. https://doi.org/10.1145/2330601.2330636.

Ellis, T. J., & Levy, Y. (2010). A guide for novice researchers: design and development research methods. *Proceedings of the 2010 InSITE Conference*, December, 107–118. https://doi.org/10.28945/1237.

Ferguson, R., Brasher, A., Clow, D., Cooper, A., Hillaire, G., Mittelmeier, J., Rienties, B., & Vuorikari, R. (2016). Research evidence on the use of learning analytics. In *A European framework for action on learning analytics* (Issue 2016). https://doi.org/10.2791/955210.

Gautham, A. (2018). *Popular learning analytics tool.* https://playxlpro.com/popular-learning-analytics-tool/

Levy, P. (1997). Education and training : New technologies and collective intelligence. *Prospects, XXVII*(2), 249–263.

Nielson, B. (2019). *The top 5 learning analytics.* https://www.yourtrainingedge.com/the-top-5-learning-analytics/

Omedes, J. (2017). *15 Strategies you can follow today to successfully deploy your learning analytics tool.* https://www.iadlearning.com/learning-analytics-tool/

Ringtved, U. L., Wahl, C., Belle, G., & Clemmensen, A. L. (2017). Development of students learning capabilities and professional capabilities. *Design LAK17*, 2–3. https://sites.google.com/site/designlak17/

Ryann, K. E. (2020). *Choosing a learning analytics tool.* https://www.td.org/newsletters/atd-links/choosing-a-learning-analytics-tool

Siemens, G. (2013). Learning analytics: The emergence of a discipline. *American Behavioral Scientist, 57*(10), 1380–1400. https://doi.org/10.1177/0002764213498851

Wahl, C., Bellè, G., Clemmensen, A. L., & Ringtved, U. (2013). Developing a learning analytics tool. In *American behavioral scientist* (Vol. 57, Issue 10). https://doi.org/10.1177/0002764213498851.

Chapter 6
Other Technology Approaches to Learning Analytics

6.1 Introduction

This section discusses some of the fundamental technologies and processes on which the remaining sections of this chapter can be understood.

6.1.1 Big Data

What is Data? "The quantities, characters, or symbols on which operations are performed by a computer, which may be stored and transmitted in the form of electrical signals and recorded on magnetic, optical, or mechanical recording media" (Sanders, 2016).

What is Big Data? The term "Big Data refers to any set of data (Klašnja-Milićević, Ivanović, & Budimac, 2017) that is so large or so complex that conventional applications are not adequate to process them." The term also refers to the tools and technologies used to handle "Big Data." Bigdata examples include the volume of data shared on the internet, watched YouTube videos, Twitter updates, and smartphone location data. Data created by learning environments have begun to increase the need for big data technologies and tools to deal with them in recent years (Sin & Muthu, 2015).

According to Gartner (Gartner, 2020), the definition of Big Data – "Big data is high-volume, velocity, and variety information assets that demand cost-effective, innovative forms of information processing for enhanced insight and decision making." Big data refers to massive, complicated data sets that need to be processed and analyzed to disclose useful information to businesses and organizations.

However, some simple tenets of big data make it much easier to respond to what big data is (Rai, 2020):

- It refers to a vast volume of data that continues to expand exponentially over time.
- It is so big that traditional data processing methods cannot be used or analyzed.
- Includes data mining, data storage, data processing, data exchange, and viewing.
- The term includes all-inclusive data, data frames, and methods and techniques for data processing and analysis.

6.1.1.1 Why Is Big Data Important?

Big data is not just how much data a company has but how a company uses the data that it collects. Every business uses data in its way; the more effective a company uses its data, the greater its potential. The Organization will collect and analyses data from any source to find responses that enable (Research Data Alliance, 2020):

1. *Cost savings*: Certain big data tools such as Hadoop and cloud-based analysis can provide companies with cost advantages as vast volumes of data are being collected, and these tools can also help find more effective ways to do business.
2. *Time reduction:* The high speed of tools such as Hadoop and in-memory analytics can easily detect new data sources, enabling companies to analyze data instantly and react quickly based on information.
3. *Understanding the market dynamics:* You can better grasp the existing market environment by analyzing big data. For instance, by observing consumers' buying habits, a company may find out the most popular goods and manufacture products according to this pattern. It can thus get ahead of its rivals.
4. *Online credibility control:* Big data tools can measure emotions. Therefore, you will gain input on who tells the organization what. If you want to track and enhance your company's online presence, big data tools will help.
5. *Use Big Data Analytics to improve consumer acquisition and retention:* The consumer relies on the most valuable asset. There is no single organization that can assert success without a strong customer base. However, with a client base, the intense competition facing a company cannot afford to neglect. If a company slowly understands what its customers want, then selling low-quality goods is very straightforward. Ultimately, the consumer's failure occurs, which has a detrimental impact on overall company performance. The use of big data helps organizations to identify different patterns and trends specific to consumers. It is essential to observe consumer behavior to cause loyalty.
6. *Big data analytics can help solve the advertiser's dilemma and provide marketing insights:* Big data analytics can help alter all transactions. This involves the opportunity to fulfill consumers' needs, improve the organization's product line, and maintain successful marketing strategies.

6.1 Introduction 163

7. ***Big Data Analytics as a catalyst for new goods:*** Big data's ability to help businesses reinvent and redevelop their goods is another significant benefit of big data.

6.1.2 Types of Big Data

Now that you know what big data is, let us look at the types of big data (Rai, 2020):

1. ***Structured:*** Structured is one of the bigdata types, and structured data means information that can be processed, stored, and recovered in a fixed format. It refers to highly ordered data which can be stored and retrieved by simple search engine algorithms easily and seamlessly from a database. For example, the employee's table in a corporate database would be arranged, as the employee's information, employment, wages, etc. are organized.
2. ***Unstructured:*** Unstructured data refers to data without some particular form or structure. This makes processing and analysis of unstructured data very complicated and time-consuming. Email is an unstructured data example. Two primary forms of big data are structured and unstructured.
3. ***Semi-structured:*** The third form of big data is semi-structured. Semi-structured data is for data containing structured and unstructured data, both of the above formats. To be exact, it refers to the data not listed under a single repository (database) but includes essential information or tags that segregate individual elements within the data.

6.1.2.1 Characteristics of Big Data

In 2001, Gartner analyst Doug Laney listed Big Data's 3 'V's (Fig. 6.1) – variety, velocity, and volume. These characteristics are necessary, in isolation, to know what big data is. Let us take a closer look at them (Research Data Alliance, 2020):

1. ***Variety:*** A variety of Big Data refers to structured, unstructured, and semi-structured data obtained from various sources. Although data can only be collected from spreadsheets and databases in the past, today, data can be collected in various forms such as emails, PDFs, photographs, images, audios, social media posts, etc.
2. ***Velocity:*** Velocity refers primarily to the speed at which data is generated in real-time. It involves the transition rate, connecting incoming data sets, and activity explosions at varying speeds in a broader context.
3. ***Volume:*** We already know that Big Data means vast amounts of data produced daily from different sources, such as social media sites, business processes, equipment, networks, human interactions, and so on. A vast quantity of data is contained in data stores.

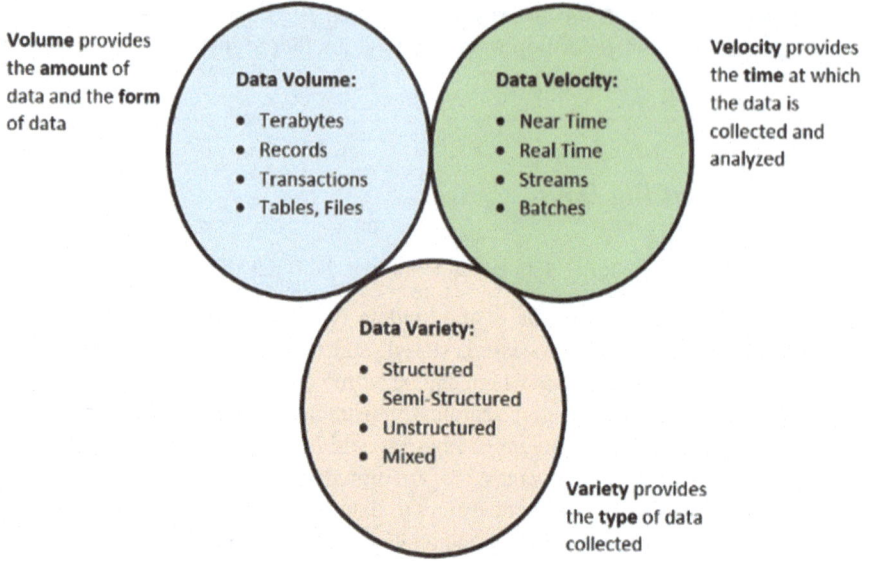

Fig. 6.1 The three V's of Big Data (Research Data Alliance, 2020)

6.1.2.2 Advantages/Features of Big Data

Big data provides a number of the following advantages (Rai, 2020):

- Predictive analysis is one of the main benefits of big data. Big data analysis tools can reliably predict outcomes so that companies and organizations can make better decisions while also maximizing their operating performance and reducing risks.
- Using Big Data analysis tools, organizations worldwide are streamlining their digital marketing campaigns to improve the overall customer experience. Big Data gives insights into the needs of consumers and helps businesses to develop their goods and services.
- To be specific, Big Data incorporates applicable data from many sources to produce highly useful insights. Nearly 43% of companies lack the tools they need to filter out irrelevant data, which ultimately costs them millions of dollars to have valuable information from the bulk. Big data tools will help you minimize this and save you time and money.
- Big data analytics could allow businesses to produce more sales figures that would raise profits. Businesses use Big Data analytics tools to understand just how well their products/services perform on the market and how their customers react. The best way to spend your time and resources is to do so.
- You can remain a step ahead of your rivals with big data analytics. You can scan the market, see what kind of deals and incentives your competitors have, and then make better incentives for your clients. Big data analytics will allow you to learn how to help consumer preferences and provide you with a highly 'personalized' experience.

6.1.2.3 Major Application Areas of Big Data

Many that use Big Data know exactly what Big Data is. Let us look at some of the major application areas (Rai, 2020):

1. *Healthcare:* Big data has already begun to make an immense difference in the health sector. Health practitioners and HCPs are now able to provide individual patients with customized health treatment with predictive analytics. Also, health wearables, telemedicine, remote monitoring – all powered by big data and AI – helping to enhance living conditions.
2. *Academia:* Today, big data also helps to boost education. Training is no longer restricted to the classroom's physical limits – many online training courses can be learned. Academic institutions invest in digital courses enabled by Big Data technology to help emerging students grow all-round. After that, some of the areas of education have been changed by improvements inspired by big data.
   - Customized and diverse systems of learning
   - Material for reframing courses
   - For Rating Schemes
   - Career prediction
3. *Banking:* The banking sector uses big data to detect fraud. Big data tools can detect fraudulent behavior in real-time effectively, such as credit/debit card violence, inspection monitor archival, customer statistic fault alteration, etc.
4. *Manufacturing:* According to the TCS Global Trend Report, the most significant big data manufacturing gain is enhanced product quality and supply strategies. Big data helps build a clear system in the manufacturing industry, thus avoiding uncertainty and incompetence that can adversely affect business.
5. *IT:* One of the world's most comprehensive big data users, the IT companies use big data to optimize their processes, increase employee efficiency, and reduce business risks. By integrating big data technology with ML and AI, the IT industry continuously pushes creativity to find solutions, even for the most challenging issues.
6. *Retail:* Big data has changed the way conventional retail stores in brick and mortar operation. Over the years, retailers have collected huge numbers of data from local population surveys, POS scanners, RFIDs, customer loyalty cards, inventories of stores, and so forth. Now, they have begun to use this knowledge to build customer engagement, increase sales, increase revenue, and provide excellent customer support. Distributors use smart sensors and Wi-Fi to monitor customers' movement, the most popular aisles, and how long customers stay in the aisles. They also collect social media information to understand what consumers feel about their products, services and tweak their product design and marketing strategies.
7. *Transportation:* For the transportation industry, Big Data Analytics has enormous value. In countries worldwide, big-data technologies are used by private and government-run transportation firms to refine road planning, track traffic,

control road congestion, and enhance services. Transport networks are now using Big Data in the field of revenue management, pushing technical advancement, improving logistics, and, of course, gaining market leadership.

6.1.3 Data Analytics

All businesses in the world today produce vast quantities of data from different sources. This data is beneficial to companies who have the resources to capitalize on it, whether it is focused on corporate structures itself, social media, or other online outlets, smartphones, or other clients/edge computers or sensors and instruments like the Internet of Things. Data analytic is the general toolbox for these tools.

The term data analytics refers to the use of different techniques that find meaningful patterns in data. It is a mechanism in which data are turned into insight and foresight. Data analytics tools help us explain what happened in the past, obtain insights into the present, and forecast the future with specific techniques (Tsai, Lai, Chao, & Vasilakos, 2015).

The data analytics area is not recent. It has been used for decades in the corporate world. Data analytics can be as simple as surveys to assess the average age or analyze other consumer metrics. A linear regression chart in an Excel spreadsheet will illuminate the patterns in sales. However, the world of data analytics never stands still as old as it is. It is continually growing as businesses apply advanced analytical techniques such as business intelligence applications and in-house data real-time analysis.

6.1.3.1 Why Is Data Analytics Important?

As a vast amount of data is generated, a business enterprise needs to gather valuable insights. Data analytics plays a vital role in the development of your business. Here are four significant factors that make data analytics necessary (Kappagantula, 2019):

- **Collect Hidden Insights:** Hidden insights are obtained and then analyzed for business requirements.
- **Generate reports:** reports from the data are generated and forwarded to the respective teams and individuals for further actions for a high level of business growth.
- **Business Research:** Market analysis may be carried out to identify competitors' strengths and weaknesses.
- **Improving business requirements:** Data analytics enables businesses to improve customer requirements and experience.

6.1 Introduction

6.1.3.2 Types of Data Analytics

Four key data analytics types (Fig. 6.2) are available (Rai, 2020): descriptive, diagnostic, predictive, and prescriptive analytics. Each category has a different purpose and role in the process of data analytics.

- *Descriptive analytics* helps to address questions about what happened. These techniques summarize broad datasets to explain stakeholders' performance. These techniques can track successes or failures by creating key performance indicators (KPIs). In many sectors, metrics such as return on investment (ROI) are used. To measure performance in specific industries, specialized metrics are created. This method includes data collection, data processing, data analysis, and data visualization. This process gives a profound insight into past performances.
- *Diagnostic analytics* helps address questions as to why things happened. These methods complement more straightforward empirical explanations. They take the results from descriptive analytics and analyze the cause deeper. The performance metrics are further analyzed to figure out whether they have changed or worse. This usually takes place in three steps:

  - Recognize data anomalies. These shifts in a metric or a specific market may be unpredictable.
  - Data was collected related to these anomalies.
  - The statistical methods are used to determine relationships and patterns that specifically explain these anomalies.

- *Predictive analytics* helps address questions about what will happen in the future. These techniques use historical data to assess patterns and to assess if

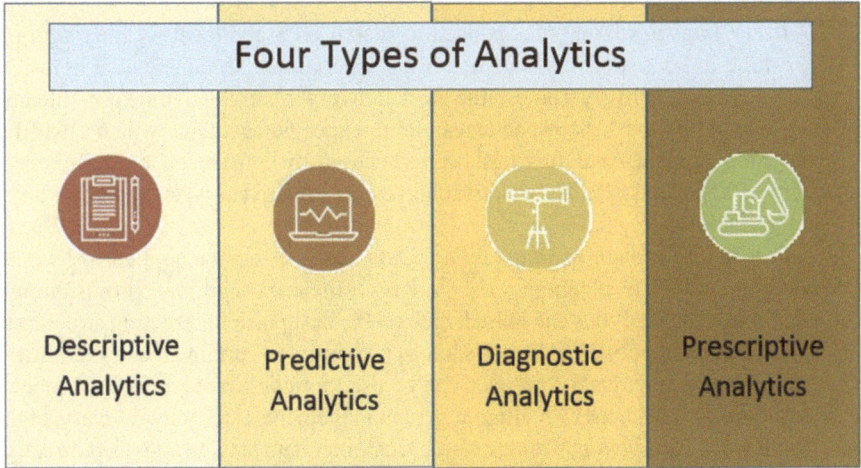

Fig. 6.2 Types of data analytics (Intellipaat, 2017)

they will recur. Predictive analytical tools offer useful insight into future trends, including several statistical and machine learning techniques, such as neural networks, decision trees, and regression.
- ***Prescriptive analytics*** helps answer questions about what should be done. Data-driven decisions can be taken by using insights from predictive analytics. In the face of uncertainty, this helps organizations to make educated decisions. Machine learning techniques that can identify patterns in massive data sets are used for prescriptive analytics. By evaluating past actions and events, it is possible to estimate the probability of various effects.

These types of data analytics offer insight into the need for organizations to make accurate and successful decisions. Used together, they provide a comprehensive view of the needs and opportunities of an organization.

6.1.3.3 Areas for Data Analytics Applications

Below is the list of top fields (Patel, 2018) in which data analytics was widely applied and still holds significant potential for continued development and progress.

1. ***Policing/Security:*** Advanced data and text mining tools have made it easier to detect offenders and predict illegal behavior. Data analytics tools for detecting crimes and the tracking of contact by suspected terrorists were commonly used. Through applying predictive analyses to geographical and historical data, forecasts of crime and possible target areas can be made more accurately.
2. ***Banking and finance:*** Advanced-Data Analytics can help banks easily detect the correlation between knowledge and market prices in solving many business problems. Applying data analytics to consumer data obtained during a loan application and data linked to their recent spending helps infer future default customers.
3. ***Delivery Logistics:*** Analytics is used to search GPS and local weather data in real-time to boost delivery logistics firms' operational efficiency as it helps to find adequate delivery routes, the best delivery times, and transport means while avoiding the loss of packages and unexpected accidents which cost life and money. Data Analytics has been successfully introduced by companies such as UPS, DHL, FedEx, etc. to achieve cost-effectiveness, customer loyalty, and reliability.
4. ***Planning and growth of smart cities:*** Data analytics can be applied in several ways to smart city planning, costs, energy efficiency, and web provisioning. Modeling data analytics can help decide on the best place for erecting structures while preventing potential issues such as proximity to certain areas or facilities and overcrowding. Data Analytics can be used to monitor resources and incorporate energy efficiency, intelligent grid management, electricity delivery, etc.
5. ***Customer Relationship Management:*** Customer data may be analyzed directly and indirectly to expose customer actions and preferences. Data analytics can

expose e-commerce and retail application patterns, identify potential buyers, optimize pricing models, build personalized and real-time deals, etc.
6. ***Healthcare:*** Healthcare analytics is rising rapidly. Clinical analysis, supply chain analysis, financial analysis, fraud, and HR analysis are the major focus areas. Data analytics can be used to forecast disease outbreaks, classify their real source and potential areas in which they can spread, and save thousands of lives at once.
7. ***Web/Internet Search:*** Companies like Google, Bing, Yahoo, etc., use high-data processing to crawl and index reliable and accurate internet sites. Due to the Internet-scale and the growth rate, these companies have recognized the need for faster digital scanning and indexing and chosen to lead Big Data Analytics research and development.
8. ***Education:*** Educational data mining and analytics are designed to forecast learning activity, evaluate education support's impact, and advance scientific learning knowledge. The next step in the education sector is an insightful curriculum that can adapt to students' needs, living environment, learning speed, and previous knowledge. Data analytics will enable institutes to develop learning experience in line with students' and teachers' abilities, learning styles, and preferences.
9. ***Research and development:*** Researchers spend a great deal of time testing, iterating, refining, and repeating while creating a solution to a specific business problem. Researchers will speed up their study by reimbursing varying data with automated model generation and training with data analysis applications.
10. ***Bioinformatics:*** Biological data mining and analysis can reveal valuable knowledge of inferences in the protein structure, gene discovery, gene interaction network reconstruction, etc. In particular, predictive analysis can be useful in disease detection, forecasting, treatment progress, prediction of subcellular protein position, etc.

The desire to improve understanding about the past, the present and the future encourages continuous improvement in data analytics. These innovations are essential in cases that cannot be understood simply by addressing straightforward issues. There are few hard-and-fast "laws of nature" in the business world that can tell you what will happen with utter certainty. To achieve this higher understanding, businesses must collect and analyze data using state-of-the-art techniques. Moreover, that takes us to data science.

6.1.4 Data Science

Data science is a state-of-the-art data processing. It is a process of testing, analyzing, and experimenting with new data processing methods and new ways of applying them (Weihs & Ickstadt, 2018). As the name suggests, data science is, at its heart, a discipline that incorporates existing scientific analysis approaches (Fig. 6.3).

Data scientists are now developing new algorithms to provide insight and understanding and assess these methods' effectiveness and the accuracy of the findings. If methods are commonly considered useful, they become more widely recognized and add to the array of data analytics tools.

While every company should use data analytics in its operations, analytics is increasingly necessary when companies undertake digital transformation. As they evolve, businesses should continually advance their analytical capabilities. One way is to employ data scientists. Strong business data cultures should include data scientists who actively seek to improve the ability to use mature, validated research methods for large organizations.

6.1.4.1 Importance of Data Science

Now, let us see some of the reasons why data science is becoming increasingly important (Morrison, 2019). Data science has come a long way from the last few years and thus becomes an integral part of understanding different industries' workings. Below are some reasons why data science will still be an integral part of the global economy.

1. With the aid of data science, businesses will achieve a deeper and improved knowledge of their consumers. Customers are the cornerstone of every product and play a significant role in its success and failure. Data Science allows companies to connect in a modified manner to their customers, thereby confirming the better product quality and power.
2. Data Science enables brands to tell their tale clearly and attractively. This is one of the reasons for its success. By using these data inclusive, the brands and businesses will share their story with their audiences, thereby creating stronger product connections.

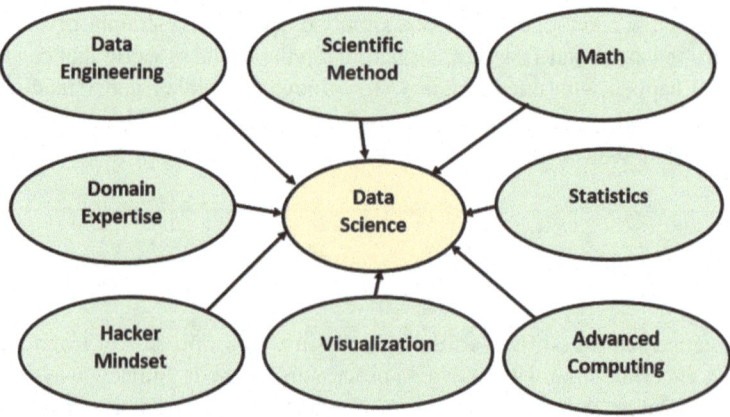

Fig. 6.3 Common disciplines of Data Science (Castrounis, 2020)

6.1 Introduction

3. One of the essential characteristics of data science is that it can be used in virtually all forms of industries such as travel, health care, and education. With the aid of data science, companies can quickly evaluate and efficiently solve their challenges.
4. Data science is available in almost all areas at present, and a large number of data are present in today's world; and if properly used, this can lead to success or failure of the product. If data is appropriately used, it will be critical in the future for achieving product objectives.
5. Big data are constantly growing and emerging. Big data helps companies address complex IT, human resources, and resource management complex issues and successfully use various regularly created tools.
6. In all sectors, data science gains prominence and plays a vital role in every product's functioning and development. Therefore, the data scientist also needs to fulfill an important task in handling data and to provide solutions to specific problems.
7. The retail sectors were also influenced by data science. Take, to take an example; the older people had a significant encounter with the local vendor. The seller was also able to satisfy the needs of the customers in a personalized manner. However, this focus has now been lost due to the rise and increase of supermarkets. However, with the aid of data analytics, sellers will communicate with their customers.
8. Data Science helps companies develop this partnership with customers. Through data science, businesses and their suppliers will understand how consumers use their goods.

6.1.4.2 The Data Science Life Cycle

Data science typically has a lifecycle of five stages (Berkeley, 2018) (Fig. 6.4)

1. *Capture:* data acquisition, entry, signal reception, extraction of data.
2. *Maintain:* data warehousing, data cleaning, data storage, data analysis, the architecture of the system
3. *Process:* Data mining, clustering, modeling of data, data summarization
4. *Communication:* data reporting, visualization, business intelligence, decision-making
5. *Analyze:* exploratory, predictive analysis, regression, text mining, qualitative analysis.

All five phases require various strategies, programs, and, in some cases, skills.

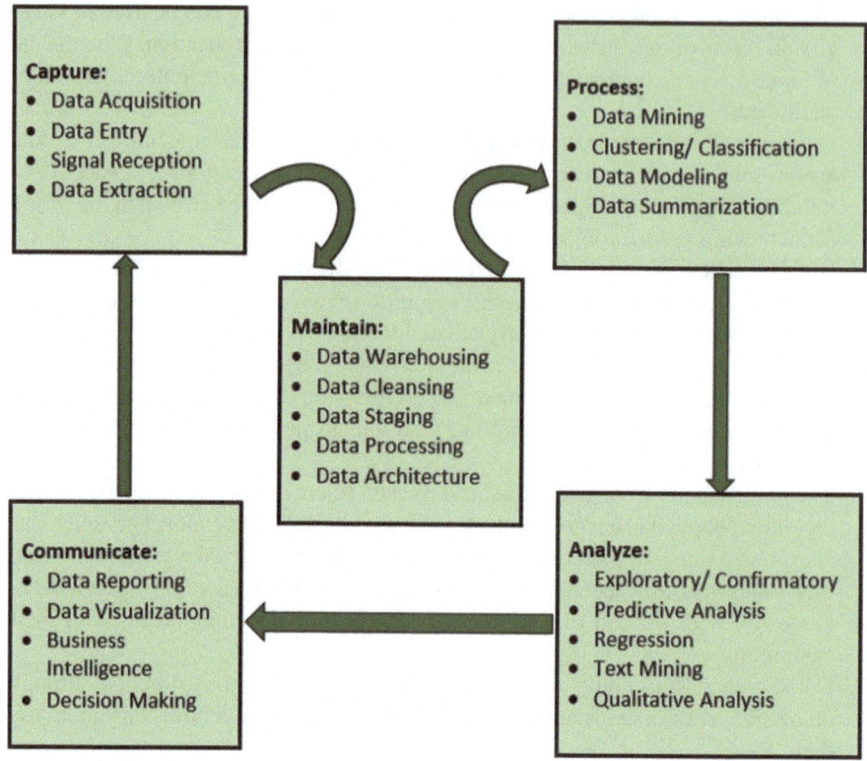

Fig. 6.4 The data science life cycle (Berkeley, 2018)

6.1.5 Data Engineering

Data engineering (Fig. 6.5) is an essential tool for data processing and data science, even though it does not attract the main headlines. Data engineering renders data usable in basic terms. It transforms structured, unstructured, and semi-structured data from various systems and silos into a set of useful and consistent data that can extract information and value in application and algorithm (Eze, 2018).

Data engineering includes work to clean datasets — often much work while juggling several different data sources and/or data with missing values, errors, and even biases. For instance, if you run analytics on recent sales in homes, you would like to correct or delete any record at a price of zero. These incorrect price data could skew the results if used in simple calculations, such as the average house price, so the data engineer works to extract them from the data set or (better), if possible, to fix them. Such data errors may have hidden consequences that cannot be readily seen in more advanced data analytics findings. However, by using the data, they may have serious consequences.

6.1 Introduction

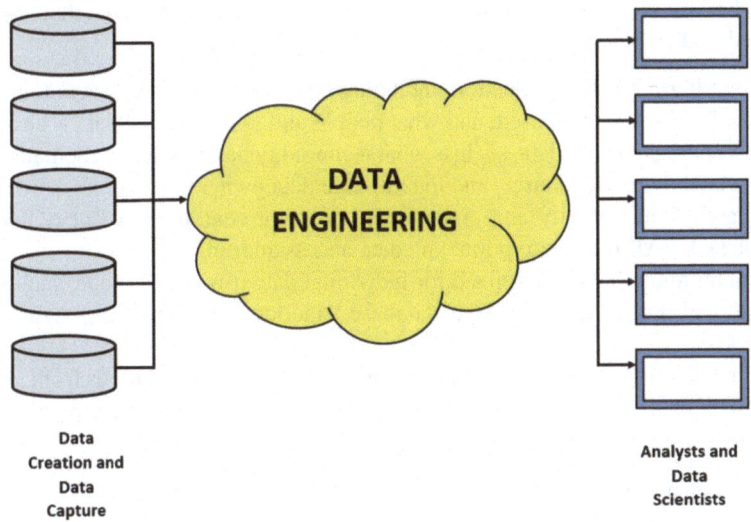

Fig. 6.5 A conceptual view of data engineering (Dremio, 2020)

While you have heard the word more frequently in recent years, data engineering is not new. It has been around for as long as we have digital records. However, data engineering is increasingly needed today as businesses combine, curate, update, and scrub various data from an ever-growing variety of sources. For advanced data analytics applications, like machine learning and deep learning, this phase is often essential. Data engineers need to delete inaccurate information, fix gaps, and ensure the data does not bias with the results.

6.1.5.1 Data Engineering Responsibilities

Data engineering organizes data to allow the use of other structures and people. You deal with several different data users, including (Dremio, 2020):

- *Data Analysts* answer specific data questions or generate reports and visualizations that make it easier for others to understand the data.
- *Data scientists* address questions that are more nuanced than analysts – a data scientist, for example, may create a model to predict which consumers are likely to buy a particular item.
- *System Architectures* are responsible for bringing data into their applications. For example, an e-commerce store could give discounts according to the user's purchasing history, and a system architect develops the infrastructure to measure that discount.
- *Business Leaders* understand the value of the data and how others use it.

Each of these groups is interested in data engineering to understand their particular needs. Their roles are:

- Data criteria for data collection, including how much time the data is to be processed, how it is to be used, and what people and systems need data access.
- Preserving data metadata, such as what technology handles data, schematic, size, protected data, data source, and the ultimate data owner.
- Maintain data security and governance, utilizing centralized security controls such as LDAP, data encryption, and data access auditing.
- With unique systems optimized for individual data use, data storage, such as the relational database, the NoSQL database, Hadoop, Amazon S3, or Azure Blog Storage.
- Data collection for specific requirements using data access methods from various sources, data transformation, enriching, data description, and data management in the storage system.

To deal with these tasks, they carry out many different tasks. Such examples are:

- *Acquisition:* Data from different systems are supplied.
- *Cleansing:* Errors detection and correction.
- *Conversion:* Converting data from one format to another format.
- *Disambiguation:* Interpreting data that have multiple meanings.
- *Deduplication:* Removal of duplicate data copies.

Most or all of these tasks are widely used for any data processing task.

6.1.6 Artificial Intelligence

Artificial intelligence refers to computing systems that can reason and take classifications and decisions that are usually human intelligence necessary (Shabbir & Anwer, 2015). Popular uses of AI include image recognition and classification, speech recognition, and language translation.

Though people may hear of AI as being modern, it has been with us since the 1950s. When computers came into existence, people felt that machines could be programmed to think as humans do.

Different approaches to AI (Boisseau & Wilson, 2019) have been developed over the years to make computers more rational or better than people. Expert systems were one solution that experienced some traction a few decades ago. These systems adopt a pre-programmed rule set developed by humans to perform tasks independently of humans. For example, we have all expert systems in automatic responses, such as those we can communicate if we call a customer service desk and have to use menu options in button presses. Many of these are now being updated using natural language processing – based on profound learning, to be more versatile, efficient, and less stressful, provided that processing of the natural language is improved over time.

6.1.6.1 Importance of AI

Although there are several reasons for giving priority to AI learning, some of them are most significant (SAS, 2018):

- *AI automates repetitive learning and discovery through data.* However, AI is distinct from robotic automation powered by hardware. Instead of manual tasks automated, AI performs high-volume, computer-based tasks efficiently and easily. The human inquiry is still important to set up the framework and ask the right questions for automation.
- *AI adds intelligence.* In most instances, AI is not marketed as a single program. You will now develop the products with AI capabilities, as Siri has been integrated into a new generation of Apple devices. Automation, conversational systems, bots, and intelligent machines can be combined with vast volumes of data to enhance multiple technologies at home and on-site, from safety intelligence to analysis of the investment.
- *AI adapts to allow the data to program through progressive learning algorithms.* AI detects structure and regularities in data to obtain an ability to construct the algorithm: the algorithm transforms into a classification or predictor. As the algorithm can teach itself how to play chess, it can teach itself which product to recommend online next time. Moreover, the models adapt when new data is given. Backpropagation is an AI technique that allows the model to adapt by training and adding details if the first response is not entirely accurate.
- *AI uses neural networks with several hidden layers to explore more and more deep data.* A few years ago, it was almost difficult to create a fraud detection system with five hidden layers. With amazing computing power and big data, everything has changed. You need more data to train profound learning models since they learn from the data directly. The more details you can feed, the more reliable it is.
- *AI achieves an unprecedented precision across deep neural networks – which was impossible before.* For example, your experiences with Alexa, Google Search, and Google Images are focused on deep learning, and more specifically, we use them. Deeper learning, picture detection, and object recognition technology in the medical field can now be used to detect cancer in MRIs with the same precision as highly qualified radiologists.
- *AI gets the most out of data. In self-learning algorithms, the data itself can become intellectual property.* The answers are in the data; you just need AI to retrieve them. As the role of data now is more important than ever, a competitive advantage can be developed. Even if everyone uses similar strategies, the best data will win if you have the best data in a competitive market.

More recently, an approach known as machine learning has become a popular means of AI. More recently, a subset of machine learning, known as deep learning, has proven to be highly efficient in certain types of problems and working load – when enough data exists to train the models (the "learning" part). Therefore, AI accepts multiple approaches at a wider stage, with machine learning and deep learning being two methods that make today's AI-enabled applications possible (Fig. 6.6).

6.1.7 Machine Learning and Deep Learning

Machine learning is a subfield of AI that enables systems to learn from data and evolve without being explicitly programmed. Algorithms for machine learning use data to build and refine rules. The machine then determines how to respond based on what the data have obtained. The aim here is to let the data direct rule-making (Simeone, 2018).

Machine-learning techniques may use various data types to understand system-generated behavior and choices, including unstructured or semi-structured data.

Consider a purposely, straightforward example. With classical machine learning, you can offer a device a series of features common to cats in pictures of different animal types. You will then allow the machine to browse through animal images databases to figure out which variations of the features supplied by humans recognize all the cats in the mixture. In the meantime, the machine learning system evolves and develops as you learn from your data experiences.

Deep learning is machine learning based on a deep hierarchy of interconnected neural network layers, with the ability to learn key "features" from the systems' data. The profound learning technique takes huge quantities of data and decides the general rules and features relevant to data (Rouse, 2019). As with conventional machine learning, data direct deep learning model training.

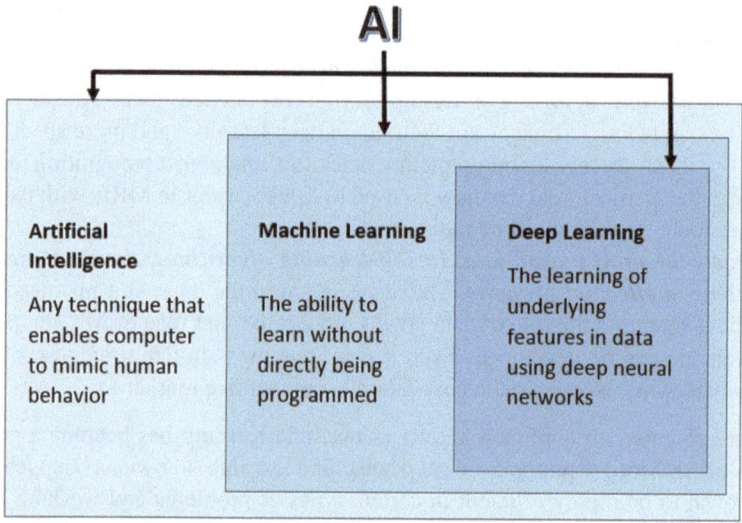

Fig. 6.6 A conceptual view of AI, ML & DL (Kharkovyna, 2019)

6.1 Introduction

Let us build on the example of our cat. If you offer sufficient images of cats to a deep learning system, the system itself will decide the properties that make a cat a cat, such as features relating to the eyes, ears, whiskers, and tail. This capacity to learn goes beyond conventional machine learning because you do not have to tell the system what it wants to be. It finds out by itself.

6.1.7.1 Elements of Machine Learning

As mentioned above, machine learning is an AI subset that is typically divided into two key categories: supervised and unsupervised learning (Heath, 2018).

Supervised Learning Training them with a vast number of labeled examples is a popular technique to teach AI systems. These machine learning systems are supplied with massive quantities of data, which have been noted to highlight the characteristics of interest. This may be named pictures to show whether a dog or written phrases have footnotes on the word 'bass' or whether they refer to music or fish. After training, these marks can then be applied to new data, such as a dog in a picture that has just been uploaded.

This teaching method of a machine by example is called supervised learning, and the task of marking these examples is typically done by online staff using platforms such as Amazon Mechanical Turk. Training of these systems usually requires a great deal of data, with some systems requiring millions of examples to help them efficiently execute a task – even though this is increasingly possible in times of extensive data and widespread data mining. Training datasets are massive and growing in size – the Google Open Images Dataset includes some nine million photos, while its YouTube-8M branded video repository connects to seven million videos branded. ImageNet, one of this type's early sites, has more than 14 million images categorized. Almost 50,000 people-most of whom were hired through Amazon Mechanical Turk-gathered over two years, reviewed, sort, and labeled almost one billion candidate images.

It may also be less necessary to access massive labeled datasets than access to large quantities of computation capacity in the long run. In recent years, Generative Adversarial Networks (GANs) have shown how machine learning systems fed a small number of marked data can create large quantities of new data to teach themselves.

This method could lead to semi-supervised learning in which systems would learn how to conduct tasks with much less marked knowledge than is currently needed for training systems using supervised learning.

Unsupervised learning However, unsupervised learning uses a different approach, in which algorithms aim to classify patterns of data and find correlations that can be used to categorize these data.

An example could be when fruits with similar weight or cars with a similar engine size are combined.

The algorithm is not set up to select certain data types in advance. It just searches for data that can be grouped by similarities, for example, Google News, which group News on similar subjects every day.

Reinforcement learning A rough analogy for enhancement is a treat for a pet when he does the trick.

In improving learning, the machine aims to optimize a reward based on its input data and ultimately undergo an attempt and error process before achieving the best possible result.

An example of reinforcement learning is Google DeepMind's Deep Q Network, which many classic Video games use to achieve the best human results. The system feeds pixels from each game and determines the distance between objects on the screen and other information.

In looking at each game's score, the machine often creates a model whose action maximizes the score in various conditions, such as the Breakout video game, in which the paddle should be shifted to intercept it.

6.1.7.2 Deep Learning Methods

Various methods can be applied to construct strong deep learning models (Margaret, 2020). These strategies include the following.

- *Learning rate decay:* The learning rate is a hyperparameter — a factor that defines the system or sets the conditions for its operation before the learning process — which checks the degree to which model experiences change when the weight of the model is modified. Too high learning rates can lead to unstable training or the learning of a sub-optimal set of weights. Too small learning rates will create a long training process that can get stuck.
- *The learning rate decay method:* also known as learning rate annealing or adaptive learning rates — is the changing phase of learning rate to improve performance and minimize training time. The simplest and most common changes to learning rates include strategies for decreasing learning rates over time.
- *Transfer learning:* A previously trained model is developed; an interface with a previously established network internals is required. Next, users feed new data with previously unknown classifications to the current network. Once the network is modified, new tasks can be carried out with more precise categorizing skills. This method's benefit is that it requires far less data than others, reducing the computation time to minutes or hours.
- *Training from scratch:* This approach requires that a developer gathers a broad data set and configures an architecture for the network, learning the features and models. This technique is particularly useful for applications with a large number of output categories and new applications. However, this approach is less popular because it needs excessive amounts of data, which takes days or weeks to train.

- ***Dropout:*** This approach aims to solve the problem of overcasting large numbers of network parameters through a random decrease of units and neural network connections during training. The dropout approach has been demonstrated to improve neural networks' performance on supervised learning tasks in fields, including language recognition, classification of documents, and computational biology.

6.2 Big Data & Learning Analytics

6.2.1 Using Big Data to Analyze Learning

Before the growth of big data, instructors had to rely on periodic tests and evaluations to assess their students' progress. Often, struggling learners were identified too late, and much effort was needed to catch up. As big data began to spread to all kinds of industries; however, the chief learning officers improved learning experiences. If we could improve student behaviors and activities and find correlations to their success or failures in learning, we would help people in their online courses become more successful. This use of big data is called learning analytics to improve online learning. This is how learning analytics operates within the LMS

Learning management systems such as Moodle and Totara collect a large number of user data. Whenever a user interacts with a learning module, forum, assessment, or communication tool, LMS records, and stores this data, these data can be sorted, filtered, and linked to specific measurements, such as activity and course completions. As models arise, facilitators and course designers can adapt the course to help struggling students succeed (Yupangco, 2017). For example, some behaviors can be used as an early warning sign that a student will fail. If a pupil shows these conducts, the trainer may be alerted to reach the pupil and intervene.

Research shows that students remember more when they are more involved in the course material. Learning Analytics enables users to understand where they are most involved with the module by tracking their activities. Then, personalized eLearning courses can be created, which break out of the one-sized paradigm. Big data in an eLearning environment creates a feedback system that helps instructors and course designers find solutions to the most frequent online learning problems.

Big data and learning analytics have the following features to develop current education technology (Kanth, Laakso, Nevalainen, & Heikkonen, 2018).

- ***Feature 1:*** Intelligent, scalable, and collaborative education platform development and implementation based on students' data. The target platform is to efficiently support the variety of courses that are best suited to the education level of doctors and to predict the real-time performance in development work as a matter of top priority.
- ***Feature 2:*** The platform envisaged will consist of a hierarchical and scalable composition of a round of exercises, tutorials, and training projects where the

highest learning results will be possible through innovative cooperation between students and teachers.
- **Feature 3:** developing a dynamic mapping matrix between students' profiles and categorizing proper exercises based on students' requirements. The aim is to automatically predict performance using deep learning and neural network techniques at the required courses.
- **Feature 4:** Establish a robust protocol to predict possible early dropouts during the course from when back-on-original paths can be within limits.
- **Feature 5:** to increase the resilience of instructional worksheets, electronic examinations, and submissions systems to achieve the highest quality during the current digitalization process and emphasize the need to weave the latest IT technology into education for more learning advantages.

6.2.2 Why Associate Big Data and Learning Analytics Together?

Big data analytics is characterized as obtaining, storing, and analyzing large sets of data ("big data"), used to identify useful information and certain trends. Also, Big Data Analytics offers the ability to understand better information that could be relevant for future decisions. For Big Data Analysts, the extraction of knowledge from data processing is essential.

Big data and analytics can be useful for a variety of higher education instructional and administrative applications. The monitoring and evaluation of learners' performance, teachers' development, production costs, commercial planning, and donor finding (van Barneveld, Arnold, & Campbell, 2012). It is essentially a requirement that the transaction process is electronic to take advantage of big data and learning analytics. Traditional face-to-face interactions can be helpful for decision making. In comparison, educational transactions must be recorded as they occur in comprehensive and time-sensitive learning analytics applications. It is possible for a course management/learning management system (CMS / LMS) and an intelligent tutoring system. Most of these systems include continuous monitoring of learning events, access to reading content, responses, posts on a forum, the resolution of tests or quizzes, and other assessments. During 15 weeks of online courses, several thousand transactions per learner could be expected. Input data for the learning analytics application can be used for tracking and analyzing these transactions in real-time. Practical values from big data can be extracted in five steps (Labrinidis & Jagadish, 2012):

1. Acquisition and recording;
2. Extraction, cleaning, and annotation;
3. Integration, aggregation, and representation;
4. Modeling and analysis;
5. Interpretation.

These five stages can be divided into two principal subprocesses: data management and data/learning analytics.

Figure 6.7 (Klašnja-Milićević et al., 2017) provides a clear indication of all phases and offers a thorough overview of all the major factors needed to consider Big Data Analytics in higher education conceptually and practically.

6.2.3 Applications of Big Data in Learning Analytics

Big data techniques can be used in different ways in learning analytics (Sin & Muthu, 2015):

- Performance prediction: Students' performance can be predicted by analyzing students' interaction with other students and teachers in their learning environment.
- Attrition Risk Detection – Students who exit courses can be predicted, and interventions can be introduced at the beginning of the course to retain students by observing their behavior.
- Data Visualization – Educational data reports become more difficult as the scale of the educational data increases. Data can be visualized using data visualization techniques so that patterns and relationships in data can be quickly detected by only looking at visual reports.
- Smart feedback — Learning systems should give students intelligent and immediate feedback on their inputs, improving student engagement and efficiency.
- Selection of courses — New courses for students based on students' desires defined by the study of their activities may be recommended. This means that students do not seek areas of interest in which they are not interested.
- Student Skills Assessment-Assessment of student abilities
- Identification of behavior of students in community-based activities or games which help to develop a student model
- Student grouping and collaboration
- Social network analysis
- Creation of concept maps
- Building of courseware
- Scheduling and Planning

6.2.4 Types of Big Data to Extract from Your LMS and How to Use It

Most LMS platforms now have strong reporting capabilities. However, to get the most out of your eLearning course, you need to know what data is worthy. This section highlights the types of big data you want to collect from your learning management system and provides advice on using this to boost your e-learning courses (Pappas, 2016).

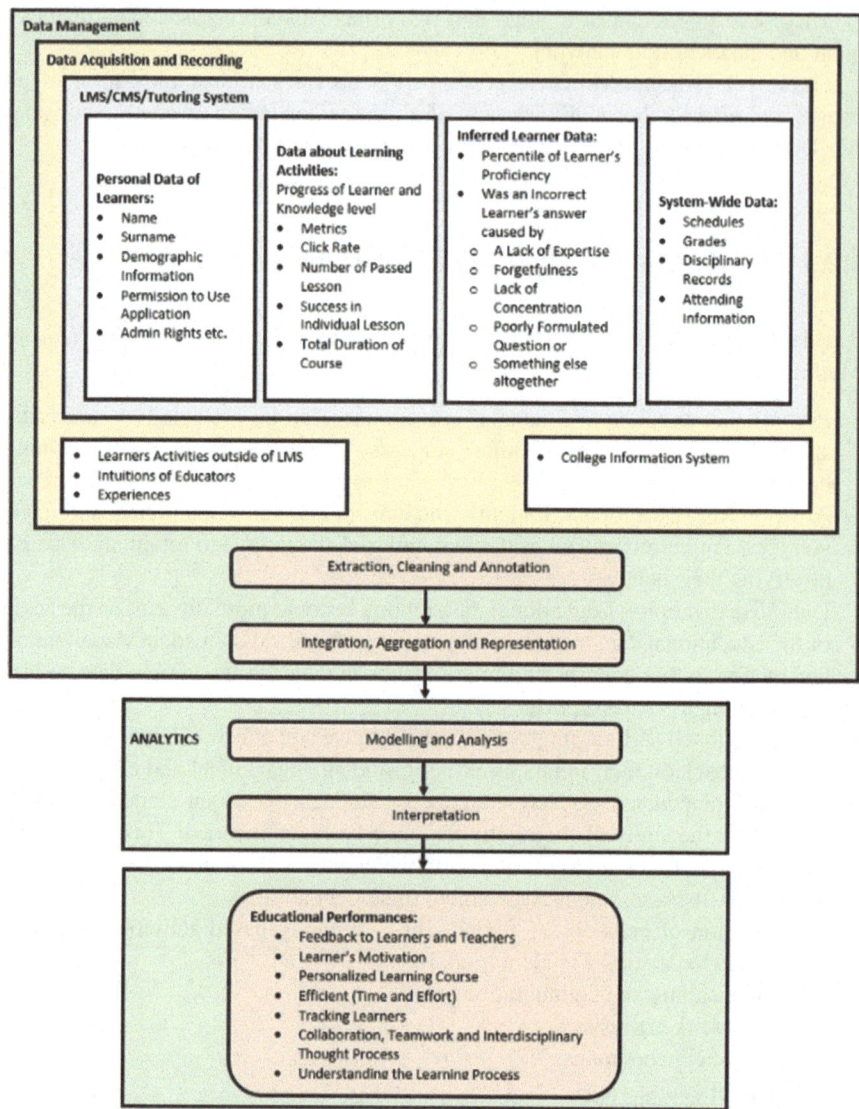

Fig. 6.7 Big data analytical platform in higher education (Klašnja-Milićević et al., 2017)

6.2.4.1 Types of Big Data to Extract

Big data is everywhere. From social media data to the monitoring of websites. However, not all numbers, diagrams, and percentages are equivalent. Only a few metrics matter where eLearning efficiency is concerned. The key is to know which data are valuable for you to use to establish actionable objectives. Below are the LMS Big Data that you can collect.

1. *Completion rates:* Are your online learners completing the eLearning course? How long does it take for each task or module to complete? LMS completion rates can answer these questions. Big Data also gives you a clear indication of eLearning effectiveness. For instance, if most online learners cannot take the eLearning course, the eLearning strategy will need to be reassessed.
2. *Performance and progress of online learners:* Are your online students going through the tasks? Or do they struggle with any elements of your eLearning course? Online student success and development assessments provide insight into learning habits, knowledge, and skills. This enables you to provide additional support and immediate personalized input when appropriate.
3. *eLearning Assessment Scores:* eLearning assessment evaluation scores give you measurable data to enhance your eLearning course design. A high percentage of grades demonstrate that your eLearning course is focused. The reverse is real, too. eLearning evaluation data also helps you define the strengths and limitations of online learners, building-specific learning pathways. For example, invite your online students to take a pre-evaluation before the eLearning course. Use your results to pick eLearning activities and modules that fulfill your requirements.
4. *Online student surveys:* Surveys are one of the most direct and observable ways of feedback from eLearning. Online students exchange truthful thoughts and feedback. You use this knowledge to create an action plan and update your eLearning template. Surveys also allow you to decide whether your eLearning course is important to your audience. Does it resonate with them, or do they find it hard to relate to your eLearning content?
5. *Feedback from peers:* This big data is harder to track. It provides a unique view of learning habits and results. eLearning sites, social media groups, collaborative projects for online groups, and online content created by learners are great peer-based feedback sources. You can go beyond LMS research to see how online students respond in social environments. However, through your LMS application, you can also perform surveys and polls to assess this useful data source.

6.2.4.2 How to Use LMS Big Data

Here we will see how to make good use of the extracted data.

1. ***Customize your approach to eLearning:*** Every piece of big data you collect helps you personalize your eLearning approach. Online student satisfaction ratings, completion times, and evaluation scores reveal strengths and improvement fields. As such, you have the opportunity to create the most valuable eLearning content. For instance, big data may reveal that there is no motivation for online learners. You can, therefore, include gaming elements to reward them and motivate them to succeed.
2. ***Identify Common Threads:*** Each graph, percentage, and feedback rating are only part of a larger whole. You will see trends and patterns that emerge when you piece them together. These are the usual threads running through your big data. They can help you identify faults in your eLearning strategy and the strong suits of your eLearning course. You may consider outsourcing if you do not have time to evaluate the data yourself. Several consulting companies can help you analyze your Big Data sources to detect significant trends.
3. ***Keep it focused:*** Sorting large amounts of Big Data can take time. You can, however, simplify the task by focusing on your goals and objectives. Which metrics are the most important? Moreover, what is the desired result? Concentrate at a time on one measurable learning goal and select only relevant data sources. For instance, overall course completion rates and online learner performance provide a complete picture but are not necessarily useful for individual assessments. To this end, you should review user progress reports to identify knowledge and performance deficiencies.
4. ***Create a plan for continuous improvement:*** Evaluation of the eLearning course is an ongoing process. As such, you need to evaluate your data regularly. Indeed, you might want to establish a timetable for how often you analyze your big data and incorporate your eLearning team. Delegate tasks and assign a metric to each member of your team. Make sure you keep your sensitive information safe. Use efficient encryption measures and give a selected group only access.
5. ***Choose Data-Rich LMS:*** LMS reports and analysis are some of the most suitable features. Identify your learning goals and objectives before you select your next learning management system to satisfy your needs. Some learning management systems, for example, have customizable metrics. This enables you to monitor training initiatives that meet your business needs and learning gaps. Take advantage of testing the reporting tools "before you buy."
6. ***Big data mining and management take time, planning, and resources:*** All your efforts, however, are rewarded through eLearning personalization and more efficient eLearning courses. In particular, if you have a robust LMS with visualizing tools to identify the shortcomings and take advantage of your eLearning data.

6.2.5 The Value of Big Data and Analytics for Higher Education

Big data provides new resources and new responsibilities for higher education institutions. Siemens and Long (Long & Siemens, 2011) reported that big data is the most widely studied method for managing massive data collection and supporting higher education.

The following are different ways of generating value for Higher Education for Big Data and analytics (Long & Siemens, 2011):

- Strategic decision making and organizational distribution of resources can be strengthened.
- You can identify at-risk students and intervene to help students achieve success. By reviewing posted conversation messages, assignments completed, and LMS messages like Moodle and Desire2Learn, educators will recognize students at risk of leaving.
- They will build a common view of the institution's achievements and challenges through open data and analysis.
- They can innovate and transform the system of college and university, academic and educational models.
- They can contribute to understanding complex issues by integrating social networks with computational networks and knowledge networks: algorithms can recognize and provide insight into data and problems at risk.
- They can help leaders' transition to holistic decision-making by analyzing scenarios and experimenting to explore how various elements connect in a complex discipline (e.g., retention of students, cost reduction) and explore the impact of changing core elements.
- You can enhance productivity and efficiency through up-to-date information and quick response to challenges.
- They can help institutional leaders establish the difficult (e.g., patents, research) and soft values generated by faculty activity (e.g., reputation, profile, teaching quality).
- They can give students insights into their learning practices and can recommend improvements. Learning-facing analytics, such as the University of Maryland, Baltimore County (UMBC) Check My activity tool, allow students to compare their activity against an anonymous summary of their fellow students.

6.2.6 Benefits of Big Data and Learning Analytics

Big data means exploring a wide variety of organizational and efficient data, gathering procedures to forecast institutional output, optimizing future outcomes, and understanding potential learning, education, and research-related issues (Hrabowski

& Suess, 2010). Also, some researchers suggested that the analytical method must be included in the framework to maximize efficiency. Several useful data features are expected in the short term to promote education (Klašnja-Milićević et al., 2017).

1. ***Reviews:*** Response information and interpretation of the context can be useful for big learning data. Learner sometimes fails in a subject but does not know why he(s) fails. It becomes worthwhile if the student looks at himself and those who have had the same experience. He or she can obtain an insight that would either explain it so that he or she is not hindered or that he or she can use it to fix it so that he or she can again succeed. The development of electronic learning modules facilitates a rational, real-time assessment of learners. Technology for data mining and data analytics will provide learners and teachers with direct feedback on educational success. This method will examine simple trends to predict learner outcomes such as dropping out, requiring additional assistance, or performing more challenging tasks. Pedagogical approaches for individual learners that seem most successful can be described.
2. ***Inspiration:*** If big data is implemented adequately, students will commit themselves to enter data because they understand how it works.
3. ***Tracking:*** To better understand students' actual habits, teachers can use big data to track a learner's experience in an e-learning course. Students are delayed as they follow the automated routes. Teachers will track the passage of learners during the entire learning process.
4. **Collaboration:** Experts from several fields must work together to ensure the Learning Management System's best operation. This facilitates collaboration, coordination, and interdisciplinary processes of thought.
5. ***Performance:*** Big data will save time and effort for several hours while trying to achieve our goals and strategies.
6. ***Customization:*** Big data can effectively approach e-learning by enabling designers to personalize courses and suit their students' individual needs. E-learning developers would also be able to establish the standard for successful and excellent e-learning courses.
7. ***Understanding the method of learning.*** By using large-scale data in e-learning, teachers may see which parts of a course or test were too basic and which sections were too difficult to solve. Other areas of the process of learners can then be studied and pages, which are often reintroduced, favorite modes of learning, recommended sections to peers, and the time of day when learning works as well as possible.

6.2.7 The Challenges of Implementation Big Data Techniques in Higher Education

Regardless of the rapid growth of applications to facilitate the introduction of Big Data technology in higher learning, a range of considerations are still required (Klašnja-Milićević et al., 2017). During the collection of data for analytics, Becker (2013) suggested three cooperation elements: timing, population, and location. Any time unit between the second and a half of the year can be described as a temporal feature. The characteristics of the community of students in the learning environments apply to the population. The location can be defined according to the learning space where students retrieve the information.

Some researchers have been recognized as significant in the critical analysis of resources and knowledge by students. Drive your learning effectively in an open networked online world. Innovative facilities and a positive attitude in an evolving and dynamic world were also illustrated (Downes, 2009; Sahlberg, 2009).

Financial investment may be one of the key challenges of applying big data analytics in higher education (Campbell, DeBlois, & Oblinger, 2007). Many institutions treat analytics rather than investment as a costly endeavor. Most of the affordability concerns the suspected criteria for costly data collection methods.

More investment is required in analytics practitioners who are qualified to use Big Data and analytics properly. They should track the entire process from the definition of important questions to creating data modeling to warnings, recommendations, and reports. Furthermore, we need expert designers and professional database managers to carry out storage and integrate data across various files and formats (Campbell et al., 2007). In addition to the skills necessary for database creation, instructional designers working with the university must consider the student behaviors relevant to their application. Great knowledge of statistics, decision trees, and strategy mapping are also important for developing a prediction model algorithm.

In implementing big data in education, the key problems can be found relating to data profiling, privacy, and pupils' rights to their behavior recording (Boyd, 2010). Even though the conventional class approach often tests learners' success and academic behavior, learning analytics is useful in a radically different level and scale method to monitor students' attitudes, which should be evaluated. Although learning analytics can be useful concerning learners' progress, the big data methodology can also be seen as an offensive to privacy that some learners would prefer not to press forward. For starters, some important questions need to be taken into account (Picciano, 2012): should students be told that they are performing their activities? How much information is required for teachers, students, parents, scholarships, and other issuers? How should competent affiliates respond? Do students need to seek support? Protection should be taken to ensure that well-known sets of learner transaction personal data are not hurt in a way that would harm people.

The masking of data at its source may help address these issues (Barlow, 2013). Masking is an innovative approach that enables big data applications while maintaining information integrity for students and teachers. New performance and competencies for ETL application software allow masking of sensitive data at the database level when putting in a data warehouse. It can be inferred that even though someone has access to the database physically, confidential details such as social security numbers would still be confused.

6.3 Data Science & Learning Analytics

6.3.1 Data Science in Education

Data scientists have discovered many innovative applications of data science in education by collecting various educational data. Big data analysis can also help the education industry address its challenges by recognizing the various types of students.

Schools, colleges, and universities have many student data to manage, for example, academic records, outcomes, degrees, personal preferences, cultural values, etc. Analysis of these data will allow you to identify innovative approaches to enhance learning for students.

Modern Data Science tools will make the education sector a huge profit. For this reason, various machine learning algorithms, such as random forests, logistic regression, decision trees, support vector machines, etc.

However, in education, there are still not many applications for data science. However, there are still several unknown data science cases that may contribute to the growth of education. A list of the advantages of Data Science in Education (TechVidvan Team, 2020) is available here.

1. ***Enhance adaptive learning:*** The student is unique to himself and has a different way of learning. Therefore, it is a very challenging job for educational organizations to choose the best means of transitioning to the classroom for all students. Today, big data and data science can help teachers use adaptive techniques in learning. Big data will allow teachers to discover students' abilities and to use them for effective teaching.
2. ***Better Parent Participation:*** Teachers may use various student data and use different analytical approaches to assess students' results. This helps educate parents about concerns that may impact their children's success in various fields such as education, sports, etc. This information can help parents keep an eye on the activities of their children. The analysis makes parents and institutions take numerous steps to improve the students' educational system's learning environment.
3. ***A good assessment of teachers:*** Data science in education allows administrators to keep an eye on teachers' practices and instructional strategies. This allows them to determine the most effective methods of teaching. The data can be analyzed in various ways to gather meaningful insights into teachers' strong and

weak areas. This helps them to improve. Analysis of the data from the attendance records, performance, reviews, etc. may be carried out.

4. ***Improve the success of students:*** Data Science in Education lets you centrally monitor the full student data to assess students' success and take effective action. This analysis will allow you to make improvements that support the students and help them overcome their problems in every way possible. For example, if a student's performance is deficient every day, Big Data and Data Science in Education can help teachers identify why and help him overcome his problems. Data science in education can help educational institutions increase student success by evaluating where they lack commitment and developing to produce better outcomes for their students.

5. ***Better Organization:*** The various data science techniques will help schools, colleges, and universities better prepare and coordinate their activities from an organizational perspective. Better organizations can also assist them in making certain crucial business decisions. The numerous data science tools will assist educational organizations in shaping their strategies.

6. ***Regular updates in the curriculum:*** Education is a large area that evolves only over time. The different educational institutions' main objective is to train their students for this competitive era's challenges. To that end, they have to keep up to date with the market requirements to create a better and efficient curriculum for their students. Therefore, educational organizations turn to data science to gain insights into the data and forecast future market trends and demand to provide the students with the necessary knowledge.

7. ***Recruitment of students:*** The Educational Institutes will use the student data to identify educational programs that are ideal for drawing many students to their institutes. Data scientists will help institutions recognize the needs of students and have the best services possible.

6.3.2 What Data Science Do with Learning Analytics

Advances in Big Data, Analytics, and Data Science, along with the vast computer processing capacity and cloud effectiveness, have provided us with great resources to push our organizations' talent development strategies to the next level. The journey starts with understanding what we want and adopting the necessary methods and instruments for achieving these objectives (Roy & Sur, 2015). Learning analytics allows future-oriented learning organizations to adapt to their talent growth activities.

1. ***Getting proactive with Learning Metrics:*** Learning analytics is essentially a starting point for an impact study of learning. Effect analysis findings "after the fact" also enable practitioners to work on measures to illustrate talent acquisition programs' market impact.

Learning analytics does more than just a pretty bow on a metric box. It goes beyond conventional impact metrics to consider the power of data in the entire process of talent creation to address crucial questions:

- Why do we need this program?
- Who needs to do what differently?
- How are we going to get them to the new performance?
- What content will drive KPIs?
- How can the impact be predicted?
- What was the impact effect, and what is next?

Through the talent acquisition process (analyzing, planning, creating, implementing, and assessing) and a new phase (define), we will gain information-driven insights into these critical issues that help learn executives produce improved and targeted business results. However, if we struggle to address the ongoing complexities of 'after-the-fact' effect analysis, practitioners will probably hurry back into tablets and surveys — those common yet insight-proof methods for monitoring outcomes.

This is why proactive metrics design is so important to every learning analytics initiative. The metrics definition sets the stage for the reasons for strategic learning programs.

2. *Incorporating learning analytics to improve outcomes:* The incorporation of learning analytics into talent growth ensures that insights are not only operable

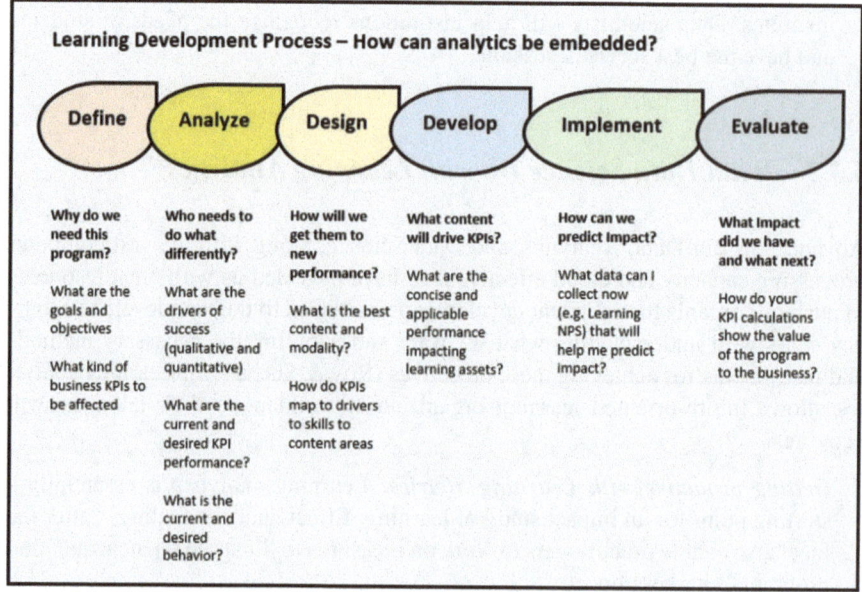

Fig. 6.8 Learning development process (Roy & Sur, 2015)

but observable. This involves calculating productivity from the viewpoint of an individual, consumer, and revenue.

As a pioneer in talent growth, the number of training hours produced is increasingly declining. Very soon, you will be able to assess the outcomes of your organizational growth by gaining input from each step of your talent development process and each learner in your programs. Figure 6.8 shows a common learning development process.

3. **Leading with Learning Analytics:** From the corner office to the back office, analytics will have, explain, and show the business value of learning techniques and programs. It is important for today's talent acquisition managers to keep up with the market by using big data to discover and solve challenges and achieve results. These managers can deliver highly customized services, which minimize costs and improve retention by using talent analytics.

6.3.3 Incorporating Data Science in Learning

The learning process in the modern education system is continuously evolving. The method is changing with data science implementation, which regulates the technical component of student awareness. By developing programming skills and techniques, knowledge has been moved to secure data platforms. (Analytics Insight, 2019) addresses the importance of applying data science in the advancement of the education system.

1. *Used to track students' special requirements:* The learning institutions are used to evaluate and analyze students using various data information science techniques. However, these were obsolete technical means that had little impact and failed to summarize all the basic trends and patterns of services widely used by students. Also, most of the methods used in student assessment were not successful.

   However, learning analytics has allowed lecturers and teachers to assess students' expectations based on performance and results assessments. In return, teacher supervision has allowed teachers to respond adequately to the anticipated need by modifying teaching methods.

   Teachers may also have an implicit prejudice against a certain number of students. However, the knowledge gained treats students with zero prejudice, which ensures that students' assessment is true and does not intervene. This provides all students with equal opportunities to learn and develop their skills.

2. *Innovations in curriculum:* Innovations in the learning sector have increased, particularly in colleges and universities. Many institutions are not up to date with these developments and have to update data science findings. It also helps to offer suitable subject courses to students.

Universities can use statistical data science to track measures to evaluate trends in the learning field. The findings allow the designers of the course to take inactive subjects. Apply predictive information analytics methods, evaluate the need for new skills, and curate relevant courses that resolve them.

3. ***Measure their instructors' efficiency:*** The success of a student depends on how the teachers teach. Many educational institutions use manual and obsolete methods of measuring the success of their teachers. For example, a student evaluation has been used to assess a teacher's teaching technique's success. However, these approaches are not effective and require time to test. However, many student reviews are a tedious task that takes longer to find a substantial assessment.

    Well, data science enables organizations to track the success of their teachers at all times. Therefore, the evaluation of school teachers using real-time information provides a detailed overview of the job results. It is also the extended use of children writing essay articles, which are later used to assess a teacher's success.

    Also, the learning institution should do the following:

    - Record accurate teacher evaluation data
    - Unstructured data storage and management
    - Analyze multiple sentiments of reviews

4. ***Significant social skills development:*** Social and cognitive skills are necessary and must be improved through education. The explanation is that a child knows how to perceive, communicate, control, and evaluate emotions. The child also appreciates the establishment of important connections with other students. This is an outstanding example of non-educational skills that play a vital role in assessing a child's learning capabilities.

In recent years, observational studies have been carried out on data used to assess the infant's social and emotional abilities. Nevertheless, organizations can now obtain information in vast amounts through advances in computer methods. The systematic knowledge of data science models and key technologies enables more comprehensive data to be collected and integrated into optimizing performance tools.

The development of data science analytics has introduced valuable techniques to many organizations. When combined, data scientists may use the derived data with analytical methods and help teachers support children.

6.4 AI & Learning Analytics

Artificial intelligence (AI) has been around for some time, along with machine learning and big data. It has influenced companies and productive industries, but its applications in the classroom and on campus have recently begun to be understood.

6.4.1 How Artificial Intelligence Helps Higher Education Management

This section gives some artificial intelligence trends that will revolutionize the management of educational resources (Sagenmüller, 2020).

1. ***Improved Student experience and services:*** According to University Business, AI can support collaboration across the classroom and in the field of higher education management. The software has expanded to include administrators and educators, and artificial intelligence is being expanded into student services, for example. The Stanford University reports showed that there are projects aimed at "model common student misconceptions, predict which students are at risk of failure, and provide real-time student feedback that is tightly integrated with learning outcomes." Rose Luckin, chair of learning with digital technologies at the UCL Institute of Education, cited the case of the University of Derby, where the student monitoring system "uses data to predict which students may be at risk of dropping out and allowing the university to intervene before that occurs." The team discusses how often students have access to and interaction with student society mentoring and counseling services. "By using these 'engagement analytics,' they can assess whether a particular student appears to be struggling."
2. ***Student Learning Analytics:*** "Artificial intelligence could play a role in the growing field of learning analytics, evaluating the quality of curricular materials, and in adaptive learning and recommendation engines," says Barbara Kurshan, a Forbes contributor. She highlights one area to bring "the vast amount of data on individual learning, social contexts, learning contexts, and personal interests together." Rose Luckin says that "there has been an enormous rise in the amount of educational data about students that are available to universities." She mentions how universities are grasping data patterns about student activity, "that are routinely recorded and analyzed by universities." The Stanford University study notes that data sets collected from large scale online learning systems "have fueled the rapid growth of the field of learning analytics. Online courses are not only good for widespread delivery but are natural vehicles for data collection and experimental instrumentation that will contribute to scientific findings and improving the quality of learning at scale." In fact, according to Chris Parr, another contributor to Times Higher Education, "Universities mine institutional data in search of gold," as the analysis of information on staff and students can help to improve recruitment and retention. He claims that universities "risk losing their competitive edge" if the information they receive from students and lecturers is not best used.
3. ***Management and organization:*** Accenture researchers Vegard Kolbjørnsrud, Richard Amico, and Robert J. Thomas, after surveying 1770 managers responsible for digital transformation, will tell the Harvard Business Review of how AI will redefine management.

Simply, "artificial intelligence will soon be able to do the administrative tasks that consume much of managers' time faster, better, and at a lower cost." But how?

- ***Delegate administrative coordination and control:*** It takes over half the time for the managers, and Artificial Intelligence will automate many of these tasks.
- ***Supporting complex decisions:*** Machine learning technologies enable machines to learn to support instead of replacing managers.
- ***Obtaining a second opinion:*** Sounding farcical, but managers will, in the future, engage in informed conversations and discussions with their computers. HBR experts say that smart machines can assist "in decision support and data-driven simulations as well as search and discovery activities."
- ***Help design new solutions:*** The application of artificial intelligence can both reduce paperwork and broaden the range of options that managers may have to develop training programs or mixed courses, as manager designers "embed design thinking into the practices of their teams and organizations."
- ***Task assignment:*** The Stanford University report goes beyond artificial intelligence applications in classrooms, highlights the use of data science to create predictive models to prioritize public policy and undertake complicated task assignments, scheduling, and planning techniques.

6.4.2 AI Is Advancing the Capabilities of Learning Analytics

"Learning analytics involves the measurement, collection, analysis, and reporting of data about learners and the contexts in which learning takes place, to improve the teaching and learning environment." AI allows learning analytics to review (North Nord, n.d.):

- What is happening (descriptive)
- why it is happening (diagnostic)
- predictive (what will happen), and
- prescriptive (what needs to happen)

Learning analytics refers to various information fields, including sociology, psychology, ethics, pedagogy, etc. The digital revolution is now possible to gather much data that can be analyzed to gain insight or even create useful tools for educational or administrative tasks. It is not easy to evaluate and get the best out of the results. Advanced data processing methods are used to efficiently control vast volumes of data in other fields, such as statistics-driven big data applications, machine learning algorithms, learning from data, and visualization tools to interact effectively with those who eventually have to make decisions. These intelligent data processing software layers will allow us to gain insights, detect learning trends, forecast future situations, or provide recommendations for maximizing the available resources. The analysis is also a significant step towards developing future AI solutions that will allow us to build avatars, for example, with the help of powerful libraries, including natural language recognition, language translation, and game theory, which simulates the behavior of a virtual teacher for students or teachers' assistant. The bright prospects for the future allow us to imagine an AI ecosystem that can overcome the numerous learning analytics challenges (Pedró, Subosa, Rivas, & Valverde, 2019).

AI is likely to advance the capability of learning analytics, but such systems need vast volumes of data, including sensitive student and faculty information, posing significant data security and privacy concerns. AI can provide just-in-time feedback and assessment. The development of AIEd (Artificial Intelligence in Education) and the availability of big student data AIEd can be integrated into learning activities for ongoing student performance analysis. Algorithms are used to assess if a student fails in an assignment or leaves a course with a high degree of precision (Zawacki-richter, Marín, & Bond, 2019).

Computer-based learning environments often capture large amounts of data on how students interact with these systems and how they perform. The data may include basic data such as the time spent in the virtual environment or the learning method, or the time spent performing tasks. Enhanced data on task success can also be given. These are typically digital data and contain text, images, and videos; all these data are also temporal. In individual learning sessions, they capture users' experiences and often include a long-term view of a student's learning experience. These data features are related to big data (Tsai et al., 2015). Data obtained during learner contact with an education system was analyzed in the field of learning analytics. The analyses of learning data can provide insights into all areas of AI application within education that can help inform the allocation of resources and enhance the learning experience for students (Long & Siemens, 2011). For example, the feedback from an automated AI-powered analysis of data collected from smart classroom sensors and other data sources can be used by individual students and teachers to focus on their learning processes and progress. Learning analytics leverages human judgment and uses automated data processing to enable this, likely using AI approaches. Learning analytics aims to acquire insights from educational experiences and be used by people to make informed choices (Southgate & Smithers, 2019).

Big data obtained from ITS or learning management systems may provide insights into how individual learning unfolds over time and under which teaching methods are successful. This data can be analyzed only through learning analytics and training approaches to data mining allowed by certain forms of AI systems using techniques like evolutionary computation and artificial neural networks (Southgate & Smithers, 2019).

AI systems need access to vast quantities of data, including confidential students and faculty personal information, depending on the application. Its use, therefore, raises several concerns about ethics, morality, and privacy that must be addressed (North Nord, n.d.). These include data protection, personal data consent, data access, possible misdiagnosis of student learning, potential failure to guide students, latent biases, and stereotyping in AI algorithms.

Besides answering the above issues of ethics, morality, and privacy, organizations that seek to incorporate and improve AI systems face several challenges. Questions include (North Nord, n.d.)

- Who is going to lead the AI initiative and champion it?
- Who will be responsible for AI policy and procedure implementation and monitoring?
- What role will the faculty play in the design and implementation of systems?
- Who recognizes the assumptions implicit in designing AI algorithms other than system developers?
- What are the ethical ramifications of incorrect diagnosis or advising for students?
- How can professional support staff be trained and retained?

Although teaching, learning, and student advising in higher education are the main AI applications, this technology reaches many other academic life areas. These tasks include the transformation of libraries, student communication, academic research, textbooks development, and external outreach.

While there are many unanswered questions about the position and management of AI, there is little doubt that technology is inexorably connected to the future of higher education. More programs and courses include AI and related topics, and current curricula will be updated to provide students with the skills required in a world where many jobs will be done by machines and new professions arise.

6.5 Machine Learning & Learning Analytics

In a wide variety of fields, machine learning techniques are used. Machine learning has the potential to have a huge effect on education. Machine learning uses mathematical methods to "learn" machines without being explicitly programmed. Machine learning is used in learning analytics and artificial intelligence in the education area. The best thing possible in education with machine learning and data science is that it will have a huge effect on student achievement and help close achievement gaps (Huebner, 2019).

"Learning analytics is the process of collecting, measuring, and using data about learners to build profiles and analyze student behavior." Machine learning algorithms are used to build such profiles and then design each student's learning paths. This method is referred to as adaptive learning. Each student can learn and work at their own pace through the content. These guidelines and routes of learning are focused on past achievements or failures. Teachers will then use this knowledge to adjust how the content is presented. In the classroom, learning analytics will collect attendance and performance data and then provide individual feedback about achievement.

Over the last few years, the use of AI and chatbots or "bots" to personalize the learning experience has increased. "Snatchbot" allows a bot to be programmed by teachers and administrators based on unique classroom specifications. They can be used as complements to the classroom to provide material for each student's needs. The use of bots will help ensure that everybody is interested in the learning process. Some teachers will perform quizzes, surveys, polls, games, and even aid students with English or mathematical problems. The bots also teach students different topics, from health and nutrition to banking and finance.

Machine learning, such as learning analytics, can also help increase the retention rate. By recognizing students "at risk," schools will reach and provide them with the support they need to excel (Lynch, 2018).

6.6 Deep Learning & Learning Analytics

Deep learning is a feature of machine learning focused on data representations. This learning can be unsupervised, supervised, and/or semi-supervised (Du & Swamy, 2014; Chapelle, Schölkopf, & Zien, 2006; Lecun, Bengio, & Hinton, 2015; Zhu & Goldberg, 2009). In other words, every deep learning model learns from experience with minimal external intervention. A computer model is generated in a typical deep learning system that can accomplish the classification task based on input images, audio, and videos. These models' training includes a deep neural network architecture and large labeled data sets (Du & Swamy, 2014; Chapelle et al., 2006). Figures 6.1 and 6.2 show the traditional machine learning methods and deep learning for the classification task, respectively (Ahad, Tripathi, & Agarwal, 2018).

Learning Analytics, which can be subdivided into the analysis of structured data (i.e., search/analyze data, for example, click streams) and unstructured data (i.e., data such as text is more difficult to manage/analyze), can also employ Machine Learning (ML) or Deep Learning (i.e., for analysis of 'more nuanced and complex behavior than machine learning offers today') (Ahad et al., 2018).

A 'data-connected' institution with real-time machine learning and/or profound learning capabilities is built to enhance learning analytics. Data sources may be rather diverse, but privacy and ethics must be carefully examined (Ahad et al., 2018).

6.7 Case Studies

6.7.1 Data Science Case Study: Georgia State University

Georgia State University (GSU) has employed various data science and machine learning tools for student data mining. This allows them to monitor courses in which the students' performance was not adequate. It contributes to implementing a backup program to fix the reason behind this to enhance student results.

They made remarkable decisions based on their analysis and found that their graduation rate between 2003 and 2014 increased from 32% to 54%. They have used student data to deal with the retention and completion of the course (TechVidvan Team, 2020).

6.7.2 Data Science Case Study: Arizona State University

Another example is the Arizona State University (ASU), one of the USA's leading universities. The Mathematics Department of ASU has developed an "Adaptive Learning" method based on student data analysis. Such that they may take effective steps to boost student results.

The system developed collected data on students, including their scores, strengths, weaknesses, cultural fields of interest, and scenarios (TechVidvan Team, 2020).

6.7.3 The University of Florida: Using Big Data Analytics to Mitigate Student Dropout

A college education is viewed as a key to a successful life. Many students enroll in universities in the expectation of a future. However, due to academic or financial difficulties, many students drop out. According to a study, in the United States, at least 54.8% of incoming students will not be able to graduate within 6 years. This incredible percentage means that industry has restricted access to qualified individuals. This will also hinder domestic development.

To solve this threatening issue, educational institutions look to data science. The University of Florida is one such institute. IBM InfoSphere is used by the University to collect, load, and transfer data from various resources. The IBM SPSS Modeler is also used for statistical analysis and data processing. The IBM Cognos Analytics (DataFlair Team, 2019) aligns these two systems.

IBM Cognos is a powerful web-based business intelligence tool that provides different reporting tools, analyzes, and monitors events through interactive viewing. The University evaluated and forecast student success using IBM Cognos Analytics. They use different variables such as students' history, age, high school grades, and economic context to determine the students' likelihood of falling. It would also allow the university to formulate its strategy and provide early support for students who are about to drop out.

6.8 Conclusion

This chapter mentioned Big Data Analytics, data science, AI, ML & DL, and how these techniques can be used to expand educational system capabilities. The value of each Learning Analytics methodology for reforming higher education practices and helping instructors improve teaching and learning has been highlighted. Different advantages and obstacles are considered. The topics discussed in this chapter will facilitate the discussion on developing effective systems of learning, based on advanced techniques for learners, teachers, curriculum designers, and institutions.

6.9 Review Questions

Reflect on the concepts of this chapter guided by the following questions.

1. Explain the differences between Artificial Intelligence, Machine Learning, and Depp Learning.
2. Define Big Data. Explain the various applications of Big Data in Learning Analytics.
3. What type of Big Data do you extract from an LMS? Illustrate how you use that data.
4. What is the need for associate Beg Data with Learning Analytics? Explain.
5. What are the various challenges of implementing Big Data techniques in Higher Education?
6. List out the various advantages of Data Science in Education.
7. How to incorporate Data Science with Learning Analytics. What Data Science do with Learning Analytics.
8. How Artificial Intelligence helps Higher Education Management?
9. Explain the role of Machine Learning & Deep Learning in Learning Analytics?
10. Describe some of the evidence of Big Data Analytics/Data Science/ML/DL for Learning Analytics.

References

Ahad, M. A., Tripathi, G., & Agarwal, P. (2018). Learning analytics for IoE based educational model using deep learning techniques: Architecture, challenges and applications. *Smart Learning Environments*, 5(1). https://doi.org/10.1186/s40561-018-0057-y.

Analytics Insight. (2019). *The importance of incorporating data science in learning for students*.

Barlow, M. (2013). Real-time big data analytics: Emerging architecture. In *O'Reilly* (Vol. 53, Issue 9). https://doi.org/10.1017/CBO9781107415324.004.

Becker, B. (2013). Learning analytics: Insights into the natural learning behavior of our students. *Behavioral and Social Sciences Librarian, 32*(1), 63–67. https://doi.org/10.1080/01639269.2 013.751804

Berkeley. (2018). *What is data science?* https://doi.org/10.7551/mitpress/11140.003.0005.

Boisseau, J., & Wilson, L. (2019). *Enterprise AI: Data analytics, data science and machine learning*. CIO. https://www.cio.com/article/3342421/enterprise-ai-data-analytics-data-science-and-machine-learning.html#:~:text=Data science is the cutting,established approaches to scientific investigation.

Boyd, D. (2010). Privacy and publicity in the context of big data. *Interpretation: A Journal of Bible and Theology*, 1–11.

Campbell, J. P., DeBlois, P. B., & Oblinger, D. G. (2007). Academic analytics: A new tool for a new era. In *EDUCAUSE review* (Vol. 42, Issue 4). Educause Review.

Castrounis, A. (2020). *What is data science? What is a data scientist? What is analytics?* InnoArchiTech. https://datajobs.com/what-is-data-science

Chapelle, O., Schölkopf, B., & Zien, A. (2006). Deep semi-supervised learning. In *Proceedings – International conference on pattern recognition* (Vol. 2018-Augus). https://doi.org/10.1109/ICPR.2018.8546327.

DataFlair Team. (2019). *Data science in education – The modern way of learning [case study] applications of data science in education*. DataFlair. https://data-flair.training/blogs/data-science-in-education/

Downes, S. (2009). New tools for personal learning. *MEFANET 2009 Conference*. http://www.downes.ca/presentation/234

Dremio. (2020). *What is data engineering?* https://doi.org/10.4324/9780429061219-2.

Du, K. L., & Swamy, M. N. S. (2014). Neural networks and statistical learning. In *Neural networks and statistical learning* (Vol. 9781447155, Issue January). https://doi.org/10.1007/978-1-4471-5571-3.

Eze, K. (2018). *The essence of data engineering*. June, 2–4.

Gartner. (2020). *Gartner glossary: Digitization*. https://www.gartner.com/en/information-technology/glossary/digitization

Heath, N. (2018). *What is AI? Everything you need to know about Artificial Intelligence*. ZDNet. https://www.zdnet.com/article/what-is-ai-everything-you-need-to-know-about-artificial-intelligence/

Hrabowski, F. A., & Suess, J. (2010). Reclaiming the Lead: Higher Education's Future and Implications for Technology

Huebner, R. (2019). *Applications of machine learning in education*. https://www.experfy.com/blog/applications-of-machine-learning-in-education

intellipaat. (2017). *What is data analytics? How does big data analytics make working so easy?* https://intellipaat.com/blog/what-is-data-analytics/

Kanth, R., Laakso, M. J., Nevalainen, P., & Heikkonen, J. (2018). Future educational technology with big data and learning analytics. *IEEE International Symposium on Industrial Electronics, 2018-June*(June), 906–910. https://doi.org/10.1109/ISIE.2018.8433753.

Kappagantula, S. (2019). *What is data analytics? Introduction to data analysis*. Edureka. https://doi.org/10.4324/9780429061219-5.

Kharkovyna, O. (2019). *Rolling in the deep learning: Basic concepts for everyone*. Towards Data Science. https://towardsdatascience.com/rolling-in-the-deep-learning-basic-concepts-for-everyone-84bdb4766d18

Klašnja-Milićević, A., Ivanović, M., & Budimac, Z. (2017). Data science in education: Big data and learning analytics. *Computer Applications in Engineering Education, 25*(6), 1066–1078. https://doi.org/10.1002/cae.21844

Labrinidis, A., & Jagadish, H. V. (2012). Challenges and opportunities with big data. *Proceedings of the VLDB Endowment*, 2032–2033. http://www.economist.com/blogs/dailychart/2011/11/big-

Lecun, Y., Bengio, Y., & Hinton, G. (2015). Deep learning. *Nature, 521*(7553), 436–444. https://doi.org/10.1038/nature14539

References

Long, P., & Siemens, G. (2011). Penetrating the Fog: Analytics in learning and education. *EDUCAUSE Review.*

Lynch, M. (2018). *8 Ways machine learning will improve education.* https://www.thetechedvocate.org/8-ways-machine-learning-will-improve-education/

Margaret, R. (2020). *Deep learning.*

Morrison, A. (2019). *Importance of data science.* ZARANtecH. https://www.zarantech.com/blog/importance-of-data-science/

North Nord. (n.d.). *Ten facts about artificial intelligence in teaching and learning.* Retrieved 6 July 2020, from https://teachonline.ca/sites/default/files/tools-trends/downloads/ten_facts_about_artificial_intelligence_0.pdf

Pappas, C. (2016). *5 Types of big data to extract from your LMS and how to use it – eLearning industry.* ELearning Industry. https://elearningindustry.com/types-big-data-extract-lms-how-use

Patel, N. (2018). *What are the top 10 areas for data analytics application.* https://www.datascience.us/what-are-the-top-10-areas-for-data-analytics-application/

Pedró, F., Subosa, M., & Rivas, A., Valverde, P. (2019). *Artificial intelligence in education: Challenges and opportunities for sustainable development.* https://unesdoc.unesco.org/ark:/48223/pf0000366994

Picciano, A. G. (2012). The evolution of big data and learning analytics in American higher education. *Journal of Asynchronous Learning Network, 16*(3), 9–20. https://doi.org/10.24059/olj.v16i3.267

Rai, A. (2020). *What is big data – Characteristics, types, benefits & examples.* UpGrad Blog. https://www.upgrad.com/blog/what-is-big-data-types-characteristics-benefits-and-examples/

Research Data Alliance. (2020). *Big data – Definition, importance, examples & tools.* https://www.rd-alliance.org/group/big-data-ig-data-development-ig/wiki/big-data-definition-importance-examples-tools

Rouse, M. (2019). *Deep learning.* SearchEnterpriseAI.Com. https://searchenterpriseai.techtarget.com/definition/deep-learning-deep-neural-network

Roy, K., & Sur, S. (2015). *Learning analytics: What does data science have to do with learning?* Association for Talent Development. https://doi.org/10.1080/00033790412331307653.

Sagenmüller, I. (2020). *How artificial intelligence helps higher education management.* U-Planner. https://www.u-planner.com/en-us/blog/artificial-intelligence-use-in-higher-education-management

Sahlberg, P. (2009). Creativity and innovation through lifelong learning. *Lifelong Learning in Europe, 1*, 53–60.

Sanders, J. (2016). Defining terms: Data, information and knowledge. *Proceedings of 2016 SAI Computing Conference, SAI 2016*, 223–228. https://doi.org/10.1109/SAI.2016.7555986.

SAS. (2018). *Artificial intelligence.* https://doi.org/10.3169/itej.72.235.

Shabbir, J., & Anwer, T. (2015). Artificial intelligence and its role in near future. *Journal of Latex Class Files, 14*(8), 1–11.

Simeone, O. (2018). *A brief introduction to machine learning for engineers* (Vol. 12, Issues 3–4). https://doi.org/10.1561/2000000102.

Sin, K., & Muthu, L. (2015). Application of big data in education data mining and learning analytics – A literature review. *ICTACT Journal on Soft Computing, 05*(04), 1035–1049. https://doi.org/10.21917/ijsc.2015.0145

Southgate, E., & Smithers, K. (2019). Artificial intelligence and emerging technologies in schools. It is a research report commissioned by the Australian Government Department of Education. August, 1–155.

TechVidvan Team. (2020). *Data science in education – A much-awaited revolution.* TechVidvan. https://techvidvan.com/tutorials/data-science-in-education/

Tsai, C. W., Lai, C. F., Chao, H. C., & Vasilakos, A. V. (2015). Big data analytics: A survey. *Journal of Big Data, 2*(1), 1–32. https://doi.org/10.1186/s40537-015-0030-3

van Barneveld, A., Arnold, K. E., & Campbell, J. P. (2012). Analytics in higher education: Establishing a common language. *EDUCASE Learning Initiative*, 1–11. https://doi.org/10.1111/j.1468-2273.2009.00438.x.

Weihs, C., & Ickstadt, K. (2018). Data science: The impact of statistics. *International Journal of Data Science and Analytics, 6*(3), 189–194. https://doi.org/10.1007/s41060-018-0102-5

Yupangco, J. (2017). *The reason you need big data to improve online learning.* ELearning Industry. https://elearningindustry.com/big-data-to-improve-online-learning-reason-need

Zawacki-richter, O., Marín, V. I., & Bond, M. (2019). Systematic review of research on artificial intelligence applications in higher education – Where are the educators? *International Journal of Educational Technology in Higher Education, 16*, 1–27.

Zhu, X., & Goldberg, A. B. (2009). Introduction to semi-supervised learning. In *Synthesis lectures on artificial intelligence and machine learning* (Vol. 6). https://doi.org/10.2200/S00196ED1V01Y200906AIM006.

Chapter 7
Learning Analytics in Massive Open Online Courses

7.1 Introduction to MOOCs

7.1.1 What Is MOOC?

MOOCs are Massive Open Online Courses (Fig. 7.1) built to accept an infinite number of registrations, facilitated fully online (Physiopedia, 2020).

Massive. since many participants often in thousands

Open. Since it takes place in a field that is open to all to read, reflect, and comment, it is accessible, and all people who take the course share material and work.

Online. Since the course is online.

Course. As it has course materials and facilitators, a start and finish date, and participants. This is an event about a subject that matters to people.

7.1.2 A Brief History of MOOCs

MOOC was coined in 2008 for an education entitled Connectivism and Connectivity Knowledge, created by Stephen Downes and George Siemens (McGill.CA, 2010). They wanted to make use of the possibility of interactions between many participants through online platforms to provide a richer learning experience than would be allowed by conventional tools. Twenty-five students attended a course by the University of Manitoba's campus, and an additional 2300 from around the world took part online. MOOCs based on interactions and connectivity is now known as cMOOCS.

In autumn 2011, Stanford offered three free online courses. Peter Norvig and Sebastien Thrun presented their Artificial Intelligence introduction for the initial

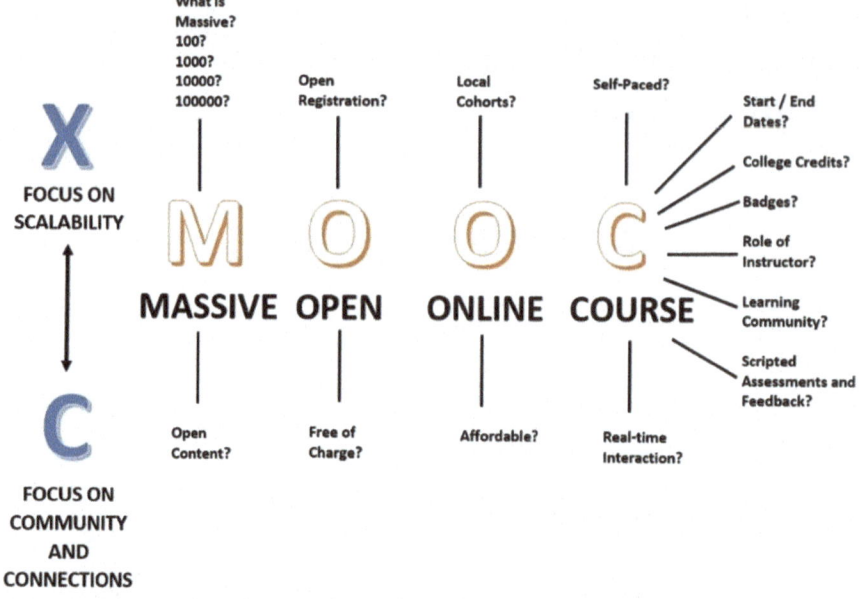

Fig. 7.1 Overview of MOOCs (Sidhartha, 2016)

registration of more than 160,000 students from around the world. More than 20,000 students completed the course. These xMOOCs concentrated less on student engagement and more on the possibility of reaching a broad audience.

In February 2012, Thrun founded a company known as Udacity (McGill.CA, 2010), which started creating and providing free MOOCs. In April 2012, the company named Coursera began with Andrew Ng and Daphne Koller, two other Stanford CS professors, who collaborated with universities in the planning and offering of MOOCs.

MIT developed MITx's MOOC platform, which was renamed edX when a partnership was formed with Harvard. There are currently over 30 university partners within the non-profit edX consortium that produces and provides MOOCs, including McGill. The project has made available an open-source platform that other organizations and individuals can use and create. The group also performs research on using emerging technology by evaluating the data it obtains from students. In reality, the consortium is the outcome of a previous MIT research project.

More than four million students have enrolled in Coursera MOOCs, and over a million students in their MOOCs have enrollment for Udacity and edX. Udacity collaborated with San Jose State to provide credit-free classes, which were low-cost and integrated MOOC resources with help from on-campus teachers and teaching assistants. Such success was indicated by Sebastian Thrun that there could be only ten institutions providing higher education in 50 years.

However, the experiment in San Jose State was less than successful, with the pass rates substantially lower in some courses than in conventional courses. Also, most

7.1 Introduction to MOOCs

MOOCs have a high dropout rate of over 90%. Thrun reported in November 2013 that Udacity has a "lousy commodity" and would reconsider vocational education. In comparison, Anant Agarwal, president of the edX consortium, emphasizes that MOOCs' availability benefits students and universities.

7.1.3 How Are MOOCs Different from Online College Courses?

A MOOC and an online college course have certain resemblances, but not the same. MOOCs vary in the following ways from online college courses (Fieland, 2020):

Similarities.

1. MOOCs are offered online.

2. The same professors who teach online college classes also teach MOOCs.

3. MOOC course materials are also the same as those for college students who study online.

4. Often, MOOCs are delivered in cooperation with universities and colleges.

5. Often, a collection of MOOCs may be provided for academic credit. However, in these circumstances, a student must be formally enrolled at a college or university and must pay tuition fees to gain academic MOOC credits.

6. MOOCs provide self-study, enabling students to complete classes and take tests on their schedule.

There are variations.

1. MOOCs are free of charge.

2. The class size of the MOOCs is infinite.

3. Anyone can join in a MOOC course even though there are not "qualified" to take it.

4. Students can always start and stop the course without any formal consequences.

5. After completing the course, a student may not have a certificate, diploma, or transcript of completion, visible or officially acknowledged.

7.1.4 Features of MOOCs

The features shared by most MOOCs are (Physiopedia, 2020):

- Participants are expected to be spread worldwide.
- The contents of the course are not contained in any location, but available across the web.
- One of the locations where the interactions occur with online classrooms includes blogs or portfolios, websites, social networking platforms, and more.
- During the course, participants and teachers compile, mix, and repurpose their content.
- Courses have no specific requirements, but participants must keep up-to-date on rough schedules.
- Most MOOCs are free; if the participant works for accreditation, there may be a fee.

7.1.5 Benefits of MOOCs to Participants

MOOCs provide participants with the following benefits (Physiopedia, 2020; Srikanth, 2017):

- MOOCs are free!
- Allow access to training and experience to which you would not have access otherwise.
- Ability to globally connect, interact, and learn with peers and colleagues.
- Build networks and links which can be established after the course is finished.
- Learn digital skills.
- Commitment to your lifelong learning (continuing education and career)

7.1.6 Benefits to Organizations Running the MOOC

MOOCs give organizations the following benefits (Physiopedia, 2020):

- Builds awareness, expertise, and culture around a subject globally.
- Promote your activities, courses, products, services, and skills.
- Advanced preparation for your students and staff.
- Training peers for possible potential hires.
- Access to those involved in research, training, etc.
- Meets the standards of corporate social responsibility.

7.1.7 Business Models Associated with MOOCs

As stated in the last section, the key advantages of operating a MOOC are often not financial. This did not, however, deter organizations aimed at developing more traditional MOOC models. MOOC's fundamental aspect is that students are free to access educational experiences, and educational institutions and suppliers of MOOC platforms are finding several alternative ways to generate revenue from MOOCs.

Approaches under consideration include (Physiopedia, 2020):

- Optional examination and credential fees
- Optional tuition fees for access to supplementary resources
- Costs for MOOC production, hosting, and distribution
- Sale of student data (e.g., to potential recruiting organizations)

7.1.8 Various MOOC Types

7.1.8.1 The Following Are the Various Categories of MOOCs (Physiopedia, 2020)

- xMOOC-The most common form of MOOC structured around the core curriculum and the central professor of predefined study materials.
- cMOOC- "Connectivity-MOOCs" look like seminar courses; course materials form part of student conversations, focused on student-to-student experiences, which are the center of learning.
- DOCC-Distributed Online Collaborative Courses are courses where students in multiple institutions access the same material, but their exact administration can differ. Students may also communicate with each other via the online component of institutions.
- BOOC-Big Open Online courses are close to MOOCs and limited to fewer than 50 students.
- SMOC-Synchronous Massive Online Courses differ from xMOOCs because the lectures are broadcast live so that students can log in or listen to the lectures at certain times.
- SPOC – Small Private Online Courses are similar to BOOCs because the classes are small, but instructor interactions are comparable to typical classroom interactions. SPOCs in the "flipped classroom" model are similarly referenced.
- Corporate MOOCs – MOOCs are usually subsidized or specially certified by employers, intended for employees' training or further education.

7.1.9 Advantages of MOOCs

Traditional MOOCs are free online university courses offered by universities worldwide that do not normally qualify for credit. They can register up to 100,000 + students, and anyone can register around the world. Usually, after registration, students work to monitor informative lectures, lessons, and exercises.

MOOCs offer numerous advantages that are worth learning. These are the benefits of MOOCs (Goldy-Brown, 2018).

1. Offer a range of subjects. College schedules are tight, so you may not be able to take every course you want. Your school may not even offer a subject that is of interest. MOOCs can assist in this. Search for interesting classes on one of the MOOC providers' websites. The topics cover yoga, personal finance, engineering, IT, composition, etc. In some cases, you can pay a college credit for your hard work. Check the transfer policy of your school before payment.
2. Let you test out your major before committing. The major you choose mostly influences the college you attend and your future career journey. High school students can complete a MOOC course to see if it is right. This risk-free, cash-free method will help you figure out what is important to choose and save you money. Starting with college knowledge means that you do not have to spend time between majors and pay for useless classes.
3. Before you enroll, familiarize yourself with college-level learning. Wondering whether a college education is right for you? With a MOOC, you will understand how high school classes are before you pay for them. The tests you take and your assignments give you an insight into what might appear in the next 4 years. Try a course at a college you plan to attend if possible.
4. Prepare yourself academically for college. Feeling unprepared for university? You are not alone. Many MOOCs are designed to fight against this unpreparedness. Some MOOCs for high school students include mathematics, composition in the first year, and precalculus. Talk to your guide or teachers to see the areas in which they recommend you to focus.
5. Learn from the world's peers. Anyone who has internet access from any country can take a MOOC class. Participants can communicate with each other via social networking and discussion threads. Like in a real classroom, you will learn from your peers and perhaps also broaden your view of the world.
6. They are open to all. One of the advantages of MOOCs is that MOOC learning will not require any prerequisite. You can register for any class regardless of background or age. Just be ready to make an effort.
7. MOOCs are available in various. Your courses are not limited to where you live. Enjoy courses taught without hesitation in foreign countries, thanks to subtitles. Subtitles make these courses also friendly for people who are deaf or hard to hear.

8. Learn a language for FREE. Rosetta Stone is expensive, and language classes in person may move too fast for you. MOOCs are a free way to learn your language. Return to lectures as required and take your time to learn rather than grapple with exams.
9. Provide FREE AP examination preparation and courses. The edX MOOC platform of Harvard and MIT provides FREE AP exam preparation and courses. Outside your high school classroom, you can learn confusing material at your own pace. These additional courses help you achieve high AP scores, which in turn give you college credit.
10. Help your college and applications for scholarship stand out. Anything you can do to show future admission counselors that you are serious about learning will help your application in high school. Knowledge gained from MOOCs also helps with department applications and interviews or interest-specific research applications. Furthermore, taking these massive open online courses demonstrates initiative and intellectual curiosity. Both of these are features of a successful student.
11. Boost your applications and prospects for your career. Employers look to their future employees for severe soft skills. More than others, some degree programs help students develop these skills—free online classes such as MOOCs help bridge the gap between college graduates and employees. EdX offers several free "soft skills" courses covering topics from teamwork to the public. This MOOC platform also offers certified paid professional programs.

7.1.10 Disadvantages of MOOCs

MOOCs also have the following disadvantages (Sidhartha, 2016):

1. MOOC offers all video lectures and slides and all associated reading resources. This offers students the opportunity not to gradually study the lectures, but the whole lecture in an entire day that does not lead to a profound understanding of the concepts.
2. Real-time question-answering is also not possible during the lectures.
3. Courses that require physical hands-on exposure (e.g., civil, mechanical, electric, etc.) are quite difficult to provide with MOOCs.
4. Effective assessment methods such as Q&A in classrooms, surprise questionnaires, and presentations are not possible.
5. There are no proper evaluation methods, as automatic machine evaluations and assessments are not effective. Peer evaluation sometimes discourages students, leading them to quit the course.
6. MOOC style of education gradually kills teacher and student care, empathy, and respect in the physical school. Only the virtual social community is increased.

7.1.11 MOOCs Pedagogy

Minimum academic support is sufficient to run a MOOC. The pedagogies that are important for MOOCs have been available for years in distance education, but they are now applied to fulfill many people's needs for a free course (Baturay, 2015). Until implementation, cMOOCs were focused on peer and socio-learning models, but the subsequent paradigm of XMOOC was focused on online learning management, including video lectures, evaluation, and messaging.

The latest courses are normally arranged weekly; students can access their sources. Some of these things include automated multi-choice quizzes, short videos, sharing of documents, and forums. Courses are based on a model of peer-learning, but the course is run by a professional. Besides asynchronous learning activities, there are synchronous learning opportunities (e.g., live seminars).

The first courses in the MOOCs contain recorded lectures, notes, and assignments that were previously released via the learning management system for campus students when the courses' layout is examined. These courses were developed over time in a video lecture format; more advanced videos with animations and simulations with their interactive characteristics are now published as MOOCs.

The majority of courses take the form of adult short learning courses, professional development, vocational students working with horses around the world, and mostly for places with no ready access to higher education institutions.

MOOCs focused on three fields of student engagement (Grainger, 2013):

- *Video lectures:* video lectures in MOOCs have different presentations, from speech heads to lecturers. Coursera provides subtitles (mainly English but other languages are introduced). The pace of the lecture videos is generally 5–10 minutes per video sample.
- *Assessment:* assignments are mainly assessed using: (a) automatically graded questions for multiple decisions or auto-graded assignments for programming, and (b) peer review assessments, where students evaluate themselves and grades based on a given rubric.
- *Forums:* forums where students answer questions posted by other students and are a significant tool for student interaction between course takers and instructors. Forums usually contain general conversation, topic-specific conversation, course input, and technical input.
- *Readings:* The majority of MOOCs do not require students to purchase books, and most readings are made available online or by trainers.
- *Live video sessions:* Live video sessions with a teacher are available as well as weekly seminars.
- *Activities:* There are several training exercises further to test their comprehension of the course's concepts.
- *Additional video resources*: scripted videos to better explain the scenes.
- *Social media:* students are encouraged to continue their talks on various social media sites such as Facebook.

7.2 From MOOCs to Learning Analytics

MOOCs and data analytics seem current to be the two most prominent trends in education technology. While the so-called "big data," in education, or "learning analytics," as it is often referred to (Siemens, 2013), is often accompanied by referrals to "disruptive innovation," (Yuan & Powell, 2013) it is also cited in lists of imminent trends in education (NMC Horizon Report, 2017). In other respects, the two developments together claim to "reverse engineer the human brain" rather optimistically (Rscapin, 2013). MOOCs and data analytics seem well suited; more data on behavior and activities by students indicate greater precision in prediction and customization, and the large numbers of enrollment in MOOCs (see (Jordan, 2014) would then deliver such a promise.

However, the connection between these apparent trends is much more profound and lies at the center of technology's main thrust in education. Like the MOOC, learning analytics promises a technological solution to the long-standing educational problems. Instead of web technology that is supposed to remove economic and geographic barriers to the elite educational institution, computational routines promise to reveal unprecedented insights into the learning process. In both these ideas, the invisibility of technology itself is common, and the emphasis is placed on the result instead of how it is produced. In view of MOOCs and data analytics, this emphasis means that we tend to see what is made visible by technology, not necessarily every aspect of the technology itself.

7.2.1 The 'Materiality' of the Video

The MOOC platforms' major providers, Coursera, edX, and Udacity, concentrate on the video presentation, a system that seems to provide a prominent window to prestigious. However, with all its visibility and supposed discovery in online education of "real humans," the video shows a remarkable disguise of the technologies that produce it.

The underlying technology needed to have a Harvard or Yale lecturer appear worldwide is not meant to be part of the MOOC story. The vast amounts of Internet infrastructure containing the video lecture or Software Codes and algorithms that make transportation possible should not be seen, experienced, or engaged. Indeed, we believe that the promotional narrative is uniform, accessible to anyone, and free of regional inconsistencies or local difficulties. Our focus should be on the lecture itself, and studies have indeed described the development of intimate relationships between students and their video-professors (Adams, Yin, Vargas Madriz, & Mullen, 2014). While this may indeed be of advantage to the learning process in some ways, it distracts attention from the contingent processes which produced video, which in itself is "just the visible surface of a large realm of software, a complex amalgam of data structures, algorithms, packages, and protocols" (Dodge, Kitchin, & Zook,

2009). Instead of just watching the video lecture, I think that you could gain important educational insights from looking around the surface.

An evident example could be the algorithms required to reproduce the video image. Nothing new suggests that coding is necessary so that "users" of technology can understand the software underpinning their digitally infused lives or videos that appear during the MOOC experiences. In the UK, coding is firmly on the political agenda and decisively on the national curriculum, Australia may follow suit. However, as Williamson clearly shows, it is not just coding that is important; it is the ideological assumptions that are already part of our teaching (Williamson, 2014). Code For Australia, this "functionalist and technician" (Williamson, 2014) thinks perfectly in its three-step process: (1) problem, (2) idea, and (3) solution. Therefore, to learn about the algorithms that can compress and decompress a MOOC video is bound up in a strong "solutionist" discourse which largely regards the world as complex conundrums, which computing provides a step-by-step solution for (Morozov, 2013). Why do we teach coding that old social issues or educational problems can be eradicated by a few algorithms and a user-friendly interface? To explore the significant benefits of learning to code, we need to ask why the technology industry is largely within a particular location with increasing claims of discriminatory work practices (Wadhwa, 2014), ageism (Scheiber, 2014), and social inequality (Gumbel, 2014). They are examples of the very actual material conditions below the slick façade of technology, such as video streaming, but they appear not to be worthy of inclusion in our education technology. Large data centers' power consumption and their significant local pollution role are a further striking example (Glanz, 2012).

Although this is not solely or directly related to MOOCs, it is precisely that type of material and reality required for a renowned professor's image to be broadcast worldwide. Far from being a benign "cloud," servers needed for global education projects like the MOOC require real locations, physical store records, and huge amounts of power, but video technology does not "reveal" any of these materials. Besides providing free, online educational content, we must also consider the hardware infrastructures that support and enable such broadcasts; what kind of access they offer locally.

The vital point in this regard is, of course not that talk on "Modern and Contemporary American Poetry" should somehow address the environmental problems raised by data storage or, indeed, the morality of Silicon Valley, instead highlighting our cultural insights into technology and how it can limit our understanding of the complexity of education. Digital "tools" may be integral to many educational tasks, but how should the pedagogy focus on the instruments themselves as a way to foster curiosity and critical awareness? We want an educational system in which students use digital tools but did not think of how these tools were developed and produced or how they were influencing or limiting the kind of tasks they could perform? The content of a video lecture is important for both educators and students, but the complex factors comprising digital video itself, as a material object, are also worthy of consideration, not only the images on the screen.

7.2.2 What Does that Have to Do with Learning Analytics?

The video lecture's analogy is significant since it points to the propensity to concentrate on the surface's image and ignore its processes. Here, the concentration on visualization is an aspect of the data analytics process that seems important to the emerging field. Like the MOOC video, "visualizations, diagrams, charts, tables, infographics and other forms of representation …make education intelligible to a wide variety of audiences" (Williamson, 2014). In reality, learning analytics continues with the visual metaphor, which is considered "essential for penetrating the fog that has settled over much of higher education" (Long & Siemens, 2014). However, this tendency to interpret educational data and the presumed validity of "seeing" user behavior must be treated carefully. The explanation is that a graphical representation not only distracts attention from algorithms that have gathered data and analyzed it often tends to obscure its condition as a designed artifact generated by data collection, categorization, and arrangement processes. In other words, visualization does not get us closer to the "true" status of the data; it offers a layer of analysis and understanding more accurately. "The capacity to mobilize data graphically as visualizations and representations, or 'database aesthetics,' amplifies the rhetorical, argumentative and persuasive function of data" (Williamson, 2014). In short, visualization is produced to tell the story that analysts want to hear, not expose reality.

Coursera and edX's emergent research is consistent with the visualization trend in analytics and generates customary "heat maps" of global MOOC participation (Breslow et al., 2013; Perna et al., 2014; University Edinburgh, 2013). Different nations are colored here according to the IP address locations registration numbers, which effectively indicate "where" MOOC students are located. However, as we look at the nuanced IP address location methods, we begin to understand the multilayered processes involved in data collection and analysis and the inconsistencies in global internet infrastructure. There is a reason why the African continent is mostly left vacant in these world views, but a graphic depiction of the statistics on the register would not really clarify anything or even give any hint about what you should do about it. Rather, the story tends to be one of global expansion, highlighting regions of corporate influence and recognizing key areas. This seems to be an excellent example of how "powerful visualizations are now being deployed to envision and diagrammatize the educational landscape 'out there,' and to make it amenable to having things done to it" (Williamson, 2014).

As if visualization is not enough, we are encouraged to consider the field of learning analytics using the now de rigueur "infographic," which, of course, provides much wider use than the humble MOOC. The importance in general on-campus programs of the maps of competence or the structures of "traffic light," as shown by Course Signals, shows the attraction for data analytics and the elegant visual layers from which we see them. We should concentrate on the graph shape or color of the show with these devices, not think about the workings below. However, who determines the most important data points, and who selects the graphic form and color, and for what reason?

It is necessary not to doubt the accuracy or the precision of the algorithmic processes at work or the successful work of these projects. Rather, the goal is to demonstrate how visualization deflects focus from process and system issues and renders the surface picture uncontroversial. This is precisely the point of visualizing the data; we do not have to look at the data itself, only the much more intuitive graph. Data scientists in wider fields are starting to challenge the blind acceptance by the mass media and the public of their visualizations (Warden, 2013). Burn-Murdoch strongly positions the problem in the visualization layer, not necessarily the underlying data science. Our belief in visualization is furthermore specifically defined in educational practices: "While the text is frequently presented to students for critique, diagrams and data visualizations are overwhelmingly used simply as a medium of displaying final results" (Burn-murdoch, 2013). Graphs, diagrams, and charts are rooted in us as the unquestionable fact of the data, and, if so, how do we transcend this and establish a more meaningful engagement?

Ferguson proposes two approaches for student analytics, including incorporating learners' viewpoints and specific guidance on ethics (Ferguson, 2012). These two directions require transparency and clarity, not in the shape of more surface visuals, but as co-development activities. This means identifying simulation processes and procedures and the motivation for educational groups to take an active part in shaping them. That requires learning analytics technology that is not invisible, but "transparent, enabling learners to respond with feedback that can be used to refine the analytics, and enabling them to see how their data are being used" (Ferguson, 2012). From this viewpoint, engaging in learning analytics becomes educational in itself as students actively participate in data production and are aware of how information is produced. This may be a way to step past fixation with the picture as an unquestionable reflection of fact and into an active practice through which we consider imagery mutability and participation.

7.3 Integrating Learning Analytics with MOOCs

Since MOOCs have been built upon the global education market (Semenova, Vilkova, & Shcheglova, 2018), online learning innovations have spread over informal education and the past decade in higher education and continued professional development (The 2019 *OpenupEd t rend report on MOOCs*, 2019). Universities and vocational schools have been able to extend educational choices through the use of MOOCs in education programs (Roshchina, Roshchin, & Rudakov, 2018) and to build conditions for virtual mobility between students (Sancho & de Vries, 2013), improve access to education, and minimize university costs (Larionova, Brown, Bystrova, & Sinitsyn, 2018). Using MOOCs, universities face the problem of choosing quality courses and evaluating the productivity of online learning. To establish specific decision-making principles, the techniques for selecting online courses and the methods for determining their efficacy must be evaluated in-depth. Learning analytics in MOOCs is a key instrument for improving education quality (Lee

O'Farrell, 2017). In addition to the evaluation of learning analytics and the study of learner interaction, it also offers quantitative details on the efficacy of online methods and techniques of learning (Bystrova, Larionova, Sinitsyn, & Tolmachev, 2018). Moreover, learning analytics is a key predictor of and actively utilized to boost MOOC efficiency (Bystrova et al., 2018).

Learning analytics is based on the study of big data on MOOC learning conduct (Keshavamurthy & Guruprasad, 2014). It can provide much knowledge about the causes of success and failure in learning and predict possible learning habits. Findings are used to improve and adapt learning experiences to new environments (Lee O'Farrell, 2017).

The key goals of learning analytics are as follows (Bystrova et al., 2018):

- Collect, measure, and present user behaviour data;
- Analyse student success during the entire course;
- Analyse behavioural patterns using big data;
- Create relationships of cause-and-effect between performance measures and learning;
- Detect errors and methodological problems in MOOCs;
- Create guidelines for the revision of course content;
- Predict the success or failure of the student.

Learning analytics covers different approaches, ranging from descriptive statistics to data mining. Additional information sources and streaming data on user activity obtained through MOOC platforms can include educational institutions' administrative databases, learner and teacher surveys, pre-tested performance, etc.

If such requirements have been met, learning analytics will theoretically play an important role in online learning and MOOCs (Brouns & Firssova, 2016).

7.3.1 Learning Analytics Parameters in MOOC

Due to the abundance of data collected through MOOCs, learning analytics is an important guide for defining instructional design parameters in MOOCs that can enhance the students' learning experiences (Shukor & Abdullah, 2019). In several MOOC-related studies, parameters including the number of views, time spent viewing content, or the number of comments are used to determine the retention and participation of students in MOOCs (Jiang, Williams, Schenke, Warschauer, & Dowd, 2014). These parameters are often used to estimate the completion rate of students at the end of the course. However, little is known about how these criteria will enable educational designers and instructors to develop and update their MOOC instructional system. In this way, the instructional design will be more suited to their learners, since this design is focused on learner behavior during the course, which was called a study in "from the field" from the learner's perspective (Guàrdia Ortiz, Sangrà Morer, & Maina, 2013).

The engagement of students with course content can be calculated by evaluating the number of views. The number of students watching online learning materials in one class was collected in a study by Murray et al. (Murray, Pérez, Geist, & Hedrick, 2012), and a clear link was found between research and course materials.

Indeed, the more tools a student communicates with, the higher the probability of success in the course (Murray et al., 2012). Furthermore, the estimation of the highest average time spent among learners on the learning content is a significant measure of the learner's learning material quality. Wong (Wong, 2013) said students who spend more time on such materials give us an idea of the learning material's value.

A good online course should allow interaction between students and students and interaction between students and teachers. In every online course, features such as online discussion boards or chatting become mandatory. Online training lecturers can learn statistics about the number of comments about the overall concept of student engagement in the course. De Lange et al. (2003) found that online discussion

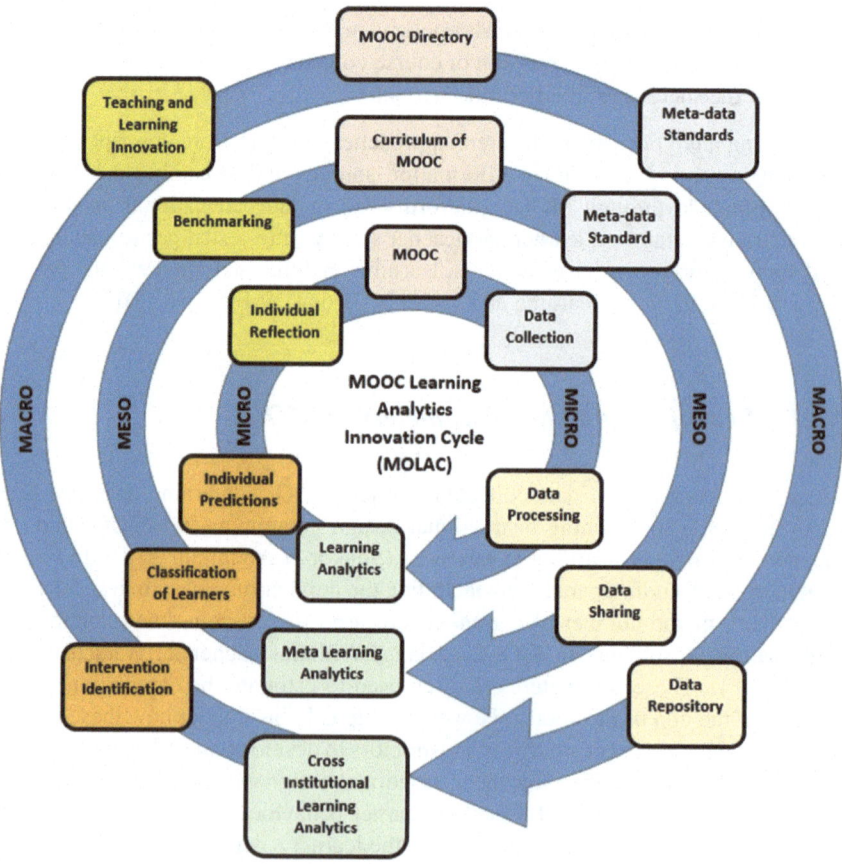

Fig. 7.2 The MOOC Learning Analytics Innovation Cycle – MOLAC (Drachsler & Kalz, 2016)

features significantly affect students' satisfaction with the course. MOOC is like many other online courses, but students' diversity has left very little room for personalized learning. Via learning analytics, trainers can learn more about their MOOC students and create an instructional design plan to suit their needs.

7.3.2 The MOOC Learning Analytics Innovation Cycle (MOLAC)

The MOOC Learning Analytics Innovation Cycle (MOLAC) (Fig. 7.2) has been developed to integrate the various domains, objectives, levels of analysis, and processes for learning analytics and MOOCs into a single picture (Drachsler & Greller, 2016). The cycle works on three levels. Data are gathered from a single course at the micro-level to promote predictions and reflection for individual students or teachers. On the meso level, educational institutions combine several MOOCs and allow data to be shared and analyzed via standard metadata beyond a single course. The combined data from different MOOCs can be used to classify learners and contributes to a more informed, data-driven approach towards the much-discussed concept of learning types and styles.

At the macro level, analysis is performed by MOOC providers, and curricula and data are shared among providers through a data repository. This type of cross-institutional learning analytics aims to identify interventions that help innovate learning and education for each institution and a wider group of stakeholders, such as the learning science community.

In this regard, the combination of MOOCs and learning analytics creates an innovative environment for educational institutions that enables initiatives and new ideas to be evaluated beyond the institution's current education structure. The majority of initiatives start with the micro-level but can ideally generalize research interest at a higher level through cross-institutional initiatives.

The European MOOCKnowledge initiative is an example of cross-institutional cooperation aimed at informing institutions about the strategic importance of the current open education strategies and providing (European) policymakers with information on the socio-economic impact of the open education sector but also obstacles to making the European higher learning system more accessible to the institutions.

7.3.3 MOOC Features for Learning Analytics

Learning analytics in MOOC tracks the behavior of a learner in a course. During the learning process, learners are tracked from the registration process, engaging in courses (video, discussions) to evaluation. Learners can view some tracking data in progress, results, completion of courses, and course statistics. etc., both for one course and all courses enrolled. Often, students are provided with additional details that alert them on top activities throughout the course.

An analysis of features offered to students across various MOOC platforms is performed (Chauhan & Goel, 2018). The analysis performed is summarized here (Chauhan & Goel, 2018).

The authors consider the features offered for a single student and all students enrolled in a course and all students of a course. They listed the characteristics for

- Single Learner Single Course (SLSC);
- Single Learner All Courses (SLAC) and
- All Learners Single Course (ALSC).

SLSC describes features to auto-reflect the learning of a person from a single course. SLAC provides information about all classes in which a student is enrolled. ALSC offers features that provide a community of students with learning, actions, and academic performance.

Also, the list of characteristics is formulated in conjunction with the learning process. Also, each feature often has a collection of parameters given to the learner as control or option. The features and parameters for various categories are shown in Table 7.1. Table 7.2 summarizes various styles for presenting the features.

The authors made a few primary findings from the review mentioned below.

- Some features are available on various channels, such as enrollment tracking, course content, forum contribution and response, specific reporting of trending, recently accessed units, the top/lowest scorer, etc.
- *Course activity* in MOOC is not so popular.
- *Assessment* information in open-source is more popular than proprietary systems.
- *Most platforms usually support • Status of progress and lesson unit.*
- The *completion status* in the proprietary platform is popular
- *Learning competency* is not a popular feature, but are supported by open-source platforms.
- *Recent activities* are a common feature of specific reporting, which is prominent among open-source platforms.
- Everybody receives the *Course information.*

Authors have also made several recommendations for learning analytics to platform providers from comparative analyses of the MOOC platforms. Features for "assessment," including quiz, assignments, and submitted assessments for the SLSC, can be included in Open edX. For all categories, the "specific reporting" feature can be implemented. Open edX also supports the ALSC group. It is also recommended that MOOC platforms have single access points for various artifacts that are visible and usable for learning analytics. For example, if a student wants to see the status of their quiz: to go where they left the last quiz, remaining to be completed, and completed all, they have to check each lesson unit and search. Controls are distributed across the system.

7.4 Benefits of Applying Learning Analytics in MOOCs

Table 7.1 The features and parameters for different categories

Category	Learning steps	Features	Parameters
SLSC (Single Learner Single Course)	Enrollment	Tracking	Total enrollment
	Course activity	Lesson unit	The score, Score details (Mean/High/Low/Score), Total, Comment, Remaining action, Deadline passed/Not released, Weight (%), Total weight (%)
		Course content	Number of videos watched/Watching, Number of slide downloads
		Forum contribution	Number of topics created, Number of comments posted, Title of topic/Post contributed to
		Forum response	Number of submissions and comments received
	Assessment	Quiz	Number of points, Grade (%), Total, Comments, Status (Completed, Overdue, Try again)
		Assignment	Grade/Score, Total, Comments, Number of assignments passed & Total, Status (Evaluation required/Not, Submitted/Not
		Assessments (Submitted)	Statistics, Recorded score, Feedback, Individual score, Time taken, Submission time
		Grades	Excursuses score, Total (%), Range, Percentage, Pass status
	Status	Progress	Completion (%), Participation threshold, Statis (Completed, Action remaining, Deadline passed/Not released
		Lesson unit	Time left, View/Completion (%), Resource status (Visited, Non-visited), Status (Completed, Action remaining, Deadline passed/Not released, Score (Subsection & problem, Total), Completed units, Release status (Lock, Unlock), Completed activities (Check, Uncheck)
		Course completion	Status (In progress, Completed), Requirement (View, Mark, Complete), Completed (Yes, No), Completion date
		Competency	Final score, Total points
	Specific reporting	Enrolment tracking	Recent learner enrolment in course
		Recent activity	Activities name (List), Update date
		Trending	Posts, Submissions
		Recent accessed unit	Lesson unit completion (%)
		Top/Lowest score	Three highest & two lowest grades (Students, Grade (%))

(continued)

Table 7.1 (continued)

Category	Learning steps	Features	Parameters
SLAC (Single Learner All Courses)	Course activity	Course	Title
		Lesson unit	Completion (%)
	Assessment	Assignment	Title, Due date
		Grades	Final grade (%), Grade required for certificate
	Status	Progress	Completion (%) or Lesson unit viewed (%)
		Completion	Completion (%)
	Specific reporting	Course	Last active/Inactive/Completed, Past/Planned/Withdrawn
		Recent accessed course	Title, Status with lesson unit (Due assignments, Ended/Not)
ALSC (All Learners Single Course)	Enrolment	Tracking	Recent enrollment in course
		Participant	Name of participants in group
	Specific reporting	Recent activity	Activities name (List), Update date
		Trending	Posts & submissions, Active learners/Teams (Today)
		Top/Lowest scorer	Three highest & lowest grades (Students, Grade (%))

7.4 Benefits of Applying Learning Analytics in MOOCs

Learning Analytics is also studying student data on online platforms to uncover secret trends and discover practices paradigms. To improve learning and quantify learning environments, the needs for Learning Analytics arose. (Khalil, Taraghi, & Ebner, 2016) conducted a comprehensive analysis of the use of Learning Analytics on MOOC platforms. Their research also indicates that, between 2013 and 2015, the combination of Learning Analytics and MOOCs resulted in the largest number of citations from Google Scholar (http://scholar.google.com).

Online distance learning platforms such as MOOCs provide a rich source of potential for knowledge mining. Learning Analytics researchers can create enormous data logs using mouse clicks, forums, quiz results, login frequency, time spent on tasks, and monitoring videos interactivity. When properly viewed, this knowledge database will help scientists from different fields of computer science, pedagogy, statistics, machine learning, etc., directly participate in the pursuit of student success. Learning analytics benefits in MOOCs are infinite.

Here are the key advantages of using learning analytics in MOOCs from (Khalil et al., 2016):

- **Prediction:** one of the most common goals in both learning analytics and educational data mining. Techniques are used to determine when an online course is going to drop by a participant. This could be achieved by an analysis of student conduct, test results, and video skips. The monitoring of previous students'

7.4 Benefits of Applying Learning Analytics in MOOCs

Table 7.2 Various styles for presenting the features

Category	Learning steps	Features	Parameters
SLSC (Single Learner Single Course)	Course activity	Lesson unit	List, Table, Color variance
		Course content	Table
	Assessment	Quiz	Table, List
		Assignment	Table, List
		Assessments (Submitted)	Table, List
		Grades	Bar chart, List, Table
	Status	Progress in course	Bar chart, CheckBox, Progress bar, Doughnut chart, Check/Uncheck, List
		Lesson unit	List, CheckBox, Color variance, Bar chart, Doughnut chart, Progress bar, Check/Uncheck
		Course completion	Table, Vertical bar, Color variance, Horizontal bar, Doughnut chart, Check/Uncheck
		Competency	Text
	Specific reporting	Recent activity	List, Table, Text
SLAC (Single Learner All Courses)	Course activity	Course	List
		Lesson unit	Bar Chart
	Assessment	Grades	Text, Table, List
		Progress	Doughnut chart, Part viewed, Color variance
	Status	Completion	Percentage completed, Part viewed, Color variance
	Specific reporting	Course	List
ALSC (All Learners Single Course)	Specific reporting	Recent activity	List
		Trending	List
		Top/Lowest scorer	List

behaviors based on particular modules allows researchers to forecast potential actions, such as falling off a course or identifying at-risk students. Learning Analytics is also used to forecast success and motivation. Further projections on video consumption in a course and relative interest in forums for discussion can be studied.

- **Recommendation:** MOOC platform actions can be compromised for a recommendation. One example is when a MOOC provider advises students to use their previous registered courses for learning materials. Additionally, a student who addresses a particular question may be recommended in discussion forums.
- **Visualization:** The monitoring of previously described acts produces several records through learning analytics. Participants will obtain visualizations through dashboards that promote perception, reflection, and understanding. On the other

hand, analyzing data through the visualization of plots helps researchers identify patterns and eventually gives MOOC participants feedback and reflection.
- *Entertainment:* gamification makes learning more enjoyable in MOOCs, which gives students an increased incentive and completion rate. Such tools can be badges, reward marks, progress bars, or colorful measurements.
- *Benchmarking:* benchmarking is a learning process accessible by learning analytics, evaluating courses, videos, assignments, and MOOC platforms. Therefore, we can recognize learning disabilities and weak points in video lectures or online courses. Constructive feedback is then provided, resulting in an improved education system.
- *Personalization:* Learners will shape their personal MOOC experience. Developers may create a collection of customized products on the MOOC platform through various learning analytics techniques. A student can, for example, prefer a portion of a video or bookmark an article or text. Also, he can personalize alerts and add video annotations.
- *Improving involvement:* the interaction was an enticing subject for MOOCs. By data mining techniques such as clustering, we may put participants into a subset of students or identify experiences into videos, activities, and quizzes because of potential MOOC design initiatives or because we are researching the students' catalog needs.
- *Communication information:* Learning Analytics requires the gathering and analysis of data from sources. It is also used to submit information to various MOOC stakeholders in the form of statistical analysis. Like web analytics, students can track their activities and, for example, via dashboards and analyze general statistics. Teachers and policymakers may use descriptive statistics to create an analysis of MOOCs.
- *Cost saving:* Because Learning Analytics offers data analysis software, it opens the doors for a large inspection service that enables poor MOOCs to be identified. Decision-makers can then easily assign resources.

7.5 Major Concerns of Implementing Learning Analytics in MOOCs

While Learning Analytics has many advantages in terms of an education data stream, the constraints have been established recently (Khalil et al., 2016). Learning Analytics is powered by a broad data collection and process to resolve privacy and ethical concerns. A climate of insecurity among Learning Analytics practitioners as well as decision-makers is slowing down its steep growth (Hendrik Drachsler & Greller, 2016). Through our experience, we urge educational organizations, which stand for confidentiality, honesty, and availability, to follow the security model CIA.

We list the key concerns (Khalil et al., 2016) about the implementation of Learning Analytics in MOOC platforms in this section:

- **Security:** the preservation of student records in Learning Analytics application databases are central to their private information. Therefore, companies should not often bother maintaining database configuration. Infringements of confidential information may also occur.
- **Privacy:** Learning Analytics will disclose students' personal information. Sensitive information such as addresses, names, or emails may be used in the MOOC datasets. Privacy can be regarded as both a threat and a constraint in learning analytics.
- **Ownership:** "Who owns the analyzed MOOC data," questions can arise at any time. Participants tend to keep their details private while maintaining accountability, includes the consent policy. Also, MOOC providers are allowed to remove or de-identify their participants' personal information.
- **Consent:** Data ownership related. Not every MOOC provider makes the use of student data transparent. Policies with legislation frameworks should include personal information collection guidelines and information use definitions, such as research purposes or third-party sale of information.
- **Transparency:** Hidden procedures can mask biased decision-making when analytics on educational data sets are used. Similarly, providers must report their approach to gather, evaluate, and use participant data when Learning Analytics is used on MOOCs. Simultaneously, when the algorithms or methods for learning analytics are proprietary, a balance should be created.
- **Storage:** As long as MOOCs are available to the public, thousands of students can take a single course. Big data storage could be expensive, bloated, complicated, and difficult to handle. Personal data often no longer than required must be stored.

7.6 Limitation of Applying Learning Analytics in MOOCs

A crucial element in learning analytics is the quest for data consistency. However, Learning Analytics is adversely affected when data records have missing segments or corrupted information. Furthermore, providing a holistic analysis of students in online courses cannot be extracted solely from their left MOOC traces. Are there assurances of the outcomes of the Learning Analytics? What about precision?

This section summarizes some of the constraints that Learning Analytics can have through its use in MOOCs (Khalil et al., 2016).

- **False Positives:** decision-making based on small sub-sets of data by analysts or directors can lead to quick decisions, which could result in "false positives." The precision of any upcoming decision in a MOOC system would, therefore, be affected. Learning Analytics is also not always precise.
- **Fallacy Analytics:** Analytics can fail, and therefore, incorrect interventions or predictions will take place. Failures could occur during the main Learning Analytics cycle processes. Potential examples of faulty analysis are incorrect

behavior in collecting data from the MOOCs, flaws in processing or filtering, and misinterpretation of data. The findings via visualizations can also be displayed on the same page. Visualizations are a fantastic way to display details, but it may be difficult for the end-user to play with scales or to use 3D figures (student, instructor, decision-maker). Fallacy analysis can be unintentional and not deliberate, but it can be detrimental to various stakeholders and non-economic to the MOOC organization if analyzing data based on fallacy analytics. Fallacy analytics as a learning analytics tool by misusing statistics corrupt and pollutes the study records and wastes other researchers' time and resources.

- *Bias:* Learning Analytics can demonstrate important prediction and recommendation outcomes. It can also prove the relationship between behavior in forums and results, or watch videos and MOOCs. Collected data "could feed," but this goes back to the researcher or decision maker's deliberate desire. The bias against a certain hypothesis and the inner desire to prove the student theory contributes to biased learning analytics.
- *Meaningful data:* Learning Analytics uses quantitative analysis findings mainly. Qualitative approaches have not yet produced sufficient results. Learning analytics can be ineffective and effortless if meaningful information is difficult to extract.

7.7 Tools that Support Learning Analytics in MOOCs

In 2014, the Universidad Autónoma de Madrid (UAM) joined the edX Consortium (https://www.edx.org/school/uamx). Several 15 MOOCs have since been created and offered free, and various studies in the field of learning analytics based on the MOOCs in the UAM in edX are being created, and the following tools support learning analytics in MOOCs (Cobos, 2018):

- *Open-DLAs:* Open Dashboard for Learning Analytics, where descriptive-analytical methods were used to determine how learning takes place.
- *edX-MAS+:* edX MOOC Model Analyzer System, predictive analytical techniques were used to build predictive models and foresee what could happen.
- *edX-WS:* edX MOOC Warning System, where perspective analytical methods were used to identify learning-enhancing strategies.
- *edX-CAS:* edX MOOC Content Analyzer System, a Web-based framework used as a tool to evaluate textual content in MOOC courses.

7.8 Cast Study: Online Learners and their Persistence Within Online Courses Offered on the Coursera Platform

The case study is focused upon "What We Can Learn From Historic MOOC Data: Findings From Our Participation in the AIM Analytics Dropout Prediction Challenge." (Quintana, Schulz, & Tan, n.d.).

7.8.1 Motivation

Yuanru Tan, Learning Design and Accessibility Fellow, and the Learning Experience Designer Rebecca Quintana, decided to learn how data scientists solve learning analysis concerns, such as recognizing which students are in danger of not completing a course, to enhance the course design. Data scientist Kyle Schulz also signed up for the AIM (Academic Innovation at Michigan) Analytics challenge and aimed to translate his previous experience in predictive analytics into a new area (online courses) to learn more about the subject space and compete for prize money.

7.8.2 The Challenge

The challenge focused primarily on online students and their success in the online courses offered on the Coursera platform. The majority of these initiatives account for just a small percentage of students who remain involved in the course. For the competition, the first 4 weeks of learner data from a random subset of courses were presented, and each student in the courses was asked to predict the probability of persistence (described as showing some behavior during the last week of the course).

7.8.3 Goals

They began with two mutually beneficial goals in mind early in the competition:

7. To understand what can be learned from historic MOOC data about the evolution of course design and
8. To build a model to find out which learner habits have important effects on the course's success rates.

7.8.4 Process and Outcomes

They used log, clickstream, and demographic data from a University of Michigan MOOC on Social Network Analysis (SNA) and an unpublished MOOC course for their goals. To understand how courses were structured (and therefore how learner behavior could differ), they also studied the two SNA courses' design. One was Applied Social Network Analysis in Python, published on Coursera in 2017. Another course was Social Network Analysis, which employs the theory and computational tools for social network analysis to provide a meaningful overview of the Internet-fueled social and information networks.

7.8.5 Learning Design Approach and Outcomes

Yuanru and Rebecca used a method for the visualizing course structure (Quintana, Tan, & Korf, 2018; Seaton, 2016) to compare the historic SNA MOOC with the contemporary SNA MOOC.

1. **Video production styles:** Social network analysis tended to have longer, 15–25 minutes-length videos, whereas Applied social network analysis in Python tended to have much shorter, 7–12-minute videos. U-M has moved from a more informal style to a more standard mode in terms of formality, with an instructor lecturing from various campus locations, where the instructor is filmed in a studio setting.
2. **The students' commitment:** Social network analysis required students to acquire and use external software to the platform and use their personal information within assignments. Applied Social Network Analysis in Python offered platform-based data and software, thus reducing participatory barriers. The length of the MOOCs has also changed: the historical MOOC lasts 9 weeks, and the current version lasts only 4 weeks.

7.8.6 Learning Analytics Approach and Outcomes

Before embarking on the model's training task, they examined recent learning analytics research on student behaviors and their associations with MOOC results. Guided by literature and their preliminary analysis, they undertook a brainstorming activity that proposed additional elements that could complement the persistence factors already established.

They have introduced a gradient-boosting algorithm (XGBoost) with a new arsenal of feature vectors to allow them to analyze:

- the overall accuracy of their persistence prediction,

- the performance of their method of prediction relative to other models published;
- the relative importance in their final model for all the features.

The two most powerful predictors of the features they implemented were:

1. The timestamp of the last interaction between a learner and the platform (i.e., their last click) and
2. The timestamp of the last "in-video" quiz submission.

Although they did not discover new persistence factors, their final model was the first place in the competition!

7.9 Conclusion

In the past 15 years, educational technology has gained great importance. Currently, the framework of education technology includes numerous engaging online environments and fields. Learning analytics and Massive Open Online Courses (MOOCs) are two of the emerging topics that are most relevant in this field. Since they are open to everybody at no cost, MOOCs attract hundreds and hundreds of thousands of people. Experts from various disciplines demonstrated considerable interest in MOOCs as the phenomenon grew rapidly. Indeed, MOOCs have proved themselves to scale-up education in various fields. Their advantages are crystallized by improving educational performance, cutting costs, and expanding accessibility.

The large datasets of MOOC platforms require advanced tools and methodologies for further study because of their exceptional massiveness. This reflects the key importance of learning analytics. MOOCs offer various challenges and practices for learning analytics to address. Given this, this chapter combines both fields to investigate further steps in learning analytics capabilities in MOOCs. This chapter's main focus was to integrate learning analytics into MOOCs and look at the advantages and challenges afterward.

7.10 Review Questions

Reflect on the concepts of this chapter guided by the following questions.

1. Define MOOCs. List the features of MOOCs.
2. Describe the benefits that MOOCs provide to organizations and participants.
3. List and explain various types of MOOCs.
4. Write a short note on MOOCs Pedagogy.
5. What are the various Learning Analytics parameters used in MOOCs?
6. With the help of a diagram, explain the MOOC Learning Analytics Innovation Cycle – MOLAC.

7. What are the benefits of applying Learning Analytics in MOOCs?
8. List and explain the major concerns of implementing Learning Analytics in Cs.
9. Summarize the various limitations of applying Learning Analytics in MOOCs.
10. Describe the various tools that support Learning Analytics in MOOCs.

References

Adams, C., Yin, Y., Vargas Madriz, L. F., & Mullen, C. S. (2014). A phenomenology of learning large: The tutorial sphere of xMOOC video lectures. *Distance Education, 35*(2), 202–216. https://doi.org/10.1080/01587919.2014.917701

Baturay, M. H. (2015). An overview of the world of MOOCs. *Procedia – Social and Behavioral Sciences, 174*, 427–433. https://doi.org/10.1016/j.sbspro.2015.01.685

Breslow, L., Pritchard, D. E., DeBoer, J., Stump, G. S., Ho, A. D., & Seaton, D. T. (2013). Studying learning in the worldwide classroom: Research into edX's first MOOC. *Research & Practice in Assessment, 8*(Summer 2013), 13. http://www.rpajournal.com/studying-learning-in-the-worldwide-classroom-research-into-edxs-first-mooc/

Brouns, F., & Firssova, O. (2016). The role of learning design and learning analytics in MOOCS. *Proceedings of the 9th EDEN Research Workshop*, 327–334. http://dspace.learningnetworks.org/bitstream/1820/7034/1/EDEN_Design_and_analytics_in_MOOCs.pdf

Burn-murdoch, J. (2013). *Why you should never trust a data visualisation.* 1–6.

Bystrova, T., Larionova, V., Sinitsyn, E., & Tolmachev, A. (2018). Learning analytics in massive open online courses as a tool for predicting learner performance. *Sotsiologicheskoe Obozrenie, 17*(4), 139–166. https://doi.org/10.17323/1814-9545-2018-4-139-166

Chauhan, J., & Goel, A. (2018). A feature-based analysis of MOOC for learning analytics. *2017 10th International Conference on Contemporary Computing, IC3 2017, 2018-Janua*(August), 1–6. https://doi.org/10.1109/IC3.2017.8284331.

Cobos, R. (2018). *Examples of tools that supports learning analytics in MOOCs.* Emadridnet. Org. http://www.emadridnet.org/index.php/en/jobs/28-eventos-y-seminarios/1069-examples-of-tools-that-supports-learning-analytics-in-moocs

de Lange, P., Suwardy, T., & Mavondo, F. (2003). Integrating a virtual learning environment into an introductory accounting course: Determinants of student motivation. *Accounting Education, 12*(1), 1–14. https://doi.org/10.1080/0963928032000064567

Dodge, M., Kitchin, R., & Zook, M. (2009). How does software make space? Exploring some geographical dimensions of pervasive computing and software studies. *Environment and Planning A, 41*(6), 1283–1293. https://doi.org/10.1068/a42133

Drachsler, H., & Kalz, M. (2016). The MOOC and learning analytics innovation cycle (MOLAC): A reflective summary of ongoing research and its challenges. *Journal of Computer Assisted Learning, 32*(3), 281–290. https://doi.org/10.1111/jcal.12135

Drachsler, Hendrik, & Greller, W. (2016). Privacy and analytics – It's a DELICATE issue a checklist for trusted learning analytics. *ACM International Conference Proceeding Series, 25–29-Apri*(April), 89–98. https://doi.org/10.1145/2883851.2883893.

Ferguson, R. (2012). Learning analytics: Drivers, developments and challenges. *International Journal of Technology Enhanced Learning, 4*(5–6), 304–317. https://doi.org/10.1504/IJTEL.2012.051816

Fieland, M. (2020). *The ultimate MOOC handbook.* Accreditedschoolsonline. https://www.accreditedschoolsonline.org/resources/moocs/

Glanz, J. (2012). *Power, pollution and the internet.* New York Times. http://nyti.ms/SkoL83

Goldy-Brown, S. (2018). *11 Benefits of MOOCS (Massive Open Online Courses) | Plexuss.* https://plexuss.com/news/article/benefits-of-moocs

References

Grainger, B. (2013). *Massive open online course (MOOC) report*.

Guàrdia Ortiz, L., Sangrà Morer, A., & Maina, M. (2013). *MOOC Design principles. A pedagogical approach from the learner's perspective*. May 2014.

Gumbel, A. (2014). San Francisco's guerrilla protest at Google buses swells into revolt. The Guardian. https://www.theguardian.com/world/2014/jan/25/google-bus-protest-swells-to-revolt-san-francisco

Jiang, S., Williams, A. E., Schenke, K., Warschauer, M., & Dowd, D. O. (2014). Predicting MOOC performance with week 1 behavior. *Proceedings of the 7th International Conference on Educational Data Mining (EDM)*, 273–275.

Jordan, K. (2014). Initial trends in enrolment and completion of massive open online courses. *International Review of Research in Open and Distance Learning, 15*(1), 133–160. https://doi.org/10.19173/irrodl.v15i1.1651

Keshavamurthy, U., & Guruprasad, D. H. S. (2014). Learning analytics: A survey. *International Journal of Computer Trends and Technology, 18*(6), 260–264. https://doi.org/10.14445/22312803/ijctt-v18p155

Khalil, M., Taraghi, B., & Ebner, M. (2016). *Engaging learning analytics in MOOCS: The good, the bad, and the ugly*. 3–7. http://arxiv.org/abs/1606.03776

Larionova, V., Brown, K., Bystrova, T., & Sinitsyn, E. (2018). Russian perspectives of online learning technologies in higher education: An empirical study of a MOOC. *Research in Comparative and International Education, 13*(1), 70–91. https://doi.org/10.1177/1745499918763420

Lee O'Farrell. (2017). *Using learning analytics to support the enhancement of teaching and learning in higher education*. National Forum for the Enhancement of Teaching and Learning in Higher Education.

Long, P. D., & Siemens, G. (2014). Penetrating the fog: Analytics in learning and education. *Italian Journal of Educational Technology, 22*(3), 132–137. https://doi.org/10.17471/2499-4324/195

McGill.CA. (2010). *A brief history of a brief history*. Popular Science.

Morozov, E. (2013). To save everything, click here: Technology, solutionism and the urge to fix problems that don't exist. *Information Polity, 18*(3), 275–276. https://doi.org/10.3233/ip-130311

Murray, M., Pérez, J., Geist, D., & Hedrick, A. (2012). Student interaction with online course content: Build it and they might come. *Journal of Information Technology Education:Research, 11*(1), 125–140. https://doi.org/10.28945/1592

NMC Horizon Report. (2017). NMC horizon report: 2017. In *NMC*. https://library.educause.edu/-/media/files/library/2017/2/2017horizonreporthe.pdf

Perna, L., Ruby, A., Boruch, R., Wang, N., Scull, J., Evans, C., & Ahmad, S. (2014). The life cycle of a million MOOC users. *MOOC Research Initiative Conference*, 33.

Physiopedia. (2020). *Introduction to MOOCs features of MOOCs benefits of MOOCs to participants benefits to organisations running the MOOC*. https://www.physio-pedia.com/Introduction_to_MOOCs

Quintana, R. M., Schulz, K., & Tan, Y. (n.d.). *What we can learn from historic MOOC data: Findings from our participation in the AIM analytics dropout prediction challenge*.

Quintana, R. M., Tan, Y., & Korf. N. (2018). *Visualizing course structure: Using course composition diagrams to reflect on design*. Paper presented at the Annual Meeting of the American Educational Research Association (AERA). April 13–17. New York.

Roshchina, Y., Roshchin, S., & Rudakov, V. (2018). The demand for massive open online courses (MOOC): Evidence from Russian education. *Voprosy Obrazovaniya, 2018*(1), 174–199. https://doi.org/10.17323/1814-9545-2018-1-174-199

Rscapin. (2013). *How data is driving the biggest revolution in education since the middle ages*. http://venturebeat.com/2013/12/04/how-data-is-driving-the-biggest-revolution-in-education-since-the-middle-ages/%0ARelated

Sancho, T., & de Vries, F. (2013). Virtual learning environments, social media and MOOCs: Key elements in the conceptualisation of new scenarios in higher education: EADTU conference 2013. *Open Learning, 28*(3), 166–170. https://doi.org/10.1080/02680513.2014.888000

Scheiber, N. (2014). *The brutal ageism of tech*. New Republic. http://www.newrepublic.com/article/117088/silicons-valleys-brutal-ageism

Seaton, D. (2016). Exploring course structure at HarvardX: A new year's resolution for MOOC research. Retrieved from https://vpal.harvard.edu/blog/exploring-course-structure-harvardx-new-year%E2%80%99s-resolution-mooc-research

Semenova, T., Vilkova, K., & Shcheglova, I. (2018). The MOOC market: Prospects for Russia. *Voprosy Obrazovaniya, 2*, 173–197. https://doi.org/10.17323/1814-9545-2018-2-173-197

Shukor, N. A., & Abdullah, Z. (2019). Using learning analytics to improve MOOC instructional design. *International Journal of Emerging Technologies in Learning, 14*(24), 6–17. https://doi.org/10.3991/ijet.v14i24.12185

Sidhartha. (2016). *MOOC: Advantages and disadvantages*. Igniteengineers. https://www.igniteengineers.com/mooc-advantages-and-disadvantages/

Siemens, G. (2013). Learning analytics: The emergence of a discipline. *American Behavioral Scientist, 57*(10), 1380–1400. https://doi.org/10.1177/0002764213498851

Srikanth, M. (2017). The Advantages and disadvantages of MOOCs for learning. *Infopro Learning*, 1–5. http://www.infoprolearning.com/blog/advantages-and-disadvantages-of-moocs-massive-open-online-courses-for-learning/

The 2019 OpenupEd t rend report on MOOCs. (2019).

University Edinburgh. (2013). *MOOCs @ Edinburgh 2013 – Report # 1*. 42. https://doi.org/10.1056/NEJMp1202451.

Wadhwa, V. (2014). *Enough is enough, Silicon Valley must end its elitism and arrogance*. The Washington Post Innovations. https://www.washingtonpost.com/news/innovations/wp/2014/01/27/enough-is-enough-silicon-valley-must-end-its-elitism-and-arrogance/?arc404=true

Warden, P. (2013). *Why you should never trust a data scientist "Pete Warden's" blog*. https://petewarden.com/2013/07/18/why-you-should-never-trust-a-data-scientist/

Williamson, B. (2014). *The end of theory in digital social research?* Connected LEarning. https://clalliance.org/blog/the-end-of-theory-in-digital-social-research/

Wong, M. (2013). *Online peer assessment in MOOCs: Students learning from students*. Centre for Teaching, Learning and Technology Newsletter. http://ctlt.ubc.ca/2013/03/28/online-peer-assessment-in-moocs-students-learning-from-students/

Yuan, L., & Powell, S. (2013). MOOCs and disruptive innovation: Implications for higher education. *ELearning Papers, In-Depth, 33*(2), 1–7.

Chapter 8
The Pedagogical Perspective of Learning Analytics

8.1 Introduction to Pedagogy

8.1.1 What Is Pedagogy?

People often speak about their 'pedagogical approach' to teaching. But what does it mean? Pedagogy is clearly defined as the method and practice of teaching. It includes (TES, 2018):

- Teaching styles
- Teaching Theory
- Feedback and assessment

When people speak of the teaching pedagogy, they refer to how teachers convey the curriculum material to a class. When a teacher prepares a lesson, they consider multiple ways of presenting the material. This decision is taken based on their teaching interests, knowledge, and the context they teach.

Differences in the age of pupils and the content of pupils will affect the teacher's pedagogical practices. Teachers will use studies from several different academic backgrounds to inform their decisions and educate these age groups by their experience. For example, an EYFS instructor may refer to cognitive development studies and adult-directed play's performance. The choices will be the pedagogical principles, and every teacher will, over time, establish his pedagogical principles.

8.1.2 Importance of Pedagogy in Teaching

Using successful pedagogical methods, students can obtain learning outcomes and their maximum intellectual potential. Quality education offers a good base for learning. It helps students develop advanced concepts and skills. The correct pedagogy helps teachers to observe their students' academic success. The following points stress the importance of pedagogy (Yadav, 2020).

1. A carefully designed pedagogy increases teaching consistency. It makes the student more open to learning. This increases the involvement of the student in the teaching-learning process.
2. A suitable pedagogy helps educate students with various styles/skills. Students gain a deeper knowledge of the subject. This, in turn, means that the learning objectives of a curriculum are achieved.
3. A correct pedagogical approach is needed for students with special needs, students from disadvantaged groups, viz. females, or minorities. They are invited to be part of the mainstream learning culture.
4. A well-developed pedagogy encourages students to achieve higher cognitive abilities, i.e., analysis, synthesis, and evaluations. Knowledge, comprehension, and application are cognitive abilities of the lower order in Bloom's taxonomy.

8.1.3 Factors Affecting Pedagogy

Different factors impact pedagogy (Fig. 8.1) in a phase of teaching. Some obvious factors are subject, curriculum, learning motivation, and instructor's skills. Student learning patterns and facilities availability also affect pedagogy. Some of these considerations are discussed in the following points (Yadav, 2020).

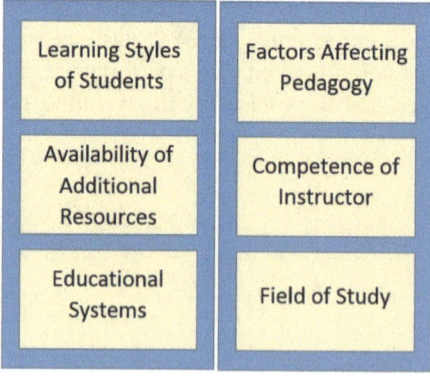

Fig. 8.1 Factors affecting pedagogy (Yadav, 2020)

8.1 Introduction to Pedagogy

1. *Teacher competence:* a professional teacher motivates students, keeps them interested and willing to learn. Such a teacher uses a wise mix of abilities, skills, and experience.
2. *The student's learning styles:* an awareness of students' learning styles allows teachers to follow a pedagogical approach. A pedagogical approach that complements student styles helps to speed up the learning process. It motivates and keeps students engaged in learning.
3. *Field of Study:* The field of study also affects pedagogical options. For example, physics needs a theory and laboratory balance. Political science does not require laboratory sessions. In addition to theory and laboratory sessions, the architecture includes field visits.
4. *Additional tools availability:* projectors, virtual labs, etc., contribute to broadening the reach of the teaching-learning process. Such educational opportunities keep learning and students alive.
5. *Education System:* education system regulations, curriculum requirements, etc. often impact the pedagogical approach. For example, a test that tests a student's ability to remember facts discourages the teacher from applying a pedagogy that improves superior thought.

8.1.4 Pedagogical Approaches

8.1.4.1 What Is the Pedagogical Approach?

1. The broad principles and methods used in teaching. Goodyear (2005) suggests that the pedagogical approach can be divided into Pedagogical Philosophy (describes the beliefs about how people learn) and a High-Level Pedagogy (to explain a broad approach between philosophy and action).
2. The educator agrees to promote contact between learning, dedication, teacher-student, student-student, or student-content (Brown & Eaton, 2020).

8.1.4.2 Types of Pedagogical Approaches

Successful pedagogical approaches are important to the efficient delivery of knowledge to students. The choice of a particular pedagogy depends on several factors. Pedagogy relates to each other teachers, students, and learning. It leads to academic success. Educationists often encourage teachers to develop their pedagogical approach. Some pedagogical methods (Yadav, 2020) are more common and omnipresent.

1. *Constructivist approach:* The student is the center of the learning process. Based on their present and previous experience, the student generates new ideas and concepts. The mentor promotes the process simply through the creation of

activities. Students find out and learn by troubleshooting. Learning might take place at a slower pace because of restricted discussions between the student and the teacher.
2. **Reflective approach:** Teachers periodically track their teaching pedagogy under the reflective approach. You track and monitor the suitability of your pedagogy in an educational setup. This method is more appropriate for trainee teachers as a model approach.
3. **Collaborative approach:** Students are expected to work together in small teams in the collaborative approach. Students may have various skill levels. The reason is that separated students do not learn as well as students in a squad. This small team can also include an instructor and a researcher in a research-oriented setup.
4. **Integrative approach:** The integrative approach concerns real-world classroom education. The students, therefore, find the teaching in the classroom more interesting and important. The students study a subject to enhance their skills. This method generates students' interest in mathematics and science.
5. **Inquiry-based approach:** This approach places the student at the center. To find a solution, students ask questions, use logic and problem-solving skills. The method focused on inquiries can be of four types: confirmation, structured, guided, and open.

8.1.4.3 Additional Pedagogical Approaches

There are other ways to identify pedagogical approaches (LearningPortal, 2018):

- *Teacher-centered pedagogy:* This pedagogy puts the teacher at the forefront of the learning process and generally relies on techniques such as whole-class lectures, rote memorization, and chorus responses (i.e., call and answer). This method is also criticized, in particular, if students only do lower-class tasks and are fearful about the teacher. However, classroom teaching may be successful if teachers ask students to elaborate on key ideas and not just lectures.
- *Learner-Center Pedagogy:* This pedagogic approach includes many related concepts (e.g., constructivist, student-centered, participatory, active) but typically use learning theories to imply that learners should be an active part of the learning process. Therefore, students use previous knowledge and new experiences to construct knowledge. The instructor supports this process but also establishes and structure the learning conditions. Significant studies and funding have supported learner-centered pedagogy for economic, cognitive, and political reasons in recent years. Some research indicates that this method can be very effective, but it is also difficult to calculate reliably. Teachers often find it difficult to move from pedagogy focused on teachers to educational pedagogy, and so significant help might be required if this is an essential goal for a given education system.
- *Learning-centered pedagogy:* Learning-centered pedagogy is a relatively recent term that recognizes pedagogy that is both learner-centered and teacher-centered, but teachers have to consider local circumstances, including the number of

students in the classroom, the physical environment, the availability of teaching and learning materials, etc. It recommends that teachers be versatile and adjust their pedagogical methods carefully, depending on the school setting.

8.1.5 Standards of Effective Pedagogy

Do you have these five principles of teaching? Take a deep dive with this self-check, originally made by the Center for Research on Education, Diversity, and Excellence at the University of California (Teaching Tolerance, 2020).

1. ***Joint Productive Activity:*** Teachers and Students Producing Together. Learning occurs most easily when experts and novices work together to accomplish a shared product or purpose and are inspired to support one another. The general concept of teaching is "assisting"; hence, joint productive activity (JPA) optimizes teaching and learning. Working together facilitates dialogue in immediate problems, which teaches vocabulary, meaning, and values. Learning through "joint productive activity" is intercultural, characteristic of human, and potentially "hard-wired." Parents with very young children, pre-schools, graduate schools, adult learning, work-related and service-learning, on-the-job training — in all schooling, aside from the tradition in K-12 — are distinguished by this form of "mentoring" and "learning" in action.

    There is generally little joint activity in schools, which creates common interactions and, therefore, no common meaning, encouraging students and teachers to establish common understanding structures. Joint interaction between teachers and students helps to establish a shared background in the classroom. This is particularly important if the teacher and the students do not have the same history.

    Joint activity and disclosure permit the highest degree of academic achievement to solve real-world issues using formal, "schooled," or "scientific" ideas. The continuous link between scholarly concepts and daily concepts is central to how mature scholarly thinkers comprehend the world. Both students and teachers should share these collaborative practices. Only when the instructor shares the interactions will the form of conversation arise that creates basic skills.

    Joint Productive Activity Indicators. The Teacher:

    (a) Designs instructional activities involving cooperation between students to achieve a joint product.
    (b) The time required to satisfy them meets the demands of the shared productive operation.
    (c) Arrange classroom seating for individual and community students to interact and work together.
    (d) Participates in joint constructive practice with students.

(e) Organizes students through different communities to facilitate engagement, such as friendship, mixed academic abilities, language, project, or interests.
(f) plans to operate in groups of students and switch from one task to another, for example, from large groups to small groups for cleanup, dismissal, and similar.
(g) Manages access to materials and technologies for students and teachers to promote collaborative, productive practices.
(h) Monitors and encourages effective student cooperation.

2. *Language Development:* Developing Language Across the Curriculum. Developing skills in instructional languages should be a meta goal of all educational activities during the school day. If teaching is bilanguage or monolingual, literacy is the key to school success. School awareness is inseparable from language and thought. Everyday social language, formal academic language, and subject lexicons are crucial to the success of education. Language acquisition at all levels — informal, problem-solving, and academic — must be facilitated not by exercises and decontextualized guidelines but by use and intentional interactions between teachers and students. Lecture and writing should be taught in particular curricula as well as incorporated into each field of material.

How language is used in a school debate, such as questions and responses, obstacles, and representations, is often foreign to English learners and other students at risk of education failure. However, their own culture can be effectively connected by building learning contexts that evoke and build on language strengths for children in academic disciplines.

Language production and literacy as meta goals also include the special language genres required to learn science, mathematics, history, art, and literature. Successful mathematical training is focused on the capacity to "speak mathematics," as well as on the mastery of the language of instruction. In all subjects, it is possible to read, write, speak, listen, and lexicons, and indeed all subject matters can be taught as if they were a second language. Joint development activity is an ideal place for establishing the vocabulary of the field of activity.

Language Development Indicators. The Teacher:

(a) Listen to students who speak about common subjects like home and culture.
(b) Answers the talk and questions of students and makes changes' in-flight' during conversations that directly relate to students' commentary.
(c) Supports the development of written and oral languages in deliberate conversations and writing by modeling, eliciting, checking, reiterating, clarifying, challenging, praising, etc.
(d) Interacts with students in ways that value student speech expectations that are different from teachers' expectations, such as attendance time, eye contact, turning, or concentrating.
(e) Connects students' language with knowledge teacher literacy and content field through speaking, listening, reading, and writing activities.

8.1 Introduction to Pedagogy

(f) encourages students to use the language of material to convey their understanding.
(g) It provides students with regular opportunities to communicate with each other and with the instructor during educational activities.
(h) Promotes the use of first and second languages for teaching.

3. **Contextualization:** Making sense: Linking schools to the lives of students. In daily settings, the high literacy targets of schools are better accomplished. This contextualization uses the information and skills funding of students as a framework for new knowledge. This approach encourages pride and trust and increases school results.
Rising contextualized education is an ongoing recommendation by researchers in education. Schools generally teach rules, abstractions, and verbal descriptions. Schools need to support at-risk students by offering interactions that display abstract ideas applied and extracted from daily life.
"Understanding" means linking new learning with previous experience. Helping students develop these relationships improves newly learned skills and enhances student interest in learning activities. Scheme theorists, cognitive scientists, behaviorists, and psychological anthropologists believe that school learning becomes meaningful by linking it to students' personal, family, and community experience. Successful education teaches how to draw and apply the abstractions of schools in the real world. Parent and community collaboration will show acceptable engagement patterns, interaction, awareness, and interests that mean literacy, numeracy, and science to all students.
Contextualization Indicators. The teacher:

(a) Starts activities with what students already know from home, community, and school.
(b) Develop educational programs that are relevant in terms of local community values and awareness for students.
(c) Acquires local values and information by listening to pupils, parents or family members, group members, and reading-related documents.
(d) Helps students communicate and apply their learning in their homes and communities.
(e) plans to build community-based learning opportunities together with students
(f) provides opportunities for parents or relatives to take part in educational programs in the classroom.
(g) Activities vary from mutual and cooperative to individual and competitive interests for students.
(h) Varied discussion forms and interaction to include the students' cultural preferences, including co-narration, call-and-response, and choral.

4. **Challenging activities:** Teaching Complex Thinking. Students at risk of failure, particularly those with poor standard English skills, often forgive academic difficulties if they have limited capacity or are forgiven for genuine appraisal of

success because the evaluation tools are insufficient. This weakens both expectations and reviews, with the inevitable consequence of impending achievement. While these measures are often the product of benevolent intentions, the effect is to deny many different students the essential needs for success — high academic expectations and substantive evaluations that provide input and support.

Educational experts strongly agree that students at risk of education failure need cognitively demanding training, education involving reflection and examination, not just routine, comprehensive training. This does not mean ignoring or storing multiplication tables, but it does mean pursuing the deepest possible scope of fascinating and relevant materials beyond the curriculum's level. In educating students at risk of educational failure, cognitive sophistication has been implemented in several respects. For example, a bilingual program itself poses cognitive difficulties that make it superior to the monolingual approach.

Working with a cognitively challenging curriculum requires diligent work leveling so that students are encouraged to stretch. It does not mean exercises for drilling and killing or daunting challenges that deter effort. The right balance and adequate assistance are a genuinely cognitively, demanding task for the teacher. Challenging Activities Indicators. The teacher:

(a) Ensures that students – with any subject – see the whole picture as the basis for understanding the parts.
(b) Presents demanding student success expectations.
(c) Designs teaching activities that encourage comprehension of students to more complex levels.
(d) Allows students to grasp more complex understanding by building on their previous achievement.
(e) It offers straightforward, direct input on how students' performance corresponds to the tough expectations.

5. *Instructional Conversation:* Teaching Through Conversation. The best way to think and share ideas is through dialogue, questions, and sharing ideas and information. In the Instructional Conversation (IC), the instructor listens attentively, guesses about the expected importance, and changes the answers to students' effort, such as graduate seminars or between mothers and children. The instructor relates the school's formal knowledge to the pupil, the family, and the student's knowledge. The IC offers opportunities for the development of languages of instruction and subject matter. IC is a collaborative and supportive event that develops a sense of intersubjectivity and community. IC individualizes training; is best exercised during joint productive activity; is suitable for the production of languages; and offers a responsive contextualization and an accurate, cognitive challenge.

This concept could seem paradoxical; instruction implies authority and preparation, while conversation implies equality and reactivity. However, the IC is focused on assumptions that vary fundamentally from conventional lessons. Like parents in natural education, teachers who use them believe that the student has more to say in the mind of an adult beyond the established answers. The adult listens attentively, guesses the context, and changes answers to assist the student — that is to say, engages in conversation. This dialogue demonstrates the learner's awareness, skills, and beliefs – the community – so that teachers can contextualize teaching to suit the student's experience base.

The educational discourse is unusual in US schools. Learning is also achieved through the recitation script in which the teacher assigns and reviews frequently. Classrooms and schools are turned into communities for learners by such dialogue teaching when teachers decrease their distance among them and their students by creating lessons from mutual knowledge of each other's experience and ideas and making teaching a warm, interpersonal and collaborative activity.

Instructional Conversation Indicators. The teacher:

(a) Arrange the classroom to accommodate normal and frequent interaction between the teacher and a small group of students.
(b) Has a strong academic aim that drives student discussion.
(c) ensures that student speech takes place at higher rates than teacher speech.
(d) Guides the discussion to include the opinions, assumptions, and rationales of students using texts and other material help.
(e) ensures that all students are included according to their interests in the discussion.
(f) Listen closely to determine the level of comprehension of students.
(g) Supports students to teach them by questioning, restating, appreciation, motivation, etc.
(h) Guides students to create a product reflecting the goals of the instructional discussion.

8.1.6 *The Future of Pedagogy in Education*

In the last 100 years, the world has changed drastically, and the teaching style of the past had to adapt significantly to hold the people of the future up and represent them.

Changes include strong demographic changes, numerous modern families, population migration, more trained parents, mothers with strong job commitments but also homework commitments, health concerns such as growing child obesity, technological trends, and access, technological lack of data security, and economic shift from the local resource to the global economy of information, changing modalities. The biggest influence on learning is mutual effectiveness. As educators, all factors that enhance learning and have the greatest impact must be acknowledged and enforced (Barton, 2019). These are the iceberg tips of the many reforms that are happening to enhance learning for all students.

As an educator, we need to improve and adapt our instruction to all students continually. We must help students understand what they understand and why and whom they can do next or who should ask to help improve self-efficacy (Barton,

2019). Our enthusiasm and knowledge are unbelievably high and must continue to inspire our students.

The days of working in isolation as a teacher have ended; communication and collaborations are essential to improving collective productivity learning and working together to 'know your effect.' Student-centered coaching is one of the strongest methods of gathering, evaluating, and engaging in all school cultures.

It is important to design pedagogies that produce meaningful learning through educational concepts, skills, content, assessment, learning, and teaching.

8.2 Learning Analytics Based Pedagogical Framework

Learning analytics is an evolving technical practice and a multidisciplinary research discipline to facilitate successful learning and learning knowledge. Ville Heilala has incorporated the knowledge discovery process, pedagogical knowledge concepts, learning analytics ethics, and microservice architecture in his design science research (Heilala, 2018). The outcome is a pedagogical learning analytics framework. The system aims to use learning analytics in practice.

Automated and ethical learning analytics are designed to address ethical, analytical, and automated problems. Automated and ethically performed learning analytics will provide teachers with new and practical insights by using applicable learning process insights. Ville Heilala referred to this form of research as pedagogical learning analytics (Heilala, 2018). It can be represented as a process cycle (Fig. 8.2).

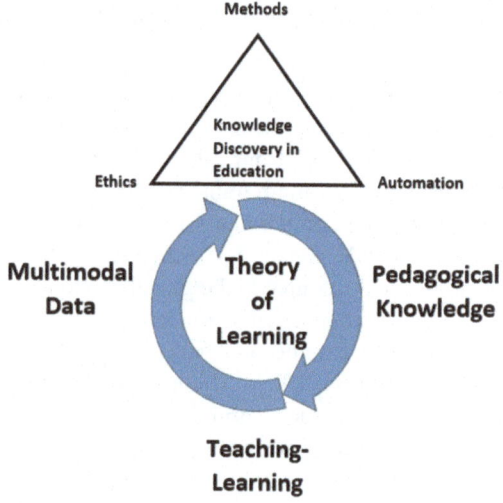

Fig. 8.2 Conceptual model of pedagogical learning analytics cycle for providing novel and useful knowledge about learning processes (Heilala, 2018)

8.2.1 Pedagogical Learning Analytics

Pedagogical learning analytics uses the educational knowledge discovery process to provide valid, innovative, and valuable knowledge that teachers can use to build and enhance teaching-learning situations and environments across subjects (Heilala, 2018). Combining this definition with the philosophy of the learning analytics cycle (Clow, 2012) and broadening the meaning of education data with multimodality (Blikstein & Worsley, 2016), Ville Heilala sketches the concept model of pedagogical learning analytics cycle (Fig. 8.3).

The focus of the pedagogical learning analytics study cycle (Fig. 8.3) is on scientific theory and knowledge about learning (1). An ultimate understanding of how people learn provides the basis for pedagogical learning analytics. For example, learning theories might guide as to what types of data are required. The actual learning occurs when students and teachers take action to teach and learn to achieve successful learning (2). These activities generate multimodal data of different kinds (3), which are collected and registered. The ethical and automated information retrieval method uses knowledge discovery and data mining (4). The knowledge discovery process outcomes are pedagogical knowledge (5), which leads to teaching and learning. Pedagogical learning analytics can be constructive feedback as new information about learning generally may lead to knowledge gained from the knowledge discovery process.

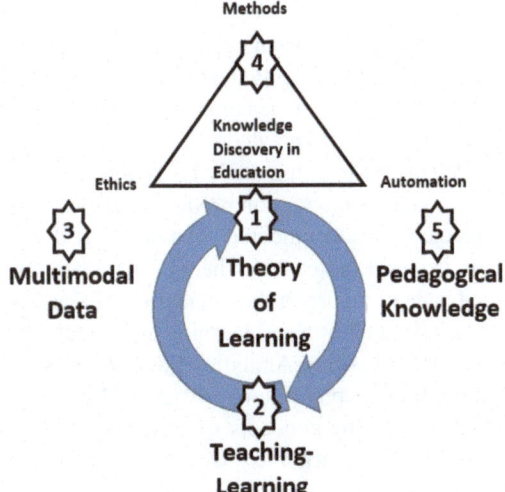

Fig. 8.3 Pedagogical learning analytics cycle (Heilala, 2018)

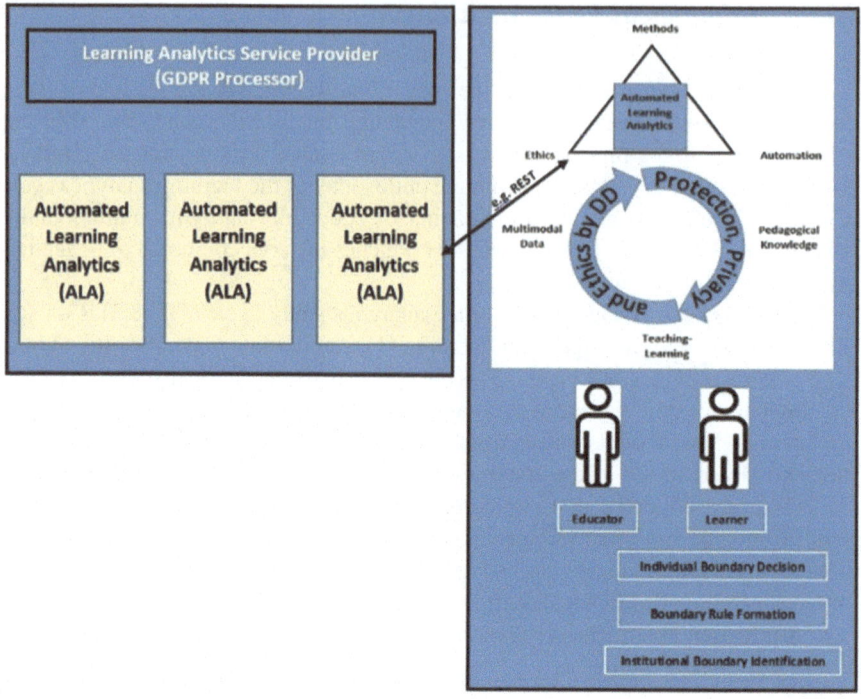

Fig. 8.4 Framework for pedagogical learning analytics (Heilala, 2018)

8.2.2 Framework for Pedagogical Learning Analytics

The definition of pedagogical learning analytics (Heilala, 2018) is based on the framework (Fig. 8.4). Pedagogical learning analytics is an analytics cycle that provides teachers with pedagogical knowledge. Teachers will use this expertise for their pedagogical knowledge base as a building block.

Pedagogic learning analytics begins with the relationship between teaching and learning. This interaction produces various types of multimodal data tracks that are collected and documented. The automated educational knowledge discovery process is based on learning theory. The analytics create educational information that the teacher can use in the interaction of teaching-learning.

Legal regulation and learning analytical ethics (e.g., GDPR) constitute the basis for LAP (Learning Analytics Policy) and system design as a whole. The system design follows protection, privacy, and ethics principles by design and default. The LAP defines the concepts used in educational institutions for the use of learning analytics. The learner assesses these values with his personal privacy needs.

Educational organizations may use external service providers to supplement their analytical repertoire. A service provider can be treated as a GDPR data processor when the data is only used on behalf of an educational institution and not for any other purpose. In any event, the processor must comply with legal requirements, policy on learning analytics, and other agreements with educational institutions.

Automation uses the architecture of microservices. The advantages of the design are derived from studying analytical services. They can be programmed with various programming languages as autonomous and decoupling services. Analytical tasks can be divided into separate services, and more complex services can then be created. Services communicate via Representational State Transfer that enables the architecture of client-servers and a standardized interface. Therefore, services are also replaceable and upgradable as they rely on each other and clients' implementations.

8.3 Pedagogical Interventions

Wise (A. F. Wise, 2014) stresses the general value of intervention design, putting it within the wider landscape of the field of learning analytics and then discusses particular issues of intervention design for students to use learning analytics. Four principles of pedagogical learning analytics intervention design to support the productive use of learning analytics by students that can be used by teachers and course developers are introduced.

- Integration
- Agency
- Reference Frame
- Dialogue

Furthermore, three main processes for engaging students are described:

- Grounding
- Setting goals
- Reflection

These principles and processes form a preliminary model of student intervention design for pedagogical learning analytics, provided as a starting point for further inquiry.

8.3.1 Classes of Pedagogical Interventions

Two classes of pedagogical interventions were defined by Wise (A. F. Wise, 2014).

1. ***Pedagogical interventions for Teachers:*** Lockyer and his colleagues examined many of the key questions relating to the teachers' use of learning analytics (Lockyer, Heathcote, & Dawson, 2013). Their approach to the understanding and flow problems consisted of harmonizing learning analytics with the learning

design process. This produces a unified cycle in which teachers record their pedagogical intentions through learning design, which then provides the conceptual basis for the questioning and the interpretation of the theoretical knowledge presented (Dawson, 2011). Lockyer and colleagues underline the need to define, before time, what tasks trends of successful (or unsuccessful) student participation in the pedagogical design are anticipated and to use instruments like checkpoints and process analysis to look at these at certain points during the learning activities (Lockyer et al., 2013). This is significant because, depending on the task design, the same pattern of a task in a system can be considered more or less productive.

In answering questions of interpretive structures and the flow of action, Lockyer's model describes a pedagogical intervention by which teachers will systematically attempt to use analytics as a productive aspect of their daily teaching practice (Lockyer et al., 2013). Of course, other pedagogical interventions can also encourage teachers' use of learning analytics, but this is currently one of the few explicitly defined models.

2. *Pedagogical Interventions for Students.* Contrary to teacher use, student intervention design has received less consideration. In many situations, merely having well-designed analytics is considered to be enough for effective use. There are also many reasons to address this. One of the major problems is that students are often not aware of their teachers' pedagogical aims and, therefore, are not aware of the instructional activity's learning objectives and the development patterns of participation. The strong metacognitive skills required in analytics to be a tool for reflection and self-regulation are further challenges for students (Butler & Winne, 1995). Although teachers may have had training or knowledge of reflecting (Schon, 1986), students also fight as self-regulating students. The difficulty of understanding pedagogical intentions, identifying effective market patterns, and activation of self-regulatory challenges indicates that students themselves are unlikely to know how or why to use analytics. However, they also provide opportunities to make the students more active partners in managing their learning. The precise relationship between students' participation in an educational activity and their perception of the activity and its meaning (Knowlton, 2005) will enhance the ability to match student actions and the educational target by communicating pedagogical intentions. Also, being involved and engaged in directing one's learning promotes better learning processes and outcomes more generally (students' participation Dawson, 2011; Zimmerman, 1990), so that students can continue to gain in other academic areas as part of their use of analytics, especially by increasing customized methods of learning that position area Finally, encouraging students to be part of their learning training will enable analytics to act as an agent of empowerment instead of enslavement.

In the light of such possible benefits (A. F. Wise, 2014), it answers concerns about intervention design for student use of learning analytics and provides a collection of pedagogical concepts and processes that teachers and course developers should use to promote the efficient use of student learning analytics.

Although the traces, analytics, and particular intervention of learning analytics needed in a given situation are unique to that context, the study model can be defined in terms of general principles and processes that can be extended to a range of learning contexts for the framing of interpretive behavior by students.

8.3.2 Principles for Pedagogical Learning Analytics Intervention Design

Principle 1: Integration The integration theory is fundamental to the basic definition of pedagogical intervention design. This suggests that the pedagogical intervention design is intended to provide an atmosphere for the operation in which analytical instruments, data, and reports are taken up. Simultaneously, the integration theory says that the research should be an integral part of the activity linked to objectives and aspirations in this context. This principle explicitly tackles the challenge of helping students understand pedagogical intentions and helps avoid the rigidity of interpretation by establishing a local context to understand the data. It also facilitates the incorporation of analytical software into the learning environment operation flow. It also offers a way of customizing analytics so that the same analytical suite in different contexts can be used in different ways.

The basic principle of integration is that the use of learning analytics must be understood and that the students must recognize these relations as an aspect of the learning design itself. For this reason, the teacher or learning designer needs to determine in the plan of a learning event which metrics (of those offered by any method used) are to concentrate on in a given situation based on the intent of the education operation and to define the productive and unproductive trends in these metrics. This preparation process is related to the principle of aligning learning analytics with learning design as part of the teacher pedagogical intervention model (Lockyer et al., 2013).

The pedagogical learning analytics intervention design requires two additional main elements and selecting metrics and predicting patterns. A strategy to communicate the link between learning analytics and learning activity with the students is the first additional aspect so that the link between goals, actions, and feedback is clear. This is conceptualized as a process of Grounding.

The second aspect is understanding when and how students can work with the selected analytics concerning the learning environment's activity flow. In certain situations (for example, with students who have encountered self-regulation), it might be good to provide students with a background at the beginning of their learning experience and leave them alone to determine whether analytics can be incorporated into individual learning processes. However, it can be helpful (or even necessary) to direct students when the study can be consulted in certain situations. This can be enforced by creating a schedule or timescale for control points that make sense of the operation involved. The problem of temporal integration is part of the Goal-Setting and Reflection process.

Principle 2: Agency Learning is a students' task to excel (Zimmerman, 1990). The opportunity to assist the learner in effectively controlling his learning process is a central attraction to learning research (Govaerts, Verbert, Klerkx, & Duval, 2010). Therefore, the Agency's principle aims to encourage learning analytics interventions that promote rather than hinder students' production and self-regulatory skills. This also answers fears that analytics is another master for students to serve rather than a power tool. In thinking of the student agency, there are two important elements: firstly, the interpretation agency (what the information is given means, how does this contribute to what is important to me in this situation), and secondly, the agency to respond to the measure. Each of these components is addressed through the processes of Goal-Setting and Reflection.

Principle 3: Reference Frame In addition to the two main Integration and Agency principles, there are two other intervention design principles to encourage the production use of analytics. The first is the reference frame principle. A benchmark is essentially the point of reference on which students concentrate on their study.

Firstly, the course instructor defined the theoretical activity patterns as efficient, which serve as an absolute point of reference for comparison. The second is a previous activity for a student that is a relative point of reference for comparison. The teacher may choose to emphasize one another, depending on the nature of the analytics' use. The third frame of reference that can be used is the one used by other students. Aggregate performance information for other students is also given in analytical frameworks and can show a student where they are compared to other students in a class (Govaerts et al., 2010) but can have some negative potential effects as well (A. Wise, Zhao, & Hausknecht, 2014). So how other students' comparison system is put in an essential component of pedagogical intervention design.

Specifically, other students' performance can motivate underperforming students who may first not understand how their actions are guided towards others. However, this reference system can also lead to competitive conduct or be overwhelming and intimidating for some students. Also, aggregated class statistics like averages are likely to become goals for students, which may or may not be sufficient based on the class's activity profile. When students only find out the method, the analytical patterns shown cannot be ideal or practical goals at the beginning of a course. Furthermore, measurements of the class's central tendency (especially the average) can be affected by some students' activities or inactivity. Recent work looking at student activity MOOCs reveals that a considerable proportion (40–80%) of the population participating in the course study did so to "sample" the course (Kizilcec, Piech, & Schneider, 2013); in this case, central tendency metrics will be a flawed benchmark for one's activities.

A number of the above-mentioned problems can be solved by the careful design and refining of analytical tools, e.g., processing data to provide aggregate measures for only similar categories of students or to provide aggregate variance measures

8.3 Pedagogical Interventions

and core trends. However, intervention designs often have an important role in helping students prioritize the benchmarks, peers, and expectations for their actions and recognize the principles and limitations of peer references given within a particular context. This knowledge is available in advance as part of the initial goal-setting process, during the learning activity, or through the individual dialogue mentioned below.

The Student Activity Meter, for example, is a learning analytics system that offers learners route maps, bar charts, and coordinate displays showing how they compare with their peers about metrics such as working time, the number of seminars they attend, and the number of services they use (Govaerts, Verbert, Duval, & Pardo, 2012). This toolkit advocate using a peer comparison system when analyzing the data, although the line chart enables students to observe shifts in their work habits over time.

This analytical tool's pedagogical action may take many different forms to promote effective comparative behavior while protecting against a detrimental competitive mindset. External expectations for planned operation can be set in certain courses. If, for example, it is understood that there are a limited number of resources to be consulted in general for a project to succeed, this amount can be stressed to students as a fixed guide for measuring progress from the outset. Similarly, if the teacher knows that students appear to be more effective if they are engaged in a smaller number (rather than several brief ones) of intensive work, then they can be encouraged to work towards a line chart pattern which involves periods of steep rise rather than an only higher time.

If absolute metrics are more difficult to provide, a pedagogical intervention can concentrate on the individual frame of reference, specifically requiring that students keep track of their progress or progress towards the community and to set targets for them. Another strategy may concentrate on collaborative efforts to allow the class to use analytics as a diagnosis community to help each other move forward. Each intervention design's main purpose is to help students avoid the simplistic mindset of "more (than other students) is better."

While it is necessary and useful to know where one is about his or her peers, in some cases more than other cases (usually or for that particular student) may still be inadequate, in others everyone is already far beyond the limit, making additional effort to boost a particular metric waste effort. If all students always strive to overpower everyone else, it can also unintentionally produce an attractive impact.

Principle 4: Dialogue The introduction of learning analytics includes questions of power and access to analytics (Duval & Verbert, 2012). The concerns relating to these questions can be answered to some extent by the concept of dialogue; that creates a space to negotiate the understanding of analytics, in which data serves as a tool for reflection and discussion, rather than for the teacher, data on the students are collected. This complements the agency concept in which students are encouraged to set targets and focus on their analytics and encourages students to engage in this process.

Since many online journaling tools such as wikis and blogs encourage interactivity between individuals, a dedicated space for reflection can easily be used as a common space between students and teachers, or even between student groups. For example, as an example of a purposely generated space, EnquiryBlogger has provided teachers (and other students) with functionality to access and comment on blog entries and search for entries with unique learning provisions (Ferguson, Buckingham Shum, & Deakin Crick, 2011).

There are numerous benefits to dialoguing the process of reflection. First, a shared journal provides an audience for writing and encourages the student to hear his voice. In particular, students should include details that the teacher does not understand on its own (e.g., "I was having a very rough time in this section of the assignment," "I have tried extra hard this week," "I know I need to express my thoughts even more, but I do not always feel sure I have the right idea"). Secondly, it provides the teacher (or designate) the opportunity to review student interpretations of targeting and analysis and react as appropriate to resolve confusion, repair uncertain interpretations, or realign objectives.

Finally, in some situations, students can define targets based on their analytics, but they do not know how to advance them, so a dialogical space encourages them to ask for guidance, and the teacher can provide suggestions or solutions. Via collaborative journal writing, the process of reflection (Andrusyszyn & Davie, 1997) can be actively encouraged, and a checkpoint for students' positive self-regulatory routes. Also, the analytics itself facilitates discussion by serving as a third "voice" in the conversation.

This gives the teacher a neutral object to which he can refer in conversation usefully (for example, "you see that your level of attendance is different from that of the rest of the class" instead of "you need more participation"). The biggest obstacle in applying the dialogue theory is the question of scale. The instructor will communicate reasonably much with all the students in a small class, but as the student-teacher ratio increases, it becomes more challenging and is not feasible for large open online courses. However, two potential alternatives to facilitate analytical dialogue may be conceivable. First of all, a tiered structure may provide the principal dialogue partner for teaching assistants or student leaders with problems or questions posed to the teacher if appropriate.

Secondly, students may be able to help each other in some situations through partnership or triad models. The problem here is the students' lack of expertise and ability to effectively help each other, so this strategy will better work with students who are reasonably experienced in analytics to support their learning.

8.3.3 Processes for Pedagogical Learning Analytics Intervention Design

Process 1: Grounding There are three elements which students need to recognize to use analytics effectively to participate more effectively in a learning activity:

1. the purpose of the learning activity,
2. the characteristics of what is known as productive engagement in the activity and
3. How this is expressed by the learning analytics given.

Such understanding can be established in many ways. The objectives of the learning activity can, for example, be explained and explained to students according to the criteria of the learning background (student maturity, the class size, mixed or completely online format, time available, etc.) or maybe jointly decided by the teacher and the students. Similarly, active participation characteristics can be brainstormed and then finalized by the group or just given a justification. Both of these exercises (which aim at a mutual understanding of the teacher and students' intent and process) are also useful for helping students participate in the desired manner before the research is applied and can be implemented fairly in many ways, both face to face and in digital environments. Furthermore, the analytics available must be related to the accepted attributes of effective participation. The extent to which the various metrics' measurement specifics will be clarified and analyzed will differ according to the students' level, time available, and perceived value. Of aspect mentioned here is a compromise between the efficiency of presentation and profound student involvement. However, irrespective of the founding process's intent, a common understanding of the qualities of effective participation in the activity is established as a framework for the study.

Another important argument here is that it is a valuable exercise to see which metrics serve as measures and emphasize any qualities of efficiency that cannot be taken by the metrics to connect the analytical products available with the qualities of the production commitment. In applying learning analytics, one significant issue is that measurement can alone determine how people participate in the learning activity, and so will "become what we measure," even though these measures capture only some aspects of the overall activity (Clow, 2012; Duval & Verbert, 2012). It is also necessary for students to know what the analytics they use do not catch. It is also beneficial to take different steps so that no analytics are the only priority (A. Wise et al., 2014). To offer a clear example of the principle of integration and grounding processes, take the Uatu analysis framework for Google Docs (McNely, Gestwicki, Hill, Parli-Horne, & Johnson, 2012) to imagine collaborative writing. To facilitate the formative evaluation of cooperation between learners, the framework constantly collects and stores data on user inputs, changes in documents size, and time from Google Docs. The database visualizations include the document's revisions as they had happened over time and indicate who made those revisions when the revisions took place, the scale, and the amount of time spent.

If the teacher imagines that this tool will be used as part of an online postsecondary history class, he may first incorporate collective writing to improve subject awareness and comprehension of key issues through the continuous expansion of key themes across the course term.

She will then provide students with specific instructions about what is anticipated and what will be measured, e.g., the frequency, size, and consistency of the feedback. In this respect, the study should be incorporated to explain how the input visualizes the document's collaborative structure and how it applies to participation requirements. For example, as students go through the semester, the teacher will add to the document by defining or adding a theme every week to explain each contribution's amount of detail. The Uatu framework does not currently include quality measures, which should be addressed as an essential factor for the operation, although it is not included in the measures. This may also be addressed in cases where the analytical method offers details on the quality of contributions. This introduces analytics as to the knowledge that has a simple meaning in the sense of this unique collaborative writing practice. With other students and another form of writing, a different intervention design will inspire the same analytics suite productively in an alternative context.

Process 2: Setting goals In self-regulation, students direct their learning process through the concept of goals and the active work to achieve them (Schunk & Zimmerman, 2003). Goals will inspire students to make greater efforts to predict themselves and to track their accomplishments. In particular, self-set goals lead to increased self-efficiency, which influences learners' effort and commitment to meet the challenges (Zimmerman, Bandura, & Martinez-Pons, 1992). However, students need guidance to develop proximate and clear goals with the right learning level (Schunk, 1990). It might seem like these discussions are superfluous, as students will all strive to optimize each of these qualities after gaining a common understanding of the purpose of educational activity and the qualities of output participation.

However, this statement is unnecessarily simplistic as students can often set their objectives for a learning activity, others less so in line with the activity's educational goals (Butler & Winne, 1995). Moreover, each student has a different starting point and skills they have to learn so that each student has different aspects of the learning activities that need more focus than others, even to achieve the same end state. This indicates the need for many potential output and development profiles rather than for a common purpose and direction to be pursued by all students.

For these purposes, a key aspect of the learning analytics organization starts with an individual target concept to establish a personal meaning for analytics. By making individual objectives an explicit and organized part of the learning experience, learners are asked to consider the specified tasks, identify their strengths and limitations, and set clear and proximal objectives. Importantly, the process of setting goals should be linked to and followed by the establishment of the target of learning operation, as described in the integration principle. This allows learning analytics to facilitate the generation of precise and proximate objectives as they provide consistent indices for the setting of targets.

The actual goal-setting process does not have to be carried out explicitly in the learning analytics system, although there are many benefits to this, namely the ability to endorse initial goals and consistent reference as analytics are checked. nStudy, a web-based toolkit designed to help students learning online content by annotating (e.g., creating tags, notes, and definitional terms) and connect these knowledge objects to construct concept maps and the like (Winne & Hadwin, 2013). While efforts are still ongoing to improve learning analytics for the system, nStudy supports learners to achieve goals through a process that enables them to identify themselves and offers tools for showing importance, difficulty, target date, and current status. An educator who uses nStudy to teach could organize this goal-setting functionality specifically into some points in the term, requiring students, for example, to set goals at the beginning of each section of the course. There are also possibilities to exchange details on the entire class's aggregated goals using such a method. Whether this is helpful or harmful for setting goals and learning remains an open question of science. Objective notes in nStudy are easily identified, modified, and related to other objects in the system. After the system's analytical features are given, reports or a dashboard may also be connected to the targets, enabling reflection of the analytical indicators, along with particular purposes and goals.

Process 3: Reflection When set, the goals drive how students engage with education resources and activities, and the input generated by analytical technology will be a significant moderator for students to track and measure their progress towards their objectives (Locke & Latham, 2006), and decide when they have to update or modify the goals themselves. This series of activities include the review of information on recent learning activities and a data-informed reflection method. Reflection was long considered an important aspect of building one's understanding from a constructivist perspective; in turn, reflections can also be used more efficaciously to support learning as one's understanding grows (McAlpine & Weston, 2002). However, reflection historically relied upon the student's own set of events, which have not been especially good studies (Veenman, Van Hout-Wolters, & Afflerbach, 2006). Thus, learning analytics provides an essential advantage in supporting the reflection process based on more detailed results. In addition to setting goals, however, students need guidance in learning when and how to focus on and take action based on analytics. This is important, particularly because online activities can occur anywhere and sometimes never anywhere (Jun, 2005); conversely, attention to the constantly available analytics can draw from involvement in the activities. Thus, explicit time, space, and guidelines for reflection on analytics are needed to promote effective reflective practice. Time may be highly organized by focusing on particular course activity or offering suggested guidance to students. It is necessary to provide analytical feedback quickly enough to affect the methodology (Shum & Crick, 2012) and at a level that makes sense for analytics to analyze in a specific context. The time-frame over which the data are analyzed can dramatically impact the results, particularly for analytics that track larger constructs (Zeini, Göhnert,

Hoppe, & Krempel, 2012). The pace of study or access and reflection depends on the context, but creating a clear schedule prevents overwhelming students or render them over-reliant or analytical (Buckingham & Ferguson, 2012).

The notion of a dedicated space for reflection often encourages the actual execution of the method and the reflection of learners to look back on their success in learning over time. With historical documents, students can see their progress (or lack thereof), track their priorities, and get a clearer understanding of their learning activity participation. The most obvious alternative is maybe a blog format, with students who can express, refine, and represent their views, ideas, and opinions through writing in a journal (Ferguson et al., 2011). However, a wiki can also be used effectively for this reason (A. F. Wise, Zhao, & Hausknecht, 2013). Blogs and wikis also allow for interactivity between learners or between the student and the teacher and thus allow reflective journal writing to become a collaborative or dialogue-based practice (Andrusyszyn & Davie, 1997).

Finally, students need support in the reflection process. Many of these recommendations can take the form of just-in-time reminders to look back at their goals, evaluate previous analyses, and think about their success and the need for more effort. Reflective guidance may also be given by clear questions of reflection or a formal reflective method when needed. Another alternative is integrating reflection support into the analytical framework or implementing an analysis of the reflection process itself. The EnquiryBlogger framework supplies a reflective journaling approach, enabling students to mark their entries with a variety of useful learning arrangements (e.g., critical curiosity, strategic awareness), and offers visual analytics reflecting this understanding of their learning power (Shum & Crick, 2012).

8.4 A Preliminary Model of Pedagogical Learning Analytics Intervention Design

The problems associated with each of the above concepts are not separate and are, in fact, very closely connected. The reflection process, for example, is related to objectives, uses a reference frame, and is discussed with the teacher as part of a conversation, while integration is, in part, a meta-organizing concept that encapsulates all other concepts. A preliminary model incorporating the pedagogic learning analytics intervention design elements for students in Fig. 8.5 reflects these relationships (A. F. Wise, 2014).

This model is not an endpoint but a starting point to stimulate attention to intervention design in learning analytics. This model needs to be implemented, reviewed, validated, updated, and the awareness of other variables that can help students make use of learning analytics is needed.

To develop their more general usefulness and recognize the additional factors required to apply it and adapt it effectively to various learning analytical contexts, further applying the pedagogical intervention design models in other educational

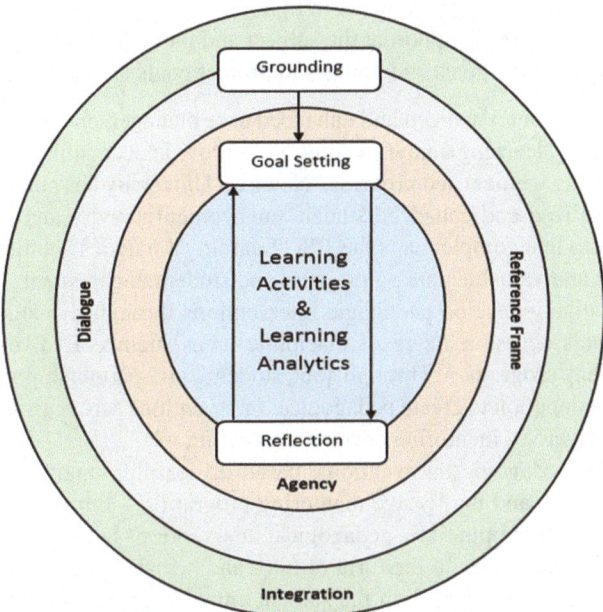

Fig. 8.5 A preliminary model of pedagogical learning analytics intervention design (A. F. Wise, 2014)

contexts involving various learning analysis applications and learners' populations is necessary.

8.5 Case Study: Newman University Birmingham's 'Collaborative Development of Pedagogic Interventions Based on Learning Analytics'

The project "Collaborative development of pedagogic interventions based on learning analytics" from Newman University Birmingham aimed to use student engagement activity data to drive pedagogic innovation.

8.5.1 Aims and Objectives

The main aim of the project was to enable more students to fulfill their potential. Emergent results indicate that this has been accomplished using the university's student-staff partnership framework to establish and incorporate data-informed tutor and peer-led mentoring systems. In light of student engagement results, these provide tailored personal support at the subject and modular levels.

The original project goals and updates to project goals are given here:

1. 'Implement a contextualized and enhanced case management system to complement the JISC learning analytics solution to provide accessible and usable data on student engagement and progress.' Newman University has purchased SEAtS: a contextualized and enhanced student engagement activity and case management system that complements the JISC Learning Analytics solution; this offers accessible and valuable data on progress and student engagement.
2. 'Collaboratively develop pedagogic interventions through five student partnership projects across a range of discipline areas include Evolve's mentoring development program' - Through four student-staff partnership projects, they work in conjunction to create pedagogical interventions across a variety of areas, including Evolve's mentoring development program.
3. 'Implement pedagogic interventions, based on learning analytics, across four discipline areas and the Evolve mentoring program' — through seven student-staff collaboration initiatives, pedagogical interventions have been carried out in three disciplinary areas in the form of tutor and peer-led mentoring systems for a full academic year, based on the student engagement results, and the Evolve Mentoring Program.
4. 'Evaluate the interventions through five student partnership projects'– evaluation of the mentoring interventions in another four student-staff partner projects.
5. 'Improve student retention & performance data on the participating programs' -confirmation that student retention & performance in participating programs have been improved.
6. 'Develop and disseminate five student-produced case studies of pedagogic interventions to enhance student progression based on learning analytics.' Project findings have been disseminated internally and across the sector by seminars, conference papers, and article submissions and continue beyond completing the formal project.

8.5.2 Key Milestones

The project worked in three separate phases:

Phase 1 (December 2016–July 2017)
The project steering group and the internal institutional reporting mechanism have been developed. The Learning, Teaching, and Assessment Committee collected and agreed upon the following policy, student guide, and FAQs:

- Using Student Engagement Data policy
- Supporting student learning through information: a student guide
- Using Student Engagement Policy FAQs

Staff/Student Partnerships. Two student/staff workshops were conducted to help student/staff teams establish how to consult with students. They also initiated a discussion of the different pedagogical approaches to help the students in other situations. Student-staff projects across three subject disciplines and Evolve surveyed the student body on the most successful approaches for students experiencing issues in this area. An additional workshop complemented this on 17 June, which disseminated the first consultation results and improved piloting interventions in Phase 2. By 30 June 2017, Phase One project reports from each region have been sent to the Academic Practice Unit.

Preparation of data. The cross-departmental work between IT employees, then Student Records, and the Academic Practice Unit was carried out to identify and collect the data necessary to migrate Moodle and student records into the Jisc Learning Analytics warehouse. This included validating the data after they were sent to the warehouse via Jisc software to test data integrity. Key project employees at Jisc Pathfinder and Analytics network meetings continued involvement. Part-time job description decided on the role of the developer of IT analytics.

Case Management System. A webinar with Unicon on the Student Success Platform's institutional usage revealed that it was not adaptable in the UK's anticipation. The decision not to use SSP was followed, and market research on other CMS used in the sector was carried out. Jisc proposes 'Co-tutor': as a potential alternative to a sector-developed system.

Phase 2 (August 2017–October 2017)

Staff/Student Partnerships. A student/staff workshop was organized to show how student interaction data could be used as a basis for pedagogical interventions. In September 2017, Phase Two applications were submitted to the Academic Practice Unit detailing the planned actions to be carried out across Evolve, English, Youth and Community Service, Sport, and Health. In September 2017, the piloting of data-informed peer and tutor-led mentoring systems started. The assessment started simultaneously with pilots through interviews and focus groups.

Data. Continued compilation and student activity data validation. Data Explorer testing and initial discussions with Jisc on library data migration into Learning Records Warehouse. Part-time IT Analytics developer job advertising is done. Jisc Pathfinder and Analytics network meetings continued attendance.

Case Management System. JISC and Newman's interactions with the co-tutor failed to create a feasible framework. Software demonstration and initial discussions with SEAts. Additional CMS exploration within the sector.

8.5.3 Significant Inputs or Outputs

The project had to adjust repeatedly but delivered its main inputs and outputs. The most important feedback and subsequent outcomes of the project were to create, execute, and assess pedagogical interventions by creating a student engagement data and case management system and leading student partnerships.

Management of student engagement data. When the project started, the data challenges' magnitude created sufficient data on student participation, gathering it, validating it, and migrating it. Members of the core project team have done extensive work to accomplish this. This helped to create a single warehouse for truth data with Jisc. In addition to the development of accessible data, adequate data collection and use policies had to be created and enforced by the university. Jisc has done extensive development work to provide user input on its data warehouse and the Data Explorer system. Due to the delay in developing a functional system, JISC systems were used for a large part of the project, but SEAtS was eventually embraced by student interaction data and case management IT system. This required additional funding for the project by the University. Due to the delayed introduction of the case management system, SEAts has not yet been completely incorporated as originally intended with Newman University systems, although these efforts continue to underpin the project's feasibility.

Student staff partnership work. Four phases one student staff collaboration projects were undertaken, covering English, Youth and Community Work, Sport and Well-being, and Evolve. This collected student feedback about what would be effective pedagogical interventions to benefit students in their fields. Academic practice and the Tutor for Transition and Retention offered preparation and development for these and further project iterations. In Step II, these four groups adopted the suggested interventions. Due to the delay in determining a suitable IT framework, some funding has been reallocated to support three academic areas in the second round of intervention projects in the second half of 2017/18 at the interim report stage. Finally, in phase three, the student assessment programs were performed in all four regions. A total of 15 student-staff collaboration initiatives were undertaken in all.

The student-staff collaboration projects' learning was substantial, and the students were the main contributors to the project's distribution and assessment. Student stakeholders have engaged completely in the design, implementation, and assessment of individual and general projects. Their voice spread beyond Newman through workshops and other distribution events in Europe through the HEFCE Catalyst Fund.

The experience gained from working with students in collaboration facilitated closer and substantive connections between student-staff partners, leading to a shared understanding of each other's circumstances and obligations. Moreover, work within the university has helped the catalyst project establish multidisciplinary connections, which has generated interdisciplinary awareness between different staff and student groups, promoting student partners' personal and professional growth and improving their university evaluations.

8.5.4 Key Findings

It was found that using student engagement data to inform proactive peer and tutor-led subject-specific mentoring can assist in supporting the student transition into and through level four studies. The Catalyst project's qualitative evidence indicates that staff/student-student relationships will be established, a feeling of alienation reduced, and a sense of membership in new HE students promoted. Quantitative analysis shows an improvement in assessment submission rates and a substantial decrease in withdrawals and suspension at level 4 among the subjects concerned.

To make effective data-informed mentoring, it should be part of the university's larger support mechanism, as part of an integrated mentoring system where anyone can use, for example, not just those defined from engagement data. Also, a 'one size fits all' approach does not allow such pedagogical innovation to be built across all students' disciplines and communities. Such activities must be versatile and informal from the beginning to allow adaptation to the cohort, discipline, and need.

Staff stated that the provision of data-informed mentoring has been of value in several ways. In general, and significant, it has made it possible to promote student participation and experience as a learning environment.

On an individual level, the staff has recognized several accomplishments, including pro-active help for mentees and an organization that prioritizes work and home living. Qualitative data collected have enabled students to feel more able to cope with the transition to HE, create confidence, and understand how the university 'worked.'

Although this Catalyst project's emphasis does not lie in, the subject-specific awareness created by staff and students and between mentor and mentee has increased participation through discussions of the modules and specific evaluations. This has resulted in a further discussion of modules/courses/lecturers amongst mentors/mentors that can be very encouraging – i.e., the mentor shares his (relative) wealth of knowledge with the mentees and staff. The value of the subject-specific nature of mentoring is underlined in turn: it would be challenging to reach some kind of students who did not take the same/similar courses and went beyond superficial and signposted levels.

It is commendable to follow working methods that facilitate collaborations between students, technical staff, and support staff from various disciplines. This includes funding, trusting, listening, and working in ways that break down conventional power relationships. The human relationship at the sharp end of meeting student needs is central to the effective use of interaction data in pedagogical interventions. While big data will help prioritize assistance where it is needed the most, the most important thing for student development and achievement is caring human interaction.

8.6 Conclusion

The growing prevalence of learner-centered forms of learning and the increase in the number of students involved in various digital platforms and instruments contribute to an ever-rising stream of learning data. Learning analytics will better understand and forecast learning and success by the learners, teachers, and institutions. This chapter highlighted the value of pedagogical systems focused on learning analytics and pedagogical intervention design for students to use learning analytics.

8.7 Review Questions

Reflect on the concepts of this chapter guided by the following questions.

1. What is Pedagogy? What is the importance of Pedagogy in Teaching?
2. List and explain the factors that affect Pedagogy.
3. What are the various Pedagogical Approaches? Describe.
4. What are the standards for Effective Pedagogy? Explain in brief.
5. Write a note on the future of Pedagogy in education.
6. What do you mean by Pedagogical Learning Analytics? Describe.
7. With the help of a neat diagram, explain the Pedagogical Learning Analytics cycle.
8. Explain the framework for Pedagogical Learning Analytics.
9. What are the various classes of Pedagogical Interventions? Explain.
10. List and explain the principles & processes for Pedagogical Learning Analytics Intervention Design.

References

Andrusyszyn, M., & Davie, L. (1997). Facilitating reflection through interactive journal writing in an online graduate course: A qualitative study. *International Journal of E-Learning. Distance Education, 12*(1), 103–126. http://search.ebscohost.com/login.aspx?direct=true&db=ehh&AN =12900501&site=ehost-live

Barton, T. (2019). *Pedagogy in education.* Serve Learn. https://servelearn.co/blog/pedagogy-in-education/

Blikstein, P., & Worsley, M. (2016). Multimodal learning analytics and education data mining: Using computational technologies to measure complex learning tasks. *Journal of Learning Analytics, 3*(2), 220–238. https://doi.org/10.18608/jla.2016.32.11

Brown, B., & Eaton, S. E. (2020). Using a community of inquiry lens to examine synchronous online discussions in graduate courses. In L. Wilton & C. Brett (Eds.), *Handbook of research on online discussion-based teaching methods* (pp. 229–262). IGI Global. https://doi.org/10.4018/978-1-7998-3292-8.ch010

References

Buckingham, S., & Ferguson, R. (2012). Social learning analytics published by: International forum of Educational Technology & Society Linked references are available on JSTOR for this article. *Journal of Educational Technology & Society, 15*(3), 3–26.

Butler, D. L., & Winne, P. H. (1995). Feedback and self-regulated learning: A theoretical synthesis. *Review of Educational Research, 65*(3), 245–281. https://doi.org/10.3102/00346543065003245

Clow, D. (2012). The learning analytics cycle: Closing the loop effectively. *ACM International Conference Proceeding Series*, 134–138. https://doi.org/10.1145/2330601.2330636

Dawson, S. (2011). 'Seeing' networks: Visualising and evaluating student learning networks final report 2011 report authors: Dr Shane Dawson Ms Aneesha Bakharia Professor Lori Lockyer Ms Elizabeth Heathcote.

Duval, E., & Verbert, K. (2012). Learning analytics research issues. *E-Learning & Education, 1*(8), 7–11.

Ferguson, R., Buckingham Shum, S., & Deakin Crick, R. (2011). EnquiryBlogger: Using widgets to support awareness and reflection in a PLE Setting. *Proceedings of the The PLE Conference 2011, September 2015*, 28–32. http://oro.open.ac.uk/30598/

Goodyear, P. (2005). Educational design and networked learning: Patterns, pattern languages and design practice. *Australasian Journal of Educational Technology, 21*(1), 82–101. https://doi.org/10.14742/ajet.1344

Govaerts, S., Verbert, K., Duval, E., & Pardo, A. (2012). The student activity meter for awareness and self-reflection. *Conference on Human Factors in Computing Systems - Proceedings, 110067*, 869–884. https://doi.org/10.1145/2212776.2212860

Govaerts, S., Verbert, K., Klerkx, J., & Duval, E. (2010). Visualizing activities for self-reflection and awareness. *Lecture Notes in Computer Science (Including Subseries Lecture Notes in Artificial Intelligence and Lecture Notes in Bioinformatics), 6483 LNCS* (June 2014), 91–100. https://doi.org/10.1007/978-3-642-17407-0_10

Heilala, V. (2018). Framework for pedagogical learning analytics. *University of Jyväskylä Faculty of Information Technology*, 1–84.

Jun, J. (2005). Understanding E-dropout? *International Journal on E-Learning, 4*(2), 229–240.

Kizilcec, R. F., Piech, C., & Schneider, E. (2013). Deconstructing disengagement: Analyzing learner subpopulations in massive open online courses. *ACM International Conference Proceeding Series, February 2014*, 170–179. https://doi.org/10.1145/2460296.2460330.

Knowlton, D. S. (2005). A taxonomy of learning through asynchronous discussion. *Journal of Interactive Learning Research, 16*(2), 155–177.

LearningPortal. (2018). *Effective and appropriate pedagogy*. Learning Portal. http://learningportal.iiep.unesco.org/en/issue-briefs/improve-learning/teachers-and-pedagogy/effective-and-appropriate-pedagogy

Locke, E. A., & Latham, G. P. (2006). New directions in goal-setting theory. *Current Directions in Psychological Science, 15*(5), 265–268. https://doi.org/10.1111/j.1467-8721.2006.00449.x

Lockyer, L., Heathcote, E., & Dawson, S. (2013). Informing pedagogical action: Aligning learning analytics with learning design. *American Behavioral Scientist, 57*(10), 1439–1459. https://doi.org/10.1177/0002764213479367

McAlpine, L., & Weston, C. (2002). Reflection: Issues related to improving professors' teaching and students' learning. *Teacher Thinking, Beliefs and Knowledge in Higher Education*, 59–78. https://doi.org/10.1007/978-94-010-0593-7_4

McNely, B. J., Gestwicki, P., Hill, J. H., Parli-Horne, P., & Johnson, E. (2012). Learning analytics for collaborative writing: A prototype and case study. *ACM International Conference Proceeding Series*, 222–225. https://doi.org/10.1145/2330601.2330654

Schon, D. A. (1986). The reflective practitioner: How professionals think in action. *The Journal of Continuing Higher Education, 34*(3), 29–30. https://doi.org/10.1080/07377366.1986.10401080

Schunk, D. H. (1990). Goal setting and self-efficacy during self-regulated learning. *Educational Psychologist, 25*(1), 71–86. https://doi.org/10.1207/s15326985ep2501

Schunk, D. H., & Zimmerman, B. J. (2003). Self-regulation and learning. In *Handbook of psychology self-regulation* (pp. 59–78), Wiley: New York, United States.

Shum, S. B., & Crick, R. D. (2012). Learning dispositions and transferable competencies: Pedagogy, modelling and learning analytics. *ACM International Conference Proceeding Series, May*, 92–101. https://doi.org/10.1145/2330601.2330629

Teaching Tolerance. (2020). *Five standards of effective pedagogy*. Teaching Tolerance. https://www.tolerance.org/professional-development/five-standards-of-effective-pedagogy

TES. (2018). What is pedagogy? *Pedagogical Seminary*. https://doi.org/10.1080/08919402.1905.10534667

Veenman, M. V. J., Van Hout-Wolters, B. H. A. M., & Afflerbach, P. (2006). Metacognition and learning: Conceptual and methodological considerations. *Metacognition and Learning, 1*(1), 3–14. https://doi.org/10.1007/s11409-006-6893-0

Winne, P. H., & Hadwin, A. F. (2013). nStudy: Tracing and supporting self-regulated learning in the internet. *Midlands State University Library, 28*, 293–308. https://doi.org/10.1007/978-1-4419-5546-3

Wise, A., Zhao, Y., & Hausknecht, S. (2014). Learning analytics for online discussions: Embedded and extracted approaches. *Journal of Learning Analytics, 1*(2), 48–71. https://doi.org/10.18608/jla.2014.12.4

Wise, A. F. (2014). Designing pedagogical interventions to support student use of learning analytics. *ACM International Conference Proceeding Series*, 203–211. https://doi.org/10.1145/2567574.2567588

Wise, A. F., Zhao, Y., & Hausknecht, S. N. (2013). *Learning analytics for online discussions: A pedagogical model for intervention with embedded and extracted analytics* (p. 48) https://doi.org/10.1145/2460296.2460308

Yadav, K. (2020). *Effective pedagogical approaches*. Evelyn Learning. https://evelynlearning.com/effective-pedagogical-practices/

Zeini, S., Göhnert, T., Hoppe, U., & Krempel, L. (2012). The impact of measurement time on subgroup detection in online communities. *Proceedings of the 2012 IEEE/ACM international conference on advances in social networks analysis and mining, ASONAM 2012*, 389–394. https://doi.org/10.1109/ASONAM.2012.70

Zimmerman, B. J. (1990). Self-regulated learning and academic achievement: An overview. *Educational Psychologist, 25*(1), 3–17. https://doi.org/10.1207/s15326985ep2501

Zimmerman, B. J., Bandura, A., & Martinez-Pons, M. (1992). Self-motivation for academic attainment: The role of self-efficacy beliefs and personal goal setting. *American Educational Research Journal, 29*(3), 663–676. https://doi.org/10.3102/00028312029003663

Chapter 9
Moving Forward

9.1 Self-Learning and Learning Analytics

One of the key goals of education is to help students improve their own abilities to learn effectively. However, this is not an easy mission. Students have to acquire various skills to set targets, monitor their progress towards these objectives, correct performance if necessary, and analyze outcomes when concluding the next performance. You will need to find ways to move forward if you are confused or otherwise stalemate in the learning process. Understanding how to help students improve these skills was a central challenge for many researchers in education and learning psychology. These attempts were mainly found in self-regulated learning (SRL) (Panadero, 2017), which we term Self-Learning or Independent Learning.

9.1.1 Self-Regulated Learning Across Educational Environments

Self-regulated learning has a long history, and over the last two decades, it has become a major focus in education-psychology (Panadero, 2017). Self-regulated learning is characterized as "self-generated thoughts, feelings, and actions that are planned and cyclically adapted to the attainment of personal goals," according to Zimmerman (Lodge, Panadero, Broadbent, & Barba, 2019). SRL models consistently demonstrated their significance and effect on student success and learning (Lodge et al., 2019). SRL has become more common in computer-based learning environments in recent years.

This development is also related to a wider discussion of how technology affects the learning process. There are many main explanations. Educational institutions at all levels are under rising pressure to offer high-quality education to a growing number of students with greater effectiveness. The rapid speed of change in the world makes it difficult for students to prepare for their careers and live in a dynamic social and economic milieu. Students who complete formal education may expect retraining and/or change over their working lives, likely more than once. This continuous need for education led to introducing concepts such as the twenty-first-century skills that are transferable skills that underly lifelong education (Aspin, Chapman, Hatton, & Sawano, 2012).

Lodge et al. (2019) and others say that SRL is key to allowing students to manage this new reality. It is also clear that SRL has a role to play in seeking to understand complex issues. It is easy to be fooled without having sufficient ability to decide how much you do or do not do about a subject. Some claim that skill is a form of critical thinking or digital literacy (Miller & Bartlett, 2012). Whatever the mark, it is a matter that students increasingly need the capacity to learn, upgrade, and judge complex and structural concepts.

As we discussed, this is a challenge given the kind of digital environments in which students study. Importantly, all stages of education are becoming omnipresent interactive learning environments. Where once the word 'blended learning' has been used to describe a formal education system in which innovations are combined, almost all formal and informal learning can now be included in the phrase. This technological explosion causes some important side effects that have significant repercussions while considering SRL. These include increased criteria for self-directed students (Hoffman & Ritchie, 1997). Increasingly adaptive and personalized interactive learning environments enable students to participate in successful SRL (Greene, Moos, & Azevedo, 2011) and face obstacles as they learn, such as avoiding multifaceted or accessing social media temptations.

Another result of this is that teachers find it more difficult to track student development. When students engage more and more with interactive worlds, the contact between students and teachers decreases proportionately. Therefore, teachers who work in such environments have trouble deciding when intervention is appropriate (Arguel, Lockyer, Lipp, Lodge, & Kennedy, 2017). On the other hand, certain of these settings can evaluate students and recognize those who require intervention. Ever-expanding class sizes amplify this added complexity for teachers. Providing individual students with personalized intervention, as required, is an extremely challenging challenge for teachers in physical and virtual classrooms in the twenty-first century. A particular promise of learning analytics is the opportunity to encourage students to improve their SRL skills, free teachers to intervene more focused and complex.

When trying to understand the consequences of students spending time in different learning environments for SRL, it is helpful to consider student growth levels of granularity. It is reasonably straightforward to obtain a significant student accomplishment at the macro level by analyzing how they advance academically. In the sense of higher education, this reflects the successful completion of the subject/unit/module. Therefore, early use of Learning analytics focused on this macro-level analysis (e.g., Macfadyen & Dawson, 2010). While it is relatively easy to see signs that students will struggle at this level to self-regulate learning, it is difficult to decide why. Many factors may lead to students' success that cannot include their self-regulating ability in their studies.

On the other hand, it has been effective to evaluate how students participate in self-regulated small-scale lab-based observation studies at the microlevel. For example, Antonietti, Colombo, and Di Nuzzo (2015) researched self-regulation processes when performing a digital learning challenge involving various multimedia content mixtures. The laboratory-based environment in which this study took place permitted the collection of rich physio-logical, behavioral, and self-reporting data. Multiple SRL indicators are much easier to obtain in managed environments of this kind, a privilege that "in the wild" does not afford digital environments. Extensive work is also done by nStudy et gStudy (e.g., Perry & Winne, 2006) and by Azevedo, Johnson, Chauncey, and Graesser (2015) by Phil Winne. However, it is complex to translate data from laboratories like these into the real world to use education technology (Lodge & Horvath, 2017). A highly managed environment will help better understand how SRL students participate in digital and online learning, but it is unlikely that the SRL student can have clear answers.

Consequently, the interest and need to help SRL in digital environments is growing alongside an interest in understanding what these environments mean for SRL. Helping students navigate digital knowledge channels that are constantly ambiguous and contradictory is crucial to their long-term learning. More and more critically, students must develop cognitive task abilities that cannot be automated soon. Dealing with difficult, systemic information is not currently or possibly feasible for computers soon. However, dealing with such concepts requires an advanced SRL power. Together, educational researchers and educators must concentrate on improving SRL in digital settings, including how learning analytics can be used to support this imperative.

9.1.2 Learning Analytics for SRL

Learning analytics to support SRL usually has two elements: a calculation and a recommendation (Winne, 2017). The calculation, for example, a notation about presence, count, proportion, length, probability, is based on traces of acts performed during one or more episodes of analysis (Roll & Winne, 2015). A numerical report with or as visualization may be submitted. Examples may be a stacked bar chart showing relative proportions of highlights, tags, and notice produced during the analysis of each of several Web pages, timeframes marked with dots to indicate when specific traces were formed, and a node-link graph showing links among words in a glossary with heat map decorations showing how often each term was operated on while studying.

This aspect represents knowledge identifying COPES in the history of a student relationship directly or by the transformation. Table 9.1 displays illustrative trace data that could be mirrored.

A "simple" history of trace data mirrored back to a learner can be affected or contextualized by other information: features of materials such as length or a readability index, demographic data describing the learner (e.g., prior achievement,

Table 9.1 Analytics describing COPES facets in SRL (Winne, 2017)

S. No	COPES facet	Description
1.	Conditions	Presence/absence of a condition within a learning episode Onset/Offset along the timeline in a study or across a series of episodes
2.	Operations	Frequency of SMART operations (see Table 9.2) Sequence, pattern, conditional probability one SMART operation relative to others
3.	Product	Presence Completeness (for example, number of fields with the text entered in a note's schema) Quality
4.	Standard	Presence Precision Appropriateness
5.	Evaluation	Presence Validity

hours of extracurricular work, postal code), or other characterizations of leaners such as disposition to procrastinate, a degree in a social network (the number of people with whom this learner has exchanged information) or context for study (MOOC vs. face-to-face course delivery, opportunity to submit drafts for review by peers before handing in a final copy to be marked) (Table 9.2).

The second element of Learning analytics about SRL is a recommendation – what improvements can be made to learn and improve it. Three aspects of COPES can be managed directly by learners: operations, standards, and certain circumstances. Products are only indirectly controllable since their features rely on (1) circumstances under which learners, under particular information chosen for operations, may choose to vary; (2) what operations they choose to enforce in manipulating information. Evaluations are calculated by the match between product attributes and the basic criteria for certain items accepted by the learner. Recommendations on changing conditions, operations, or standards can be focused on results from mining data that are not influenced by theory, study findings in learning, and combination.

If a recommendation is given or not, changes in the student's conduct trace a student's assessment that (1) prior learning methods were not adequately productive or acceptable, and (2) the student expects that the recommendation or its adaptation would benefit from a shift. Learning analytics in this sense update external conditions previously and deliver new internal conditions. Together, there is a potential for intervention, but this is only for two reasons. Firstly, students should not know how to make a recommendation or how to do so. Second, they monitor their learning because students are agents.

Therefore, learning review provides students with the ability to practice SRL, but they choose what to do. This logic has a significant corollary. If a learning analytic is provided without a recommendation for intervention, there is an incentive for a learner to study alternatives beforehand and now choose to practice by themselves.

Table 9.2 SMART cognitive operations (Winne, 2017)

S. No.	SMART cognitive operation	Description	Sample traces
1.	Search	Directing attention to particular information	Opening successive bookmarks using a search tool
2.	Monitor	Comparing information presentations in terms of standards	Highlighting text (the information highlighted meets a standard, e.g., important)
3.	Assemble	Relating items of information	Tagging Assigning two bookmarks to a titled folder
4.	Rehearse	Maintaining or re-instating information in working memory	Reviewing a note Copying, then pasting
5.	Translate	Transforming the representation of information	Paraphrasing Describing a graph, equation, or diagram in words

In other words, encouragement and current learning tactics may be examined by omitting recommendations and guidance for action.

9.2 Life-Long Learning and Learning Analytics

Lifelong learning is a term that incorporates a wide range of learning formats and is generally considered as education throughout the lifetime (Kalz, 2015). Lifelong learning may occur outside an education institution (non-formal) or accidentally and not intended (informal) in the formal sense organized by an educational institution. Every purposeful learning activity carried out permanently to develop knowledge, talents, and abilities can be considered lifelong learning. Due to global demographics, environmental imperatives, the prevalent access to knowledge through digital technologies, and the pace of innovation in science and technology, lifelong learning is critical in the twenty-first century. As a result of these factors, there is a growing need to equip people with knowledge in educational institutions and train them to upgrade their knowledge, skills, and competencies and accept responsibility for learning throughout their lives.

The (Kalz, 2015) describes the elimination of obstacles to lifelong learning as a significant point of action to be addressed by R&D and society in general.

- Poor family learning culture
- Lack of funding for lifelong learning
- Learning providers not adapted to students' needs
- Inadequate information systems to draw learners to learning
- Distance from the provision of education

- Lack of facilities at home
- Belief that the benefits system discourages learning

Although educational institutions emphasizing supporting short episodes of learning have generally offered the learning technology, little attention was paid to supporting the diverse spectrum of environments, lives, and individual characteristics of learners. Koper and Tattersall (2004) argue that time frames and the episodic and multi-institutional character of lifelong learning have not historically been expressed in conventional technical learning.

In the area of technology-enhanced learning (TEL), in recent years, a range of research recommendations have been established that help solve today's challenges by lifelong learners. This segment explains the use of learning analytics for lifelong learning.

The modeling and understanding of learner behaviors and contexts are one of the challenges in the field of TEL. Since lifelong learners may constantly change their learning context, location, goals, learning environment, and learning technology, it is not easy and promising to consider the learner's current situation to personalize and adapt to the learning environment. A lifelong learner can start his or her day on a trip by reading a working textbook on his or her tablet computer, continue working on a particular problem in a professional social network and participate in an online master class on a subject he or she wants to develop expertise in the evening. These brief episodes of 1-day learning reflect a symbolic image of lifelong learning as a whole. Learners are interested in various learning environments, different learning formats, and various learning technologies. The study, design, and identification of the learner context have historically been approached from the perspective of adaptive hypermedia (AH) under the learner paradigm (Brusilovsky & Henze, 2007). Using an analysis of the student behaviors and contexts, algorithms have been developed to predict the learner's behavior, provide instructions for the learning process, or personalize the learning presentation. However, in this work, there is a major limitation. The processing and rationalization of data work well in closed environments, including a particular electronic learning environment (for example, a learning management system). However, the incorporation of data from various learning contexts, as presented above, poses limitations. This is the 'open corpus problem' (Brusilovsky & Henze, 2007). Open corpus AH operates not on a closed collection of resources identified at the time of design but on the premise that learning resources and the meaning of learning context continuously change and expand.

Several initiatives for lifelong learner modeling have been launched to resolve this problem and to enable customization. A learner model is a total of all the information that a software system has about a learner. This model is continuously updated during learning and should represent the current state of learners' knowledge. While conventional learner models were closed and used only by technological infrastructure, newly open learner models for learner use were suggested and evaluated. The user is presented with the current state of such a learner model and various ideas about the advantages and the administration of such an open learner model. Bull and Kay (2010) define autonomous open learner models as totally

9.2 Life-Long Learning and Learning Analytics

controlled by learners rather than system-controlled or cooperatively controlled learner models. This approach solves the customization barrier of technical lifelong learning and gives learners control over their digital representation in a learner model.

Kay (2008) goes one step further in this approach and aims to connect and integrate learner models from different contexts into long-term learning models that incorporate lifelong learners' multiple contexts. In addition to collecting and storing such data, she also proposes incorporating lifelong learner model representations into lifelong learners' work contexts. This direction is also discussed in a relatively young research topic in the field of TEL known as 'Learning Analytics' (Griffin, McGaw, & Care, 2012). Learning analytics take advantage of available broad datasets (in terms of learners, classes, actions, etc.) to provide input for various stakeholders (learner, instructor, organization) in the form of practical visualizations. Although many projects in the field remain within the conventional limits of educational segments or organizations, many authors advocate a more open approach to learning analytics that is potentially useful in the context of lifelong learning (Shum & Ferguson, 2012). Approaches that track and collect students' behaviors in various TEL environments have particular potential to allow students to link different learning contexts (Romero-Zaldivar, Pardo, Burgos, & Delgado Kloos, 2012). Therefore, open student models and learning analytics reflect new technical solutions that can help learners link their knowledge from their learning experiences in various learning environments and contexts and dismantle personalization obstacles to lifelong learning.

Today's research focuses on open learning models and learning analytics to improve understanding of the learning process itself and its impact on metacognition. On the other hand, the assessment contexts were chosen predominantly concentrate on schools' context, and the transition of outcomes to authentic lifelong learning contexts cannot be accomplished without limitations. A relatively high visual literacy level is a constraint for both methods discussed here to use the data representation supplied. Therefore, some problems in open learning models and learning analytics relate to promoting learners' visualization methods and data on learning activities.

9.2.1 Establishing a Lifelong Learning Environment Using IoT and Learning Analytics

Cheng and Liao (2012) jointly considered IoT (Internet of Things) and learning analytics techniques to evaluate students' learning process for lifelong learning support.

They used IOT and learning analytics techniques to build the environment ELLA (Environment for lifelong learning using learning analytics) that combines devices such as mobile devices, KIOSK, copy machine, RFID locker, Dom-air-conditioner, school bus, VOI, SMS, information service, web terminal, vacancy in the classroom,

classroom entrance, garage, student ID, electronic student ID, library, etc. Teachers may use these devices to teach their students, pick their teaching strategies, and provide different information and teaching contents according to the learning strategies.

The learning analytics system will collect IOTE data and provide the instructor with learning success and outcomes interpretation. The instructor will change the teaching methods and instructional practices and increase learning efficacy through the learning analytics framework's recommendations. Also, students could benefit from the learning analytics framework and improve their learning performance and quality.

As for learners, ELLA has the following features:

- In this environment, learners can access all their physical resources through their student ID or NFC cell phones.
- IOT technique has been used to store and evaluate all records of students' physical resource usage in schools in this environment.
- Learners can use mobile devices to access all kinds of resources and reviews and recommendations given by ELLA on the internet.
- Prior arrangements can be made before classes by pre-visual data generated by teachers.
- They can give teachers feedback and information and build learning activities on the internet at any time through mobile devices.
- They can use the mobile device to record the entire learning process and put them in LMS (including video recording).
- They can use mobile devices and the Internet to chat and video call online at any time with their classmates and teachers.
- They can engage in cooperative learning, debate, and exchange of experiences with their classmates.
- They can exchange information and share their records.
- The learning process will be saved permanently in LMS.
- They can monitor and examine all sorts of learning data in detail, including participation, conversations, practice, purchasing physical books, and even data copying and course material arrangements.

ELLA had the following characteristics for teachers:

- Teachers can access the physical tools they need to learn through their Instructor ID or NFC mobile phones.
- Teachers can upload or share all kinds of learning resources using a Mobile Device.
- They will collect feedback from students using mobile devices and engage in their study activities in ELLA, and give suggestions at any time.
- Teachers can always access students' real-time activities and historical learning records through ELLA.
- They can make online conversations and video calls with students at any time through the Internet.

- They will cooperatively learn, chat, and exchange experiences with students through this environment.
- Teachers can exchange information and documents with students.
- Their instructions will always be saved in LMS.
- All their teaching records, including discussion, guidance, copying of data, and the arrangement of contents, can be documented and examined in detail through this environment.

9.3 Present and Future Trends of Learning Analytics in the World

9.3.1 Trends that Influence Learning Analytics

Data has become an integral component of organizations in recent years. Trainers and L&D practitioners will use the power of Big Data to assess how well online training programs influence learners. The learning analytics market is primed for huge growth, with many developments shaping the future of learning analytics in organizations.

It would be correct to suggest that learning analytics can turn learning experience for students in an organization. The following trends (eThink, 2019; Katambur, 2020) influence learning analytics and add a new dimension to online training.

1. *Personalized learning:* The days when a one-size-fits-all training curriculum was administered to the students have gone. The emphasis is now on customized learning, with online education services designed for various students or classes. Learners in an organization should pursue their own course of learning at a comfortable rate. The quality and quantity of knowledge obtained from analytics offer insight into learners' preferences and learning styles. For instance, if learning analytics suggests that a student spends too much on a given portion of the e-learning course, videos, or links to additional material may enhance the student's understanding of the contents.
2. *Cloud Analytics:* More organizations can opt for cloud analytics as the data volume grows rapidly. With the growing security and efficiency of cloud computing, the use of data analytics with cloud computing increased. An LMS like Effectus, for example, can be installed on a cloud server, and the data monitored can be used for gaining insight into the status of online training programs. Cloud-based systems offer a flexible framework to store data and provide an efficient solution for data analytics.
3. *Self-service analytics:* Learning measurements are important in an organization to operate the L&D unit. Many organizations depend on LMS to determine the business effect of learning. However, according to a Bersin survey, 69% of organizations do not have analytical skills. Does this suggest that organizations must start employing more data scientists to make their data meaningful? Not at

all, since self-service analytics will help here. In order to make efficient use of self-service analytics and to make informed decisions, L&D practitioners and functional managers do not need to have IT or statistical context. Modern LMSs are well configured with dashboards and reports to reliably inform you about your organization's online training programs' status. Reports can be personalized with the support of an LMS vendor if appropriate.

4. *Machine Learning:* In learning analytics, there is a vast amount of training data that can be difficult to track and evaluate. For educational leaders to make the most of these data to understand and improve student learning, practitioners of learning analytics now aim to machine learning algorithms and approaches. Machine learning already influences many fields, including personalized learning, prediction of test results, risk determination of students, rise in graduation rates, and more. Learning analytics draws significant numbers now – all areas related to machine learning – from fields such as predictive modeling, statistics, and computer science. Therefore, integrating these two fields makes sense and is potentially the future of smart learning analytics.

5. *Deep Learning:* Deep learning is one development that will undoubtedly affect future years on learning analytics. With deep learning, data parameters are set such that the computer recognizes patterns after data runs across several processing layers. Deep learning algorithms are potentially one of the most useful methods for big data analytics. Deep learning is quite useful for the study of how people speak, read, and learn. Human intervention is not required because the machine can predict what learners know and do not know by reacting to tests and engaging with learning material. At present, the only thing not conducive to deep learning is that it is too costly.

6. *Self-regulated learning:* There are significant variables in self-regulated learning that could affect student progress. Why did one learner not successful in completing their learning activities while others succeed? To provide individual students with the best resources, the institutions need to consider certain variables, recognize trends, and resolve their educational design weaknesses before it is too late. By incorporating learning analytics, educational decision-makers may now evaluate student data from students enrolled in a course – be it online, in-class, or blended – to provide instructors and designers the knowledge they need to direct strategies for greater student retention and performance. Integration with key IT infrastructure, such as the institution's LMS, is important in providing seamless access to all applicable educational data.

7. *Predictive analytics:* Training programs are not limited to classrooms in an organization. The way corporate training is provided shifts from Massive Open Online Courses (MOOCs) to eLearning courses and enhanced reality. L&D managers are also required to answer questions like:

   - Will the online training program give a successful return on investment?
   - What training strategy fits best for each segment of the workforce (e.g., new hires, leadership teams, sales teams, etc.)?

Predictive analytics can be used to boost the participation and retention of learners. Predicting whether an employee can pass an online evaluation or whether their participation level can decrease will help trainers develop their training programs. Effective training programs were known to boost retention rates for workers. Predictive analytics are definitely useful to tailor training material to meet business goals.

8. ***Journey Analytics:*** Learning is no longer seen as a siloed process but as an interactive, interlinked experience in a learner's education career with an institution or organization. That is why learning analytics breaks down data silos and weaves together every point with which students interact. By linking learning data normally divided between different systems, leaders can now interpret and use this collective knowledge to improve the learner experience.

Throughout their full academic lifetime, for example, the Blue Student Journey Analytics (SJA) solutions allow students to access an "always-on" listening platform, automated input collection processes, and decision support – ensuring that institutions have all the knowledge they need to see the whole picture. Many companies still collect a fraction of the potentials of learning analytics, and their capacity is still to be completely exploited. Instead of relying on experience and intuition, companies can use learning analytics to rapidly detect trends that provide insight into the state of organizational online training. In general, learning analytics helps educators and L&D managers have more productive training and training services to benefit modern learners.

9.3.2 Education and Learning Analytics Market (Forecast 2016–2026)

The report (Transparency Market Research, 2020) provides a detailed market assessment. It does this by in-depth qualitative perspectives, historical data, and true market size forecasts. The report estimates have been produced using well-established research methodologies and assumptions. This is used as a repository for analyses and knowledge on any aspect of the market, including but not limited to regional markets, technology, styles, and applications. The following gives an overview of the EDA Market for 2016–2026 (Transparency Market Research, 2020).

The education sector is constantly changing because of rising industry digitalization and mobile devices' adoption by users. The number, variety, and speed of data generation are growing rapidly. These data can be used and analyzed easily to provide powerful insights into user behavior, interests, and future actions. Students who use different educational hubs such as digital channels or university campuses to study leave data footprints during their studies. Universities use this knowledge to consider how students learn and refine their solutions to increase student experience. The educational hubs use education and learning analytics to understand products and their clients better.

Analytical tools enable the education sector to improve its productivity, recognize opportunities and developments, and become more creative. The education sector is rich in data as universities use it and generate vast amounts of data every day. Furthermore, the data produced vary from the socio-demographic information (gender, education level, age, language, etc.) to statistics (frequency and time of use, number of clicks, response time), or performance indicators (for example, test results) to behaviors (machine or individuals' interactions). This knowledge can be used to experiment with various forms of training with students to assess their reaction time, customize and improve their training, and provide them with daily feedback. Education and learning analytics can play an important role in the education field, providing students with better input, retention, improving teaching and learning, and recording attendance information.

Significant factors driving the market in education and learning analytics include the need for data-driven evaluations to enhance education quality and increase mobile learning. The lack of knowledge of analytical solutions among end-users and the need for high-quality professionals to manage and deploy analytical solutions are key obstacles in the market of education and learning analytics.

Based on its part, research, end-use industries, and regions, the global education and learning analytics market can be segmented. The demand for education and learning analytics can be split into software and services in terms of components. The services segment can be further divided into professional and managed services. Professional services include consultancy, integration and implementation services, training, and support services. The global market for education and analysis can be divided into a premise, cloud-based, and hybrid solutions based on software. As far as analytics is concerned, the demand for training and learning analytics can be categorized into the predictive analysis, prescriptive analytics, descriptive analysis, etc. The global education and learning analytics market are divided into K-12, higher education, enterprise, and more based on end-use industries. The enterprise segment can also be divided into large and small, and medium-sized enterprises.

The global education and learning analytics market in North America, Europe, Asia Pacific, Middle East & Africa, and South America can be segmented in terms of region. Business growth in North America is largely due to high technology investment in the region's education field. Developments in IT infrastructure and an increase in propensity to implement BI and analytics in the region are likely to affect the demand in Europe and Asia-Pacific.

IBM Corporation, SAS Institute, Microsoft Corporation, SAP SE, Oracle Corporation, Tableau Software, Blackboard Inc., MicroStrategy Incorporated, TIBCO Software Inc., Alteryx, and Qlik are major players in world education and learning analytics. These businesses invest heavily in research and development to integrate emerging technologies and develop innovative products into their solutions. Also, players enter into strategic alliances with other players to extend their reach and gain market share across the globe.

9.3.3 Learning Analytics in the Future

While Learning Analytics is now in its infancy, learning institutions should be careful: in the end, the way all education is conducted would revolutionize. This section gives you some insights into possible learning research (Alexander, 2018).

1. *Improved institutional interconnectedness*: The future of Learning Analytics will be how organizations realize the value of creating a coherent, diverse, and integrated learning framework. This daunting concept parallels Brown (2017), who notes that its brick components' interoperability in a cohesive learning ecosystem is the key to the next generation digital learning environment (NGDLE).
2. *Computers understanding at an equivalent level*: Natural Language Processing (NLP), for instance, breakthroughs have the potential to transform Business Intelligence (BI); Tirosh (2017), for instance, believes that the interaction capacity of machines is as much essential as human interactions (i.e., through chatbots).
3. *Trying to find out what 'the' humans are 'really' thinking or feeling*: The 'Holy Grail' of Learning Analytics will attempt to understand the person qualitatively; however, around 200,000 anthropocentric years on Earth have transformed person battle experiments into very cunning and very talented people to conceal their true thoughts and intentions. Moreover, while biometric solutions (e.g., iMotions) are rapidly emerging and are believed to have tremendous potential in Learning Analytics, it is not easy to interpret the data.
4. *Research paradigm assumptions are actually important*: In a world of infinite structured and unstructured data, research approaches in LA analyses need to be carefully considered; for example, the ontology of Nature of Truth is objective and singular (with an inductive methodology of cause and effect) or subjective and multiple (with inductive emerge patterns)

9.4 Measuring Twenty-First Century Skills Using Learning Analytics

The unparalleled possibilities of collecting knowledge on learning and contexts have drawn considerable interest in education. Using data analytics and machine learning approaches, many important questions in education have been answered. Learning analytics can be used to evaluate skills in the twenty-first century, according to Dragan Gašević (2019).

One of these skills, now known as the twenty-first century's skills, is collaborating, solving problems, searching for knowledge, thinking critically and creatively, and efficiently self-regulating learning (Griffin et al., 2012). Their significance in the policy and research frameworks has been stressed, and many employers have strong expectations of these skills required for various jobs. This capacity also enables equal involvement in society and access to numerous public services.

Education organizations at all levels have various services to help improve these skills in response to these demands. Sophisticated approaches to the assessment of twenty-first-century skills were also proposed with increasing focus by policymakers and employers (Wilson & Scalise, 2015).

However, there has been considerably less progress in evaluating methods that chart the progress of 21st skills growth "in the wild." For example, the Organization for Economic and Co-operation and Development (OECD) has carried out (complex and collaborative) problem-solving measurements through the Program for International Student Assessment (IPSA). In highly trolled conditions, PISA can be carried out where only predefined messages can be used for communication among human collaborators (Rosen & Foltz, 2014), and the actual collaboration evaluates potential digital-human-collaboration issues (e.g., uncooperative, incompatible) through the joint work between human and computer agents (Rosen, 2014). Moreover, relatively little work has been done in learning environments where pedagogical frameworks can vary from very formal approaches to collective learning through students' concerns needing support from their peers in their classes or a larger social network.

Learning analytics provides promising methods for evaluating 21st skills in authentic contexts (Buckingham Shum & Deakin Crick, 2016). Learning analytics harnesses big data's power to establish measurement techniques - collected as a digital footprint of learners' use of technology – by operating on the intersection between machine learning, measurement sciences, and learning sciences. Recent research has brought promising progress in the validity assessment of learning analytics to provide effective means for the developmental evaluation of skills of the twenty-first century.

9.5 Moving Forward

Present developments in learning analytics research concentrated less on technical advancement and more on the teaching and learning philosophy and concepts. Srećko Joksimović, Kovanović, and Dawson (2019) outlined four promising fields of investigation.

1. **Learning analytics for supporting student learning**: To date, research and development in learning analytics feedback and dashboards have been more focused on teachers instead of customized students. With large data at hand, it became obvious that it was not enough to recognize underlying data trends and forecast future effects. It is also important to recognize custom approaches to learning data presentations that draw on existing academic expertise and practices and do not generate an abundance of information. Also, existing dashboards do not help metacognitive skills development, provide information about successful learning tactics and techniques, and trigger serious problems in their assessment. Thus, there are increasing demands based on dashboards for learning analytics in the literature on learning processes and efficient studying and feedback methods.

2. **Grounding learning analytics in educational theory**: The lack of theoretical support for its study is a common criticism of learning analysis. For instance, the creation of student performance and retention predictive models relies on simple learning proxies. Trace data for students are primarily reported counts in a particular technology. To understand what constitutes a realistic measure of learning, the applicable theory needs to be combined with the analytics involved. Predictive modeling is designed to minimize bias and uncertainty, thus sacrificing theoretical precision for better empirical precision. However, to gain successful insights to advance the learning process, it is explanatory power (theory) that plays this role. In learning analytics, a theory's value is often derived from the principle of truth in educational measurement. The extent to which theory and data endorse the understanding of the measurement is seen as validity.
3. **Learning analytics for feedback provision and instructional interventions**: The emphasis is mainly on the formative assessment of learning (i.e., assessment of the student's learning) and assessment as learning, i.e., assessment as a particular learning activity) and not on the usual summative assessment of learning (i.e.., assessment as a measurement of student's knowledge). This is mainly due to learning analytic methods and techniques that offer students and teachers timely, realistic, and personalized perspectives. There has been a big initiative to move beyond grades to recognize students at risk to evaluate critical thinking, innovation, teamwork, and other high-level processes.
4. **Learning analytics for understanding student emotions**: Emotion is one of the fundamental elements influencing online learning. Every learning activity is typically based on certain emotional responses, either positive (for example, joy, pride, satisfaction) or negative (anger, frustration, anxiety). Several efforts have been made to broaden the most widely adopted method to trace data to recognize learning processes to isolate affective aspects from student experiences with technology. One of the drawbacks of this reexamination is that interaction studies between data and emotions are normally performed in a laboratory where affective states (such as anger, anxiety, or boredom) are reported using different decision protocols or self-reports. The interplay between study and emotion research in learning analytics and multimodal study research has provided exciting new directions. It attempts to detect the effect of body signals that have been made using multiple protocols for classroom observation or coding documented interactions.

9.6 Smart Learning Analytics (Smart LA)

Since its inception, LA has continued to demonstrate its significance in the educational sector. To better understand and improve learning environments (Siemens, 2012), LA requires measuring, collecting, analyzing, and reporting contextual learner data (Siemens, 2012). LA will create better learning environments tailored to its individual needs, talents, and interests (Clow, 2013; Siemens, 2012). When all learning tasks are conducted at a finer degree of granularity – including episodes of study by students, episodes of assessment preparation and completion, and teaching episodes – the personalization of learning experience can be increased in order to generate insight/conception about what learners know and how to facilitate constructional learning (V. S. Kumar et al., 2016).

Recent learning models have been moved from rote learning to inclusive and personalized learning. Therefore, it addressed a fundamental question about how students can make learning practical and meaningful. Tests and/or examinations focused on memorization are becoming increasingly clear that they do not help learn and apply knowledge effectively. Hwang, Tsai, and Yang (2008) and Yahya, Ahmad, and Jalil (2010) argue that students are enthusiastically inspired to learn when they see learning to be important and significant. Lage, Platt, and Treglia (2000) and Sampson, Karagiannidis, Society, and Economy (2002) stress the importance for all students of inclusive learning. Education priorities should also concentrate on how students can be helped by highlighting their unique strengths and weaknesses. Also, learning should be accessible where there is a possibility and should not be limited to a fixed time or place. Such an opportunistic learning mechanism needs the omnipresent presence of learner help, including timely input and technical aid. Contemporary models of learning transition towards more omnipresent and contextualized learning – where personalization means that the students can learn at their own rate and receive individual input addressing individual strengths and shortcomings, leading to the idea that it is more difficult to forget the learnings that take place spontaneously in real life (Sampson et al., 2002).

The idea of "smart learning" has also grown as learning conceptualization has shifted. Since adaptation and personalization have emerged as two main components of smart learning, experts have highlighted the value of using technology to enhance learning (Gros, 2016). A successful technical design goes beyond merely using state-of-the-art training technologies to encourage intelligent behavior, integrating various collective technologies (Höjer & Wangel, 2015). Under the theme of 'smart learning,' concepts like 'seamless learning' and 'ubiquitous learning' have appeared. Sharples et al. (2013) argued that seamless learning allows a person to continuously experience learning in a mixture of places, times, technologies, and social environments. Ubiquitous learning can be seen as a learning experience that is more time and space distributed, such that students can learn in environments where the line between work and play and public and private is established. Essentially, "smart learning" not only emphasizes technology-enhanced learning but provides a way to improve information through the incorporation of different technologies, environments, and components.

Researchers and educators have focused on incorporating a "smart" element into LA. Smart learning is a LA subset that supports such processes and features of smart learning (Giannakos, Sampson, & Kidziński, 2016). Educators may use Smart LA to define and evaluate student comportment, educational merits, and suitability of learning environments and collect information from different sources to distinguish traces that promote educational support (Kinshuk, 2017). Big data creation and emerging modes of information communication and sharing have laid the foundations for more immersive and personalized learning. Data on learner capabilities and competencies and environments where students use particular technologies are useful for evaluating learner behavior, experiences, interests, and skill level changes. As a result, teachers can track each student's learning pattern – i.e., "a network of observed study activities that lead to a measurable chunk of learning" (Kumar et al., 2016), which is a significant data source for the LA. Learning traces allow for personalization so that individual students with different learning styles can follow different approaches, even for the same learning activities.

Many researchers have researched areas such as how teachers can use LA to develop student abilities, build smart environments, and apply emerging technologies. However, few researched Smart LA's ability to facilitate engaging and personalized learning, i.e., smart learning. In the current work, Boulanger et al. (2015) have analyzed Smart LA with a Smart LA framework SCALE case study and its efficiency in improving student outcomes. Giannakos et al. (2016) have also discussed the Smart LA principle of video-based learning.

9.6.1 Key Features of Smart LA

A comprehensive analysis of learners and environments is part of Smart LA (Kumar, 2018). Smart LA includes many types of data to identify traces of learning that inform the creation of better learning environments. Researchers and/or teachers face the task of finding and collecting applicable data sources and efficient data processing and interpretation as it is available.

Teachers, students, and parents will observe improved learner learning abilities by observing the subsequent learning traces. A residue of learning is generated when both finely-grained student teaching and research findings are collected and interpreted at various times. These real-time findings will help personalized learning that meets the needs of individual learners. This can be an individual undertaking (i.e., instructor, student, or parent) or a collective effort. With Smart LA, researchers can accurately evaluate and predict the essence of learning, including learner effort and performance, in different environments. Consequently, different organizations should provide sufficient administrative support based on policies aimed at competency-based learning. The main features of Smart LA are as follows (Kumar, 2018).

1. ***Learner awareness:*** Smart LA encourages understanding of acute learning. Learners are best served by their own success in the course of learning. Students who know their learning behavior may monitor their progress and seek appropriate assistance to develop their learning habits. Smart LA makes students more conscious of ways to perform best. One of Smart LA's feedback channels is to imagine the improvement in learning. Such visualization should be carefully planned so that efficient pedagogical approaches become feasible for smooth communication between students, teachers, and the analytical framework.

Diverse data sensors provide learner information such as performance, metacognitive capacities, cognitive ability, learning strategies, successful state, and physiological symptoms. Smart LA will use these data sets to personalize the study experience. Personalization starts in many cases with learner modeling, which derives students' attributes from raw data sets and the importance of learning strategies. Models arise in learner modeling from the study of interactions between learners with their learning environments that expose important learner information such as knowledge levels, weaknesses, and misconceptions. A learner model continuously updates the sensor data, and Smart LA gives students access to such models, which individualize learning experiences and empower students to reflect, prepare, and track their own learning.

2. *Sensitivity to technology:* Technology is essential to Smart LA. Sensitivity to technology ensures the most efficient use of software and promotes the personalization of content and learning. Users need to consider the key features of various technologies and equipment incorporated in Smart LA and e-learning applications to best leverage their resources and customize their functionality dynamically. Teachers, for example, should know what device or technology their teaching is best supported. Feature refers to tools integrated into a device or software that allows it to perform its tasks. Features include display capabilities, audio, video capabilities, multi-lingual capabilities, and platform consistency. Another notable problem is the centralism of big data. Smart LA is powerful in its ability to merge various data sources. Technological developments mean that people can access smart LA software from various devices while collecting generalized knowledge remains key. Continuous data analysis often allows pedagogical scientists or the system to acquire new knowledge structures from the analyzed data and create more knowledge structures that support the learner's dynamic adoption.

3. *Location awareness:* Location-based technology promotes location-based learning. The former helps to classify learners' locations while using the software and the latter transfers information by identifying wireless interface and sensor networks that constantly adapt to the user location. Existing wireless technologies provide GPS, Wi-Fi, RFID, and Bluetooth positioning systems to track user positions automatically. Location – both the learners' physical place and learning opportunities – is critical to contextual learning. Location-sensitive learning opportunities are growing. For example, recognizing students with identical characteristics and learning interests in neighboring locations enables them to relate to their shared learning benefits.

4. *Surrounding awareness:* After developments in location-aware technology and devices, the concept of mobile learning originated. Mobile learning refers to the ease at which learning travels at learners and is not limited to mobile learning. Furthermore, mobile learning is not technology but the nucleus of learning. It deals with "mobile" learners. In essence, technology offers learners the ability to learn in various environments, while mobile learning facilitates the development of specific training programs focused on both the learner-specified goals and certain context-aware information systems in different fields. The word

"context-aware" refers to providing knowledge related to their tasks within unique contexts for users. Mobile learning includes students in their surroundings, encourages authentic, collaborative experiences and informal learning. Embedded in the community, learning lets students learn, however they wish. Real-life physical objects are now becoming important vehicles for location-based adapted learning.

For example, museums are used to connect QR codes to various display boards, both indoor and outdoor. Learners with smartphones or the like will gain additional knowledge and communicate with digital representations of displayed objects by scanning QR codes. Such well-designed mobile learning systems exemplify both ubiquitous and personalized learning. For example, if a user scans the same QR code repeatedly, a well-designed customized system can recognize the user's study progress and adjust subsequent information rather than always providing the same information.

Understandably, knowledge cannot be divorced from the cultivation of intelligent learning environments. Combining the benefits of physical and multiple virtual learning environments – assisted by the holistic internet of things and certain ubiquitous sensing devices – ensures the whole toolkit for knowledge of meaning. Students can learn at their own speed with location awareness, and teachers can track students' progress, adapt feedback, and support to the applicable big data from their respective smart learning environments. The collection and review of student data offers a deeper understanding of learning experiences and encourages personalized instruction, introducing appropriate and effective learning opportunities into the learning environment.

9.7 Case Study. Learning Analytics to Support Self-Regulated Learning in Asynchronous Online Courses: A Case Study at a women's University in South Korea

In this study, Kim, Yoon, Jo, and Branch (2018) used learning analytics to investigate SRL in an asynchronous online course. For this analysis, student log data were used to detect unknown but current SRL patterns. Specifically, student SRL profiles were first observed using their accumulated log traces, and their SRL processes were analysed over time using log variables and cluster membership every week.

This study's background was an introductory course on business statistics for undergraduate students at a private women's university in South Korea. The courses were compulsory for students who majored in business but were available to other students as an optional course. The courses' contents were provided asynchronously online except for four special face-to-face meetings; two were intended to teach students the assessment style and provide specific information on the course, while the other two were intended for mid-term and final exams. In addition to the two tests, students had to apply two different tasks to solve statistical problems relevant to what they had learned from the video lectures. The course used the university LMS, where students watched the teacher's pre-registered video lectures and downloaded the related course materials; new lecture videos and material were uploaded regularly. The teacher made daily announcements on the course schedule, deadlines, technical problems, changes to the course, and main updates. A Q&A board was set up to encourage students to ask questions or comment on the course content.

At first, 382 students were registered for two semesters, 188 in the first semester and 194 in the second semester. However, in the first semester, only 106 students and 178 students in the second, along with their consent form, returned the completed survey, allowing 284 student data in additional analyses. All 284 participants were graduates; of these, 45 (15.8%) were fresheners, 76 were sophomores (26.8%), 73 (25.7%) were juniors, and 90 (31.7%) were seniors. They came from 45 different majors, and only 11 (3.9%) of them were business major students. Also verified that nobody took the course in both the semesters. The students are well aware that the log data are only used for testing purposes and that they are not seen or used for grading by the teacher.

The data used for this analysis included student logs and survey responses consisting of an SRL questionnaire and demographic questions. They analysed the data and identified three distinct profiles of online self-regulation with distinct interaction patterns. Students with self-regulation actively pursued assistance, but students with weaker self-regulation abilities did not actively seek assistance in online discussions.

This study's results gave an extensive account of pupils' various learning habits with various SRL profiles. This study will help us understand how students with different SRL profiles behave differently over the entire course. The research and practice contributions of this study can be summarised as follows.

1. Firstly, this study helps develop successful online learning environments to consider potentially different SRL profiles for students. The proposed log variables can guide future research and practice and promote more debate about how students with different SRL profiles can deliver customized interventions. This research will inform the design of successful SRL support by linking student SRL profiles, actual behaviours, and learning outcomes.
2. Second, proof-based learning analytics was conducted to structure log variables that mirrored theoretical and empirical evidence from the previous research. Therefore, this study's results contribute to the knowledge base so that students can better understand how they learn and how education can be structured to help SRL in asynchronous online courses. Also, it offered opportunities for future studies to analyse SRL in similar online environments in terms of selecting indicators and linking them with the current theoretical framework.
3. Third, this research applied an innovative analytical approach to student SRL trends over time. Clustering and classification methods were combined to assess student behaviour predictors' contributions at various times. Nonparametric methods have made it possible to evaluate the highly correlated unstructured

dataset for which conventional parametric methods cannot work adequately due to the high probability of infringing modelling assumptions. Using the one non-parametric classification model that included all of the predictors, the probability of Type 1 errors occurring during each week of the course was decreased. Finally, this study showed the ability of learning analytics to discover emerging SRL trends.

9.8 Conclusion

There has been a growing interest in learning analytics in technology-enhanced learning (TEL). LA methods share a shift from data to analysis to action to learning. The environment of TEL is evolving, and this should be reflected in future LA approaches to better learning experiences. In this chapter, we presented a summary of the range of possibilities opens up by LA. We explored some promising avenues for future LA research. That includes self-learning, lifelong learning, and smart learning. We also presented a summary of the present and future developments of Learning analytics in the world. This chapter added a lot to LA research because it offers a more substantial and forward-looking view of LA and its related developments and provides a promising path for the twenty-first century in this emerging field.

9.9 Review Questions

Reflect on the concepts of this chapter guided by the following questions.

1. What is Self-Regulated Learning (SRL)? Describe its importance.
2. How will Learning Analytics be used for SRL? Explain.
3. What do you mean by Lifelong Learning? What are the various barriers to it?
4. How do you establish a Lifelong Learning environment? Explain the role of Learning Analytics in doing so.
5. Write a note on the present and future trends of Learning Analytics in the World.
6. What are the past and future trends in Learning Analytics Market? Provide a brief report.
7. How will Learning Analytics be used in measuring twenty-first Century skills? Explain.
8. What is Smart Learning Analytics (Smart LA)? List and explain the key features of Smart LA.

References

Alexander, C. (2018). *Trends in learning analytics: Educational institutions take heed - eLearning industry.* 2018. https://elearningindustry.com/trends-in-learning-analytics-educational-institutions-take-heed

Antonietti, A., Colombo, B., & Di Nuzzo, C. (2015). Metacognition in self-regulated multimedia learning: Integrating behavioural, psychophysiological and introspective measures. *Learning, Media and Technology, 40*(2), 187–209. https://doi.org/10.1080/17439884.2014.933112

Arguel, A., Lockyer, L., Lipp, O. V., Lodge, J. M., & Kennedy, G. (2017). Inside out: Detecting learners' confusion to improve interactive digital learning environments. *Journal of Educational Computing Research, 55*(4). https://doi.org/10.1177/0735633116674732

Aspin, D. N., Chapman, J. D., Hatton, M., & Sawano, Y. (2012). *Second international handbook of lifelong learning.* Springer: Springer Dordrecht Heidelberg London New York

Azevedo, R., Johnson, A., Chauncey, A., & Graesser, A. (2015). Use of hypermedia to assess and convey self-regulated learning. In *Handbook of self-regulation of learning and performance* (p. 13109) https://doi.org/10.4324/9780203839010.ch7

Boulanger, D., Seanosky, J., Pinnell, C., Bell, J., Kumar, V., & Kinshuk. (2015). SCALE: A competence analytics framework. In *State-of-the-art and future directions of smart learning.* (Issue October, pp. 19–30). https://doi.org/10.1007/978-981-287-868-7

Brown, M. (2017). The NGDLE: We are the architects. *Educause Review, 52*(4). https://er.educause.edu/articles/2017/7/the-ngdle-we-are-the-architects%0Ahttp://files/4246/the-ngdle-we-are-the-architects.html%0Ahttps://er.educause.edu/articles/2017/7/the-ngdle-we-are-the-architects

Brusilovsky, P., & Henze, N. (2007). Open corpus adaptive educational hypermedia. *The Adaptive Web, 4321*(January 2007), 325–341. https://doi.org/10.1007/978-3-540-72079-9

Buckingham Shum, S., & Deakin Crick, R. (2016). Learning analytics for 21st century competencies. *Journal of Learning Analytics, 3*(2), 6–21. https://doi.org/10.18608/jla.2016.32.2

Bull, S., & Kay, J. (2010). Open Learner Models. *Advances in Intelligent Tutoring Systems, 308*(September), 301–322. https://doi.org/10.1007/978-3-642-14363-2

Cheng, H. C., & Liao, W. W. (2012). Establishing an lifelong learning environment using IOT and learning analytics. *International Conference on Advanced Communication Technology, ICACT*, 1178–1183.

Clow, D. (2013). An overview of learning analytics. *Teaching in Higher Education, 18*(6), 683–695. https://doi.org/10.1080/13562517.2013.827653

eThink. (2019). *3 new learning analytics trends driving education.* https://ethinkeducation.com/blog/learning-analytics-trends-driving-education/

Gašević, D. (2019). Using learning analytics to measure 21st-century skills. *Research Conference, 2019,* 46–50.

Giannakos, M. N., Sampson, D. G., & Kidziński, Ł. (2016). Introduction to smart learning analytics: Foundations and developments in video-based learning. *Smart Learning Environments, 3*(1). https://doi.org/10.1186/s40561-016-0034-2

Greene, J. A., Moos, D. C., & Azevedo, R. (2011). Self-regulation of learning with computer-based learning environments. *New Directions for Teaching and Learning, 119,* 1–7. https://doi.org/10.1002/tl.449

Griffin, P., McGaw, B., & Care, E. (2012). *Assessment and teaching of 21st century skills.* Cham, Switzerland: Springer.

Gros, B. (2016). The design of smart educational environments. *Smart Learning Environments, 3*(1). https://doi.org/10.1186/s40561-016-0039-x

Hoffman, B., & Ritchie, D. (1997). Using multimedia to overcome the problems with problem based learning. *Instructional Science, 25*(2), 97–115. https://doi.org/10.1023/A:1002967414942

Höjer, M., & Wangel, J. (2015). Smart sustainable cities: Definition and challenges. In *Advance intelligent systemes and computing* (Vol. 310, August). https://doi.org/10.1007/978-3-319-09228-7

Hwang, G. J., Tsai, C. C., & Yang, S. J. H. (2008). Criteria, strategies and research issues of context-aware ubiquitous learning. *Educational Technology and Society, 11*(2), 81–91.

Joksimović, S., Kovanović, V., & Dawson, S. (2019). The journey of learning analytics. *Mind, Culture, and Activity, 2*, 37–63. https://doi.org/10.1080/10749039.2019.1686028

Kalz, M. (2015). Lifelong learning and its support with new technologies. In *International encyclopedia of the social & behavioral sciences: Second edition* (Vol. 13, 2nd ed.). Elsevier. https://doi.org/10.1016/B978-0-08-097086-8.92006-3

Katambur, B. D. (2020). *5 Trends that Influence Learning Analytics*. https://blog.commlabindia.com/elearning-development/5-trends-that-influence-learning-analytics

Kay, J. (2008). Lifelong learner modeling for lifelong personalized pervasive learning. *IEEE Transactions on Learning Technologies, 1*(4), 215–228. https://doi.org/10.1109/TLT.2009.9

Kim, D., Yoon, M., Jo, I. H., & Branch, R. M. (2018). Learning analytics to support self-regulated learning in asynchronous online courses: A case study at a women's university in South Korea. *Computers and Education, 127*, 233–251. https://doi.org/10.1016/j.compedu.2018.08.023

Kinshuk. (2017). *Improving learning through smart learning analytics (Power Point Slides)*. http://www.ouhk.edu.hk/URC/Sym_OIE_2017/files/Keynote_Kinshuk.pdf

Koper, R., & Tattersall, C. (2004). New directions for lifelong learning using network technologies. *British Journal of Educational Technology, 35*(6), 689–700. https://doi.org/10.1111/j.1467-8535.2004.00427.x

Kumar, K. (2018). Advancing learning through smart learning analytics: A review of case studies. *Asian Association of Open Universities Journal, 13*(1), 1–12. https://doi.org/10.1108/aaouj-12-2017-0039

Kumar, V. S., Kinshuk, Pinnell, C., & Paulmani, G. (2016). Analytics in authentic learning. *Lecture Notes in Educational Technology, 0*(9789811059292), 75–89. https://doi.org/10.1007/978-981-10-5930-8_6

Lage, M. J., Platt, G. J., & Treglia, M. (2000). Inverting the classroom: A gateway to creating an inclusive learning environment. *Journal of Economic Education, 31*(1), 30–43. https://doi.org/10.1080/00220480009596759

Lodge, J. M., & Horvath, J. C. (2017). Science of learning and digital learning environments. In *From the laboratory to the classroom: Translating learning sciences for teachers* (pp. 122–135), Routledge – Taylor & Francis: England, UK.

Lodge, J. M., Panadero, E., Broadbent, J., & de Barba, P. G. (2019). Supporting self-regulated learning with learning analytics. In *Learning analytics in the classroom* (October, pp. 45–55). https://doi.org/10.4324/9781351113038-4

Macfadyen, L. P., & Dawson, S. (2010). Mining LMS data to develop an "early warning system" for educators: A proof of concept. *Computers and Education, 54*(2), 588–599. https://doi.org/10.1016/j.compedu.2009.09.008

Miller, C., & Bartlett, J. (2012). "Digital fluency": Towards young people's critical use of the internet. *Journal of Information Literacy, 6*(2). https://doi.org/10.11645/6.2.1714

Panadero, E. (2017). A review of self-regulated learning: Six models and four directions for research. *Frontiers in Psychology, 8*(APR), 1–28. https://doi.org/10.3389/fpsyg.2017.00422

Perry, N. E., & Winne, P. H. (2006). Learning from learning kits: gStudy traces of students' self-regulated engagements with computerized content. *Educational Psychology Review, 18*(3), 211–228. https://doi.org/10.1007/s10648-006-9014-3

Roll, I., & Winne, P. H. (2015). Understanding, evaluating, and supporting self-regulated learning using learning analytics. *A Time for the Humanities, 2*(1), 7–12. https://doi.org/10.2307/j.ctt13x0cd3.6

Romero-Zaldivar, V. A., Pardo, A., Burgos, D., & Delgado Kloos, C. (2012). Monitoring student progress using virtual appliances: A case study. *Computers and Education, 58*(4), 1058–1067. https://doi.org/10.1016/j.compedu.2011.12.003

Rosen, Y. (2014). Comparability of conflict opportunities in human-to-human and human-to-agent online collaborative problem solving. *Technology, Knowledge and Learning, 18*(3), 147–164. https://doi.org/10.1007/s10758-014-9229-1

Rosen, Y., & Foltz, P. (2014). Assessing collaborative problem solving through computer agent technologies. *Research and Practice in Technology Enhanced Learning, 9*(3), 389–410. https://doi.org/10.4018/978-1-4666-5888-2.ch010

Sampson, D., Karagiannidis, C., & Kinshuk. (2002). Personalised learning: Educational, technological and standardisation perspective. *Interactive Educational Multimedia: IEM, 39*, 24–39.

Sharples, M., Mcandrew, P., Weller, M., Ferguson, R., Fitzgerald, E., & Hirst, T. (2013). *Innovating pedagogy 2014* (issue November). The Open University: United Kingdom.

Shum, S. B., & Ferguson, R. (2012). Social Learning Analytics., *15*(3), 3–26. https://doi.org/10.1145/2330601.2330616

Siemens, G. (2012). Learning analytics: Envisioning a research discipline and a domain of practice. In *2nd international conference on learning analytics and knowledge* (pp. 1–8). https://doi.org/10.1007/s11434-007-0406-7

Tirosh, G. (2017). *Why natural language processing is the future of business intelligence | sisense*. DZone.Com. https://www.sisense.com/blog/heres-natural-language-processing-future-bi/

Transparency Market Research. (2020). *Education and learning analytics market - global industry analysis, size, share, growth, trends, and forecast 2018–2026* (pp. 1–8), Transparency Market Research: Albany NY – 12207, United States.

Wilson, M., & Scalise, K. (2015). Assessment of learning in digital networks. In *Assessment and teaching of 21st century skills* (pp. 57–81). https://doi.org/10.1007/978-94-017-9395-7_3

Winne, P. H. (2017). Learning analytics for self-regulated learning. In *Handbook of learning analytics* (pp. 241–249). https://doi.org/10.18608/hla17.021

Yahya, S., Ahmad, E. A., & Jalil, K. A. (2010). The definition and characteristics of ubiquiteous learning: A discussion. *International Journal of Education and Development Using Information and Communication Technology, 6*(1), 117–127.

Chapter 10
Case Studies

10.1 Recommender Systems Using Learning Analytics

10.1.1 Austin Peay State University: "Degree Compass" and "My Future"

Degree Compass This case study (Game Changers: Education and Information Technologies, 2012) explains the Degree Compass course recommendation system introduced by Austin Peay State University. The system guides students in courses that complement their established talents and match their selected curriculum. Degree Compass blends hundreds of thousands of grades with each current student's transcript to make individual recommendations. The strongest suggestions are about a course that a student should graduate, which are core at the university curriculum and the student's major. The student is immediately projected to excel. This form of academic recommendation will encourage a student's progress in graduation and shorten the time to graduation, thus lowering higher education costs. Austin Peay succeeds Degree Compass and the model through support other institutions of higher education as well.

Students who pursue higher education face the sometimes-daunting challenge of taking a degree. In the face of a wide variety of choices that might fulfill degree criteria, which is the best way to succeed? How should the courses be conducted? Courses also offer no hint of what the course would entail but instead include several technical words incorporated in the course. Consultants are well qualified to guide them in their fields. But most programs require students to take classes from across the entire university continuum, and consultants find it challenging to provide valuable guidance in other disciplines.

All of this implies that the student has picked a major that suits well. In reality, many students have undecided or realized their college career is not what they expected afterward. Complete College America recently revealed that, on average, students take up to 20% more classes than they need to complete — not because they want a new class, but because they had to reconsider their plans several times. A semester of extra study plays a vital role in a setting that has significant consequences for a student's chances of completing a degree.

What seemed important was a system that could take advantage of previous experiences to start a better-informed dialogue between students and advisors. This system will allow consultants and students to prepare plans for future semesters, with data on courses or even undergraduates, where previously students with similar programs, grades, and courses have succeeded.

Degree Compass System How it operates. Austin Peay State University (APSU), Clarksville, Tennessee, inspired with reviews from companies including Netflix, Amazon, and Pandora, developed a course recommendation system called Degree Compass, which successfully integrates existing students with courses that best fit the skills of the students and a program of study for upcoming semesters. The model blends hundreds of thousands of previous grades with each student's transcript to make individual recommendations for current students.

Unlike systems recommending films or books, this system does not rely on which classes students like more than others. Instead, predictive analysis approaches based on the grades and the registration data are used to identify courses according to factors that assess how each course will help students progress through a selected program. The system chooses the courses that are ideally suited for the course series of the student program and are the most central in the university curriculum as a whole from those that contribute specifically to the student's curriculum. This ranking is then superimposed on a model that predicts the courses in which the student is most likely to meet the best grades. Using this approach, the system makes its strongest recommendations for courses that a student must complete, which are fundamental to the university curriculum and the major, and in which students are required to excel academically.

Each student's suggested course list is conveniently shown on the university portal's secure side on a web-based GUI. This interactive interface gives information on the curriculum, specifications, and role of the courses in the graduate program and classes' availability in future semesters. The same details can also be found on the APSU mobile application PeayMobile. Faculty consultants can access Degree Compass as a tool for academic advising to complete material available to faculty members when providing advice to their advisees.

Degree Compass also offers a range of enterprise-scale reports that provide department heads and advisors with strategic knowledge. These reports contain data that allow for targeted interventions. For example, a report enables the institution to strengthen its Early Warning System at the beginning of the semester by using projected course grades to recognize students who may benefit from teaching support or academic support.

Is it working? The key reason for student achievement and growth is the system's ability to position students in the most competitive classes. The faculty and students both embrace and engage easily with the GUI. The grade-prediction model offers a reliable estimation of a student's final grade. As compared to real-world student grades, it is found that 90% of the time, the model correctly predicted courses in which students earned a C or better — on average, C grades or better were predicted within 0.56 letter grades. Also, by evaluating students' actual grades from their semester classes, the grades in classes recommended did not recommend the student average of 0.46 in a letter grade higher than those in courses.

Challenges Faced This system's critical challenge was developing a statistical model to predict the potential levels of a student to a reasonable tolerance based on the transcript and legacy data of the university. A secondary difficulty was creating a system for sequential courses focused on a single major and the entire university curriculum. After these models had been designed and tested, the system had to be implemented entirely and interacted smoothly with APSU's course management system.

Will it function somewhere else? As APSU discusses the challenges of interfacing with computer systems and adjusting to other institutions' curriculum, the challenges of replicating Degree Compass in other institutions remain entirely solved. The system played a central role in the successful completion of the Complete Innovation Challenge application, which has been given a $1,000,000 prizes for three other campuses – a university and two community universities – by Complete College America and the Bill & Melinda Gates Foundation to fund the Degree Compass.

Future Because of the Degree Compass program's encouraging acceptance and outcomes, Austin Peay launched a similar 'My Future' program (Hannover Research, 2016). Students who have already chosen a subject receive additional information on concentrations and graduation trajectories and career information, such as ties to the United States Department of Labor Statistics for related occupations and jobs availability. Students without a chosen field of study or considering another field can receive proposals for different areas they are likely to excel, similar to the Degree Compass predictive subject ratings.

10.1.2 Student Advice Recommender Agent (SARA): University of Saskatchewan

SARA is the computerized Student Advice Recommender Agent (Fortenbacher & Pinkwart, 2015), who has been offering customized advisory messages to students at BIOL 120 at the University of Saskatchewan since autumn 2014. Based on every student's background, interests, achievement levels, and academic activity, SARA tries to build messages that can give every student valuable academic advice every week in this comprehensive multi-sectoral course. SARA collects information on students' online behavior in the BIOL 120 and their ratings on quizzes, laboratories, and assignments to link each individual with the helpful tools to optimize their overall biological performance.

Every week, a new message from SARA is displayed on the BIOL 120 Blackboard site of each student. The message may point the students to online tools, peer learning opportunities, academic advice, or study tips. By clicking the SARA link in the blackboard's left menu, students will be able to look back at all SARA messages so far. If students wish to explore further, they can also see what kind of messages SARA sends to other students.

SARA is a software agent, and SARA's advice might not be ideal at times – may be more effective advice may be offered. This is why students can browse SARA's advice to others-or ask SARA if they so desire. A real human instructional support professional in biology will answer questions to SARA.

SARA is a groundbreaking project initially piloted in 2014 in Biology 120 at the University of Saskatchewan. The SARA project team consists of biology, computer science, education, and artificial intelligence experts – all of whom work together with the Biology Department and the Student Learning Services to provide you with a better learning experience. Also, in select First-Year Engineering and Chemistry courses, SARA has been used.

10.1.3 Personalized Pathway Planning at Open Universities Australia

Open Universities Australia (OUA) is a network of seven Australian universities in distance education. Study materials or a combination of printing, CD, and DVD are available in full or in part online. Qualifications as modular courses are offered. Students may select how many units they learn simultaneously, but it can be challenging to plan a route through the appropriate modules for their qualifications. Personalized Adaptive Study Success (PASS) (JISC, 2016i), enables each student to personalize the study experience, particularly about their study path. It seeks to assist and support students in difficulty by proposing alternative modules that are more suited to their needs. Risk-related students are also known.

In a conventional linear curriculum, bad performance on one module reflects on student results in subsequent modules, and a demanding student will not be able to fit the rest of the cohort. PASS, however, supports a customized and adaptive learning course. A poor student can study additional modules to improve the area before retaking the original module. PASS will suggest an alternate study path at any point where the student is perceived to need assistance.

PASS uses data from several sources, including OUA customer partnerships and affiliate colleges, the apprenticeship management framework, and research profiles for each unit and program. The analysis consists of three profiles: the student profile (location, socio-demographic, prior knowledge, etc.), the learning profile (usage of online content, assessment, online forums, etc.), and the curriculum profile (module and software specifications, alternative pathways, etc.) The learning analytics engine is an analysis of the combination of statistical and qualitative data. This is built for micro, meso, and macro interference, for example, to recommend a student an additional mathematics module or to provide proof that a part of the curriculum can be revamped.

PASS uses the performance of a learning analytical engine to inform a personalization engine and a adaption engine. The personalization and adaptation engine provides the student dashboard in the online learning environment with suggestions for content and activities. Students, facilitators, and educational designers are presented with dashboards. These can be personalized by adding and moving tiles, including summaries, suggestions, and warnings, with different functions.

One of the project's findings is that it is essential to prepare the stakeholders for practical insights from learning analytics. The interaction and fragmentation of knowledge and its qualitative characteristics were a significant challenge for this project. The models mixed numerical and qualitative data to construct a more accurate image of the learner's condition. Semantically rich data from forums of discussions and answers to open-ended evaluations, for example, allow for a deeper understanding of learners' skills and needs.

10.2 Learning Analytics in Higher Education

10.2.1 The Impacts of Learning Analytics on the Higher Education Sector

Dietz-Uhler and Hurn claim in their research study (Dietz-Uhler & Hurn, 2013) that some learning analytics consequences include enhanced transparency, higher retention rates, and better student performance. In addition to helping individual students improve their academic performance, learning analytics may also help management improve their decision-making process. Also, learning analytics provides the managers with the critical knowledge they need to distribute capital effectively. The use of learning analytics in higher education will also allow management to recognize the institution's problems and achievements, increasing the organization's competitiveness. Learning analytics has helped faculty members recognize students who may be at risk in their learning. The faculty members were able to develop interventions and methods to support these students during the learning process. The faculty has also used learning analytics to transform pedagogical methods and build strategies to help students gain insights into their performance and learning. Using learning analytics, higher educational institutions have also developed models that display the behaviors of active students (Smith, Lange, & Huston, 2012). The pattern may include details about the number of times a good student has access to the panel posts and the exam duration, among other items. A professorship is likely to inspire students to participate in such conduct if it constructs a paradigm that represents a good student's behavior. It may also test the actions of students who do not comply with this specific model.

In their research study (Greller & Drachsler, 2012), Greller and Drachsler have observed that learning analytics has allowed the faculty to recognize gaps in learners' understanding and knowledge. Knowledge of such shortcomings would enable teachers to focus on individual learners and improve their academic performance and progress. Similarly, in their research study (Wolff, Zdrahal, Nikolov, & Pantucek, 2013), Zdrahal, Nikolov, and Pantucek argue that higher education institutions could understand their students through learning analytics. The main objective of using learning analytics is to understand students' actions by analyzing their data (Ifenthaler & Yau, 2020; Ifenthaler, Yau, & Mah, 2019). The study of the student data allows the faculty to determine how students communicate with VLE and how these experiences influence the ultimate performance of a learner. Adejo and Connolly noted that LA's use in higher education facilities has allowed teachers and faculty members to recognize the obstacles learners face during their learning process (Lester, Klein, Rangwala, & Johri, 2017). They also mention that learning analytics have helped to increase retention rates for students. Close monitoring of learners' persistence and learning will allow higher education stakeholders to identify unnecessary emotional states and disorderly conduct among students.

Consequently, it could be possible to identify students at risk by recognizing such conduct for faculty members (Verbert, Manouselis, Drachsler, & Duval, 2012). Factors that may cause a student to leave school may also be detected and handled promptly. The faculty members will, in turn, build strategies to support students who can leave the learning institution. These interventions or follow-up activities may take the form of, among others, counseling services.

10.2.2 The Challenges of Learning Analytics in Higher Education

(Lester et al., 2017) In their research, learning analytics is intended to provide substantial benefits for both students and teachers in the learning institution. However, the implementation and application of learning analytics in higher education have been adversely affected by various challenges. The first problem highlighted by Lester et al. in 2017 is the heterogeneity of databases and data. Vast quantities of educational data are typically distributed through many heterogeneous databases in various formats. The vast databases are also difficult to incorporate into the school.

The second problem is that learning analytics has no suitable technological architecture. Such a situation threatens the implementation and application of LA technology in higher education. The third problem is the question of data ownership. The data obtained from the different learning institutions databases and obtained using questionnaires and surveys typically have ownership problems. The question of data ownership must be clarified. The other problem examined (Lester et al., 2017) in their research is privacy. Themes such as data profiling, and access must be dealt with before an educational institution chooses to use learning analytics. The educational administrator must create protocols and structures in a learning institution to monitor student data access and use.

10.2 Learning Analytics in Higher Education

The topic of consensus-based research is a significant factor influencing LA's implementation in the education sector (Ferguson, 2012). The lack of a formal structure currently exists that can help incorporate learning analytics into the educational system. The generalization of tools and software is the other significant factor challenging the implementation and application of learning analytics in the education sector. Several high schools have learning analytics in their system introduced and used. Examples include Purdue University, Open University Australia, and Wollongong University (Lester et al., 2017). It should be remembered, however, that these LA technologies are typically unique to educational institutions. Notably, educational institutions cannot adapt to LA technology developed by other universities due to geographical, economic, and social factors that affect such technologies. To be efficient and competitive, LA needs to answer the challenge of adaptability. The last challenge that has affected LA technology application and implementation is insufficient faculty and teaching personnel's insufficient preparation in applying LA tools and techniques.

10.2.3 Case Studies

10.2.3.1 Traffic Lights and Interventions: Signals at Purdue University

At Purdue University, Indiana, the institutional goal was to use business intelligence to increase student performance at the course level, thus increasing retention and graduation rates. The Signals system (JISC, 2013) attempts to help students advance rapidly enough to seek help and improve their likelihood of grade or pursue a different path.

Signals mines SIS, VLE, and grade book details to create an indicator of the "traffic light" that indicates how each student is considered at risk. The teacher will then take a variety of interventions. The predictive algorithm is based on student success (points earned so far), effort (VLE interaction), previous academic background, and student attributes (e.g., age or credits attempted). These components are weighed and incorporated into the algorithm that produces the required traffic signal. Red suggests a high probability of ineffective yellow possible problems and green a high likelihood of success.

Potential issues in the second week of the semester are reported. Teachers can therefore decide to interfere in different ways, for instance, by posting the signal on the student's home page, e-mailing, or arranging a meeting. Positive feedback is sent as a green light, which a positive message will reinforced by the teacher.

An alert message will give negative feedback. Student performance, final-grade measurements, and behavior, and VLE and aid search behavior interactions have been evaluated with signals. Two semesters of data showed that in those courses using Signals, Cs and Ds were consistently higher than Ds and Fs. Meanwhile, students who received automatic interventions sought assistance faster and more often than those who did not.

Two years of results have been tracked and seemed encouraging. In biology, the pilot signals produced 12% more grades of B and C than among non-pilot students and 14% lower grades of D and F. There was also a 14% rise in students withdrawing early enough to avoid impacting their overall grade point (GPA) grades. When they realized their degree of risk, it also seemed that students appeared to alter their behavior, thus enhancing their efficiency. Students in pilot groups requested support sooner and more often than not. And after the interventions ended, these students were 30% more likely than those in the control group to seek help.

Signals had a significant advantage in that student who used Signals used the subject support desks and extra tutoring sessions, mostly poorly attended. Signals were also shown to enhance contact between students and teachers. Meanwhile, teachers accepted that students appeared to display progress in commitment and thought about their tasks earlier by using cues.

The opinions of Learners on Signals were also sought. In five semesters, more than 1500 students were surveyed anonymously to collect feedback on their use of signals. Most felt that the automated notifications and alerts they received were a form of personal interaction with their teacher, which reduced the feeling of "just a number." They considered the messages and the lighting details beneficial and useful to alter their behavior and wished for even more specific information about improving them.

10.2.3.2 Analyzing the Use of the VLE at the University of Maryland, Baltimore County

The University of Maryland, Baltimore County (UMBC) a public research university with 12,000 students has had rising VLE use but no evidence that it enhances learning. In an educational research project, the associations between VLE data and final grades were examined and how the predictions are best used to help students. It also examined possible approaches and how effective data-based teaching activities can be identified (JISC, 2016b).

As a first move, students with C grades or higher used VLE 39% more than those with lower scoring. If less successful students had noted the difference in VLE use, would they have changed their habits? The Checks My Behavior (CMA) method was developed to help students equate their VLE activities in a course with a synthesis of the entire cohort.

After a pilot, the tool was deployed across the institution with an advertisement campaign and a VLE gradebook link. In 1 year, 45,000 visits were made to the CMA tool page. In a cohort of new UMBC students, 92% used the VLE, while 91.5% used the CMA method. Those that used the tool were 1.92 times more likely than those who didn't use a C grade or higher. The students can pay attention to input from the CMA tool that a staff member cannot hear or acknowledge.

The tool could also draw on "obsessive status-checking tendencies" of students to provide regular feedback which is not cost-effective if employees are involved. As a precaution, successful students prefer to embrace new tools in more significant measure than hard-working students.

A more thorough review of the VLE log files showed that one teacher had an exceptionally high student involvement level. He used the 'adaptive release' feature of Blackboard, so the students had to take questions about course material before accessing the assignments. Usually, students in the adaptive release sections were 20% higher than in other sections. They did better than those who had not used adaptive releases when those students went to their next course. Therefore, analytics revealed efficient learning design and a general conclusion: efficient implementation of a VLE tool in a pre-conditional course will lead to better results in this course and subsequent courses. It was also proposed that specific VLE operation types may promote better participation, which in turn contributes to better levels.

Future improvements have been proposed, in particular, a consent mechanism for resolving privacy issues by adding two checkboxes to the tool: 'It's ok to track my usage of this site' and 'It's ok to follow up with me for an informational interview.' Additional scheduled changes provide an analysis of the frequency and length of VLE use as opposed to other devices and warnings sent to individuals when their VLE operation falls below the target level (model from the rest of the cohort). It also aims to provide the students with a facility to exchange information with staff and encourage them to intervene when their VLE behavior falls below a certain amount.

10.2.3.3 Identifying at-Risk Students at the New York Institute of Technology

New York Institute of Technology (NYIT) is a private university with 13,000 students in the United States and abroad. By creating their predictive model, NYIT has been able to classify risk students with a high level of precision in partnership with counseling staff (JISC, 2016h). In the first year of their research, the goal was to improve students' retention by developing a model for recognizing the most in need of support individuals and providing information on each student's condition to assist support counsellors in their work. The process included collecting data, the analytical process, and the output processing in a beneficial format for the counselling staff. There are two explanations for this approach: however accurate the predictive model could be if the counseling staff were not willing and able to integrate it into their daily work, and without time-consuming manual intervention, the model had to work quickly and automatically.

The problem definition came from the users: the student support consultants. An external supplier of IT solutions worked with NYIT personnel to define, deploy, and analyze the required data. The design process was an iterative loop, with NYIT consultants at every point involved. The model was designed within the NYIT so that the database, forecast model, and front end of the consultants were all on the same platform.

The model used four data sources: admission application data, registration/placement test data, all students' surveys, and financial data. The latter was included because the rate of completion was known to affect the student. The model has been educated on a variety of records of previous students in NYIT. A total of 372 variants of four mathematical approaches were compared to see which modeling of the risk best depends on the other characteristics (coming grades, finance, etc.).

The models have been tested for precision and recall to assess the match between student conduct. The model's best edition had a recall of 74% and a precision of 55%. This is very strong compared with a similar model, independently developed at Western Kentucky University (WKU). The WKU model was based on pre-registration data only. Therefore, the increased recall of the NYIT model is considered because of the inclusion of financial and student survey data and the type of model used. It means that three of those students were correctly projected to be at risk for every four students not returning to study in the following year.

The results were displayed on a dashboard with and for student support staff. A simple table showing whether they are to return to study the following year, the percentage trust in that model prediction, and, most importantly, the reasons for the prediction, is a simple one-line for each student. The counsellor then has the basis to discuss his condition and future plans with each student.

10.2.3.4 A Fine-Grained Analysis of Student Data at California State University

The Ph.D. project of John Whitmer has observed student behavior at California State University, Chico. This is a medium-sized campus in the northwest of the state with a full-time population of 14,640 students. Whitmer studied the entire community of 377 students on a new course designed to view a much more profound use of learning technologies (JISC, 2016g). His study sought to tackle factors contributing to student achievement more extensively than the more complex approaches taken by some other researchers. He assumed that most of the VLE data in current learning analytics programs had been overlooked, and there was no reason for the inclusion of certain variables and not others. He divided VLE interventions into broader categories, e.g., listed posting as an interaction practice for a debate. He also considered nine traditional student variables, including sex, whether in a minority racial/ethnic group, revenues, high school grades, and whether the student was the first in a family to study.

Whitmer points out that earlier studies have consistently shown a much more significant association between student characteristics and student performance than single demographic variables. If the student's race, income, and gender are used, predictions should be much stronger than using one of these variables. Seven of the nine student variables were statistically important. VLE use, however, was a better indicator of student progress than commonly used demographic and registration data to classify students at risk. It has also been found that the use of individual VLE resources varies widely between students but is less widely used within the specified categories, i.e. administration, evaluation, content, and involvement. Whitmer therefore advises that predictive analytics should not be carried out at the level of individual instruments.

Total Hits is the most important indicator of student performance and Assessment Activity Hits are near seconds. Whitmer points out in his results that total VLE hits are an excellent starting point for predictive modelling and early warning systems. All of the above variables except Total Hits have been used to perform a multivariate regression. It was found that 25% of the final grade variance was clarified. Another 10% applied the predictive relation to the degree to all the student characteristic variables in the study.

Overall, Whitmer concluded that the use of VLE is connected with student achievement. What his research does, however, is to measure the difference between the different types of VLE use and thus allow teachers to track their students' efforts and to have risky students flagged them. He found that more than four times the VLE variables were as closely correlated with achievement as demographic variables. The use of VLE is a proxy for student effort and therefore a good indicator of the last degree. It indicates that students do more than their histories or past performance on a course. A further finding was that use of VLE is less successful for risk students: the impact of VLE use by risky students (based on minority status and income), relative to non-risk students, has dropped by 25%.

10.2.3.5 Transferring Predictive Models to Other Institutions from Marist College

The Marist College (New York State Liberal Arts Institution) led the Open Academic Analytics Initiative (OAAI), which developed an open-source early warning solution for higher education (JISC, 2016j). The predictive model was moved to multiple institutions effectively and intervention methods were tested to support at-risk students. The technologies are now being used as part of Jisc's learning analytics architecture in UK universities. The first predictive models were based on Marist College results. Based on the Purdue approach, data sources included demographic information such as gender and age, aptitude information, such as high school scores, and different aspects of VLE use. The models were used in two community colleges and two state universities with a significant number of low-retention ethnic minors to research the models' portability and the efficacy of interventions with risky students.

Researchers found that the three most critical indicators to predict student progress were scores, the grade point average as well as the current academic status. The model was trained using Marist College data and was distributed to partner colleges and universities. It has been found to be transferring well, with about 75% of at-risk students in three of the four institutions. The researchers predicted a much greater disparity between institutions and Marist because of the disparity between student cohorts, type of institution and teaching practices. They believe that it was their first project to recognize partial contributions to students' final grade, as entered in the VLE Gradebook method, as the primary indicator to assess students at risk. This encourages teachers to take action much earlier than before in the semester.

Students who were then exposed to one of two separate intervening techniques were officially considered to be at risk. The first group got a message saying they are in danger of not finishing the course and giving advice on how to boost their chances. The second was targeted at the online support community with open educational tools in fields like studying skills, time management, stress reduction, algebra, statistics, writing, and research. Colleagues and support staff also provided opportunities. Both interventions included structured text, which with each message becomes more serious.

In 2012, two separate cohorts, 1739 and 696, were split into three groups: Students who received a call, those targeted at the support environment and a control group that did not receive interventions. There were no variations between the two treatment groups overall, but the final level increased by 6% for those who were exposed to control intervention in one course. Another result was that in the intervention community the withdrawal rates were higher than among control subjects. Students who choose to leave early rather than risk later should clarify the differences. The Marist researchers conclude that the predictive model enables students to have earlier input on their progress and resolve problems in advance. They also note that some students seem "immune" to interventions. They found that very few students who did not respond to the first treatment improved after the second or third intervention.

10.2.3.6 Enhancing Retention at Edith Cowan University

In Perth, Western Australia, Edith Cowan University (ECU) has a diverse community of students, primarily from non-traditional backgrounds. The strategic priorities are maintaining strong teaching quality records and helping students improve retention through Connect for Success (C4S) an institution-wide predictive learning analytics initiative. The C4S (JISC, 2016f) technology automatically detects students who may need assistance. The organizational structure allows support personnel to contact a wide range of students and perform many interventions for each. Governance, control systems, organization, coordination and risk management involved a staggered program over 2–3 years. This offered time for technology advancement and a framework for changing management in order to help staff and create new positions in the student-facing teams.

The University has invested heavily to determine which student variables are better suited to predicting attrition. Although the research review identified some common factors (including grades, university entrance scores and linguistic skills) in students' attrition in other institutions, students' departure or absence are different and the factors that depend on one another. Therefore, ECU agreed that the compilation and review of institutional data were necessary to classify the students most likely to need help accurately. For the first three semesters of an ECU student's period, statistical models were developed based on more than 200 student variables. The models used ECU SIS data, including details on population and development, divided into undergraduate and postgraduate courses. Six models have been developed in total to predict retention. As a consequence, for every new and continuing student registered in an undergraduate course, ECU has a probability ranking.

In a regular report, the predictive model recognizes students who may need assistance. This is checked by two staff who make sure no student is approached twice or too often. Personalized e-mails are then sent to the students who provide support.

If students do not answer the initial email, a similar message is contacted by telephone. A dashboard helps support staff to record and track each student's contacts and support. They may develop an action plan that agreed with the student which could include appointments or interventions to specialist support services.

Critical success factors included: training and professional support staff, collaborations with institutional stakeholders, awareness of consistent responsibilities and boundaries with other ECU facilities, workflow processes on a regular basis and good support from the management. The challenges included: data integrity (manual selection in the early stages, understanding of it was an issue), re-sourcing at peak periods (for example, during Orientation), systemic integration of information systems and 'student suspicions.'

Roughly 700 students were approached via e-mail and/or telephone and were offered the chance to opt for an initiative to support their studies. The institution estimates 20% of students opted in to meet the take-up rates for similar programs at other universities.

10.2.3.7 Early Alert at the University of new England

There are about 18,000 students at the University of New England, New South Wales, Australia with a high number of part-time and external or mixed-graduates. The socio-economic status of 20% of students is poor. The key driver was the need to recognize students who struggled so that they could get help promptly. In the past students who were at-risk appeared to be found after they had not submit the assignment or attended a class. Many students who were off-campus were also difficult to observe. The goal was to establish a "dynamic, systematic and automated mechanism to achieve the learning well-being of every student" (JISC, 2016e). Three strands were there:

e-motion Each student has a collection of emoticons and a text box on their website. They may choose to record how you feel every day (happy, neutral, unhappy, very un-happy) connected with their current module. The Student Support Team contacts all students with a negative emotion within 24 hours. 17–20% of students who record "unhappy" or "very unhappy" are the team's case. Thirty three percent of these require several contacts.

The Vibe Students' statements are added into a word cloud, which is updated every 10 minutes, in the text box alongside the emoticons, so the entire student cohort can see what their peers are thinking. This word cloud serves as a barometer for students' welfare and normalizes student experience, since the larger the word, the higher the number of students. The text entries on each student's portal page also give the support team a regular update on student problems and concerns.

The Automatic Wellness Engine (AWE) Every night, analyses data from seven systems and runs a model based on 34 triggers which indicate risky behavior. These metrics are based on actions, not demographics. The data sources include e-motion student entries, class attendance, previous study history, previous results, career applications and online student portal access trends, and other University websites. Also included are previous AWE ratings. Time series and trend analysis are used to determine the intervention ranking. The AWE can still run the model, even when a student doesn't provide direct feedback through e-motion. The student support staff dashboard is updated every morning to determine increasing students need support. An automated email, accompanied by phone calls and additional support, is used in the first instance.

Initial AWE trials lowered the attrition from 18% to 12%. Qualitative feedback from students shows that Early Warning has effectively strengthened students' sense of community and increased the incentive to share their study expertise. Students' feedback was "overwhelmingly optimistic," suggesting they appreciate constructive support. Other aspects of the method are effective when automatic input on the cohort motivates students instead of the personnel's direct interference.

Another essential aspect of Early Warning is the importance of learning analytics in a broader social media strategy. Multiple channels establish a sense of community and the support staff's participation as a routine (not only in times of crisis). The staff use Facebook, Instagram and a blog to connect daily with students and interfere with the AWE if needed. Students are more open to the process because they know the staff by name.

10.2.3.8 Developing an 'Analytics Mind-Set' at the Open University

Open University, UK, has more than 200,000 students studying part-time degree, postgraduate and sub-degree qualifications. It invests extensively in a strategic learning analytics program to improve student achievement through the incorporation of evidence-based decision-making on all levels. Due to funding changes, the retention of qualifications is now a strategic challenge for the institution; retention of students is particularly demanding if they are locally distributed, are part-time students, and generally have several years to graduate.

In ten main fields, the University strengthens its institutional capacity to improve the foundations for the productive use of learning analytics. These are grouped into three main strands: data availability, research and insight development, and processes that influence the performance of the student. At the macro level, incorporating details on the student learning experience offers strategic goals to consistently improve student experience, retention and development. At the micro-level, analytics are used in student, module and certification levels to perform short, medium and long-term interventions. One of the goals is to establish a 'analytical mindset' around the university such that staff integrate evidence-based decision making into their regular activities (JISC, 2016c).

Understanding the effects of initiatives is an essential objective. There are a wide number of interventions within the University. Earlier, it was difficult to decide how a single action influenced students' performance and so a more cohesive image was created with the learning analytics approach. Data from SIS, VLE and other platforms is collected. Many dashboards, reports and software are being created for a variety of users, including senior management, school support staff, academics and students, to access analytical outputs easily. For example, the dashboard support staff helps staff to handle a standardized intervention program. A student dashboard helps students to track the progress of their study paths and make informed choices. Predictive analysis is being developed to model students' development at the individual and institutional module levels and based on previous cohorts in similar modules.

At the curriculum stage, faculty use analytics to inform the design changes and evaluation of the learning modules. Analytics may also recognize effective learning designs that enable best practice to be shared (Ifenthaler, Gibson, & Dobozy, 2018). Learning analytics was seen by the University as an ethical method, with an emphasis on the student as an active participant. The Policy for the Ethical use of Student Data for Learning Analytics' goes beyond legal requirements. This approach also acknowledges that, however good the models, a student is more than a data collection, and that elements of student experience will still be beyond the area of learning analytics. Key factors influencing student performance are now adequately well known to guide strategic planning priorities.

10.2.3.9 Predictive Analytics at Nottingham Trent University

Nottingham Trent University (NTU) has launched an institution-wide dashboard to improve its 28,000 students' academic experience by fostering dialogue between students and staff, one of the most influential learning analytics projects in the UK. The main goals were: enhancing retention, growing the sense of belonging to a community and improving attainment (JISC, 2016d).

Previous institutional research has shown that somewhere in the first year up to a third of the students have considered leaving at some point during their first year. These doubters were less confident, less engaged, developed poorer ties with colleagues and tutors, and were more likely to retreat early in the final analysis. Instead of "doubters," who most wanted it, students who asked for guidance were helped by tutors but did not ask. There are four main dashboard features designed to accomplish these goals. Stu-dents and staff can see exactly the same details, the dashboard sends an email warning when student involvement ends for 2 weeks, the dashboard enables students to write down accepted activities when they interact with students. The tool itself is simple to use with a low effect on academic time for training and use.

Demographic data have not been used in the model intentionally because a student can only alter their actions and not their context, and there is the dashboard to inspire students. One in five commitment ratings is issued to each student: High, Good, Partial, Low and Not Fully Enrolled. The dashboard helps students verify their participation and tutors to address the students' success with them. Two graphs showing progress that indicates engagement, contrasts individual students with the rest of the cohort and indicates the student's engagement level. In order to obtain a deeper understanding of the recent commitment, the tutor should train down to the stage below the grade.

The pilot showed that a greater effort was positively connected to success and achievement in four courses. Examining a much wider dataset for students of the first year found that a student's dedication was much more important than data such as history or entry qualifications. In the final year, there has been a strong correlation between the commitment and the final qualification: 81% of students have a high average degree with an honors degree of 2:1 or the highest award, while only 42% of students have a low average degree.

In a first-year student survey, 27% said their behavior had changed in response to dashboard results. Some students have done more academic tasks, for example, independent study, but these are not calculated in the dashboard. Others fought for the highest ranking. However, there is a risk of partiality here because the dashboard will help students express and express themselves. In the coming years, NTU will discuss these concerns in far more depth.

Another effect is that tutors adjust the way they interact with students due to analytics. They conclude that enhanced knowledge on individuals enables them to more accurately tailor their interventions. Most tutors in the first pilot once a week used the dashboard with a marginal effect on their workload; one third of the tutors contacted students because of their engagement details.

10.2.3.10 Analyzing Social Networks at the University of Wollongong

The University of Wollongong, New South Wales, Australia is a public study university with more than 30,000 students. The central premise of the Social Networks Adapting Pedagogical Practice (SNAPP) initiative is that collaborative learning is necessary to foster students' comprehension. SNAPP (JISC, 2016a) analyses interactions in on-line forums to display trends and relationships as social network diagrams in real time.

The teacher usually moderates these forums while students deal with specific learning tasks or have general discussions about the topic or administrative issues. The timing and consistency of the lecturer's interventions will significantly affect the learning experience of the student. There are hundreds of participants in some of these forums which makes it difficult for a teacher to control the action.

Teachers can track relationship evolution by comparing diagrams over time. The software SNAPP is used as a diagnostic method to help instructors identify students who are separated from the main discussion or to understand how the overall trend progresses (Are many students dominating? What is the scale of peer discussion?). Instructor visualization may also be used to focus on learning design and even redefine the role for a potential cohort.

While primarily intended to encourage interaction in real-time, teachers mostly used SNAPP after completion of their courses for reflection. This was useful for professional growth, as network patterns imply different moderation modes, e.g. if a teacher responds to individual students and does not promote broader debate. SNAPP was felt to be helpful in real-time in identifying isolated students, especially in broad forums during busy times. Some teachers showed their student groups SNAPP network diagrams as part of a discussion of how to contribute to an online platform.

SNAPP was suggested to be marketed as a reflective teaching tool and to highlight the value of learning design in professional development. It was felt that there was a need to increase understanding of common patterns of interaction among staff and to understand how, as a facilitator, one can participate in a conversation that shows unwanted patterns of social interaction.

The SNAPP project showed a clear correlation between students' learning orientations and the platforms they often use. For example, people with a strong emphasis on learning preferred learning discussions and resource sharing. Students with a success orientation focused on the discussion of administrative and appraisal forums.

SNAPP software is a web browser extension that collects data from the selected forum automatically and shows the relationships as social networking maps. SNAPP targets student engagement data as a commitment measure and develops a visualization framework that operates through many third parties' platforms and variants. This approach can be used to add other features to a VLE.

10.2.3.11 Learning Analytics Practice at the Flinders University (West, Luzeckyj, Searle, Toohey, & Price, 2018)

The Learning Analytics Community of Practice The Learning Analytics Community of Practice (LA CoP) has played an important role since its creation in bringing together key university people with an interest in the area. Since the Flinders University has declared learning analytics as a key strategic direction and is beginning to invest more in the field, the LA CoP is expected to continue to play a significant continuous role in shaping future learning analytics developments at Flinders.

Application of learning analytics in a flipped classroom Since the unit started in 2008, live lectures have been given to a gradually diminishing audience each week. In 2016, the teaching team agreed to revamp the subject to increase overall student participation and give students an opportunity to discuss classroom challenges while teachers were present. Therefore, the standard lectures were replaced by a "flipped class." The LMS teaching team assessed the LMS students through the study of learning analytics and the contrast with final topic grades. As anticipated, unit grade increases were seen with increased video access. Student involvement was also assessed by the frequency of physical attendance and an increase in last grade was also observed in contrast with the final subject grades as physical attendance improved. Unfortunately, however, in final subject ratings or test scores, no overall improvement was seen compared to the previous year following completion of the flipped classroom.

Learning Analytics for a First Year Psychology Research Methods Topic In this unit, the professor carefully structures formational tests and recognizes concepts in which students seem to struggle by the use of learning analytics. A study workshop will be held at the end of each semester to study these areas and propose new revisions and procedures to explicitly resolve these problems. Also, with the method changing from year to year, the instructor was able to use various methods to teach the identified problem areas and then use learning analytics to compare the relative benefit of these various approaches.

10.2.3.12 Learning Analytics Practice at Murdoch University (West et al., 2018)

Learning Analytics Production at Murdoch University The Murdoch University has built and implemented learning analytics at a relatively early level. The key focus to date was investigating students' attrition, but a Student Analytics Committee was created to investigate more widely in the field of learning analytics. So far, it has established and instigated many projects involving the use of existing LMS instruments and functions. It also establishes a long-term strategy on learning analytics within the educational technology context that includes the steps taken by other universities and the evolving learning analytics innovations in the landscape of education technology. Aspects of this long-term strategy should be:

- push the use of established resources in learning analytics and related 'know-how' inside schools ('quick wins')
- provide the necessary information and perspectives on the function of the broader Student Analytics and Student Success Initiative
- investigate and/or contribute to the development of LMS and related educational technology capabilities for learning analytics.

Learning Analytics in a Multi-mode IT Unit This unit is available at campuses, off campuses (external/distance/online), and international campuses in Singapore and Dubai. It was planned to be available in mixed mode from the ground up. Students have preparatory materials that include readings, lectures for all students, a short video series, and a pre-workshop quiz. On-campus students and international campus students will be given workshops consisting of a computer laboratory session followed by a group discussion/tutorial session. Off-campus students engage in the same computer lab session and in an online discussion forum. Students then have to complete post-workshop tasks. Due to the diversity of modes of distribution, it was determined that it would be necessary to understand items and events to research when used (in the timeline of the offering of the unit) and what forms were more used (e.g., videos, online quizzes).

10.2.3.13 Learning Analytics Practice at Charles Darwin University (West et al., 2018)

Institutional Development The Charles Darwin University is a dual sector institution that utilizes the power of education technology to provide students across the Northern Territory and beyond with and sustain learning opportunities. The combination of the education technology suite with a large external cohort of students means that a large part of teaching is digitally recorded in the systems. This is a good example of how learning analytics are used for a range of reasons, including improved learning and education and retention.

Charles Darwin University has done extensive work in the creation and implementation of learning analytics in the organization. The main focus of the work was on LMS and SIS data integration. The two programs provide a significant part of the knowledge about learning and teaching and the types of questions that teaching staff wants to answer. The result was that a wide range of reports was adapted, both for vocational education and training and teachers of higher education and several classes, faculty and university reports, which could be used for several different purposes.

Tertiary Enabling Program Given the high attrition rate in the TEP and the supporting programs across Australia, this project aims to identify possible factors contributing to attrition rates and key periods when attrition-occur. The aim is to use this information to help students if they need it to complete their program successfully.

This project builds on research on the relationship between LMS access frequencies and timelines and academic success to recognize crucial time points. This offers valuable information to enable teachers to intervene efficiently and to serve students better. This information is also applied to ongoing program assessments and is used to advise ongoing curriculum development and teaching practice. Although work began in one TEP unit, this project has been extended into other units in the program.

Use analytics for grade boundary decision-making This case study discusses the use of learning analytics to support students during the semester and inform and promote academic decisions on degree levels while a student is on a grade level. This nursing unit, entirely external through LMS, has a consistent sequential framework including weekly self-assessment quizzes and adaptive releases, ensuring that several data points can be readily viewed as historical student progress and performance record. To provide early warning emails to students and guide students at information sources of assistance to help them get on track (or help them to cope with life-related issues), the success dashboard (showing the various types of user activities) and the retention center are used to locate students who are deemed to be at risk based on a set of configurable guidelines. A combination of the Student Snapshot report, the grade center's download, and early progress warnings are uncommon and effective in promoting transparent and reasonable decision-making.

10.3 Other Evidence on the Use of Learning Analytics

10.3.1 University of Technology, Sydney - Learning Analytics in the Context of a Data-Intensive Strategy (Ferguson et al., 2016)

Introduction In 2011, the Australian University of Technology Sydney (UTS) pledged itself to be a data-intensive university. This policy, led by Deputy Vice-Chancellor and Vice-President Professor Shirley Alexander, uses university data to help university stakeholders' decision-making processes.

A dedicated organization, the Connected Intelligence Center (CIC), was founded as part of this strategy in August 2014. In response to the increasing importance of data in UTS learning and research, CIC was developed. It leads the UTS learning analytics initiative and is the gateway to the learning.futures program, which is shaping the future of UTS student learning.

Context UTS is a University in Australia, which was established in 1988 and enrolled 40,636 students by 2015. Since 2008, the University has invested AU$1 billion in campus renovation. In addition to its campus training facilities' renovation, UTS has also renovated its learning activities, led by its Learning2014 plan and its predecessor.

Deputy vice-chancellor and Vice-President (Teaching and Learning) Shirley Alexander launched the initiative to become a data-intensive university. The goal was to build a university where employees and students would use and reuse data and store and curate, submit, and develop research tools to analyze data regardless of the data's size and diversity. The curriculum represented an understanding of the abundance of data in society, and that this growth has repercussions for the whole of the university, how it functions as an institution, what and how it prepares students to plan for the future, and how scientists are to work in the future.

In 2010–2013, the project started with a series of in-house projects where computer science researchers evaluated the potential of data mining techniques for student retention issues. Learning analytics was developed in 2011 as a human-centered area for the integration of data science with education. Within UTS, data becomes increasingly apparent as a university business, learning, and research priority.

These factors contribute to the Data-Intensive University (DIU) strategy and the opening in 2014 of the Connected Intelligence Centre (CIC). The institute's name reflects the UTS staff's decision to identify this as a related intelligence project instead of a data-intensive university project. This was because the term 'data-intensive university' might alienate certain people. Simultaneously, 'connected intelligence' better represents the project's strategic goal to undermine the impact of the data revolution on education.

The CIC operates outside university faculties as a hybrid research laboratory that performs applied research and offers selected courses. Its core audience is made up of UTS students and workers. The facility is directly part of the Deputy Vice-

Chancellor (Education and Students) portfolio. CIC cooperates with the Advanced Analytics Institute, the business unit, and the UTS data warehouse business intelligence unit in addition to the faculties.

The CIC has close partnerships with industry and the government outside the academic sphere. These partnerships are evident in its collaborations with corporate partners and in the interest of corporate partners in the Master's program in data science and innovation, which fills a skill gap that currently opens up with data scientists. External collaborators – including major consulting firms, government agencies, start-up companies, and NGOs – contribute to the education and the registration of their employees.

Design and implementation phase CIC is currently based on research on the next generation's learning analytics tools and training students in a data-intensive environment.

Early learning research work at UTS focuses on students' turnover, the so-called "killer subjects," which disincentive students and engagement patterns. CIC now is focusing on analytics and collaboration on social media. Their current emphasis is on UTS graduate attributes, the twenty-first century's essential qualities to both staff and students. This goal stems directly from UTS learning.futures creative strategy, which transforms the university's learning spaces and practices to positively impact student satisfaction and commitment75 positively.

One of the main development fields is the design of analytics that provide students with learning experiences. Academic writing analytics, for example, was built to help students' expertise in analytical and reflection. Student organization development and resilience are fostered with student profile analytics. In this field, CIC uses participatory design approaches to include all stakeholders in the analytics design.

One of the main CIC research projects focuses on the potential of automated written analysis using different technologies to provide students with constructive input on their draft. This could be draughts of conventional academic writing, but could also be draughts of more personal reflective writing, which is really important for reflective students and how they are thinking of how they grow as learners.

In designing this invention, the CIC involved many stakeholders. The planning process involved pedagogical experts specialized in reflective writing and providing the basis for teaching reflective writing. The process also included academics from various faculties who gave specialist expertise. The academic writing tool uses a language platform sponsored by a corporate research laboratory that now incorporates additional language technologies. The challenge here was to match standardized language technology, part of which is focused on a company-wide partner language platform, with academic requirements. CIC has chosen a product co-design method involving the business partner and UTS academics and students.

Another big CIC project uses the CLARA self-evaluation survey method, a method designed to make students aware of their learning (the patterns of their minds). The survey tool framework creates 'learning power' profiles for each student and recommends strategies based on the learning profiles.

This self-assessment method for learning power is focused on education research and has been in progress for 15 years. It is a primary survey platform from a technological point of view.

One main improvement was introducing a flexible method that provides the centuries of students who use the tool with mentoring and training. This was a challenge because mentoring is hard to scale up. For instance, 900 first-year science students performed self-analysis using the survey method. It is not possible to 900 undergraduates to perform a 1:1 coaching discussion. CIC, therefore, engaged in developing a coaching program by the Science Faculty. It educated students in the methods associated with the tool for the third and fourth years and exposed them to fictional students with fictional learning power profiles, to promote reflection. These people were based on reports of the types of students studying their courses by academics.

A large variety of stakeholders engaged in the entire innovation process. Academics have been interested in the concept of students. Educated senior students in coaching. UTS Peer Mentoring administers the entire peer training program.

On the teaching side CIC offers a a Master in Data Science and Innovation program, a Ph.D. program, and an elective course. This course is part of the learning. futures strategy which increases the level of data literacy in the university. It teaches staff and students basic statistical principles and enhances their data literacy and their capacity to disagree about and criticize types of data prevalent to everyday life.

Experience While CIC exists only since August 2014, some findings can be taken from the University's collaboration.

CIC meets UTS staff to address both input and the relatively new learning analytics concept and what it can mean by learning and teaching. Many educators are pleased with the function of the CIC in learning analytics. For example, they see tremendous promise in the CIC's academic writing analytics tool because it provides students with instant feedback at any time of the day or night on draught documents that cannot something academics can provide. Students' feedback is also overwhelmingly positive. Initially, some educators were worried with data processing and often about reductionist education. When they engaged with CIC staff, they were told that they were really involved in education. This scattered fears that analytics required some kind of learning and brought about a shift in learning analytics expectations.

Although the transition from the old learning and teaching method to the new system was a general challenge, these challenges are not unique to learning analytics. Learning and teaching are incorporated in the organizational processes and information systems built by one style of pedagogy. Learning.futures approach contributes to the transition in organizational processes and information structures to modern pedagogies.

Policies The University's existing policies are seen as excellent facilitators for student research and CIC study. The strategy of UTS learning.future considers learning analytics to be important. It states that quick formative feedback, authentic evaluation and more data analysis are needed to allow students to learn qualities, such as higher graduate attributes, that prepare student for the data-saturated society.

While senior managers have launched the program, it is not a top-down approach but instead incorporates bottom-up creativity by working together with academics and early adopters to show the university how good learning analytics look. These success stories allow the University to buy more and more people into analytics.

In addition to UTS, policy changes at the national level would be required to adjust current evaluation views. As evaluation influences teachers' and students' actions, old evaluation techniques will restrict the potential of learning analytics and learning technology. Learning analytics will assist in moving education to more genuine learning forms that equip and evaluate students with the twenty-first century competencies, which are essential in their future lives.

10.3.2 *The Apereo Foundation Learning Analytics Initiative – Open-Source Software and Architecture as an Option (Ferguson et al., 2016)*

Introduction Apereo launched in 2014 the Learning Analytics Initiative (LAI) to speed up the growth of the software of learning analytics, promote pilot studies at member organizations, and discourage duplication of software and institutional innovations. Apereo Foundation is an umbrella group to facilitate the creation and maintenance of open-source software "for the academic enterprise" and its surrounding communities.

LAI's training came from discussing an open learning analytics framework within the international Society of Learning Analytics Research (SoLAR). One challenge that members saw in the field at the time was that the use of fragmented learning analytical systems was not a feasible long-term solution. An integrated platform was needed to combine all data with data mining tools in one place. Another main driver was the collaborative culture of the foundation, since Marist College (United States), University of Amsterdam (NL), University of Hull (UK) and Unicon (USA) thought that their work could be combined with the creation of a coherent forum for promoting learning analytics activities.

The Learning Analytics Initiative started with identifying five major parts of an effective learning study platform: Collection, Storage, Study, Communication, and Action. Data from various learning systems must be collected and aggregated in a centralized storage portion. Next, it takes an analytical aspect to make sense of the results. The analysis results should be transferred to a dashboard portion for the instructor, administrator, or student for communication. Finally, components such as advice and interventions are required to start actions. Projects are initiated under the Apereo umbrella to cover each of these five regions.

Context The Apereo Foundation is a system organization for developing and maintaining open-source software 'for the academic enterprise' and its surrounding communities. It also integrates an incubator phase throughout the transition to a sustainable product, where new open source technologies can be sponsored. The Learning Analytics Initiative has funded two products: the Student Success Plan for student support case management and a Learning Analytics processor, which manages analytical workflow and focuses on quantitative student data modeling.

Discussions leading to the Apereo Foundation were initiated in 2010. The initial impetus was a merger between Sakai (an open-source learning management system) and Jasig (a non-profit organization, US). Since 2006, both organizations have worked closely together to develop open-source education solutions. In 2012, Apereo was officially created and called. Today, Apereo operates as a global network of more than 180 collaborators on six continents, each contributing to various educational initiatives and communities. There is currently a good representation in the United States and Europe organization. Moreover, Apereo ventures have ties to more than ten company affiliates.

The underlying aim of Apereo is to encourage open-source collaboration between these stakeholders. This means that open-source software creation (which includes open licences and open source code) and community building are two important elements. In Apereo's larger education programs, learning analytics constitute only one component or culture within the foundation.

Student Success Plan (SSP) and Learning Analytics Progress (LAP) are perhaps the largest learning analysis projects developed by Apereo. These programs are two independent projects, but they can be integrated with each other under the Apereo and LAI umbrella. Using this model, institutions can adopt or integrate one or the other software with existing programs in its entirety. Both programs are open source and can be adapted to individual institutions' specific needs, in line with Apereo's mission.

SSP is a funded project that has been implemented in around 50 organizations, mainly in the US. The program consists of case management software that includes a set of tools to promote students' success. These tools help fields like academic advising, student services, coaching or counselling, accommodation for people with disabilities, and data grouping. Therefore, SSP works in the LAI system's compilation and processing and offers guidance for intervention for students' enrollment.

Learning Analytics Progress focuses on the statistical modeling of student performance and completion, and it falls into the framework's analysis and communication elements. The program is intended to help consolidate big data in educational institutions for early alerts and data visualization with the ultimate objective of providing intervention resources.

Design and implementation process Projects within the community of Apereo are being incubated. The program needs to be widely developed and a potential candidate for large-scale adoption to move to this stage (e.g., the Learning Analytics Processor). To complete the incubation, the project must comply with an established exit criteria list which is endorsed by Apereo. This approval is an indication of the maturity and longevity of the program. The incubation process also contributes to a joint infrastructure to evaluate and implement Apereo initiatives and offer comprehensive global collaboration.

In the operations of Apereo, a variety of other components play a role. First, the use of standards and community building that encourages universities to collaborate and work together. Secondly, the transferability of their predictive models to student performance between universities. An empirical study at Marist College in the USA, for example, analyzed how well Apereo models work when they are built and then implemented in another institution. The initial results were positive. Finally, the Apereo architecture allows several types of dashboards to be built to fit individual, organizational needs. This makes it more economical to use open-source software from Apereo than to create a new dashboard from scratch.

Many of Apereo's new learning analytics work includes expanding existing systems and planning for major deployment. For example, Jisc worked closely with the Society in UK to establish a national initiative for learning analytics using Apereo software. The UK is Apereo's first national project, but it is already being considered in other nations. Therefore, Apereo operates in expectation of broad-scale use on scale systems to a cloud-based application.

We take more action to translate this online culture into face-to-face contexts. Apereo will hold an annual international conference and numerous regional and community-specific conferences. These also include networking and icebreaker exercises to promote dialogue and collaboration. Webinars (online lectures), hackathons (collaborative computer coding events), workshops, seminars, and showcases are also arranged. The incubation process also allows people to work together on both face-to-face and online projects.

Experience The impact of the learning analytics activities of Apereo has been significant, especially given that it is a relatively young base. As far as software is concerned, the Student Success Plan is a fully functional basic framework that can very much be changed to suit the individual institutions' needs and cultures. It has been adopted by approximately 50 institutions, primarily in the USA, and the Foundation aims to implement it in the future with more institutions.

The work of the Foundation on initiatives such as Learning Analytics Progress contributed to a national initiative in the United Kingdom. The increased cooperation between the institutions and stakeholders has also had a significant effect since Apereo is currently the only global open-source learning analytics initiative. Foundation members also co-create, co-author and peer review in ways that are unlikely to occur in the commercial sense and are not feasible before the development of Apereo. The Apereo model shows a base with many strengths as a global community initiative developed by volunteers (workers from other institutions). In the next 10–15 years, Apereo aims to become the primary platform for open learning analytics projects, offering a longitudinal data system over the learner's lifecycle.

Policies Several policy-led initiatives are seen as critical for Apereo's potential progress in the field of learning analytics. One of the main concerns is national data aggregation and data protection policies. There is little or no real-time access to education information in many countries. In the UK, for example, the statistics on higher education are published to HESA. Still, a substantial decrease in their publication and university registration statistics in 2013 was not available until 2016. Policies and Laws are obsolete in other contexts and may pre-date the Internet. For Apereo to achieve its goals, members of the Foundation agree that a shared dictionary and data sharing policies must incorporate predictive models at an international level.

In addition to foreign and national policies, Apereo 's work's performance is influenced by individual corporate policies. Many universities do not have a knowledge policy in place. This leads to a lack of control over the data and a lack of knowledge of how to aggregate and interpret them. Institutional policies relating to data sharing, such as the Jisc Code of Practice, are essential for the learning analytics. Therefore, top-down systemic policies are main factors for active initiatives such as Apereo. To integrate Apereo with the university system, the university culture recognizes and prioritizes the importance of knowledge.

10.3.3 Blue Canary – Commercial Providers of Learning Analytics, Can Move the Whole Field Forward (Ferguson et al., 2016)

Introduction Until the end of 2015, Blue Canary was a commercial provider of personalized solutions for predictive analytics, focusing mostly on predicting which students are at risk for completing their courses. Blackboard then purchased it. The case of Blue Canary shows how a community's efforts, including donors, colleges, academics, governments, and entrepreneurs, can help develop a path to success for the start-up learning analytics company and the entire analytics field.

Context In 2011, the Bill & Melinda Gates Foundation received a million-dollar grant to build the system for Predictive Analytics Reporting (PAR). The objective was to define variables that affect student retention and success and direct decision-making to increase US post-secondary graduation rates. Data from over 400,000 student records from six universities belonging to the West Interstate Commission for Higher Education were gathered from the predictive analysis reporting framework. Each of the six participating institutions investigated or carried out analytical projects on their student results. The PAR Framework allowed them to build on this work by analyzing the trends that could come out of the six institutional data packages when a single unified sample was considered.

In 2013, one of the project participants started a Blue Canary company, based on the project's experience. Mike Sharkey, the founder, saw that a single-size predictive analytics model is unlikely to operate in any sense. Early insights into the knowledge led him to conclude that a tailored approach could be a viable strategy for a predictive analytics firm at the institutional level. One of the insights he gave was that there were many commonalities in data in the above data collection, which

10.3 Other Evidence on the Use of Learning Analytics

gathered records from two community colleges, two profit-making universities, and two public universities over 4 years. To establish predictive analytics for student retention, these commonalities, along with elements unique to the university, had to be considered.

Design and implementation phase In 2012, the Blue Canary founder gave a presentation at the International Conference on Learning Analytics and Knowledge (LAK12) of the prediction model at the University of Phoenix, and how this model differs from the system for predictive analysis reporting (PAR), which was developed. In his speech, he highlighted the low value in relation to normal practices of University of Phoeniz in some of the PAR measures used to forecast risks for the retention of students and progress towards the graduation.

In 2013, Blue Canary began to follow a bootstrap approach to develop a company to predict which students have been at-risk in terms of completion. Mike Sharkey, the company's founder, has partnered with a partner focused on markets like wellness (by a company called Clairvoyant) and jointly developed tailored analytical tools for their customers.

Blue Canary worked on the premise that the student retention issue consists of two parts. The first issue is the detection of at-risk students, and the second is the development of intervention methods to retain the students.

The company concentrated on addressing institutions' first of these issues. Therefore, Blue Canary and its client organizations partnered in the business model. The company forecast the students would be at-risk every week, and then it was up to university to intervene to keep the students at-risk. Every week it sent clients a list of students who classified predictive analytics as likely to drop out in the coming week. The goal was not to replace human beings with analytics but to improve human decision-making with data based on predictive models.

By 2014, Blue Canary began to gain traction, and brand awareness and sales force penetrated the market were the main challenges for growth. An ideal customer was part of the sales plan. The team decided, for Blue Canary, that an ideal customer will have five attributes.

They concentrated not on learning and schooling but on systemic planning and leadership.

1. An institutional aim to boost retention of students
2. Key influencers aware of the power of analytics
3. Current footprint of data
4. Action and intervention engagement of stakeholders
5. Defined purchase decision process.

Since Blue Canary saw itself as just half of the solution (the assessment of students at risk), these requirements helped make sure employees spent some time working with clients who could provide the other half. The company was looking for consumers who would buy their product effectively, have the requisite information to work with the product, take an interest in and take action on Blue Canary's predictions, and appreciate the value of prediction. The vendor alone could not solve the issue of student retention; predictive technology could only be used to help students by partnering with an organization.

Some customers have "got it" and have integrated people who can work with Blue Canary in technical work, as well as individuals who can take action based on Blue Canary knowledge. However, it was not clear who was held liable in other institutions to retain students, which made it harder for Blue Canary to provide effective service. Although the enterprise could give forecasts, institutions needed facilities and personnel to solve students' problems. The organization needed not only data but strategic leadership to collaborate with a provider of learning analysis.

In 2014, as in the previous and subsequent years, the Learning Analytics and Knowledge Conference (LAK14) included an annual data challenge which made a data set accessible to members of the learning analytics community in a specific context using the same data set. Blue Canary won the data challenge in that year and helped this relatively young company develop international market recognition. The LAK Data Challenge gives an example of how the work of those who are actively involved in a research group can be seen. The challenge also gives practitioners the ability to educate researchers of technological possibilities.

Awards may play an essential role in setting up a start-up brand. In 2015, Blue Canary's collaborator, Clairvoyant received the Governor's Celebration of Innovation (GCOI) Award in the Year Start-Up category to recognize Blue Canary's groundbreaking analytical work. The award also shows how regional funding from Arizona Commerce Authority will lead to the creation of a new learning analytical business.

Experience Blackboard purchased Blue Canary at the end of 2015, where Sharkey now holds the position as Vice President Analytics, responsible for various products like Blue Canary. He believes this allows him the ability to work on items that are not only recognized by the brand but also have sufficient marketing power to have a wider impact.

In 2016, Sharkey was one of the chairmen of the Learning Analytics and Knowledge Conference, LAK16. He considers that his role in the early years was to serve the practitioner, and he was happy to help establish his role at the conference and improve his role in advancing the sector. He sees cooperation between researchers and practitioners, as well as between the education sector and the benefit sector, as necessary to advance the field. He saw firsthand the importance of interacting with data through organizations as well as the repercussions for ethics, data security and privacy. Blue Canary deliberately avoided customer-to-client data analysis. The organization kept consumer data carefully apart and it was an essential part of its customer privacy agreement.

Policies Data privacy provides future obstacles and opportunities for cooperation between profit-making companies and universities. Blue Canary found that data security regulations limit analytical opportunities and discourage consumers from creating perspectives through organizations. Such policies may restrict vendors' ability to develop their customers' goods and eventually reduce their student benefits.

Blue Canary worked to reduce the division between researchers and practitioners and the divide between institutions and vendors. Although profit organizations do not act the same way as educational institutions, these organizations need to find a viable way to cooperate. It is essential to understand how collaboration between universities and profits can be facilitated rather than discouraged by data privacy policies.

10.3.4 *The Open University, UK – The Process of Developing an Institutional Ethics Policy (Ferguson et al., 2016)*

Introduction This study focuses on the creation of institutional policy for the ethical use of student knowledge. The Open University (OU) in the United Kingdom has collected and analyzed student information for several years and used it in several ways, including concentrating student support and retention efforts. When learning analytics became a field, the university became strategically involved in it. The need for an ethical policy on student data use stems from an increasing university understanding of the variety and amount of data collected and how it can provide students with efficient and timely guidance. Policy was released in July 2014.

Context The OU initiated a strategic initiative in early 2013 to explore learning analytics. This project includes a range of practical and technological sub-projects concentrating on designing learning analytics tools for OU staff and students. This included progress updates and visualization of data. Creating a Student Data Ethical Framework was the subject of a particular sub-project that was part of the other Student Analytics sub-projects. No external drivers, including national legislation, were involved in the policy development.

The first team was five people headed by a business school professor from the university, involved in ethical problems relevant to learning analytics. A data security specialist, the Head of the Information Office of the OU, the University Institute of Educational Technology (IET), an academic specialist on ethics and search, and a project manager from their Learning and Teaching Centre were among the team.

As the sub-project for ethical policy began, the team started looking into what was going on outside of the OU. They found that no other universities had policies on the ethics of learning analytics at the time. Many had data security policies, but none discussed exploring problems, such as classification and data ownership concerns and consent issues.

For two reasons, the implementation of the policy in the OU was deemed especially significant. Firstly, the university has an open entry policy, because students have diverse backgrounds and experiences. Second, it is a university of distance teaching because face-to-face interactions between staff and students seldom happen, if at all, compared with traditional universities. These two factors make the OU reliant on knowledge obtained for the benefit of students to make decisions. In certain cases, the information obtained through analytics is the main or only source of knowledge on student research aspects.

When the policy work began, the sub-project team members knew no other organizations who were working on similar ethical policy problems. No reference to the ethics of learning analytics had been found in a public review of institutional policies in Britain and South Africa.

OU students have been and are the key players in policy growth. University stakeholders included faculty employees, student support staff, the University of Colombia's IT unit, the University Academic Policy and Governance Unit, and the University's Pro-Vice Chancellors. The other members were the project team, which grew when a senior academic joined the OU in 2014.

Design and implementation phase The team's goal was to create a policy, but the university did not define specific criteria. The team decided that the policy should be straightforward – what the university does with student data should be clear without distress or incomprehension among students.

The policy-making process started with studying associated policies and drew on existing studies by the team leader. This led to a series of general principles. The principles outlined in Section 4 of "OU Ethical Use of Student Data for Learning Analytics Policy" document were tested, revised, and refined over time through a series of consultation with stakeholder groups.

- Principle 1: Learning analytics is an ethical practice that should harmonize with the organization's core values, such as open entry into undergraduate studies.
- Principle 2: The OU is responsible for using and extracting value from student data for students where feasible.
- Principle 3: students should not be wholly defined by their observable data or by interpretation.
- Principle 4: The intent and limits of the use of learning analytics must be clearly defined and noticeable.
- Principle 5: The University is transparent about data collection and provides students a daily opportunity to amend data and consent agreements.
- Principle 6: Students should be engaged in learning analytics as active agents (e.g., informed consent, customized learning paths, interventions), etc.
- Principle 7: Data analysis modeling and interventions should be sound and bias-free.
- Principle 8: Adoption of learning analytics within the OU calls for broad recognition of principles and benefits and the development of acceptable organizational skills.

Two dedicated online student consultation forums contributed primarily to the policy's analysis and improvement from a student's side. The forums comprised a group of volunteer students representing OU students in their entirety. This group of approximately 90 students were hired to inform the University on several issues.

In the first forum, the first draught of the principles used in the policy was discussed. These principles were posted at the platform and a set of questions to study the participants' interpretation of the principles. Issues discussed led to the drafting of the policy's initial versions.

10.3 Other Evidence on the Use of Learning Analytics

Two members of the Open University Students Association (OUSA), who had drawn up an initial version of the proposal, took part in consultations with the project team to further develop the proposal. These debates centered on the topic of consent, whether or when students would be expected to agree to their data used for learning analytics. The goal of OUSA was to ensure that the student's voice was heard and that the university understood the students' concerns about data collection and analytics.

The team performed several further meetings with different university committees and requested and obtained their approval. As the policy work continues, the team is mindful of stakeholders that may have opposing views, such as the unit responsible for registering students with the university.

One of the team's suggestions was that each student should seek informed approval so that their data can be used for analytics. However, it was described as a possible obstacle to registration because it could discourage certain students from registering. There was a solution by raising the profile and presenting it to students in several ways.

Early on, team members found that they were producing very few policy changes. The team worked to develop policy versions that are relevant and comprehensible to students. They have also been in touch with employees working on student-facing websites to highlight the policy and involve students more actively and allow them to update their own information. This concerns one of the laws surrounding students and universities' shared obligation to ensure that the information they store is up to date. Case studies and realistic advice for student-oriented staff have been created to see what policy means in practice.

The establishment of the student data ethics policy involved minimal improvements to other institutional policies. The policy team was responsible for designing the policy that went live in 2014. This proposal did not involve a consent stance and conversations on this subject continued with stakeholders until 2016. There were two key stakeholder groups with differing viewpoints on the subject of consent: students and college employees. There was no common ground, but the team was unified with the staff and recommended an informed consent role. This was officially accepted by the Student Experience Committee of the University in February 2016.

Once finalized and accepted, the policy was passed to the Maintenance and Growth Academic Policy and Governance Unit (where necessary). This unit provides the University with resources for academic and student policies, standards and processes and institutional governance and enforcement. One of the project team is this unit, which has enabled the transition from team to unit.

Experience Team members have published reports on policy formulation and have been active in similar work outside the OU. For instance, the team chair consulted on the Jisc project which led to the Jisc Code of Practice for Learning Analytics being published in June 2015. Participation in creating this code has contributed to a reflection on the OU policy's role regarding the student's consent to the use of its data for academic purposes. The Jisc Code of Practice advises that students agree to the use of their data in learning analytics. The distinction between the two positions may be because the OU has to deal with the practicalities of enforcing its legislation, but it is the organization that is responsible for enforcing the Code of Practice, and not Jisc.

Interesting and contentious legal issues continue to be studied. For example, educational institutions do not have the resources required to offer proactive support to all students defined as requiring additional support using analytics. Decisions on how to target available resources would have to be made. There are currently no standards or standards for making such a decision.

Policies Overall, the Ethics Policy Subproject team's work has not been funded and has not been constrained by current laws, although legislation such as the data protection regulations on the use of confidential data has been taken into account. The OU had policies related to how it was to use student data and how students accepted it, and one of the things the team had to do was add information to these.

Other higher education institutions should build legislation on the ethical use of student data based on this experience. In general, students must be aware that they are the main stakeholders but that other problems, including retention and completion rates, are likely to influence this field's policies' design and execution.

10.4 Conclusion

It seems clear that learning analytics is gaining traction and are likely here to stay. There are several advantages to learning analytics; it can teach our students how our students succeed. We have large quantities of data available in educational institutions. We can use this data to tell what we are doing. The core of learning analytics is in the classroom, whether face-to-face or online. Different organizations are paving the way and showing students and teachers the tremendous benefits of learning analytics. According to studies, institutions should use the data they have in their courses to enhance students/faculty's success. While obviously "small-scale," these efforts can significantly affect the institution's overall performance.

10.5 Review Questions

Reflect on the concepts of this chapter guided by the following questions.

1. What would be your approach for introducing learning analytics into an institution? What are the risks and benefits to consider?
2. Institution ABC is struggling. Identify the three main problems it's facing. What is the most important problem the institution is facing? How would you

recommend learning analytics can address this problem? Provide your reasoning for your recommendation(s).
3. A higher education institution has been experiencing problems in student retention for the last two academic years. Research suggests that introducing learning analytics will give the solution. Provide some evidences that learning analytics solved the problem of student retention.
4. A well-established institution's faculty are struggling in framing and delivering the right education content for their students. List the problems that you identify for this. Can learning analytics solve this problem. Provide some evidences.
5. A new institution is being opened up. Discuss how learning analytics will help this institution in growing up from its initiation.
6. Reread the case studies carefully. Make a note of any ideas that you think of.
7. Identify key issues, that institutions used learning analytics to solve problems.

References

Dietz-Uhler, B., & Hurn, J. E. (2013). Using learning analytics to predict (and improve) student success: A faculty perspective. *Journal of Interactive Online Learning, 12*(1), 17–26.

Ferguson, R. (2012). Learning analytics: Drivers, developments and challenges. *International Journal of Technology Enhanced Learning, 4*(5–6), 304–317. https://doi.org/10.1504/IJTEL.2012.051816

Ferguson, R., Brasher, A., Clow, D., Cooper, A., Hillaire, G., Mittelmeier, J., Rienties, B., & Vuorikari, R. (2016). Research evidence on the use of learning analytics. In *A European Framework for Action on Learning Analytics* (Issue 2016). https://doi.org/10.2791/955210

Fortenbacher, A., & Pinkwart, N. (2015). Learning analytics. *CEUR Workshop Proceedings.* https://teaching.usask.ca/about/units/learning-analytics.php#Context

Game Changers: Education and Information Technologies. (2012). http://www.unesco.org/iiep/virtualuniversity/forumsfiche.php?queryforumspages_id=25

Greller, W., & Drachsler, H. (2012). Translating learning into numbers: A generic framework for learning analytics. *Educational Technology and Society, 15*(3), 42–57.

Hanover Research. (2016). Learning analytics tools for student tracking progress. In www.hanoverresearch.com: Vol. B.

Ifenthaler, D., Gibson, D. C., & Dobozy, E. (2018). Informing learning design through analytics: Applying network graph analysis. *Australasian Journal of Educational Technology, 34*(2), 117–132. https://doi.org/10.14742/ajet.3767

Ifenthaler, D., & Yau, J. Y.-K. (2020). Utilising learning analytics to support study success in higher education: A systematic review. *Educational Technology Research and Development, 68*(4), 1961–1990. https://doi.org/10.1007/s11423-020-09788-z

Ifenthaler, D., Yau, J. Y.-K., & Mah, D.-K. (Eds.). (2019). *Utilizing learning analytics to support study success*. New York, NY: Springer.

JISC. (2013). Case study A: traffic lights and interventions: Signals at Purdue University. *Learning Analytics in Higher Education.* https://analytics.jiscinvolve.org/wp/files/2016/04/CASE-STUDY-A-Purdue-University.pdf

JISC. (2016a). *Analysing social networks at the University of Wollongong.* https://analytics.jiscinvolve.org/wp/files/2016/04/CASE-STUDY-J-University-of-Wollongong.pdf

JISC. (2016b). *Analysing use of the VLE at the University of Maryland, Baltimore County.* https://analytics.jiscinvolve.org/wp/files/2016/04/CASE-STUDY-B-University-of-Maryland-Baltimore-County.pdf

JISC. (2016c). *Case study H: Developing an 'analytics mind-set' at the Open University.* https://analytics.jiscinvolve.org/wp/files/2016/04/CASE-STUDY-H-Open-University-UK.pdf

JISC. (2016d). *Case study I: Predictive analytics at Nottingham Trent University.* https://analytics.jiscinvolve.org/wp/files/2016/04/CASE-STUDY-I-Nottingham-Trent-University.pdf

JISC. (2016e). *Early alert at the University of New England.* https://analytics.jiscinvolve.org/wp/files/2016/04/CASE-STUDY-G-University-of-New-England.pdf

JISC. (2016f). *Enhancing retention at Edith Cowan University. 2011.* https://analytics.jiscinvolve.org/wp/files/2016/04/CASE-STUDY-F-Edith-Cowan-University.pdf

JISC. (2016g). *Fine-grained analysis of student data at California State University.* https://analytics.jiscinvolve.org/wp/files/2016/04/CASE-STUDY-D-California-State-University.pdf

JISC. (2016h). *Identifying at-risk students at New York Institute of Technology.* https://analytics.jiscinvolve.org/wp/files/2016/04/CASE-STUDY-C-New-York-Institute-of-Technology.pdf

JISC. (2016i). *Personalised pathway planning at Open Universities Australia.* https://analytics.jiscinvolve.org/wp/files/2016/04/CASE-STUDY-K-Open-Universities-Australia.pdf

JISC. (2016j). *Transferring predictive models to otherinstitutions from Marist College.* https://analytics.jiscinvolve.org/wp/files/2016/04/CASE-STUDY-E-Marist-College.pdf

Lester, J., Klein, C., Rangwala, H., & Johri, A. (2017). Learning analytics in higher education. *ASHE Higher Education Report, 43*(5), 9–135. https://doi.org/10.1002/aehe.20121.

Smith, V. C., Lange, A., & Huston, D. R. (2012). Predictive modeling to forecast student outcomes and drive effective interventions. *Journal of Asynchronous Learning Networks, 16*(3), 51–61.

Verbert, K., Manouselis, N., Drachsler, H., & Duval, E. (2012). Dataset-driven research to support learning and knowledge analytics. *Educational Technology and Society, 15*(3), 133–148.

West, D., Luzeckyj, A., Searle, B., Toohey, D., & Price, R. (2018). *The use of learning analytics to support improvements in teaching practice.* Innovative Research Universities: Melbourne, Australia.

Wolff, A., Zdrahal, Z., Nikolov, A., & Pantucek, M. (2013). Improving retention: Predicting at-risk students by analysing clicking behaviour in a virtual learning environment. *ACM international conference proceeding series, January 2019*, 145–149. https://doi.org/10.1145/2460296.2460324

Chapter 11
Problems

Enhance your knowledge and further understanding of the concepts guided by the following questions.

Problem-1

Consider the data of 05 students in your class.

Student number	Number of practice tests attempted	Final score in the exam
1	2	3.5
2	3	4
3	9	9
4	1	3
5	5	6

Build the best regression model to fit this data.

Problem-2

Consider that you are a professor for a course. You have two teaching methods. You want to test which is the effective teaching method you want to consider for your future teaching. You teach Class-A using Teaching Method-1 and Class-B with Teaching Method-2. You conducted the same test in both classes for the same topic. Now you have the scores of the students if both the classes. Use any Learning Analytics tool and find out which teaching method is effective for that course.

Problem-3

You have the data of 100 students

- C1: number of hours the student logged-in in the online course portal
- C2: score in the final exam

Using this data and any Learning Analytics tool determine the relationship (build a model) between the number of hours the student logged in in the online course portal and the final exam score.

Problem-4

Consider the following data of 60 students in your class.

- C1: Performance in the final test
- C2: the number of hours spent on the learning environment
- C3: the number of quizzes attempted in the learning environment

Using this data and any Learning Analytics tool, find that which will be the more significant predictor, i.e., either C2 or C3, the students' performance in the final test.

Problem-5

You are given the following data from a study conducted with learners interacting with a learning environment.

- Student_ID
- Page_ID
- Activity_ID
- Time_Spent_on_Page

From the above data find

- What are the different ways in which learners navigate through activities in the learning environment
- In which activity do learners spend the maximum time

Problem-6

Consider a dataset that consists of students' data interacting with an Online MOOC Course. The features can be extracted from the log-data. Following are the details about the features-

- *SID*- Student ID.
- *Learn*- The no. of lessons completed by the learner.
- *Quiz*- The no of quizzes attempted by the learner.
- *Coins*- The no. of coin earned by the learner.
- *Responses*- The no of responses in the Discussion forum.
- *Activities*- The total no of activities completed by the learner.
- *Coins/act*-The no. of coins earned per activity.
- *Inactive_time*-The time for which the student has not performed any action.

Use the above features to predict the target variable.

Target- This informs whether the student will logout from the system before or after the given fixed time.

Develop a logistic regression model (ten-fold cross-validation) and then evaluate your model to answer the following questions. You can also use Weka for this purpose that was demonstrated in the course.

(Report all your answers correct to 2 decimal places)

11 Problems

- The AUC value of the model is
- The F1 value of the model is
- The Recall value of the model is
- The precision value of the model is
- The accuracy

Problem-7

Consider a dataset that consists of students' data interacting with an Online MOOC Course. The features can be extracted from the log-data. Following are the details about the features-

- *S_ID*- Student ID
- *Qualification*- This feature classifies students into three categories, Master's, Bachelor's, and Doctorates.
- *Chapters_Completed*- This represents the no. of chapters completed by a particular student.
- *No_of_post*- This informs the no. of times a student has posted in the discussion forum.
- *Marks*- The marks obtained by a particular student in the first assignment.

Use any Learning Analytics tool of your choice to visualize this data and answer the following questions.

- Find the interquartile range of "Chapters_Completed" with the help of a box-plot.
- Use the bar graph and report the percentage of the students having a Bachelor's degree enrolled in the course.
- Use a pie chart to represent the gender distribution of students enrolled in the course. What is the percentage of female students enrolled in the course?
- With the visualization chart's help, identify the percentage of males who have scored ten marks in the test.
- What is the median of marks scored by Doctoral students?

Problem-8

Consider the data of 05 students in your class.

Student number	Engagement	Scores in the mid_sem exam	Scores in the end exam
1	80	75	60
2	55	60	55
3	90	80	90
4	95	80	88
5	45	40	50
6	50	55	60
7	65	60	70
8	60	50	60

From the above data

- Consider that 'Engagement' and 'Scores in the Mid_Sem exam' are independent variables used to predict the Scores in the End exam. Find out the correlation between variables.
- If only one independent variable should be selected to predict Scores in the End exam, then what will be that variable.

Problem-9

Consider the data of 60 students in your class.

- Student_ID
- Attribute_Value_1
- Attribute_Value_2
- Attribute_Value_3

Sample Data is as follows

Student number	Score in test_1	Score in test_2	Score in test_3
1	6	6	5
2	5	2	6
3	10	3	4
4	5	3	9
5	6	5	6
6	4	2	1
7	9	4	6
8	6	7	7

From the above data find

- What percentage of students who scored two marks in Test_2 has scored 5 in Test_1
- What percentage of students scoring eight marks in Test_3
- What is the number of students that have scored five marks in both Test_1 and Test_3

Problem-10

Consider the following THREE students' interaction behavior in a MOOC course.

- S1: Read Video Quiz Read Video Forum Quiz Read Forum Quiz
- S2: Video Read Read Quiz Video Forum Read Video Forum Quiz
- S3: Quiz Video Forum Read Quiz Video Read Video Quiz Forum

By using any Learning Analytics Tool find the following

- Find the value of s-Support for the pattern "Read-Video."
- Find the value of i-frequency for the pattern "Read-Video."
- Calculate the value of s-Support for pattern: "Quiz-Video."

- Calculate the value of i-frequency for the pattern "Quiz-Video."

Problem-11

Consider that you have completed an online course and you have taken feedback from the participants about the Course Instructor as follows on a scale of 1–5 (1-Lowest and 5-Highest)

- Subject Knowledge
- Ability to Interact
- Application of updated Information
- Ability to retain the attention of participants
- Ability to answer questions
- Presentation Quality
- Communication Skill

Using the collected feedback, evaluate the performance of the Instructor as (Poor, Fair, Good & Excellent)

Problem-12

Consider that you have completed an online course and you have taken the following feedback from the participants about the Course

- Your Role (Student, Faculty, Employer, Other)
- Was the course interesting? (Yes, No)
- Did the course cover the topics given in the initial syllabus? (Yes, No)
- Rate the difficulty level of the course. (Very difficult, Difficult, Moderate, Easy, Very easy)
- Rate the clarity of the videos posted. (Not exact, Normal, Clear, Very clear)
- Rate the clarity of the audio in the video. (Not Clear, Normal, Clear, Very Clear)
- Lessons and assignments were posted on the schedule. (Yes, No)

Based on the above feedback data, evaluate whether the course fulfilled the participants' professional/personal objectives?

Problem-13

Consider that you have completed an online course and you have taken the following feedback from the participants about the assignments given during the course to the participants

- Were assignments given regularly? (Yes, No)
- Were the assignments relevant to the module taught? (Yes, No)
- Rate the difficulty of the assignments. (Very difficult, Difficult, Moderate, Easy, Very easy)
- Was sufficient time given to submit assignments? (Yes, No)
- Whether the solutions published are clear and useful? (Yes, No)

Based on data, identify the effectiveness of the assignments given during the course.

Problem-14

Consider that you have completed an online course and you have taken the following feedback from the participants about the assignments given during the course to the students

- Does your course contain a LIVE session? (Yes, No)
- Have you watched the LIVE session? (Yes, No)
- Was the LIVE session useful? (Yes, No)

Based on the above feedback, Rate the Live Session on a 1–5 scale (1-Very Poor & 5-Excellent)

Problem-15

Consider that you have completed an online course, and you have taken the following feedback from participants about the Discussion Forum ran during the course to the participants.

- Was the forum active throughout the course? (Yes, No)
- Were questions regarding the lessons/assignments posted - answered promptly and satisfactorily? (Yes, No)

Based on the above feedback, Rate the Discussion Forum 1–5 scale (1-Very Poor & 5-Excellent)

Problem-16

Consider that you have completed an online course, and you have taken the following feedback from the participants about the Material supplied during the course to the participants.

- Why would you prefer material? (It is easier to read as notes than listening to the video, Video was too long to watch, Poor internet bandwidth, Following the Professor's language was challenging, Handy for exam preparation)
- Do you watch videos along with the subtitles? (Yes, No, Maybe)
- How would you prefer to study? (View the videos alone, Study from the material alone, View the videos and learn from the material)
- Do you want the material (English) translated into your local language? (Yes, No)
- Where would you go and look for material? (Material supplied during the course, Browse Internet)

Based on the above feedback rate, the quality of the material supplied on a scale of 1–4 (1-Very Useful & 4-Poor)

Problem-17

Consider that you have completed an online course and have taken the following feedback from the participants about the course's certification exam from the participants.

- Rate the difficulty level of the exam. (Very difficult, Difficult, Moderate, Easy, Very easy)

- Rate the performance of the online exam platform. (Very poor, Poor, Moderate, Good, Very good)
- Rate the facilities and invigilation at the exam center. (Very poor, Poor, Moderate, Good, Very good)

Based on the above feedback, find the following perception of the participant.
Did the participant opt for the certification exam? (Yes, No)
If the answers to the above question are YES, find out which platform the participant would prefer in the future (Online, Offline, Traditional)

Problem-18
Consider that you have completed an online course, and you have taken the following feedback from the participants about the overall experience on the course from the participants.

- Overall, are you satisfied with the quality of this course? (Very poor, Poor, Moderate, Good, Very good)
- Online Platform/Tool/Website was easy to use. (Very difficult, Difficult, Moderate, Easy, Very easy)
- Will you continue with the future online courses? (Yes, No)

Based on the above feedback find

- which one is better? (Online Platform, Regular Classroom Classes)
- whether to continue this course in the future (Yes, No)

Problem-19
Consider that you have completed an online course, and you have taken the following feedback from the participants about the overall experience on the course from the participants.

- Overall satisfaction with the course? (Very poor, Poor, Moderate, Good, Very good)
  Analyze students' responses and group them into categories such as

- good understanding
- Moderate
- Significant difficulties

Problem-20
Consider that you have completed an online course and you have taken the following feedback from the participants about the assignments given during the course to the participants

- Were assignments given regularly? (Yes, No)
- Were the assignments relevant to the module taught? (Yes, No)
- Rate the difficulty of the assignments. (Very difficult, Difficult, Moderate, Easy, Very easy)
- Was sufficient time given to submit assignments? (Yes, No)
- Whether the solutions published are clear and useful? (Yes, No)

Based on data, identify specific questions/assignments where the students faced difficulties in responding.

Problem-21

Consider that you have completed an online course. From the log files, collect the learners' clicks on VLE activities of the course and visualize the number of clicks per activity. For example:

- Home page
- URL
- Subpage
- Resource
- Glossary
- Forum, etc.

Problem-22

Consider that you have completed an online course. Based on the queries students posted in the chatbox/forum, identify a concept or principle, your students facing significant difficulty in understanding that concept.

Problem-23

A week or two before the final exam, conduct a pre-final examination for the course you thought. Based on the performance in this exam and other mid-term examinations, identify

- at-risk students and
- the pass percentage of your class

Problem-24

Choose 1–3 problems and ask your students to solve the problem. Collect

- The number of students who responded to the problem
- Number of who correctly solved the problem
- Number of students who attempted to solve the problem but failed in achieving the correct solution

Based on this data, assess the problem-solving skills of your students and cluster them into groups.

Problem-25

During an online course, pose 1–2 questions to students and record the students' response time to those questions. Based on the responses, cluster students into slow-learners and fast learners.

Printed in Singapore by Markono Print Media Pte Ltd